Red Hat Linux Network Management Tools

McGraw-Hill Tools Series Titles:

Red Hat Linux Network Management Tools

Steve Maxwell

McGraw-Hill

New York • San Francisco • Washington, D.C. • Auckland • Bogotá • Caracas
Lisbon • London • Madrid • Mexico City • Milan • Montreal • New Delhi
San Juan • Singapore • Sydney • Tokyo • Toronto

Library of Congress Cataloging-in-Publication Data

Maxwell, Steven.
   Red Hat Linux network management tools / Steve Maxwell.
      p.   cm.
   ISBN 0-07-212262-5
   1. Linux. 2. Operating systems (Computers). 3. Computer networks—Management. I. Title.
   QA76.76.O63 M373339 2000
   050.4'469—dc21

                                                      99-088793

McGraw-Hill

A Division of The McGraw-Hill Companies

1 2 3 4 5 6 7 8 9 0 AGM/AGM 0 5 4 3 2 1 0

P/N 0-07-212260-9

Part of ISBN 0-07-212262-5

The sponsoring editor for this book was Simon Yates and the production supervisor was Clare Stanley. It was set in Sabon by TIPS Technical Publishing.

Printed and bound by Quebecor/Martinsburg.

McGraw-Hill books are available at special quantity discounts to use as premiums and sales promotions, or for use in corporate training programs. For more information, please write to the Director of Special Sales, McGraw-Hill, 2 Penn Plaza, New York, NY 10121. Or contact your local bookstore.

Throughout this book, trademarked names are used. Rather than put a trademark symbol after every occurrence of a trademarked name, we use names in an editorial fashion only, and to the benefit of the trademark owner, with no intention of infringement of the trademark. Where such designations appear in this book, they have been printed with initial caps.

 This book is printed on recycled, acid-free paper containing a minimum of 50% recycled, de-inked fiber.

To Ginny, forever and always...

Contents

List of Figures

List of Tables

xvii

Code Listings

Preface

This book addresses the fundamentals of network management from an individual component perspective. Many software tools that provide important functions and features previously found only in commercial products and solutions are publicly available. This book discusses and describes many of the discrete tools and utilities you can use to effectively manage an enterprise network, which may consist of workstations, servers, and other networking components such as switches, routers, and hubs.

During the past few years, enterprise networks have become the critical link and integral component of the information systems landscape. Gone are the days when connectivity between users was optional and network failures were a normal part of computing. In many corporations and institutions, a network outage or delay can have serious implications for the organization's ability to conduct normal business activities or communicate with their customers. In the financial community, even a relatively short network outage can result in significant financial impact.

Today's corporate and institutional networks are characterized by significant growth in the diversity and number of systems attached to these networks. This is known as *heterogeneous networking* and is quite common. It is difficult to effectively manage the many different computers, peripherals, and core devices because much of it must be done manually. A critical system or network failure can significantly impact the use of corporate services and affect the day-to-day operations of an organization. Many networks have also been deployed with very little regard for their manageability or upgrade capabilities. This makes the task of network management that much harder due to the added requirements of legacy systems.

Also, with the widespread acceptance of the Internet as the primary external communication vehicle for many companies, maintaining network up time is even more critical because users and customers are accustomed to instant access to information and services. With the small number of steps involved in accessing a site from any location in the world, a disconnection from the Internet could mean lost revenue opportunities if customers choose a competitor's site.

Due to the explosive growth in the networking industry, the computing landscape is filled with various computing platforms and systems from many different vendors. Thanks to the TCP/IP protocol suite, many kinds of computing systems and devices can be connected to the network, ranging from large mainframe systems to small handheld devices. With TCP/IP, many of these systems share common services and provide a standard framework for connectivity. Also, with common implementation of network management protocols among these systems, a standard network management model can be deployed.

This book will give you the knowledge of critical tools and the skills necessary to aid in systems and enterprise network management. The fundamental importance and goal of this book is to provide information on using software tools and related system utilities to manage a TCP/IP enterprise.

Audience

The primary audience for this book is the network manager and system administrator. If you already know the difference between the **arp** and **ifconfig** commands and have already used the **snmpwalk** command, then this book may not be for you. Others, who are new to these commands, will find the book useful because it deals with fundamentals of network management, specific networking management protocols, and software tools like the ones mentioned. It will help to serve as a launching point for those faced with supporting networks in the real world. The text focuses more on tools than lengthy detailed descriptions of protocol operations, network management design, or architecture. At a minimum, the reader should be familiar with the basics of the UNIX operating system and feel comfortable executing commands and accessing system files. Users unfamiliar with these subjects might consider examining the other titles in the series.

UNIX Versions

All of the tools discussed and examples provided in this book are from the Linux UNIX operating system. Because many of the UNIX tools are available across a wide variety of versions of UNIX, the reader will have little difficulty adapting and using the tools in their environment. Most of the software is in the form of RPM packages and can be found on the CD-ROM provided with this book. See Appendix B, "Installation Procedures," for a complete listing of the software available on the CD-ROM and detailed installation information and instructions.

Overview of this Book

The first three chapters provide an overview for the reader and focus on network management in general, the Simple Network Management Protocol, and TCP/IP networking. Since this book provides an overview of network management tools, it seems only appropriate to include introductory information on the core component of network management.

Chapter 1, "Overview of Network Management," provides an introduction to network management; it describes the basic elements and functions found in network management systems and defines specific components that will be referenced throughout the book. It establishes the basic framework for the review of additional information and advanced topics that may rest upon the base foundation. Chapter 2, "Simple Network Management Protocol," includes a detailed description of the SNMP, which is the most popular and widely implemented management protocol today. As such, it discusses the core protocol operation and explains how both network managers and agents operate in a seamless fashion. Chapter 3, "TCP/IP Protocol Suite," gives a detailed overview of TCP/IP. It covers many aspects of networking—such as IP addresses and the basic operation of TCP and other protocols—that a network administrator or system manager may need when using or administering UNIX systems.

The next two chapters focus on using UNIX software tools to manage individual and networked systems. Chapter 4, "Core System Utilities and Tools," provides a detailed overview of some of the most common UNIX utilities and tools. These include ARP, ifconfig, netstat, ping, and traceroute. Chapter 5, "Additional System Utilities and Tools," extends the theme of the previous chapter by introducing additional tools and utilities such as nmap and ethereal.

Chapter 6, "Overview of MIB-II," describes the objects available with the MIB-II object store. It is these objects that are implemented in most vendor products. Chapter 7, "Using SNMP Agents," introduces SNMP agents and their associated MIB objects. This chapter will help readers to understand the basic services and functions of agents. Chapter 8, "SNMP Tools," addresses specific tools that retrieve network management information from SNMP agents. These tools are part of the overall foundation for controlling and configuring network systems.

Chapter 9, "Web-enabled Tools," provides the necessary review of Web-based tools that promise to further enhance the reporting aspects of network management. Chapter 10, "Linux Control Panel," describes the standard control-panel package that comes with Red Hat Linux. Chapter 11, "tkined Tool—Network Editor," provides a detailed description of the Scotty network editor. This software tool can create network topology maps for monitoring and management of a diverse collection of networking devices.

Appendix A, "Tools at a Glance," provides an overview of all the tools discussed in this book; Appendix B, "Installation Procedures and Software Notes," provides installation procedures for many of the tools discussed in this book; and Appendix C , "Glossary of Networking/Network Management Terms," provides definitions for some of the most commonly used networking and network management terms.

The book contains two CD-ROMs. One CD-ROM contains the entire Red Hat 6.1 distribution. The other contains many of the tools discussed within the book. It also contains the Red Hat Linux 6.1 Powertools distribution.

Conventions

The following conventions are used in this book:

- Code line, functions, variable names, and any text you see onscreen appear in a special `monospace` typeface.

- File, button, icon, and menu names are also set in a `monospace` typeface.

- Program, utility, and tool names are set in normal font and either capped or left lowercase as the industry dictates (such as MRTG and ntop).

- New terms are in *italic*.

- If you are instructed within the body of a paragraph to type any text, the text you must type will appear in **boldface**. For example, "Type **./mysqlshow**." Usually, however, the line is set off by itself in a bolded, monospace typeface, as shown in the following example:

```
./mysqlshow
```

- Commands and keywords are set in **boldface**.

Acknowledgments

Many thanks to Ginny, my wife, for her valuable assistance and constant, witty satire during the development of this text. Also, to the three best kids that I have ever come to love and grow up with: Lisa, Matthew, and Joshua. You help make life worth living. The author wishes to thank the McGraw-Hill production staff for their outstanding efforts in preparing the manuscript. Special thanks to Simon Yates, the Senior Editor, for managing and believing in the UNIX Tools series and coordinating the fine art of book publishing. Also, many thanks to Bob Kern for expert craftsmanship in putting this book together. Thanks also go to Sandra Henry-Stocker for poring over the manuscript during the review process and Lynanne Fowle for typesetting the book and handling all the little details that were required.

Special thanks to JC, without whom I could do nothing, and for making this entire thing a reality.

About the Author

For the last 15 years, Steve Maxwell has been involved with the design, deployment, and management of enterprise networks in a variety of companies and institutions. He has helped build and support networks and systems for Lisp Machine, BBN, Boston University, Stratus Computer, 3Com, and others. Also, while at 3Com, he has helped deliver network management products and gained insight into the fundamentals and strategies needed to effectively address the network management requirements of large heterogeneous networks. Steve Maxwell currently lives in the Orlando, Florida area with his wife and their three ever-growing kids.

Steve welcomes feedback—please send comments and suggestions about this book to: sjmaxwell@worldnet.att.net

Red Hat Linux Network Management Tools

Overview of Network Management

On a conceptual level, a network management system addresses three fundamental areas: performance monitoring, configuration management, and diagnostic management. Some network management systems provide all these services, while most individual tools address only one or two.

Each of these areas is part of an overall puzzle, as shown in Figure 1.1. A network management system must function in all three areas and provide the tools necessary to implement effective network management. If one of the areas is not covered, the network management picture is incomplete and the solution is inadequate. That is to say, without tools to support critical network management functions, the overall network management effort will be hindered. One of the goals of this book is to address each of the management areas by describing tools that implement one or more of the network management functions. However, because some of the tools presented are available within the public domain, not all areas will be covered by an appropriate network management tool.

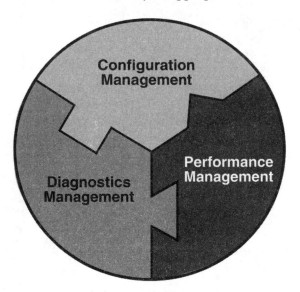

Figure 1.1 *Three elements of network management.*

Performance management includes the ability to keep tabs on the general efficiency or health of the network from the perspective of an enterprise or an individual device. It involves the collection and subsequent analysis of traffic patterns to alleviate network bottlenecks and solve related problems, such as when a file transfer between two systems takes longer than it should or database updates to a remote site time-out on a periodic basis. Solving these and other problems requires obtaining adequate historical performance information and conducting trend analysis on the data collected. By proactively conducting performance reviews, the network administrator or designer can plan for network growth in a more consistent, timely, and strategic fashion.

Configuration management involves ensuring that each network device or system contains the appropriate configuration and correct version of operating system software. For instance, say we need to enable security parameters on a set of networking devices. Sometimes changes are made to individual devices, while at other times changes are propagated to a large number of systems. In these cases, the network management system must ensure that these changes are made correctly and efficiently.

Diagnostic management involves troubleshooting network failures, software problems, and other issues and problems that affect normal operation of the network or its components. It also involves effectively managing the many different types of problems and issues that result from software- and hardware-related failures. Network problems vary in complexity and can range from a simple hardware failure to a protocol-related problem. It is the goal of the network management system to isolate, describe, and, in some cases, repair the problem.

A significant challenge in network management is keeping pace with improvements and advances in network technology as a whole. With the deployment of virtual local area networks (VLANs), where network topologies can be defined and modified very quickly and individual devices and workstations are moved around the network logically rather than physically, the need for robust and functional management is critical. With the migration from standard wide area network (WAN) topologies, the creation of virtual private networks (VPNs) where a public network is used as the basis for networking infrastructure, and the eventual wide-scale implementation of storage area networks (SANs), network management must again play an important role in shaping the administration, support, and day-to-day operations of the network.

With these factors in mind, we present a review of the major components of a network management system with an emphasis on specific system functionality.

Network Management Components

To understand how a network management system functions, we must first consider the individual elements that make up such a system. Generally speaking, a network management system consists of the following four components:

- managers

- agents

- management information bases (MIBs)

- proxy agents

The first three components are required elements in most networking management systems. The remaining element, proxy services or proxies, is optional because these services tend to be very specialized and might not be required in most network environments.

Managers

Network management software includes important functionality to assist the network administrator in the day-to-day tasks of managing the network or individual devices. Network manager software queries agent entities on a regular basis to collect vital information. A manager might *poll* many agents on a regular basis to collect a variety of information regarding the operating state, present configuration, or performance data. Figure 1.2 shows the relationship between a manager and an agent from a high-level standpoint. The manager uses the information collected to determine the general health of individual network devices, a portion of the network, or the network as a whole.

Agents

Network management agents are software modules that reside in network devices such as UNIX workstations, personal computers, network printers, routers, switches, and other networking devices. Agents have access to the operational state, device characteristics, system configuration, and other related information, as shown in Figure 1.3. Agents are the information brokers for each managed network device; they respond to requests for specific

Figure 1.2 *Manager/agent relationship.*

information and are usually polled by one or more network managers. Agents are responsible for the interface between the management software and the device in which the agent resides. Agents can control the functions of network devices by manipulating the database of information stored in the management information base (MIB) contained within the device.

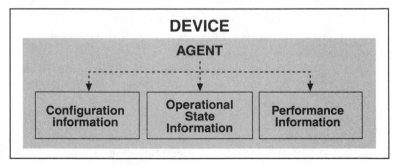

Figure 1.3 *Agent within a networking device.*

The external behavior of network management agents is the same across different vendor products if the agent supports a standard protocol like Simple Network Management Protocol (SNMP). SNMP agents understand both the language and the type of questions a manager can ask. It is possible to deploy a network management system from one vendor, third-party network applications from another, and agents from a host of additional vendors and ensure communication among all components. SNMP provides the framework to permit communication and understanding among many disparate devices, software, and systems.

The internals of many networking devices—such as routers, switches, and hubs—are proprietary by design, and the agent component is provided by the network equipment manufacturer as part of the base system or as an optional upgrade module. In many cases the agent is embedded in the operating system of the device and usually provides minimal configuration options. This is in sharp contrast to computer operating systems such as UNIX, where the agent is provided as a standalone system program and the user has much more control over the system's operation and configuration. Under the UNIX system, several agents are available from both commercial vendors and the public domain. In contrast, no public domain agents are available for most networking hardware products.

It is the responsibility of a network management agent to convert the network manager's request from a standard network format, retrieve the desired information, and send back a valid response. In some situations, the manager might request the agent to perform some action by setting the value of a management information base (MIB) object. For example, if an agent receives a request to reboot a device, no return message will be sent, but the agent will attempt to satisfy the request, provided the security requirements are met. Only with additional polls to the device would the manager actually know whether the device was restarted.

Equipment vendors define the objects their agents manipulate or support, which poses some interesting problems for agent developers. How does a vendor determine agent functionality? Generally, the vendor seeks customer advice and, in an ideal world, attempts to mimic hardware functions. That is, they try to enable the agent to support the hardware function or services as close as possible given marketing and engineering constraints. However, this goal isn't always practical or attainable; hardware designs generally change too quickly, and agent software might not keep pace with hardware improvements. Also, network management as a whole is still in its infancy, and not all equipment vendors operate with the realization that agent development is as critical as hardware product development. In other words, having the fastest device on the market in many situations is more important than providing a fully functional agent.

Usually only a single agent operates within a networking device. However, some of the more expensive high-end equipment may have more than one agent available. There are several reasons to use multiple agents. First, multiple agents provide a level of added redundancy and, thus, resiliency against failures. Should one of the modules/agents fail, another will take over the required task, thus ensuring continued agent availability and operations. Second, additional agents can have a positive impact on performance where polling is concerned. It may be more efficient, for example, to poll two independent agents versus just one. Third, the hardware design or architecture could warrant multiple independent agents.

Regardless of the reason, having more than one agent introduces some unique problems and issues for a network management system. For one thing, multiple agents can appear to the manager as different devices. This can cause problems for the application that collects inventory information because the number of devices recorded by the application differs from the actual number of hardware devices installed on the network. Multiple agents also force the network administrator to execute tasks with all the agents in mind, not just a single one, thus increasing the complexity of network management.

Agents tend to be very static in nature; they support a fixed set of functions or objects. With many networking devices, the agents can only be modified or upgraded by the vendor of the device. This is somewhat unfortunate because it is helpful to add additional agent functionality without waiting for the vendor to provide updates. However, a small number of agents are extensible and can be configured to support additional functionality. Generally speaking, agents that reside on UNIX systems or other operating systems have one or more files that control some of the operational or configuration aspects of the agent. The system agent that is available for Linux, for example, is highly configurable. Many extensible agents are only available for generic operating systems such as UNIX, versus specific devices like Cisco routers or Brocade Fibre

Channel switches. Extensible agents provide the ability for the user to plug in new capabilities without resorting to building or upgrading to another version of the agent. Figure 1.4 shows a functional overview of this type of agent. As you can see, the extensible component is simply an add-on to the agent. In many cases, it requires additional configuration parameters and commands to be added to the agent configuration file.

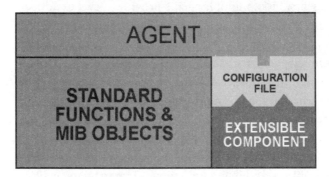

Figure 1.4 *Agent functional diagram.*

Management Information Base (MIB)

The MIB defines a database of objects that can be retrieved or manipulated by a network management system. Figure 1.5 shows the relationship of the agent and MIB objects. The MIB is a storehouse of information and can contain literally thousands of objects that the network manager can use to control, configure, and monitor devices by manipulating the objects directly. MIB objects are made available to a network management system via the agent. It is the responsibility of the agent to maintain the MIB object consistency regardless of the number of objects.

Several common standard MIBs have been defined, which include specific objects that must be supported in networking devices so that they are compatible with the SNMP protocol. The most widely implemented and common MIB is MIB-II. Many additional MIBs have been developed and documented in Request for Comments (RFCs) to address different networking components and technologies. Table 1.1 shows a sample list of these MIBs. As you can see, MIBs are available for a diverse collection of services, networking protocols, and architectures.

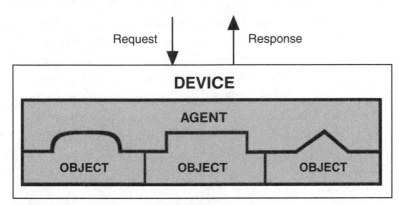

Figure 1.5 *SNMP agent and MIB objects.*

Table 1.1 *List of standard MIBs*

MIB	Description
FDDI MIB	Provides access to Fiber Data Distribution Interface (FDDI) network management functions
Host-Resource MIB	Provides access to system objects that are related to memory, disks, processes, and other system-related information
ISDN MIB	Used to provide management of Integrated Service Digital Network (ISDN) nodes
DNS Resolver and Server MIB	Provides management capabilities for the Domain Name Service (DNS)
MIB-II	Provides access to system-level objects that include network protocols, network interfaces, and generic system information
Printer MIB	Provides access to common printer management functions

Additionally, many vendors have developed their own proprietary MIBs. These MIBs define additional objects that are not found in the standard MIBs. These additional MIBs are necessary to take full advantage of vendor-specific management functions that may be available. Because MIBs are written in a standard language, they can be used with many different network management tools and products. Many networking equipment vendors like 3Com, Brocade, Cabletron, and Cisco, as well as computer manufacturers like HP, IBM, and Sun, have developed their own MIBs. Table 1.2 shows a sample of proprietary MIBs that are available from some of these vendors.

Table 1.2 *List of proprietary MIBs*

MIB	Description
3cProd-mib	3Com Switching Systems MIB for Core Builder Switch products
3cWeb-mib	3Com Web Server MIB
Cisco-mib	Cisco Router MIB
snmpdx.mib	Sun Master Agent MIB
swmib	Brocade Switch MIB

Proxy Agent

A proxy agent[1] bridges the gap between standard network protocol managers and legacy systems that do not directly support such standards. The term proxy agent can also refer to an agent that supports more than one network management protocol. Figure 1.6 shows the basic functions of a proxy-based system. Proxy agents provide a migration path from older standard protocols to newer versions without upgrading the entire network. For instance, over the past few years a significant amount of work has been focused on establishing improvements to the SNMP protocol.

When newer versions of SNMP become available, it is desirable that existing network devices will be upgraded. However, when

---

1. The term proxy as used here is not related to the proxy servers used today in many enterprise networks that provide protocol filtering, security, and other related services to hide the details of an internal network to the outside world.

these enhancements are made available from equipment vendors, it is reasonable to assume that not all products will be upgraded to support the new protocols. Some vendors will provide updates to their products while others will not; it is a matter of product viability and economics. It is possible that critical devices, such as high-end routers, will be upgraded, while other products will be made obsolete. As a result, organizations must address the issue of supporting different versions of SNMP for the foreseeable future. The proxy mechanism is one way to deal with any migration concerns because it can be used as a bridge to the older non-upgradable devices.

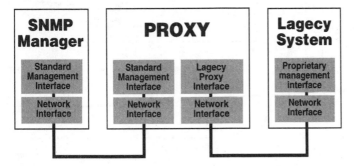

Figure 1.6 *Proxy-based system.*

It is interesting to note that a proxy-based system might also provide network connectivity to systems that do not support any standard network protocols (such as TCP/IP) and, thus, provide basic network connectivity services as well.

Manager Functions

Managers today offer a host of services to address the needs of an expanding heterogeneous enterprise network. The services provided can come from the basic management system itself or from third-party application providers, or they can be developed in-house to address some specific unique requirements. The capabilities and functions of a network manager can be grouped into three areas:

- architecture

- core services

- application

Table 1.3 lists the associated services for each of these categories, and a discussion of each category's services follows.

Table 1.3 *Manager services listed by category*

Category	Architecture	Core Services	Additional Applications
Open/Extensible Framework	✓		
Distributed/ Centralized Monitoring	✓		
Common Platforms	✓		
Fault Detection/ Resolution		✓	
Alarm Notification		✓	
Large Number of Devices		✓	
Reporting Tools		✓	
Easy-to-use GUI		✓	
Configuration Management		✓	
Network Discovery		✓	
Software Distribution			✓
Trouble Ticket			✓

Table 1.3 *Manager services listed by category (continued)*

Category	Architecture	Core Services	Additional Applications
Policy Management			✓
Advanced Alarm Processing			✓
Network Simulation			✓

Architecture

The architecture describes the basic framework and model of how the manager operates and implements the basic services needed to accomplish network management tasks. It should include:

An Open and Extensible Framework—Some managers are designed around an open standards-based framework, which can support enhancements to existing protocols and emerging technologies. An open network manager supports standards-based network management protocols such as SNMP and Common Management Information Protocol (CMIP). Today, the network management protocol of choice is SNMP. A network management system that doesn't support an open architecture and standard protocols should be viewed with suspicion because it could be difficult for the software to support enhancements in network protocols, databases, and operating system software. Managers must also support the TCP/IP Internet protocol suite and other proprietary networking protocols.

An open management system also provides integration tools and applications programming interfaces (APIs) for third-party developers to *layer* additional software solutions over the management framework. These solutions provide specialized application functions that are usually not available with the basic network management system. Depending on the level of integration, the user might not be aware of the different vendors' solutions contained within the management system.

Support for Distributed/Centralized Monitoring—Network management systems should have the ability to be deployed in a distributed or a centralized architecture. This is also known as the client/server approach and provides the means for the network management system to scale up and address additional network management requirements. In many situations, it is advisable to deploy one or more dedicated computer systems to handle the overhead associated with managing a large network. Although vendors don't always require more than one system for management tasks, it is unreasonable to assume that a single network management system can handle and support a network that consists of tens of thousands of devices. If, for the sake of argument, the platform selected could monitor that many devices, some practical considerations would warrant against using a single system.

First, in a centralized approach, the manager may poll each device from a single segment or subnetwork. This can cause serious traffic congestion for that portion of the network and significantly reduce the ability of the other devices on that segment to communicate with the rest of the network. Second, the network management system itself may be so occupied with the task of polling that it might not be able to respond to the GUI or other related management tasks. Third, using a centralized system is problematic with respect to general availability and uptime. Should the main management station fail due to a hardware or software problem that renders the system unusable, the network will be without a management platform until the system can be repaired. This may be an unacceptable situation in computing environments where system availability is critical.

Support for Common Platforms—To provide the most choices for customers, vendors of network management systems provide cross system support on the most popular operating systems and hardware platforms. Many vendors support both the UNIX and Windows NT operating systems. However, UNIX is still the most popular platform for vendors of network management systems and will continue to play an important role in the future. The most popular UNIX platforms that network management software vendors support include Solaris, AIX, and HP-UX. Due to the tremendous growth of Linux, network management software like

Hewlett-Packard's (HP) OpenView product has been ported to the Red Hat version of Linux. It is impossible at this juncture to accurately predict the role Linux will play in the network management market space. One thing is for certain: Linux is a robust, powerful, and cost-effective solution that will be deployed in many areas of computing and networking in the foreseeable future.

Core Services

A network management system usually provides a fundamental level of services. These basic services are typically considered the minimum amount of functionality that a network management system needs to deliver to accomplish simple management tasks. As such, it may be assumed these capabilities are available in most enterprise management systems. To some degree, vendors compete in the industry by providing more significant core service offerings and by ensuring availability of third-party products. Services may be supplied with the basic system or as additional optional components. Additional basic services may include the following:

Fault Detection and Resolution—Network faults are problems or conditions that occur in the network. These include configuration problems, overloaded devices, devices that have crashed due to software or hardware problems, and many other network-related problems. Due to the large size and complexity of many enterprise networks, the management software must provide a mechanism to detect, report, filter, and, in some situations, resolve network failures and problems. For example, when a critical system depletes the available disk space, the network management system should attempt to address the problem by executing a system utility to remove unnecessary files. Also, as with most enterprise networks, the number of networking faults is directly proportional to the number of monitored devices, which can be quite large. Inadequate handling of these faults can impact the ability of the network support staff to respond to the problem.

Alarm Notifications and Processing—Along with fault detection and resolution, a manager should provide a mechanism to respond to detected errors and conditions. An alarm is a programmed response to a network condition. Alarms connect the network condition to some action that will address the problem.

For example, an alarm is generated when a critical server becomes unavailable to the network and activates the pager of the system administrator, providing notification of the failure. Events, on the other hand, are specific conditions that are not always considered critical and might not warrant immediate notification or reaction. A change to the configuration of a device or a decrease in the load of a server can be considered a network event. For events such as these, it may be reasonable to simply log these events for future review.

Support Large Number of Devices—Managers are designed and required to handle a significantly large number of active devices. It is not uncommon for a manager to support hundreds or even thousands of devices from a theoretical standpoint. However, as a practical matter, managers are normally not configured to poll extremely large numbers of devices due to network performance considerations.

Reporting Tools—One of the most significant requirements of a network management system is its ability to effectively produce reports. The types of reports considered essential include performance, configuration, inventory, and fault. In many cases, the most critical area for reporting is related to performance. Network management systems can collect a large amount of performance statistics. An easy-to-use and flexible facility is required to assist with determining the general health of the network so that potential bottlenecks can be pinpointed quickly and easily. Also, the reporting software should handle inventory requirements in order to assist, for example, with determining device revision information needed to help with networking upgrades.

Easy to Use Interface—Typically a manager has a graphical user interface (GUI) to ease administration functions and tasks. Presently, network management systems are undergoing a transformation with respect to interfaces. Many network management vendors provide both native GUI support and Web-based interfaces for their products. Some vendors have taken the GUI concept to its fullest potential, and many have been successful in marrying disparate network devices to share a uniform view for management and control. This has been a tremendous advantage in managing the network from a remote or help-desk standpoint. The

Web model will certainly change the way network management has traditionally been done. However, it may be some time before network management products have completely migrated to a Web-enabled interface.

Performance Monitoring and Measuring—One of the most significant areas that cause network administrators trouble is managing network performance. Some network management system vendors provide tools to collect and analyze network performance information. This information is vital in diagnosing performance-related problems and aids in the proactive planning of network upgrades and/or other enhancements to improve network performance characteristics. Performance tools are aided by special hardware (and sometimes software) products that collect performance information on a continued basis. These devices, often referred to as network probes, are installed on the network or embedded with other devices like routers and switches. These probes listen in on the network and collect performance information and packet-level communication between network nodes. The network performance tools interact with these devices, poll the probes for performance data, and provide robust reporting and graphing capabilities.

Configuration Management—Enterprise networks often consist of equipment that requires custom configuration information to control the functionality and to correct system operations. A network management system must provide support for device configuration changes. For example, it is not uncommon to update one or more configuration parameters across a larger number of devices. In this case, it would be advantageous for the manager to handle this task in a logical, uniform manner. Network management systems are often criticized for their lack of sophisticated configuration management support. However, tremendous progress is now being made to address the complex task of configuration management and support.

Network Discovery—Due to the sheer volume of devices contained in an enterprise network, it is unreasonable to manually add all the devices to a network management system. Therefore, managers provide the ability to automatically look up or *discover* an entire network or a special class of devices. The network discovery process generally takes time and can consume a significant amount of network bandwidth. Care should be exercised when conducting the discovery process, as it can adversely affect network performance. After the discovery process is finished, the devices are placed in special views, which are usually arranged by subnetwork.

Additional Applications or Services

Often network management systems are deployed in environments where additional services and functions are necessary to address the unique business processes and support structure within an organization. These services will extend the usefulness and capabilities of a basic network manager by providing value-added applications that are layered onto the network management system. These applications may be available from third-party providers or from the vendor of the network management system itself. In many cases, network management vendors will seek solution partners to provide specific business software that will complement and integrate with the network management system.

The level of integration from third-party products will depend on the core services of the network management system, the effort involved with integrating into the management system, and the product functionality. Depending on the management system, integration from one vendor could mean having the ability to invoke software functions from a common menu, or it could mean gaining access to the database.

Some of the more popular applications and services that are available include:

Software Distribution—In large computing environments, it is necessary to have an automated mechanism to maintain software across the the many computer systems found on the network. With many sites, the network contains personal computers, workstations, and servers, each supporting one or more different operating systems. To address software manageability for those systems, network management systems provide automated software distribution software that can be used to load operating system patches and application software at the push of a button. Imagine, for instance, having to install a third-party application on 100 systems. Without network management software to *push* the application to these systems, the only alternative is to install this software by hand or build a custom installation script to do the job. Accomplishing this task manually requires a significant amount of time and effort. Because network administrators already have too much to do, having management software can positively impact this situation.

Trouble Ticketing—This application provides the ability to track and manage network events and failures in an automated fashion. When trouble ticketing is integrated with a network management system, certain network events or alarms can trigger the creation of a ticket that will notify the appropriate party or individual regarding the network problem. One problem with using this automated approach is the possibility of creating unwanted or invalid tickets. For example, should a building lose power momentarily and portions of the network reboot, many tickets could be generated because a large portion of the network was unavailable. Clearly it would be sufficient for a single ticket to be generated versus tickets for all possible devices. Some trouble ticket systems have the ability to filter incoming alarms based on user-defined criteria or other conditions. As a result, a filter could be created to measure the duration of an outage and, only after establishing the period of time elapsed, generate the appropriate ticket. When used carefully, this filter can provide a fully automated way to dispatch key personnel when network problems occur, without the requirement of a dedicated call support center.

Policy Based Management—Policy management is a relatively new aspect in network management. A policy involves establishing a resource profile or access domain for an individual user, group, or system. It might also contain user information such as access rights, privileges, Email identification, and so on. In particular, policies can be used to define the network from access control lists (ACLs) to broadcast domains. A broadcast domain describes the area or number of devices with which a system is permitted to communicate. Also, virtual local area networks (VLANs) and virtual private networks (VPNs) make use of policies to help define or shape the network and establish and enforce service-level agreements (SLAs).

Advanced Alarm Processing—Sometimes the basic alarm handling within the core management product doesn't provide the customization or functionality needed to address specific requirements. As a result, more advanced alarm-processing capabilities might be required. For example, it might be necessary for the alarm software to provide better mechanisms for alarm notification. Sometimes activating a pager is inappropriate, particularly in a lights-out, automated operation. Instead, the alarm software should be intelligent enough to make decisions about how to best resolve the issue. This can include running an external program or script, or initiating a fail-over sequence.

Network Simulation—Network simulation software emulates the behavior of a real network environment. In certain situations, it is advisable to model a network design or upgrade before any changes are made to the existing network. By interfacing with a network management system, the network simulations can be more realistic and dynamic because they are based on information about the actual devices and network topology, rather than static generic information.

## 02

Simple Network Management Protocol

The Simple Network Management Protocol (SNMP) provides the low-level framework for many network management systems. SNMP is widely implemented and can be found in a large variety of different networking devices and systems. Today, SNMP is considered the management protocol of choice for network hardware vendors, network management vendors, software application developers, Internet Service Providers (ISPs), and end users.

Why is SNMP so popular? First, SNMP is simple to implement compared to other network management architectures or protocols. The protocol, MIBs, and associated framework can be run on anything from low-end personal computers (PCs) to high-end mainframes, servers, and network devices such as routers and switches. An SNMP agent component doesn't need to occupy a large *footprint* in terms of memory and doesn't require significant processing power. SNMP can generally be developed very quickly on target systems, thus increasing the time-to-market for new products and enhancements. When SNMP was first introduced, other management mechanisms were available, but SNMP proved to be more flexible and easier to implement. It is true that SNMP lacks certain features found in other network management protocols (such as OSI, for example), but its simple design, extensibility, and ease of use minimize any possible drawbacks.

Second, SNMP is free and in the public domain. As a result, no single vendor can claim ownership of the protocol, nor can it be copy-protected by any company or individual. The only way to influence or change SNMP is to engage in the standards process of the Internet Engineering Task Force (IETF), which can be a daunting task. The IETF is one of the standards bodies for the Internet. Vendors may choose to make proprietary changes to SNMP. Such changes may prove futile, however, because these vendors must lobby other vendors and users to support their nonstandard enhancements, which defeats the purpose of having a standard in the first place.

Third, SNMP is well documented (via RFCs, articles, and textbooks) and well understood in the industry. This provides an established foundation for continued enhancement and adoption.

Finally, SNMP can be used to control a variety of devices. It is even finding its way into nontraditional equipment such as telephone systems, environmental control equipment, and just about anything else that can be attached to a network and requires management or control.

SNMP Operation

SNMP defines the packet format and information exchange between a network manager and associated agents. At its core, SNMP manipulates objects within the MIB of the agent and, as a result, can manage a variety of tasks defined within the agent. The SNMP protocol and related components are described in a number of RFCs. Any SNMP-compliant agent can communicate with any network management system that supports SNMP. The management system is responsible for asking questions of the agents. This is also known as polling the agent. If the agent supports standard MIBs, then the management system simply requests one or more objects from the agent. If the agent supports nonstandard MIBs (i.e., vendor-specific MIBs), then the manager must have a copy of the agent MIB to correctly interpret the supported agent objects.

One of the reasons SNMP is considered *simple* is because it provides three general-purpose operations that can be applied to agent objects. These operations, or functions, are at the heart of SNMP; they are set, get, and trap.

Set: A management system may update or change the value of an object that is contained in an agent. The set operation is a privileged command because, for example, it can be used to alter a device configuration or control its operating state.

Get: A management system may obtain or read the value of an object that is contained within an agent. The get function is the most common SNMP operation because this is the primary mechanism used to obtain management information from network devices.

Trap: An agent may send an unsolicited message to a network manager. The purpose of the trap service is to notify a network management system of a special condition or problem without the management system specifically requesting this information.

SNMP defines the relationship and message flow between manager and agent with respect to communications, as shown in Figure 2.1. As you can see, in most instances the SNMP manager directs

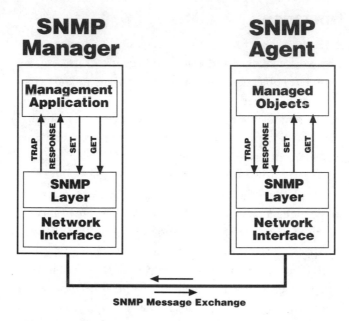

Figure 2.1 *SNMP manager and agent relationship.*

the message exchange with the agent. This is accomplished via either the get or set function. A management application requests information; the message is translated to SNMP using the SNMP layer, passed to the network interface layer, and eventually transmitted on the network. The agent receives the message on the network interface layer, passes the message to the SNMP for translation, and accesses the desired object information. The reverse process is used when the agent sends the reply from the manager.

SNMP provides the ability for the agent to send the manager asynchronous messages without specifically being polled. This is known as a *trap*. The trap provides a convenient and important way for agents to communicate without specifically being asked, and also to communicate important information or special circumstances or events.

SNMP doesn't define any additional mechanisms outside of the above-listed SNMP commands to control or issue commands to device agents. The only actions that can be applied to MIB objects are to set or get a value. For instance, there is no reboot function defined in SNMP. Instead, agent software can implement specific commands by associating MIB objects with the internal commands supported within the device. To reboot a device, the management station would alter (via the *set* operation) a specific MIB object to 1, for example. This would signal the agent to reboot the device and reset the MIB reboot object to its previous state. Note that no standard set of interfaces (or MIB objects) are currently available that can manipulate all aspects of device control. Instead, each vendor is responsible for providing this access using their own collection of MIB objects.

Management Information Base (MIB)

As previously mentioned, the MIB is a storehouse of information related to configuration, performance, and other data contained within an agent. MIBs have an organization and common structure and may contain a large number of objects separated into groups.

Organization

MIB objects are organized in a hierarchical tree structure in which each branch has a unique name and numeric identifier. Figure 2.2 shows the standard MIB organization from the root to additional branches. The branches of the tree serve as a logical grouping of related objects. The leaves, or *nodes* as they are often called, represent individual objects. Also, sub-trees are formed and represent both additional intermediate branches and connecting leaves. Objects within an MIB can be referenced by specifying each of the numeric identifiers starting with the top of the tree (or root) and proceeding to the individual leaf or object. The root of the branch is commonly written with a . (dot). Accessing MIBs is similar to referencing files within the UNIX operating system. However, one key difference is that UNIX pathnames can be expressed in absolute or relative terms. MIB objects can only be accessed in an absolute manner; the relative format is not available.

For example, Figure 2.2 shows root (.) at the topmost position of the tree and sysDescr(1) as the leaf. The common method of expressing object identifiers is to use the *dotted notation*. This notation requires that a dot separate each branch name or identifier. Often the root (.) is not expressed, as it is implied. To access

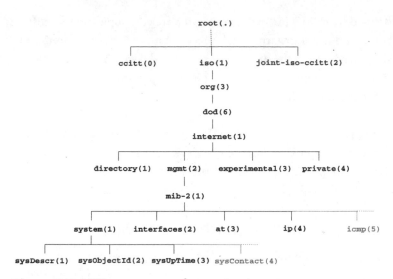

Figure 2.2 *MIB structure and organization.*

the `sysDescr(1)` object, the fully qualified identifier would be written as:

`iso.org.dod.internet.mgmt.mib-2.system.sysDescr`

This identifier is read from left to right. Objects can also be expressed in a short form by substituting the branch name with the numeric identifier associated with each identifier name. Thus, `iso.org.dod.internet.mgmt.mib-2.system.sysDescr` can also be expressed as `1.3.6.1.2.1.1.1`. These two expressions are functionally equivalent and reference the same MIB object. The reason to choose one form over the other is a matter of preference, although the numeric identifier is much more concise. However, MIB browsers can display MIB objects in either format, thus making it easy to convert from one format to the other. After using SNMP and MIBs for a short while, you will become familiar with both methods and have the opportunity to choose which style is best for you.

By using the structure shown in Figure 2.2, an SNMP manager (or MIB browser tool) can drill down into the MIB in an easy, yet concise manner. An MIB browser is a software application that traverses a MIB tree, usually showing a graphical display of branches, leaf objects, and associated values. Figure 2.3 shows a screen snapshot of an MIB browser. MIB browsers are great for probing an agent for specific information or learning the structure and format of new MIBs.

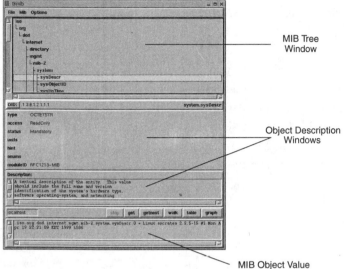

MIB Tree Window

Object Description Windows

MIB Object Value

Figure 2.3 *MIB browser.*

The MIB Browser window contains several sections, as shown in Figure 2.3. The first panel provides a hierarchical view of MIBs that can be used to *navigate* to the desired MIB object or branch. The next panel shows detailed information regarding the object. The third shows the value obtained from the MIB object specified. More detailed information regarding this tool can be found in Chapter 8, "SNMP Tools."

Object Types

Within an MIB, different object types represent data structures or values contained in an agent. The objects can represent physical agent attributes, configuration information, or other data. These object types are derived from the Abstract Syntax Notation (ASN.1) standard rules. ASN.1 provides a detailed mechanism for the implementation and encoding of basic data types that are machine-independent and can be transmitted over the network in an unambiguous way.

Why is this important to SNMP or network management? Because network management must address a heterogeneous network environment, a standard way must be provided to ensure that SNMP messages can be transmitted and understood on different systems and devices. Because various computer platforms store information differently, ASN.1 provides a common format. For example, an integer on one system can be expressed with the most significant digit first, while on others it might be expressed with the least significant digit first. Also, ASN.1 data types are found in MIBs. For us to understand network management, we must be able to read and understand MIB objects. Without a good grasp of MIBs, it will be difficult to use SNMP tools and software to manage a network effectively.

Two object data type classes are defined using ASN.1:

- universal types

- application types

The universal class consists of primitive types that can be used to build additional data types of objects within an MIB. Table 2.1 lists some of the available simple data types found in the universal class.

Table 2.1 *Universal data types*

ASN.1 Data Type	Description
INTEGER	A data type representing a cardinal number, where no limitation is made on the level of precision that might be required to represent an integer value
OCTET STRING	A data type representing zero or more octets, where each octet may take any value from 0 to 255
NULL	A data type meant as a placeholder, but currently not used

Table 2.1 *Universal data types (continued)*

ASN.1 Data Type	Description
OBJECT IDENTIFIER	A data type representing an authoritatively named object that consists of a sequence of values that specify an MIB tree.
SEQUENCE SEQUENCE OF	A data type used to denote an ordered list of zero or more elements that contain other ASN.1 types. SEQUENCE OF contains an ordered list of the same ASN.1 type.

SNMP derives some application data types from the universal class type. These application types define additional types that can be used to represent specific values customized for use within the network management environment. Table 2.2 describes some of the application data types presently available in the application class.

Table 2.2 *Application data types*

ASN.1 Data Type	Description
Counter Counter32	A data type that represents a non-negative integer that increases until it reaches a maximum value and then resets to zero. A counter is an INTEGER that can take a value between 0 and 4294967295. A counter has no defined starting value
Counter64	Just like a counter object except that a counter64 is an INTEGER that can take a value between 0 and 18446744073709551615
DisplayString	A data type representing zero or more octets, where each octet may take any value from 0 to 255. A DisplayString is like an OctetString object

Table 2.2 *Application data types (continued)*

ASN.1 Data Type	Description
Gauge Gauge32	A data type that represents a non-negative integer that may increase or decrease and will trigger at a maximum value. A gauge is like a counter in every other aspect
IpAddress	Represents an OCTET STRING that has a length of 4 bytes (32-bits) and where each of the four octets relates to the four bytes of a standard IP address
Opaque	A data type that provides the ability to pass arbitrary information that uses the OCTET STRING data type
NetworkAddress	Can represent an address from one of several network protocol address standards. Presently, it is the same as IpAddress
TimeTicks	Represents a non-negative integer that counts time in hundredths of a second since some established epoch. TimeTicks is like a counter in every other aspect

Why include this kind of MIB detail in this book? Because the sections in the succeeding chapters will focus on using network management tools that manipulate MIB objects, it seems reasonable to present the types of objects that might be encountered. It is therefore important that the reader understands the different types of objects and why values from these objects are in a certain format or structure. Of equal importance is the access mode of MIB objects, which is discussed below.

Sample MIB Object Listing

Because MIB objects are an important component of network management, some of the chapters in this book specifically describe MIB definitions as they relate to system agents and net-

work management tools. Therefore, when discussing MIBs, the
common format shown below will be used:

Object Name: sysDescr

OID: system.1

Object Type: Octet String

Access Mode: read-only

Status: current

Description: A description of the agent device or entity. This
value should include the full name, identification
of the system, hardware type, operating system,
and network software. It is mandatory that this
only contain printable ASCII characters. A sample of this object includes the following obtained
for the Linux system agent: Linux socrates
2.2.5-15 apr 19 22:21:09 EDT 1999

This format includes the *object name*, *OID string*, *object type*,
access mode, *status*, and *description*. The *object name* is the name
used when querying an agent for this particular object. In this
example, the sysDescr object is a string that contains a general
description of the device or agent contained within the device. The
object identifier string, or OID string, shows which group the
object is contained in and its logical position in that MIB hierarchy.
In this case, it is the first object in the system group. This group can
be found within the standard MIB-II definition.

The *object type* is OctetString and can be as long as 255 characters. Recall that Table 2.2 lists the definitions of these ASN.1
types. The *access mode* indicates how the manager or other tools
may manipulate the object. It is very common for those new to
SNMP to attempt to alter non-writable objects. In this case,
attempting to alter the sysDescr object will cause the agent to
respond with not writable or another error message.

The status field indicates if the object is current or historic.
The current status means that the object is presently available
within the agent as described within the MIB. That is, if the MIB
represents that agent, then all objects labeled as current will be

implemented within that agent. Other values can also be used to indicate additional states of the objects. For example, the `obsolete` reference indicates that the object is no longer supported within the MIB. The `deprecated` reference can be used to aid interoperability with older versions or implementations of the agent.

The *description* field provides an overview of the object, purpose, and a sample value if appropriate. In the above example, when the `sysDescr` object is queried, it returns the agent operating system (`Linux`), the hostname the agent resides with (`socrates`), operating system version information, and date information.

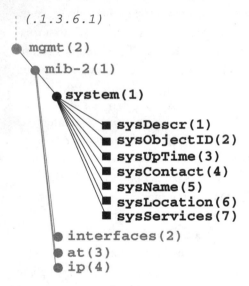

Figure 2.4 *Sample MIB structure.*

Another way this book describes MIBs is with a hierarchical graph showing each of the objects laid out in a tree structure. Figure 2.4 shows the general format. In particular, it shows the MIB-II objects found under the `system` group. As you can see, the formatting includes the use of closed circles (●) and closed squares (■). The squares represent discrete objects such as `INTEGER` and `OCTET STRING`, but not tables or other groups of objects. The circles represent groups of objects or tables. Also, gray lines and objects that are peripheral further indicate the structure needed to navigate to the group in question. These objects and associated lines that are of interest are drawn in black. Included with these objects is the member index (in parentheses) that shows the relative position of each object within the tree structure. Thus, `sysContact(4)` is the fourth object within the `system` group.

Tables

As noted above, an MIB may contain objects that represent physical characteristics of a device or other information contained within an agent. These objects can either be in the form of discrete elements (i.e., individual objects like `sysDescr`) or, in some cases, two-dimensional tables. Tables store related information that might contain several instances or copies of an MIB object. The best way to illustrate the use of a table is by examining a table within an actual MIB.

Defined in the MIB-II standard is the `interface` group that has the object identifier defined as `1.3.6.1.2.1.2` or `iso.org.dod.internet.mgmt.mib-2.interface`. Objects within this group represent physical network interfaces and related information installed within a networking device. Performance-related information is also collected and stored within this group.

For each interface within a network device, the following information is used to describe the nature of the interface and associated configuration:

- *Description:* general description of the interface

- *Type:* the type of interface, such as Ethernet or TokenRing

- *Mtu:* the maximum transmission size

- *Speed:* the transmission speed of the interface

- *Physical Address:* the datalink protocol or hardware address

- *Administration Status:* the current administrative status of the interface

- *Operational Status:* the actual operating status of the interface

- *Last Change:* the time when the interface became operational

Additional objects within the table store the following performance-monitoring information:

- number of octets received or sent

- number of unicast packets delivered to or sent from higher-level software

- number of non-unicast packets delivered to or sent from higher-level software

- number of inbound/outbound packets discarded

- number of inbound/outbound packets containing errors

- number of inbound/outbound packets discarded due to bad protocol

- length of the output packet queue

Figure 1.5 shows the structure of the interface group. Tables are used to contain interface information because networking devices can contain many interfaces. For example, a router or switch device can contain literally dozens of interfaces, often supporting different network protocols such as Ethernet, ATM, or FDDI. Using a table provides a straightforward and convenient way to access individual objects within a given interface definition.

The `interface` group includes the `ifNumber` object, which contains the total number of network interfaces within the networking device. Using the sample data contained in Table 2.3, the `ifNumber` value would be `2`. In this case, the device reports two interfaces: one defined as a pseudo-interface and the other defined as an Ethernet. It is common for networking devices to contain a pseudo-interface for internal diagnostic purposes.

The rest of the `interface` group consists of a table called `ifTable`, which contains a row for each interface defined within the device. This table is indexed by `ifIndex`, which contains a value between the range of 1 and the value of `ifNumber`. The `ifIndex` object uniquely addresses each column of the table that represents the interface.

Table 2.3 shows the entire interface group in the first column and associated values taken from an actual network device in the remaining columns. Each row corresponds to each of the specific MIB objects contained within the `ifEntry` table. Each `ifEntry`

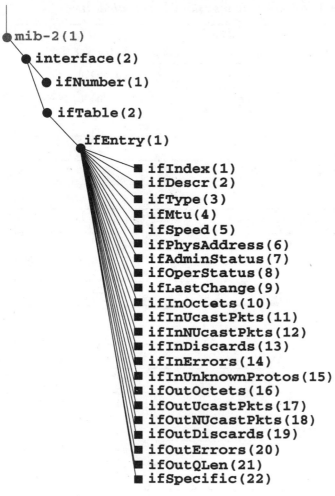

Figure 2.5 *MIB-II interface group structure.*

Table 2.3 *Interface group instance table*

MIB Objects	IfEntry 1.3.6.1.2.1.2.2.1	IfEntry 1.3.6.1.2.1.2.2.2
IfIndex	1	2
ifDescr	Pseudo Interface	Ethernet
ifType	1	6
ifMtu	1500	1500

Table 2.3 *Interface group instance table (continued)*

MIB Objects	IfEntry 1.3.6.1.2.1.2.2.1	IfEntry 1.3.6.1.2.1.2.2.2
IfSpeed	10000000	10000000
ifPhysAddress	None[a]	0x000400l0ee5d
IfAdminStatus	1	1
IfOperStatus	1	1
IfLastChange	0	0
IfInOctets	0	42617
IfInUcastPkts	445	680
IfInNUcastPkts	0	19
IfInDiscards	0	0
IfInErrors	0	5
IfInUnknown-Protos	0	0
IfOutOctets	0	42600
IfOutUcastPkts	445	570
IfOutNUcastPkts	0	94
IfOutDiscards	0	0
IfOutErrors	0	87
IfOutQLen	0	0
ifSpecific	null	null

a. Pseudo-interfaces do not normally have physical addresses associated with them. That is why no interface address is listed here.

instance represents an interface defined in the table. To access the object ifDescr for the first interface, one would use the object identifier (OID):

1.3.6.1.2.1.2.2.1.1

    or

iso.org.dod.internet.mgmt.mib-2.interface.ifTable.ifEntry.ifDescr

The `ifDescr` object provides a general description of the interface. The objects starting from `IfInOctets` to `IfOutQLen` represent traffic counters within the agent for device interfaces and can be used to measure network and device performance.

Accessing Objects

MIB objects are defined with access control information that specifies what kind of operation can be performed on the object. SNMP includes the following access control information for MIB objects:

- not-accessible

- accessible-for-notify

- read-only

- read-write

- read-create

Not-accessible objects defined within the MIB usually reference object definitions, or other object descriptions that are not objects themselves, that can be manipulated by an SNMP manager. One good example is the table data structure, where an object describes the shape or size of the table but not the actual rows or columns.

Accessible-for-notify objects are only available via a notification to a network manager or another agent. No direct polling of the object is permitted.

Read-only objects are not alterable by the network management system, but values may be obtained via a get or trap operation. Why would a change to an MIB object be prohibited? The reason is very clear: certain MIB information will never change during the life of a product. For example, the MIB object `sysDescr`, which stands for *system description*, contains vendor information for the agent. An SNMP manager should not modify this information because it would disassociate the device with the actual product vendor, thus making agent identification difficult. Also, it can adversely affect the accuracy of any software-based network inventory mechanisms. Another reason to make objects read-only is to ensure that performance information or other statistical data remains accurate rather than getting altered unintentionally.

Read-write access is necessary when a particular object must be altered to accomplish some specific goal or must be configured in a certain way. For example, it might be necessary to disable a router port due to a large number of errors detected on one of its interfaces. In this case, the network management system must change the operational status of the interface to 0, thus shutting down the physical connection until the cause of the errors is determined.

Read-create objects have the same access permission as read-only and read-write objects. Read-create access is used for objects that may be created on-the-fly. Such objects may include table row (also called conceptual row) instances, for example.

Standard and Private MIBs

As previously mentioned, MIBs are organized under a hierarchical tree structure, and a number of standard MIBs have been developed and placed under the mgmt(2) branch. Many of these MIBs were developed via the RFC process. Many different individuals or vendors assisted with their development but don't actually own them, nor can they arbitrarily make changes to them. However, many vendors and third-party software developers have developed additional MIBs to address specific functionality or services for their particular products. Many of these MIBs, known as enterprise MIBs, start under the private(4) branch of the standard MIB tree. Figure 2.6 shows several popular MIBs that can be found under this branch.

The Internet Assigned Numbers Authority (IANA) maintains a list of assigned enterprise numbers. Those wishing to obtain a number make a request to this organization and obtain a valid number. Table 2.4 shows a small sample of the numbers that have already been assigned.

Why develop enterprise MIBs? Many vendors do so because they may need specific objects for their devices that may not be defined or available within the standard MIBs. Also, vendor-specific MIBs don't need to become standards, since only that vendor and their customers actually need to use the MIBs. It only makes sense to develop standard MIBs when many vendors can imple-

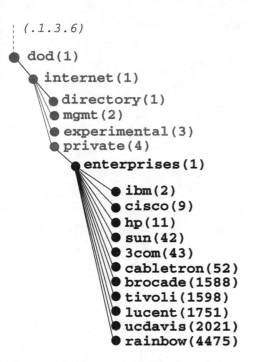

Figure 2.6 *Enterprise MIBs from private branch.*

ment the same collection of MIBs across a large number of different devices.

Table 2.4 *Assigned enterprise numbers*

Number	Vendor
2	IBM
9	Cisco Systems
11	Hewlett-Packard
42	Sun Microsystems
43	3Com Corporation
52	Cabletron Systems
1588	Brocade Communications Systems
1598	Tivoli Systems

Table 2.4 *Assigned enterprise numbers (continued)*

Number	Vendor
1751/3729	Lucent Technologies
4475	Rainbow Software Solutions

SNMP Communities

Often a network management system will be deployed in a large network environment that contains a collection of many different groups of networks and devices. Thus, it is reasonable for an enterprise network to be divided into zones or communities of users in order to partition responsibility. As a result, a `community name` can be assigned to a class of devices and provide a security boundary that helps to implement the desired communities or zones. SNMP supports this kind of security model based on community string information, which is physically added to each device within the selected community. Some practical examples include selecting a community that represents all the Cisco backbone routers and selecting another community that includes devices in just the sales department.

SNMP's present community-based authentication model is considered very weak and poses a significant security problem. The major reason is that SNMP doesn't provide any encryption facilities or other mechanisms to ensure that the community information is not simply copied from the network during an SNMP packet exchange. Using a packet capture tool, the entire SNMP packet could be decoded, thus revealing the community name. As a result of this limitation, many sites disable set operations to many of the agent devices. This has the unfortunate side effect of limiting SNMP usefulness because it can then only monitor object values and not alter them.

Overview of SNMP Versions

SNMP became generally available in 1988. Since then, it has seen widespread use and been implemented in virtually all local area networking (LAN) devices and on many computer operating systems. This popular version, known as SNMPv1, accounts for a significant portion of the installed base of agents today. Despite its popularity, SNMPv1 has several fundamental problems. First, because it lacks a robust security mechanism, it can't be used to its full potential. As a result, many vendors limit the **set** operations on agents to minimize the potential risk of a security breach. Second, SNMPv1 doesn't optimize the processing of large amounts of information, thus further restricting the use of SNMP. Third, SNMPv1's relationship between network manager and agent are well defined—agents play only a single, simplistic role of accepting commands from more management systems. This significantly limits SNMPv1 when smart agents are needed to address specific requirements for distributed network management functions. SNMPv1 also specifies a collection of MIB objects known as MIB-II. The goal of MIB-II was to provide a collection of objects that all SNMP agents can supported, regardless of which vendor implemented the agent. To summarize, SNMPv1 provides:

- the basic network management framework

- the definition of the MIB-II standard

- descriptions of the Protocol Data Units (PDUs), which include: *GetRequest, GetNextRequest, SetRequest, GetResponse,* and *Trap*

- a description of ASN.1 encoding language

To address some of the deficiencies in SNMPv1, a significant amount of effort has been made over the past few years to enhance SNMP. The first series of improvements came in 1993 when a series of 12 RFCs (1441-1452) was introduced, proposing to add PDUs and enhancements to the SNMP architecture and security model. This collection of RFCs was known as SNMPv2 Classic. At that time, many users of SNMP were anticipating these improvements and planned to implement the new version as soon as it became available.

Unfortunately, there was still much debate about SNMPv2 security and remote configuration. When it became apparent that not all the original SNMPv2 proposals were going to be widely adopted, additional work was done to define SNMP security and remote configuration management components. This led to additional proposals that included a new protocol and new MIB structure elements (documented in RFCs 1901-1908). These proposals were more popular than SNMPv2 Classic and became known as community-base SNMPv2 or SNMPv2c. The problem with SNMPv2c was that, though it was endorsed by the IETF, it lacked robust security and administration facilities.

Additional improvements to the remote management capability of SNMPv1 resulted in proposals known as SNMPv2usec and SNMPv2*, documented in RFC 1909-1910 and RFC 2222, respectively. The SNMPv2usec recommends a robust security model and administrative framework. One of the problems with SNMPv2usec is that it lacks endorsement of the IETF, which relinquished the proposal to a non-standard. The major functions of SNMPv2 include:

- expanded data types, such as 64-bit counters

- improved performance and efficiency with the *get-bulk* PDU

- event notification with the *inform* PDU

- better error handling

- more efficient row creation and deletion

Finally, in an attempt to reach some agreement between the various remote management and security proposals, another series of RFCs was written, which later became known as SNMPv3. These RFCs (2271-2275) have been put forth by the IETF as Proposed Standards, which means that they are available to the general public for review and discussion. SNMPv3 is SNMPv2c plus provisions for robust security and administration; it draws upon the SNMPv2c RFCs (1902-1908). At a high level, the SNMPv3 proposal attempts to:

- put forth a security model based on DES, MD5, and other authentication protocols

- define a view-based access control model

- redefine some of the SNMP concepts and terms

SNMPv3 has enjoyed a certain level of success in the market-place at this point, but the protocols are still quite new. Major net-working hardware and software companies already support SNMPv3 or are working on it right now. However, SNMPv3 has yet to be deployed widely within the industry; this is perhaps just a matter of time. One of the major delays for adoption of this new protocol is the cost-to-benefit ratio. For those sites that require bet-ter security today, they can upgrade to the new protocols as ven-dors make their implementation available. However, it may not be justifiable for everyone to upgrade all existing equipment to sup-port SNMPv3. The most likely approach will be to migrate slowly over time as newer products that contain SNMPv3 support are deployed. Eventually, new products will replace the older ones, and deploying the new management protocols will simply be a matter of configuration.

SNMP Protocol Operation

An SNMPv1 message contains three major components: a ver-sion field, a community field, and an SNMP protocol data unit (PDU) field. Unlike other TCP/IP protocols, SNMP packets are not of a fixed length and, instead, rely on ASN.1 formatting. Figure 2.7 shows this basic SNMP packet structure and a description of the fields (and sizes) follows.

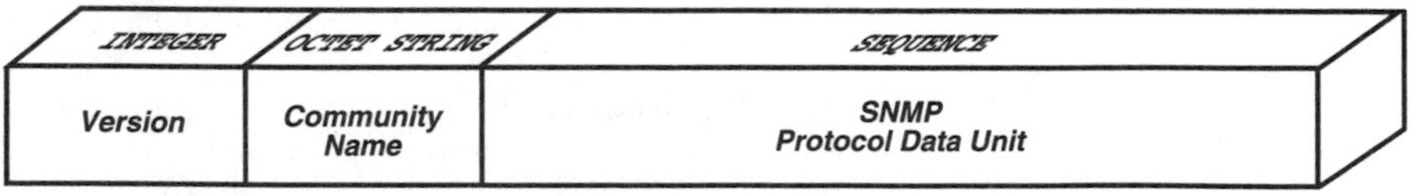

Figure 2.7 *SNMP message format.*

The format includes field names, shown in bold text, and for-matting labels (type), as shown on the top in gray text. The type shows the basic format for each of the fields. For instance, the ver-sion information is an INTEGER object. The field names are defined as follows.

version: This field indicates which version of the SNMP protocol is being used. Presently version 1 is the most widely implemented and supported SNMP protocol.

community name: The community is used as the primary security mechanism to establish authentication from a network manager to agents within SNMP. The community name or string is used as a password for which requests to access objects are permitted, based on the condition that the network manager knows the agent's password. If the agent has been configured to emit traps, an authenticationFailure trap is generated when a network manager queries an agent with an invalid community string.

protocol data units: SNMPv1 PDUs can be one of five different types and consist of request and response components. They include:

•*GetRequest*

•*GetNextRequest*

•*SetRequest*

•*GetResponse*

•*Trap*

SNMPv2 defines these additional PDUs:

•*GetBulkRequest*

•*InformRequest*

Each of the GetRequest, GetNextRequest, and SetRequest components elicits from the responding agent a GetResponse that might contain valid data or an error status.

GetRequest

The GetRequest PDU is issued by an SNMP manager or application to obtain one or more MIB objects from an SNMP agent.

Figure 2.8 shows the packet format that contains the following fields:

pdu type: indicates the PDU type is a GetRequest.

request-id: unique identifier that permits the SNMP man-
                     ager to match paired requests and responses. It
                     also aids in detecting duplicate messages that
                     may be received when using an unreliable
                     transport service.

variable-bindings: a list of requested MIB objects.

The GetRequest operation is the primary way to obtain information from agents when the objects in question are known
beforehand. For example, should the network manager decide to
retrieve `sysDescr` and `sysUpTime` objects from an agent, we can
think of the request as simply a function to include:

```
GetRequest (sysDescr, sysUpTime)
```

In this case, both of these objects are placed within the variable-
binding field when sent. The `sysDescr` object represents a string
that contains a general description of the agent, and `sysUptime`
reflects the amount of time that an agent has been running.

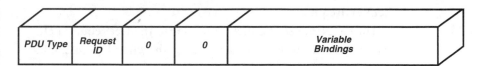

Figure 2.8 *GetRequest message format.*

When the agent receives the above message and no errors have
occurred, it will respond with the values of the MIB objects
requested via a GetResponse PDU. The GetRequest operation is
atomic. That is, either all the values requested are returned or no
values are returned. When the receiving entity responds to the
GetRequest, it includes the values in the GetResponse variable-
binding field. If, for some reason, at least one of the values cannot
be supplied, no values will be provided.

If the values requested from a manager cannot be returned by the agent, the agent will respond with an error. For example, the management system might have requested an MIB object that isn't implemented in the agent. In this case, the agent can't possibly satisfy the request, and thus an error is returned. Also, in certain situations, returning the value of a requested object fails because it might be too large to be processed by the manager.

The *variable-bindings* field includes a list of objects for which values are requested. When the agent responds via GetResponse, the variable binding includes the requested objects and associated values. Given the example above, the following GetResponse would be sent by the agent:

```
GetResponse(sysDescr="3Com Enterprise Monitor", sysUpTime\
=0000154477)
```

In this example, the agent is a 3Com enterprise RMON monitor (or network probe), as indicated by the sysDescr field. This device collects network performance and packet contents information for later analysis and reporting. The sysUpTime object contains the amount of time the agent has been up and running. The value shown in the example indicates that the device was running for approximately 15 minutes and 44 seconds.

GetNextRequest

The GetNextRequest PDU is similar to the GetRequest PDU, and the packet formats are identical, as shown in Figure 2.8. However, the GetNextRequest PDU has one difference: it is used to retrieve objects when the structure of the MIB tree is unknown. The GetNextRequest can be a great asset when it is used to discover the exact MIB structure of an agent. Why would an agent's MIB structure be unknown to an SNMP manager? SNMP provides no direct way to determine which MIBs or MIB structure is supported within an agent. Vendors are of course free to implement whichever MIBs their devices need. Therefore, the network manager must discover the supported MIBs by walking the MIB tree in an automated fashion. When the GetNextRequest is sent with a particular object, the GetResponse returns the requested object's value, plus the instance of the next lexicographic object in the MIB tree. As a result, each GetNextRequest will reveal the next object within the MIB without the manager knowing what the next object will be. The GetNextRequest operation also provides a more efficient mechanism to retrieve objects from an agent than GetRequest because it requires fewer request/response exchanges.

SetRequest

The SetRequest operation is used to alter agent information such as the value of a MIB object. The packet format is the same as GetRequest and GetNextRequest, as shown in Figure 2.8. Unlike GetRequest or GetNextRequest, SetRequest is used to alter the value of an MIB object. As mentioned before, the SetRequest requires security privileges, which are presently mapped via the community string for the SNMPv1 protocol. Therefore, the agent must validate the SetRequest community string provided before the operation is permitted to succeed. The SetRequest is also atomic; either all the values can be altered or none can. If the Set-Request is successful, a GetResponse is returned and the variable-binding list contains the objects with their new values. This is how the network manager can determine that the set operation was successful. If the SetRequest was unsuccessful, an error is returned in the GetResponse.

GetResponse

Each of the SNMP operations, with the exception of the trap, receives a GetResponse from the agent. Figure 2.9 shows the format of the GetResponse packet, which includes the following fields:

pdu type: indicates the PDU type, which is GetResponse.

request-id: unique identifier that permits the pairing of requests and responses.

error-status: indicates that an exception condition occurred while processing the request.

error-index: when an error occurrs, indicates which object variable in the variable-binding list caused the error.

variable-bindings: a list of MIB objects that are involved in the
operation.

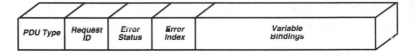

Figure 2.9 *GetResponse message format.*

Trap

A *Trap* is an unsolicited message, from an agent directed to a
network management station, that represents a significant event or
condition for which notification to the manager is considered necessary. This type of communication from the agent is asynchronous
as compared to the polling from the manager. The Trap PDU is
quite different from that of the other PDUs defined in SNMP, as
shown in Figure 2.10. Unlike the other SNMP PDUs, Trap does
not warrant a response from the receiving network. The fields
from a Trap include:

PDU Type: indicates that the PDU type is a Trap.

Enterprise: contains the MIB object `sysObjectID` of the
                   sending agent. The `sysObjectID` object
                   includes information regarding the vendor of
                   the agent that sent the Trap.

Agent-address: represents the IP address of the sending agent.

Generic-trap: one of the predefined Trap values listed in
                   Table 2.5.

Specific-trap: more detailed information about the Trap.
                   This is usually `zero` unless the generic-trap is
                   an `enterpriseSpecific` Trap. Enterprise
                   Traps are vendor-specific and may contain
                   additional agent information about the condi-
                   tion that caused the Trap in the first place.

Time-stamp: the amount of time between the generation of the Trap and when the device was last initialized, expressed in tens of milliseconds.

Variable-binding: vendor-specific information related to the Trap.

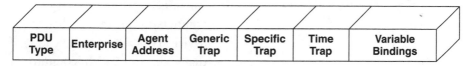

| PDU Type | Enterprise | Agent Address | Generic Trap | Specific Trap | Time Trap | Variable Bindings |

Figure 2.10 *Trap message format.*

Table 2.5 lists the seven predefined general Trap types. The enterpriseSpecific Trap type is provided as a mechanism to define custom or proprietary traps that do not fit within the other generic types.

Table 2.5 *SNMP predefined traps*

Trap Type	Meaning
ColdStart (0)	The device is restarting or reinitializing itself such that the agent or configuration may be changed. Usually, this indicates a crash or other reboot condition
WarmStart (1)	The device is restarting or reinitializing itself such that no changes are made to the agent or configuration. Usually, this implies a simple refresh or reboot of the operating system environment
LinkDown (2)	Indicates a failure on one of the device's communications (interface) links

Table 2.5 *SNMP predefined traps (continued)*

Trap Type	Meaning
LinkUp (3)	Indicates that a device's communication (interface) link is now up and running
AuthenticationFailure (4)	An authentication or security failure has occurred on the device. Typically, this indicates that an invalid SNMP community string has been used
EgpNeighborLoss (5)	Indicates that external gateway protocol (EGP) neighbor, of which the device is a peer, has been labeled down and the relationship no longer is valid
EnterpriseSpecific (6)	Indicates that some vendor-specific event has occurred. Vendors use this generic trap type to represent their own proprietary traps

GetBulkRequest

This PDU is issued by an SNMPv2 manager or application to minimize network interaction and permit the agent to return larger packets (as compared to the GetNextRequest or GetRequest), thus improving the efficiency of obtaining a large number of objects from an agent. This uses the same PDU format as most other SNMPv1 operators. The only difference is the re-naming of the *error-status* and *error-index* (from the Response PDU) fields to *non-repeaters* and *max-repetitions*, respectively. These fields are defined as follows:

non-repeaters: the number of MIB objects that should be retrieved once at most *max-repetitions:* the maximum number of times other MIB objects should be retrieved

InformRequest

The InformRequest PDU is issued by an SNMPv2 entity acting in a manager role to another SNMPv2 entity acting in the same role for the purpose of providing network management information. The major function of this PDU is to provide distributed SNMP management capabilities. Thus, an agent can implement this PDU to provide management-like services and functions. The format of this PDU is the same as for GetRequest and other related PDUs.

SNMP Response Codes

The error codes returned from an SNMPv1 agent were very limited. For example, if an SNMP manager requested the set operation on a MIB object, and the agent couldn't perform the operation as requested, the agent would reply with `noSuchName`. With the addition of more error codes in SNMPv2, the agent would reply with `notWritable` in this situation. Table 2.6 lists all of the SNMP response codes.

Table 2.6 *SNMP response codes*

Response Code	Description
SNMPv1	
`tooBig`	Returned by the agent if the response to a request would be too large to send
`noSuchName`	Returned by the agent in either of these two cases: 1) if a **set** operation is attempted for an object that is not in the MIB view, or 2) if a **set** operation is attempted for an object that is in the MIB view, but its object is `read-only`. This code is now used for proxy compatibility

Table 2.6 *SNMP response codes (continued)*

Response Code	Description
badValue	Returned by the agent that has detected an error in the PDU variable binding list. This code is now used for proxy compatibility
Read-only	Returned by the agent. This code is now used for proxy compatibility
genError	Returned by the agent when processing of a PDU fails for a reason other than what is listed in this table
SNMPv2/v3	
noAccess	The variable is outside the defined MIB view for this operation to succeed
notWritable	The variable exists within the agent, but the agent is unable to modify the object
WrongType	The value supplied is of the wrong data type, as defined by ASN.1
WrongLength	The value supplied is of the wrong length
WrongEncoding	The value supplied was not encoded correctly
WrongValue	The value supplied is not within the range required for the object type
NoCreation	The object doesn't exist and the agent is unable to create an instance of this object

Table 2.6 *SNMP response codes (continued)*

Response Code	Description
InconsistentName	The object doesn't exist and the agent is unable to create an instance of this object because the name is inconsistent with the values of other related objects
InconsistentValue	The object provided is inconsistent with the values of the managed objects
resourceUnavailable	A needed resource within the agent can't be reserved to complete the request

These codes are important because they can help you track down problems and issues when using SNMP agents and tools that communicate with agents. Determining the solution to SNMP problems is aided by knowing these message codes and understanding the difference between configuration errors with the agent versus connectivity problems between the manager and agent.

Transmission of an SNMP Message

The following series of events occurs when a network manager formulates an SNMP message:

1. The basic PDU is constructed.

2. The PDU is passed to the security service layer if available.

3. The protocol layer formats the message, including the version and community information.

4. The entire message is now encoded using ASN.1 rules.

5. The message is passed to the transport service so that it will be delivered to the receiving entity.

The following series of events occurs when an agent device receives an SNMP message:

1. A basic check is performed to ensure the message is formatted correctly. The message is discarded if any errors are encountered.

2. The protocol version information is verified. If there is a mismatch, the message is discarded.

3. The security service attempts to verify the sending entity. If this fails, a trap is generated and the message is discarded.

4. The PDU is decoded.

5. The PDU is processed.

Connectionless Protocol

SNMP is a connectionless protocol, which means that it doesn't support the concept of establishing and controlling a dedicated connection like Telnet or FTP. SNMP transmits information between an agent and a manager by the use of requests and return responses. This removes the burden from agents of having to support additional protocols and processes associated with connection-based schemes. Therefore, SNMP provides its own mechanism to address reliability and error detection.

Master and Subagent

When deploying network management software, it is common to have a single agent installed on each system that will be managed. In the case of networking devices such as network routers and switches, usually only a single agent is available. In either case, the agents will communicate with one or more network managers using the standard SNMP port of 161. For most needs, a single agent approach makes sense and is appropriate. However, there are instances when more than one agent is necessary to achieve the desired level of manageability. For example, workstation manufacturers will often provide an SNMP agent within their operating system. This particular system agent will usually support a limited number of operating system functions and parameters. If we wish to manage database services on this same system via SNMP, this will require that we install another agent to specifically monitor the database functions. This poses a problem because both agents will typically be accessed by the SNMP manager using the same standard port. Further, when the agents are started by the system, the first agent will start and open the port 161 and will operate normally. However, when the second agent starts and attempts to do the same, it will get an error stating that the port is busy and it should abort operation.

Two possible approaches can be taken to address this port contention problem. First, one of the agents can be configured to use an alternative port instead of standard 161. This solution will work if the agent can be made to support another port when it is started by the system. Many system agents do support alternative ports, but this is by no means the rule. The major drawback to this solution is that any SNMP managers used to poll the agent must now be configured to use this new port as well. This doesn't pose a significant problem when only a small number of non-standard ports are used. However, if this solution is used on a large scale, say with many agents all using non-standards ports across a large number of systems, the approach loses its appeal because of the administrative burden it may introduce.

The other solution might be considered more elegant because it involves using a master agent and one or more subagents. A master agent solves the port conflict problem by becoming the keeper of the standard SNMP port and forwards all the SNMP traffic to the appropriate subagent. Subagents are normal SNMP agents, but they are registered with the master agent and assigned nonstandard ports that are used to communicate with the master agent. SNMP messages from managers are sent to the master agent, who in turn delivers the message to the correct subagent using the port it dynamically assigned to the subagent. Figure 2.11 shows a diagram of the master/subagent architecture. One major benefit of this solution is that it alleviates the administration task of modifying the SNMP managers cited in the first solution. Also, this solution can scale very well because new subagents can be added in a straightforward manner.

On the negative side, the master agent can pose a problem because it can crash or otherwise become inoperative. This would have the adverse effect of disabling the connectivity to the sub-

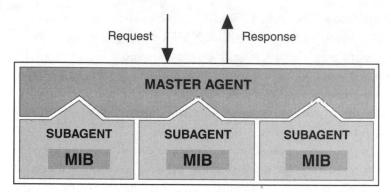

Figure 2.11 *Master/Subagent architecture.*

agents. Because this particular problem can be said of other software systems as well, the risk, although not zero, isn't necessarily a
significant factor. Also, because the master agent is responsible for
delivering the SNMP to the appropriate subagent, it takes a certain
amount of processing time and overhead. This might be a factor in
time-critical management functions.

Several proposals and products have been put forth in an
attempt to provide a standard mechanism that supports a master
and subagent architecture. These include SMUX[1](RFC1227),
AgentX (RFC2257), and vendor-specific products like master
agent on Solaris and the master agent on HP-UX. All of these
accomplish the same purpose: permitting two or more agents to
operate on the same system without port conflict problems.

1. This RFC has been promoted to historic status and as such may not receive
attention from network management product vendors.

## 03

TCP/IP Protocol Suite

As a network administrator, you will be required to interact directly with the TCP/IP protocols and related services. As a result, you will need a good understanding of TCP/IP, associated protocols, and applications. Today, TCP/IP is used extensively by many corporations, institutions, and other organizations to address their networking requirements. It is considered the protocol family of choice by networking manufacturers, operating system vendors, and users alike. In fact, the world's largest network, the Internet, uses TCP/IP exclusively.

TCP/IP Protocol Suite

If you have accessed a Web site, transferred files from an FTP server, or sent Email via the Internet, you have indirectly used the TCP/IP protocols. Fundamentally, TCP/IP provides a standard way to deliver data from one system to another without the concern for operating system differences and network hardware. TCP/IP is an acronym that stands for two separate protocols: Transmission Control Protocol (TCP) and Internet Protocol (IP). However, TCP/IP generally refers to these protocols, plus a suite of related protocols. For example, the File Transfer Protocol (FTP) uses TCP/IP and provides a basic file transfer facility across devices that support TCP/IP. If the device supports TCP/IP, it is generally assumed to support FTP and a host of protocols and other services as well.

Today, the TCP/IP suite is supported on every major computer operating system available. As such, it is considered the most popular networking protocol, and many of the same TCP/IP services are available on different versions of UNIX. This is good news, because many of the core functions of TCP/IP and applications are the same across different versions of UNIX. The operations of TCP/IP are independent of operating system or computer platform. The protocol hides the underlying operating system details and provides a common framework for establishing connectivity among systems.

Many networking devices such as routers, switches, and specialized devices implement TCP/IP protocols for local administration and control. Generally speaking, a small core set of services is available on these devices. Table 3.1 shows the list of services available on some of the most popular networking devices. As you can see, SNMP, Telnet, and FTP are the most widely implemented services.

The TCP/IP suite is built on industry standards and is documented completely in Request for Comments (RFCs). This means the protocol will remain open and standard, and no single vendor can own the protocols or develop proprietary extensions. As a result, many networking hardware vendors provide support for TCP/IP in their products.

Table 3.1 *TCP/IP protocol support for administration*

Device Type	TCP/IP Protocols
3Com CoreBuilder switch	HTTP, FTP, Telnet, and SNMP
3Com RMON probe	TFTP and SNMP
Cisco 7000 router	HTTP, FTP, Telnet, and SNMP
Brocade fibre channel switch	HTTP, Telnet, and SNMP
Lexmark laser printer	FTP and SNMP

TCP/IP is independent of the datalink protocol and can be used with many different networking technologies, including FDDI, Ethernet, ATM, TokenRing, Frame Relay, and SMDS. TCP/IP makes it possible to build a truly heterogeneous network consisting of products and network technologies from many different vendors and sources. In fact, the Internet, which is considered the world's largest network, consists of devices from many networking vendors that operate together. That's not to say the Internet doesn't have its share of networking issues or problems, but, for the most part, many would agree that interoperability between equipment vendors isn't a major factor for the established core set of TCP/IP protocols.

From a management standpoint, many of the tools used to administer TCP/IP systems are consistent across most UNIX operating system versions. These tools are described in Chapter 6, "Network Management Agents." However, one issue that can be a problem is that each UNIX operating system vendor can and does implement non-protocol details differently. For example, how the IP address information is stored on each network device is not covered by any RFC standard, nor should it be. The present TCP/IP suite provides a mechanism to dynamically assign IP addresses to devices, and it also mandates that they be uniquely assigned to each device attached to the network. However, IP addresses are stored on a local system and are not a protocol matter, but rather a network management or system configuration issue, which is traditionally resolved at the operating system level. Each operating system vendor provides its own solutions to how IP address information or other operating system parameters are to be stored.

OSI Model

Networking protocols including TCP/IP can be mapped to a general network model. This model defines the relationship and services that each protocol will provide to other associated protocols, services, and applications. The most common standard network model is based on Open Standard Interconnect (OSI). The OSI seven-layer model is represented by a series of layers stacked one upon another, which, when viewed collectively, represent the operation of an entire network. Each layer represents a unique view of the elements that make up the network. The layers of the OSI model consist of the following:

- application

- presentation

- session

- transport

- network

- datalink

- physical

Application Layer

Provides services to users that include file transfer, electronic email, remote host access, and many other services.

Presentation Layer

Is used to provide a common interface for applications to the lower layers and implement common services that might include encryption, reformatting, and compression.

Session Layer

Provides the mechanism to establish, maintain, and terminate sessions between cooperating applications.

Transport Layer

Ensures reliable, transparent data transfer, flow control, and data error detection and recovery between two endpoints.

Network Layer

Provides upper-layer protocol transparency because different network communication methodologies may be used. This layer is responsible for establishing, maintaining, and terminating connections for different networks.

Datalink Layer

Provides data transfer service on the physical link using frames; handles error detection, flow control, and related services. Some common frame types include Ethernet, FDDI, and TokenRing.

Physical Layer

Addresses the mechanism connectivity requirements (such as cables and connectors) and provides transmission of a bit stream that involves controlling voltage characteristics to produce the appropriate signals. Examples include cabling for Ethernet, Fast Ethernet, FDDI, and TokenRing.

TCP/IP Protocol Architecture

Placing or overlaying the TCP/IP suite on the OSI model helps demonstrate TCP/IP's protocol operation and its relationship to other protocols. Figure 3.1 shows a pictorial view of where TCP/IP fits into the OSI model.

As shown in Figure 3.1, the TCP/IP model consists of four layers. Each layer maps to one or more of the OSI layers, which include:

- process

- host-to-host

- Internet

- network access

Except for network access, the other three component layers are software-based and consist of programmed modules that provide

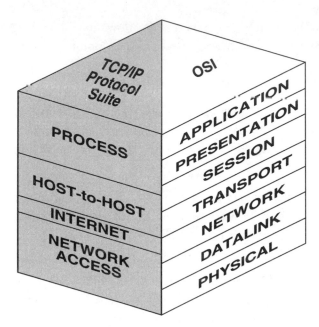

Figure 3.1 *TCP/IP over the OSI networking model.*

the required functionality. Typically, these components are incorporated into operating systems to provide generalized access.

Process Layer

This layer provides user applications and interfaces with the host-to-host layer. Additional protocols and services are also found on this layer. The process layer maps to the presentation and application layers, which are defined within the OSI model. Applications on this layer include Telnet, FTP, SMTP, and many others.

Host-to-host Layer

This layer is responsible for ensuring that data is reliable and that each higher-level service obtains the correct information from the sending entity. The protocol supported on this layer is TCP. The layer maps to the OSI transport layer. The term used to describe information on the host-to-host layer is *segment*.

Internet Layer

This layer provides an unreliable flow of information from one network to another. From an OSI standpoint, this layer is defined as the network layer. The Internet layer (or network) is responsible for routing between different IP networks. The protocol supported on this layer is IP. The term used to describe the information processed on this layer is *packet*.

Network Access Layer

The network access layer involves physical attachment to the network, which traditionally requires a hardware interface from the network to a computer's internal bus. This layer includes both physical and datalink layers from the OSI model. The network access component defines the network architecture and topology. Some examples include Ethernet, FDDI, and TokenRing. The term used to describe the information processed on this layer is *frame*. A small driver program, which is provided by the interface manufacturers, is also needed to interface the hardware to the operating system.

The TCP/IP and associated protocols can also be placed on the OSI seven-layer model, as shown in Figure 3.2. Here, we can see how the protocols and services relate to the model. The next few pages further describe the many additional services provided by the TCP/IP protocol suite.

Process Layer Services

The TCP/IP services on the process layer include end-user tools, additional protocols, and system services. Found on different UNIX platforms, TCP/IP provides a common mechanism to share files, send/receive Email, access systems remotely, transfer files between systems, and accomplish other networking tasks. Although the TCP/IP protocol and application suite is large, many UNIX system vendors provide a smaller subset of these services. Table 3.2 lists many of the core TCP/IP services generally available on UNIX systems.

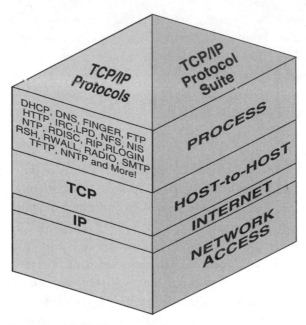

Figure 3.2 *TCP/IP protocol suite.*

End-User Tools

The end-user tools, which are common to many UNIX system implementations of TCP/IP, are applications that are generally available to normal system users. As a result, these tools do not require system root privileges for operation. For example, general users without any special consideration from an administration standpoint can invoke the Telnet and FTP commands. Some services within the TCP/IP suite refer to both end-user applications and protocols. Telnet is a good example of this because it represents both a user tool and a communication protocol. In practice, however, this isn't a big problem, because end-user applications on UNIX are lower case (such as `telnet`) and protocols are generally written in upper case.

It is interesting to note that certain organizations disable some TCP/IP services as a way of tightening security. One organization in particular did not want its users to have the ability to send or receive Email on core development systems and removed the SMTP servers from those systems. Another way that organizations typically disable services is by blocking access to system ports using a firewall device or router.

Additional Protocols

The TCP/IP suite includes additional higher-level protocols that exist above the network layer and provide the necessary details to ensure that applications can communicate. For example, the File Transfer Protocol (FTP) defines how files and associated information are transmitted across the network. The protocol handles all the details related to user authorization, naming, and data representation among heterogeneous systems.

System Services

TCP/IP system services include those facilities that are provided to all users of the system but can only be controlled by the system administrator. System services include specific system processes and special configuration files used by those processes. System network services are usually started automatically when the system is started or when the system is rebooted, but some start in response to requests.

Table 3.2 *Core TCP/IP protocols and services*

Service	Description
ARP/RARP	Address Resolution Protocol Reverse Address Resolution Protocol
DHCP	Dynamic Host Configuration Protocol
DNS	Domain Name Service
FINGER	Look up remote/local user
FTP	File Transfer Protocol
HTTP	Hypertext Transfer Protocol
ICMP	Internet Control Message Protocol
LPD	Line Printer Daemon
NFS	Network File System

Table 3.2 *Core TCP/IP protocols and services (continued)*

Service	Description
NIS	Network Information Service
NTP	Network Time Protocol
RDISC	Router Discovery Protocol
REXEC	Remote execution service
RIP	Routing Information Protocol
RLOGIN	Remote login service
RPC	Remote Procedure Call
RSH	Remote Shell Service
RWHO	Remote monitoring of users
RWALL	Remote message broadcast
RADIO	Radio transmitter/receiver
SMTP	Simple Mail Transfer Protocol
TALK	talk to remote/local user
Telnet	access to remote system
TFTP	Trivial File Transfer Protocol
WHOIS	Remote Lookup Service

The core TCP/IP protocols and services listed in Table 3.2 are
further defined as follows.

ARP: The Address Resolution Protocol provides mapping
between lower-level datalink protocols (such as Ethernet and
TokenRing) and higher-level protocols such as IP. ARP maps
datalink (i.e., hardware interface) addresses to IP addresses. The
Reverse Address Resolution Protocol (RARP) is used to go the
other way; it maps IP addresses to datalink protocol addresses.
ARP and RARP are described fully later in this section.

DHCP: The Dynamic Host Configuration Protocol provides
startup (booting) information to client systems. DHCP supports IP

address information, operating system configuration information, and other related information. From a network address standpoint, DHCP is an excellent way to manage IP addresses across an enterprise. For example, clients can dynamically obtain IP information while booting, thus removing the burden of having to configure each machine.

DNS: The Domain Name Service maps between hostnames and IP addresses. The client side provides the ability to resolve names and addresses by making requests to one or more DNS servers only. The server-side component, `named`, listens for requests and either looks up entries in a local database or contacts another name server for resolution.

FINGER: The finger services permit the lookup of user information on either a local or a remote system. The finger service isn't a protocol, just an end-user program that uses TCP for communication with the `in.fingerd` server.

FTP: The File Transfer Protocol transfers files between systems. FTP provides basic user authorization that includes using the login name and password on the remote system. The FTP interface is basic, but provides a simple way to transfer single or multiple files. The FTP server is known as `in.ftpd`. FTP supports transmission of both binary and ASCII data files.

HTTP: The Hyper Text Transfer Protocol transmits Web pages and documents from a Web server to a browser.

ICMP: The Internet Control Message Protocol is a network diagnostic facility that uses the IP protocol. The `ping` tool uses the ICMP echo request/reply protocol to determine node connectivity.

LPD: The Line Printer Daemon provides a printing facility for either the network or directly attached printers.

NFS: The Network File System facility provides file sharing between systems on a local network.

NIS: The Network Information Service is a directory lookup facility that provides client access to server databases. The types of information typically used within NIS include login, host, file sharing, and other system configuration information.

NTP: The Network Time Protocol provides an excellent way to ensure that time and date information is synchronized between all networked UNIX systems.

RDISC: The ICMP network Router Discovery Protocol finds routers and builds a table of routes to attached networks.

REXEC: The Remote Execution Service provides execution of UNIX commands on remote systems. REXEC uses a specialized authentication procedure that includes reading both the login name and password and comparing this information with the remote system. If the login information matches, the UNIXcommand is executed. The family of remote commands includes **rsh, rwho, rlogin**, and others.

RIP: The Routing Information Protocol propagates routing information between network system devices such as routers. UNIX systems support RIP as well. On some UNIX systems, if two or more network interfaces are installed, the system will automatically perform routing functions. The routing function is incorporated in the `in.routed` system process that is started when the system is initialized.

RLOGIN: The Remote Login Service accesses a remote UNIX system. It provides the same basic services as the Telnet program.

RPC: The Remote Procedure Call is a mechanism and protocol that permits the execution of procedures across the network in a neutral fashion.

RSH: The Remote Shell Service provides a shell to the remote system.

RWHO: RWHO provides a list of logged-in users on a remote system. This command is similar to the UNIX **who** command.

RWALL: RWALL provides a way to write to users on a remote system. This command is similar to the UNIX **wall** command.

RADIO: This is the radio broadcast facility.

SMTP: The Simple Mail Transfer Protocol provides the mail delivery mechanism that is used by many electronic mail packages and is the standard mailing protocol for the Internet. The `sendmail` system program implements SMTP and is responsible for mail propagation between systems.

TALK: Talk is a two-way communication facility that can be used to talk to other system users either on local or remote systems. Talk isn't a protocol, but is just an end-user system utility that uses the UDP protocol.

Telnet: Telnet is the name for a protocol and end-user system utility. The Telnet utility provides a user interface to a remote UNIX system. Users can log into other systems over the network and execute commands as if they were local to that system. Their terminal is connected via the Telnet protocol to the remote system using the `in.telnetd` server process. The Telnet protocol defines a network virtual interface that controls the flow and interpretation of a character stream between systems.

TFTP: The Trivial File Transfer Protocol provides a more simplistic file transfer facility than FTP. TFTP is considered a light version of FTP because it doesn't support a robust authorization mechanism or command set. TFTP is used mainly to download system configuration information or data.

WHOIS: WHOIS is a white pages lookup utility. The WHOIS service will search for individual users and other information from standard Internet servers.

Additional Services

Many public domain TCP/IP services and applications are also available via the Internet. Some of the resources available are improvements over the existing core set of services, while other applications provide new services and features. Table 3.3 lists some of these TCP/IP applications.

Table 3.3 *Additional TCP/IP services*

Service	Description
ARCHIE	FTP search facility
GOPHER	Document retrieval system
IRC	Internet Relay Chat service
NNTP	Network News Transfer Protocol
WAIS	Wide Area Information Servers

ARCHIE: Archie is a database of anonymous FTP sites and their contents. Archie keeps track of the entire contents of a very large number of anonymous FTP sites and allows you to search for files on those sites using various kinds of filename searches.

GOPHER: GOPHER is a document retrieval system that is available via a menu-driven interface (for character-base devices) and the World Wide Web (WWW).

IRC: Internet Relay Chat is a way to send either public or private text messages to one or more subscribers in real time.

NNTP: The Network News Transfer Protocol provides the ability to transfer news files (also known as Usenet) between a client and server.

WAIS: WAIS is another facility that helps search for indexed material and files.

Host-to-Host Layer

The host-to-host layer, or OSI network layer, is responsible for providing a robust data delivery mechanism between different network entities. The standard that provides this service is the transmission control protocol (TCP). Within a network, data can be lost or destroyed when transmission errors or network hardware failures occur. Data can also be delivered out of order and with significant delays before reaching the final destination. TCP was designed and developed to address these types of network-related problems. TCP is responsible for ensuring that data arrives in the correct order and is free from errors. It accomplishes these tasks by providing the services described below:

Virtual Connections

TCP provides a virtual connection interface to the network that is analogous to the way phone calls are established in the telephone network. Conceptually, a user calls another machine to request data transfer. After all the details of the connection setup are complete, data transmission can occur between applications. From an application perspective, the TCP connection looks and behaves as if a dedicated hardware link has been established. However, this is only an illusion provided by the TCP streams interface.

Sequenced Data

To ensure reliable transfer, TCP keeps track of the data it transmits by assigning a sequence number to each segment. The sequence number uniquely identifies each data segment within a connection and provides a positive acknowledgment to the sending entity. No acknowledgment indicates that the message should be retransmitted. The sequence number is also used to reorder any segments that might have arrived out of order. How can segments arrive out of order? Consider, for example, the network in Figure 3.3.

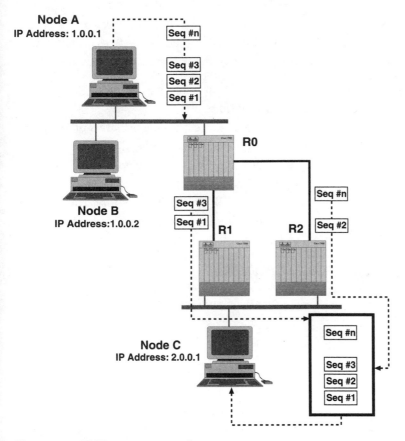

Figure 3.3 *TCP segment numbers in action.*

Because more than one network path to Node C exists, it is possible that some TCP segments might travel via router R2 instead of router R1. Should the path between Node C and R1 become temporarily heavily loaded, for example, segments may be routed via the alternate path. As a result, segments using the R2 path could arrive at the destination sooner than segments using the R1 path.

Stream Abstraction Interface

From the application layer standpoint, TCP provides a buffered byte-oriented interface between two applications or processes. The data transmitted from the source entity is exactly the same information that the destination receives. For example, if the sending entity transmitted the message `Hello World`, the destination would receive `Hello World`. As it turns out, this is a very useful and convenient feature for developing networking applications and services. Also, the TCP stream is buffered, which means that applications have more flexibility when it comes to processing the data from the network.

Ports, Sockets, and Connections

TCP ports are addresses that specify a network resource and are used to uniquely identify an individual application or service on the system. There are quite a few well-known address ports in use today, and many of them can be found in the `/etc/services` file on UNIX systems. See Appendix B for additional information regarding this file. Table 3.4 contains a partial list of some of the most commonly used TCP ports.

Table 3.4 *Common TCP ports*

Port	Application/Service
20	FTP data
21	FTP
23	Telnet
25	SMTP
53	DNS
119	NNTP
161	SNMP
80	HTTP

To further understand the function of these ports, consider the services of the UNIX `inetd` process. `Inetd` is called the super Internet server because it is responsible for connecting service requests from the network to the actual server program. Inetd knows which process to invoke because it can determine relationships between ports and services. By processing the /etc/services file and the /etc/inetd.conf configuration file, inetd can make the network request to the appropriate service as needed. Appendix B contains additional information regarding the inetd.conf file. Figure 3.4 shows the operation of inetd when a remote user requests a Telnet session.

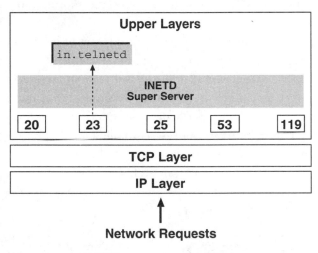

Figure 3.4 *INETD operation with Telnet request.*

It is important to understand that TCP uses a connection-oriented model whereby one network entity may call another to establish either a half- or full-duplex session. In a full-duplex mode, two independent channels are established between systems, and data can flow between the systems without an apparent interaction. In the half-duplex mode, only a single channel is established. A network entity may first establish a full-duplex session and then shut down one channel if necessary. On the other hand, a service may initially establish a single half-duplex session for control purposes and then start another channel to carry out some specific action or task. This application behavior might seem a little strange, but the FTP service, for example, operates in this fashion.

When an FTP session begins, it first establishes a single session to the destination system. This session is used for user authentication and the command interface. When the user specifies a file transfer or executes a remote command, another session is established to service the request. After the transfer is complete, the newly created session is closed. This process is repeated for each separate transaction.

Sockets are ports that the system allocates on the user's behalf when executing network applications or other services. Because the operating system generates a unique socket number, no two simultaneously running applications on the same system will have the same socket number. On some UNIX systems, the allocation of sockets begins above 1024.

In the context of a connection, TCP uses four pieces of information to uniquely identify one session from another: source IP address, source port, destination IP address, and destination port. This is important to remember because many sessions to the same application or service can be established, even from the same host. For example, two different users can `telnet` to the same destination host without any conflicts among the ports. This is accomplished by the fact that TCP uses all four addressing elements to distinguish a unique session. Figure 3.5 shows the relationship of the TCP elements in different sessions.

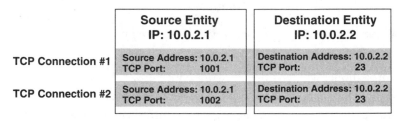

Figure 3.5 *Two TCP sessions from same source/destination.*

Positive Acknowledgment

One way TCP provides reliability is by ensuring that every message transmitted is confirmed by the receiving entity. The confirmation of TCP messages is known as positive acknowledgment and is used to ensure that the receiving entity has obtained all the segments that have been sent. When a TCP message is sent, the sending entity starts a timer. If no acknowledgment is received before the time expires, TCP assumes the message was lost or damaged in some way, preventing its delivery. As a result, TCP sends another message to replace the first and starts the timer process over again. This process continues until all segments have been acknowledged or until an internal error threshold is reached. If the sender receives no acknowledgment for outstanding segments after the internal error count has been reached, the connection will be terminated.

Establishing and Closing a TCP Connection

As previously discussed, TCP uses connections that provide a reliable, robust data transfer facility. The procedure for establishing or shutting down a connection is not a magical process. Instead, each TCP entity follows the same set of rules when creating a session or terminating one. To establish a connection, TCP uses a three-way handshake protocol, outlined in Figure 3.6.

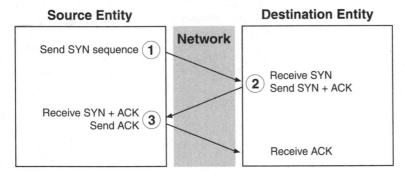

Figure 3.6 *Opening a TCP connection using the three-way handshake.*

First, the source transmits a SYN message segment. The SYN (pronounced "sin") or synchronization is a request to start a TCP session and have the SYN bit set in the code field. Next, the destination responds with an ACK segment that has both the SYN bit and ACK bits set in the code field, indicating that it has accepted the request and is continuing the handshake protocol. Finally, the source sends an ACK segment, which informs the destination that both entities agree that a connection has been established and that segments can now be transmitted and received.

To close an established session, TCP uses a modified three-way handshake, shown in Figure 3.7. First, the source transmits a FIN or finish segment (the FIN bit is set in the code field) as a result of the application wishing to close its side of the connection. Recall that TCP views these connections as full duplex; therefore, either party may terminate their side of the connection. Once the application on the destination closes the connection, TCP emits a FIN segment to the source. Next, the source receives the FIN sequence and sends an acknowledgment.

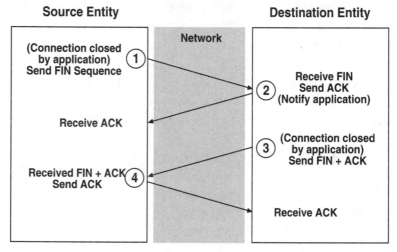

Figure 3.7 *Closing a TCP connection.*

Please note that it takes three segments to create a TCP connection, and four additional segments to shut it down. A total of seven messages are required to operate a TCP connection, not including any data transfer segments.

State Machine

The operation of TCP is best described using a state machine model, which controls the basic operation of the protocol. Figure 3.8 shows a representative picture of the TCP state machine, where each TCP connection goes through a series of defined phases. Movement from one state to another is the result of an event or transition. The label on each transition shows what TCP receives to cause the change between states. For instance, we discussed that TCP must open a connection before data can be transferred. Normally, each TCP side of the connection starts in the CLOSED state. When a connection is desired, a transition from the CLOSED to SYN

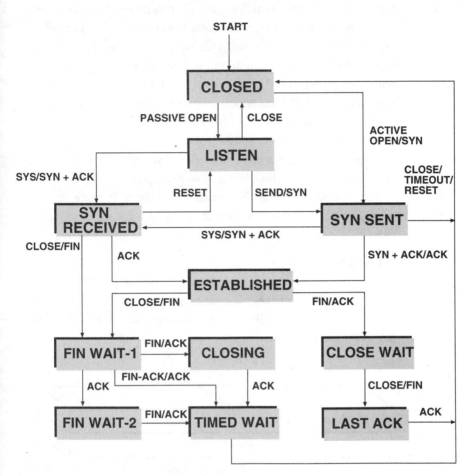

Figure 3.8 *TCP state machine.*

SENT state is made. At this point the client side sends a SYN packet. If the SYN packet is accepted, the remote side emits an ACK, which causes a transition from the SYN SENT to the SYN RECEIVED state. Once the final ACK has been received, the ESTABLISHED state is reached and data transfer may begin. When a TCP connection has been made, it will remain in the ESTABLISHED state until either side wishes to terminate the connection or some error occurs.

When a TCP connection is terminated (either by the source or destination), the connection moves to either the CLOSED WAIT or FIN WAIT-1 state. If the source sends a FIN segment, TCP transitions to the CLOSE WAIT state, which eventually terminates the connection. When the destination wants to close the connection, a change is made to the FIN WAIT-1 state. TCP has an elaborate mechanism to ensure that segments from previous connections do not interfere with existing ones. TCP maintains a timer, known as the maximum segment lifetime (MSL), which contains the maximum time an old segment may remain alive within the network. As a result, TCP moves to the TIMED WAIT state after closing the connection. It remains within this state for twice the MSL. After this, if any segments arrive for the connection, they are rejected. Why do we care about these details? Well, it sometimes is helpful in tracking down connectivity problems. The **netstat** command, for example, provides TCP port state information to assist with this type of activity.

TCP Sequence Format

TCP defines a sequence format, which includes all the necessary information to ensure that segments get to the correct destination and also contains additional control information. Figure 3.9 shows the TCP segment format.

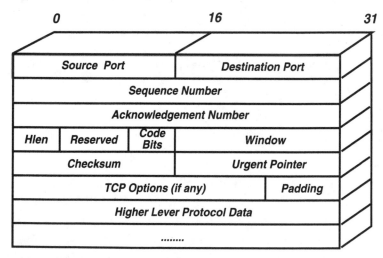

Figure 3.9 *TCP segment format.*

The TCP segment fields include:

Source Port:	the protocol (or service) that sent this segment
Destination Port:	the protocol (or service) that will receive this segment
Sequence Number:	the position in the byte stream of the sender
Acknowledgment Number:	the number of the byte that the source expects to receive in the next segment
Hlen:	integer that specifies the length of the segment header
Code Bits (C Bits):	details on the purpose and content of the segment
Window:	specification of how much data TCP is willing to accept
Checksum:	integer used to verify the TCP header and data integrity
Urgent Pointer:	field for indicating that this segment should be processed right away
Options:	details for negotiating the maximum segment size
Data:	high-level protocols or application-specific information

Code Bits

These bits indicate the type of TCP segment and how it should be processed. Table 3.5 shows established codes and their associated meanings. These codes are analogous to the type field in the Ethernet frame, which means that TCP segments are self-identifying.

Table 3.5 *TCP segment types*

Codes	Meaning
URG	Urgent pointer
ACK	Acknowledgment
PSH	Request a push
RST	Reset
SYN	Synchronize sequence numbers and start connection
FIN	Reached end of byte stream

Window

TCP has an elaborate mechanism to handle data buffering, flow control, and retransmission of unacknowledged segments. The window field helps TCP determine how much data it is willing to accept in the next segment. The data size of a transaction can significantly impact overall network and application performance. To understand why, assume for the moment that a TCP connection has been established between two nodes named socrates and durer, and that during the previous transactions, socrates has specified to durer a TCP window of 1024 (which is the default). Now, durer begins to experience high usage and begins to run low on available resources such as memory. Many reasons can cause this situation. At this time, socrates is still sending TCP messages to durer, but durer is having trouble acknowledging (or perhaps even processing) segments from socrates due to the number of the messages. Because durer is having resource problems, the next segment sent to socrates contains a smaller window size, which informs socrates that it must adjust the amount of data contained in subsequent TCP messages. After socrates receives the new window size, it begins sending durer smaller amounts of data.

After the resource limitation has been resolved on durer, either by explicit action on the part of the system administrator or by the completion of the tasks which caused the resource problem in the first place, durer sends socrates a larger window size and resumes processing as before. Without the ability for TCP to dynamically adjust the size of segments, in the example, durer would begin to drop the messages it couldn't process. This, in turn, would cause socrates to retransmit them, not only wasting processing cycles on socrates, but also wasting networking bandwidth due to the retransmitted messages.

Urgent Pointer

Because TCP provides a streamed interface, it is sometimes important that an application has a way to send an out-of-band or an urgent message to the other end of the connection without having to wait for the previous messages to be processed. An example of why out-of-band is important is when a user wishes to terminate a remote login session using Telnet. Often terminals provide interrupts or control signals, which can be used to inform applications that they should terminate. In this case, TCP uses the URG bit to indicate that this is an out-of-band segment and sets the urgent pointer to specify the position in the segment where the urgent data ends.

TCP Options

This field negotiates the TCP segment size, which is useful in a situation when it is possible to establish either a higher or lower maximum transfer unit (MTU). MTU values can be different on different physical networks. For example, ATM has a higher MTU than Ethernet.

Internet Layer

The Internet (or network of the OSI model) layer provides a delivery service that is unreliable and based on a connectionless transfer protocol. As previously indicated, the Internet Protocol (IP) operates on this layer, providing a best-effort transfer service, and is responsible for routing packets among different IP networks. IP packets may be lost, delayed, duplicated, and delivered out of order.

Two versions of the protocol have been defined. The most widely implemented version is 4 (known as IPv4) and, due to protocol deficiencies and resource limitations of this version, enhancements were made that resulted in a new version known as IPv6. However, version 6 hasn't been widely implemented within the networking industry.

The major characteristics and services of IP (version 4) include:

- unreliable delivery

- connectionless protocol

- packet travel over different paths

- address format

- subnetting

- routing

Unreliable Delivery

The term *unreliable* indicates that IP makes no attempt at guaranteeing the delivery of a packet to its destination. This is in sharp contrast to the behavior and services of transmission control protocol, which provides a reliable transfer facility that ensures message delivery. IP, on the other hand, provides a best-effort delivery facility and does not ensure packet transfer, but it doesn't capriciously discard them either. Despite the fact that IP is not reliable, it doesn't mean that data carried within an IP isn't delivered correctly. IP simply uses an upper-level protocol like TCP to ensure guaranteed data delivery.

Connectionless Protocol

IP is said to be connectionless because it does not establish a connection through which to transfer packets, which is contrary to the behavior of reliable transfer protocols. Packet delivery is based on IP address information contained within the packet itself. Each IP packet is self-contained, independent of any other packet, and not part of a pre-established agreement between network entities. Because no connection information is maintained within IP, packet delivery is simplified and more efficient.

Packets over Different Paths

With IP, packets may travel different paths to reach their final destination, even though each packet might carry a smaller portion of a much larger message. This behavior is observed when IP packets travel within an Internet. Also, packets might arrive out of order.

IP Addressing

IP defines the format of addresses and requires that each network entity have its own unique address. Addresses contain both a network and a node identification pair, which are expressed as a single number. With IPv4, 32-bits are used to represent an IP address and are expressed in dotted notation. Each address is written as four decimal integers separated by decimal points. Five different classes have been defined within IPv4. However, in practice, only the first three primary classes are used to define a network/node pair, as shown in Figure 3.10.

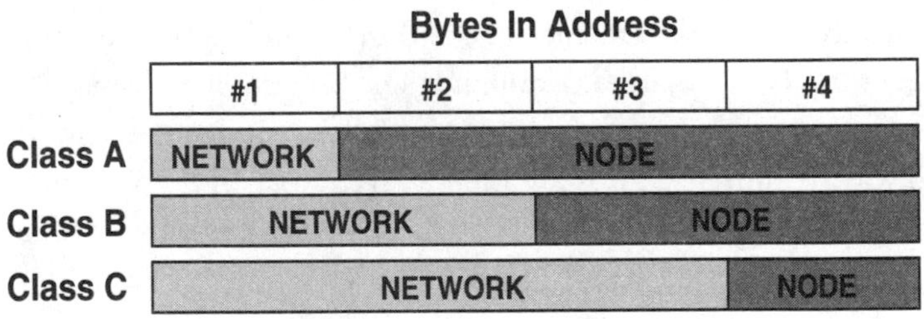

Bytes In Address

#1	#2	#3	#4

	#1	#2	#3	#4
Class A	NETWORK	NODE		
Class B	NETWORK		NODE	
Class C	NETWORK			NODE

Figure 3.10 *Three primary IP address classes.*

Each class specifies the format used to interpret how much of the address is used to represent the network and how much of the address is used to represent the node. The interpretations of addresses include:

Class A: The first byte is the network identification, and the remaining bytes specify the node. The network address range (first byte) is 1-127.

Class B: The first two bytes are the network identification, and the remaining bytes are the node. The network address range is 128-191.

Class C: The first three bytes are the network identification, and
the remaining byte is the node. The network address
range is 192-223.

Two additional (D and E) classes are defined, but they are
reserved and can't be used for normal network addresses. Class D
addresses are used for multicast support, and Class E addresses are
reserved for future use. One way to distinguish the different classes
is to use the first byte rule. With this rule, the first byte determines
to which class the address belongs. For example, using the IP
address of 10.1.3.2, 10 is the first byte of this address. The number
10 falls in the range of 1-127, so this IP address is a Class A type
and the network portion is 10, while the node portion is 1.3.2.

IP also defines some reserved addresses that include loop back
and broadcast addresses. The loopback network is defined as
address 127 and is used as a private network for internal diagnostics and support with an IP device. This network address is
reserved and is not supposed to be used as a genuine network
address. In fact, the IP protocol specifications don't recommend its
use on a live network. The loopback address can be observed by
issuing the UNIX **ifconfig -a** command. The broadcast address
defined as 255 is also considered special because it denotes a shorthand way to address all hosts within a given range. For example,
given the network of 134.110.0.0, which is a B Class network, the
broadcast address of 134.110.255.255 addresses all devices within
the entire 134.110 network. Because of the special meaning associated with 255, it should not be used as a node address.

Assignment of IP addresses is accomplished through a central
agency known as the Network Information Center (NIC). The
NIC is responsible for assigning unique IP network addresses to
any organization wishing to connect to the Internet. In many
instances, a local Internet Service Provider (ISP) will request an IP
address on your behalf or provide one of its own.

Subnetting

Subnetting is a mechanism used to divide a network into smaller
subnetworks or *subnets*. One major motivation for implementing
subnets is to distribute administration control of IP address allocation. Subnets also permit more effective use of existing addresses.

With subnets, the node portion of the IP address is divided into two sections: the subnet address and node address, as shown in Figure 3.11.

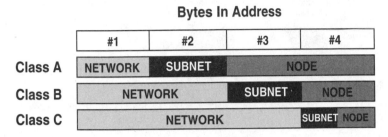

Figure 3.11 *Subnets addressing.*

To implement subnetting, the following requirements must be met. First, a subnet mask must be created for use on each of the devices that will participate within the subnet. This subnet mask is a special 32-bit address, which is expressed like a normal IP address using dotted decimal notation. As with a regular IP address, each of the octets within the subnet is in the range of 1 to 255. But unlike IP addresses, the octets represent a set of masked bits that are combined with the device's IP address to yield the subnet network. In particular, determining the subnet involves combining the subnet mask and host IP address with the Boolean and operator. Figure 3.12 shows the subnet calculation required.

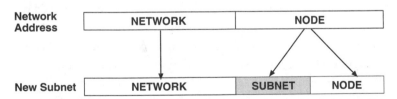

Figure 3.12 *Subnet calculation.*

Second, each device that will participate in a subnet must use the same subnet mask address. In particular, for each interface defined on the local system, the subnet mask should be defined along with other interface parameters. For instance, under UNIX the **ifconfig** command is invoked on every system interface installed in the system. The subnet mask information must be included when this system command is executed.

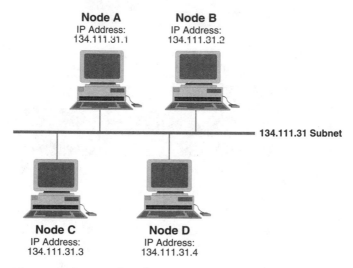

Figure 3.13 *Sample subnet.*

To further illustrate the implementation of a subnet, consider the sample network shown in Figure 3.13. In this figure, we have four devices attached to the same network. Each of the devices has already received an IP address, but now we must determine what the subnet mask should be. We have determined that the network will grow in the future and need to have enough IP addresses in the subnet for approximately 200 devices. As a result, we will need to use at least 8 bits (1 octet) for the subnet.

The IP addresses used in the sample network are of type Class B. Recall that B Class addresses are in the range of 128-191 and the first two octets are the network address (134.111), while the remaining two (31.1, for instance) are node addresses. The only place we can take bits to use for the subnet is from the host portion of the address. We simply can't use any of the network address because that area of the address is restricted. With this in mind, we need to sub divide the host portion into two, which is where the subnet mask comes into play. By using all ones (1) in the bits of the subnet fields and all zeros (0) in the bits of the node field, we can

forge the desired subnet address by converting the IP address and
subnet mask into binary:

(decimal)	(binary)	
134.111.31.1	10000110.01101111. 00011111.00000001	(IP address)
255.255.255.0	11111111.11111111. 11111111.00000000	(Subnet Mask)
134.111.31.0	10000110.01101111. 00011111.00000000	(Subnet Address)

Applying the Boolean and will produce the subnet address of
134.111.31.0. After this subnet mask has been configured on every
device within the subnet, every node will do the required and calculation to determine the subnet address to which it belongs. On
many (if not all) UNIX systems, this is an automatic task when the
system's network services are started. To summarize, to subnet a
network, include the following steps:

1. Determine the IP address class of the network you want to subnet.

2. Determine the amount of addresses you require for the subnet.

3. Determine if you can use a full octet (with at least a B Class
   address) for the subnet address.

4. Perform the Boolean and on one of the device addresses using
   the subnet mask.

5. Apply the subnet mask to all devices that will participate in the
   subnet.

The subnet mask assignment in this example was relatively
straightforward because a full octet was used for the subnet number. This also made the and calculation very simple. However, suppose we change the example by using a C Class network number
instead. The addresses we now need to assign to the sample network in Figure 3.13 include 199.81.23.1 through 199.81.23.4.
With a C Class address, the range of the first octet falls within 192-
223. The first three octets are the network address (199.81.23),
while the remaining octet (4, in this example) is the node address.
This example will complicate the subnet process a bit because we

must now split the host portion and the subnet address from just one octet. However, the same procedure applies as stated above.

In order to formulate a subnet address from a class C network address, we must borrow some number of bits from the host portion of the address to represent the subnet number. In doing so, we automatically reduce the number of IP addresses that will be free for each device within the subnet. Therefore, we need to know exactly how many devices will be installed on the subnet. To further refine our example, assume we will only need ten IP addresses for individual nodes on the subnet.

We can determine the subnet mask and other information by hand, but it is much easier and faster if we use a software program to do the calculations for us. One excellent calculator is available from the Chesapeake Web Site (`www.cci.com/tools/subcal`). This software provides the ability to subnet any valid IP address and shows us the calculations and steps involved. Figure 3.14 shows the main screen. Please note, this software can be downloaded and run from a local computer or executed directly from the Chesapeake site. Download and installation instruction for use on a local computer can be found in Appendix C.

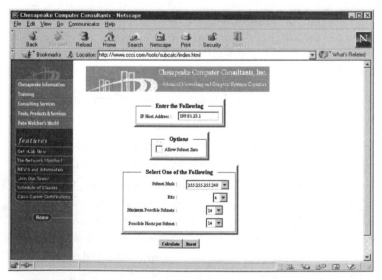

Figure 3.14 *Main subnet calculator window.*

The first field, IP Host Address, requires that we specify the IP address of one of the hosts on our network. In this case, we give it one of the node addresses from our second example (i.e., 199.81.23.1). Next, we provide some information about the subnet by entering information in the third box, labeled "Select One of the Following". We can do this in one of four ways: by specifying the subnet mask directly (Subnet Mask field), the number of bits for the subnet (Bits field), the maximum number of hosts within the subnet (Maximum Possible Subnets field), or the number of possible hosts per subnet (Possible Hosts per Subnet field). Changing one of these fields changes the other three automatically. For example, when a subnet mask is changed to 255.255.255.224, then the number of bits becomes three and the number of possible hosts per subnet goes to 30.

The relationship between these fields can be more easily seen by viewing the calculations window shown in Figure 3.15. This screen contains five sections. The first shows two lines each containing three fields, the standard IP Address (Class C Network field) class in both decimal and binary format, the Subnet and Host bits fields respectively, and the subnet mask. This is the mask that must be applied to every system that will be involved within the subnet. This subnet mask uses 28 bits and hence can be referred to as a "28-bit subnet mask." The second section contains the subnet number from the logical AND operation of the host address (199.81.21.1) and subnet mask (255.255.255.224) fields. The third shows the correct subnet mask, inverted subnet mask, and subnet number as expressed in binary. The next section contains the subnet directed address and the broadcast address. The broadcast address directs IP packets to every node on the local subnet. The final section includes the summary that contains the subnet address, the available host addresses specified with a range, and the directed broadcast address. The available host range is important because it represents the addresses that can be used by all host systems within the subnet.

Internet Control Message Protocol

As previously discussed, IP provides a best-effort packet delivery mechanism that doesn't guarantee data delivery. IP is insulated

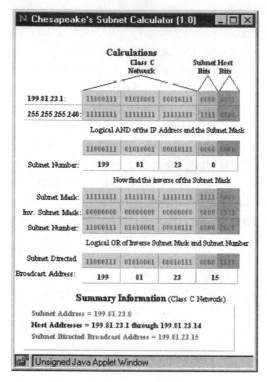

Figure 3.15 *Subnet calculation window.*

from the lower-level protocol details and makes few assumptions about the performance and reliability of the network. Data delivery is accomplished without any special coordination among other IP entities and, for the most part, operates quite well. However, conditions might exist beyond IP's control that make delivery difficult or impossible. For example, a remote host could be temporarily removed from the network or a router could become overloaded when a network-intensive application is started. IP needs a way to detect these types of problems.

The Internet Control Message Protocol (ICMP) provides a general error message facility for the IP protocol and related services. ICMP provides a way for IP entities that encounter errors to report them to the source that caused the problem. It is the responsibility of the source entity to correct the error. This might include, for example, reporting the error to a higher-level application. Table 3.6 lists some of the ICMP message types.

Table 3.6 *ICMP error message types*

Message Type	Meaning
Echo request/reply	Determine system reachability
Destination unreachable	Can't reach desired destination
Source quench	Stop sending data
Redirect	Detection of routing error
Time exceeded	Stale IP packet

One of the most popular networking debugging utilities, ping, uses ICMP to determine host reachability. ping uses the echo request and echo reply primitives that are available within ICMP to determine if a remote host is available and operating correctly on the network. Figure 3.16 shows the basic operation of the echo request and reply. A user wants to determine if Node B is available on the network. From Node A, the user enters a **ping** command that issues an echo request to Node B. If Node B is active, it responds back to Node A using an echo reply. If Node B is not active, then Node A receives no response. In this case, the request from Node A simply times out. When this occurs, the user is presented with a time out message that indicates that Node B didn't respond to the request.

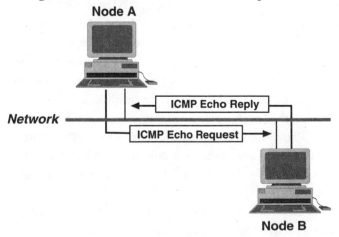

Figure 3.16 *ICMP echo request/reply.*

Destination Unreachable

When a router can't deliver or forward a packet to its destination, it will emit an ICMP *destination unreachable* message to the sender. Destination unreachable errors usually imply some sort of routing problem or error (i.e., incorrect route within a routing table). Destinations may be unreachable due to hardware failures that cause a system to become temporarily unavailable, or when the sender specifies a non-existent destination address. Sometimes it is impossible to know that a destination is unreachable unless the ping system utility is used. For example, if a user issues a Telnet request to a remote system (which happens to be connected to an Ethernet LAN), and the system has been disconnected from the network, this Telnet request will eventually time out because Ethernet doesn't support any frame acknowledgments. As a result, no destination unreachable messages will be generated because Ethernet assumes data delivery even for a node that has been temporarily disconnected from the network.

Source Quench

The source quench within ICMP provides a way to handle congestion at the IP packet level. Congestion within a network can be caused by several factors. However, one primary cause is when several systems begin transmission of data that flows through a single router, as shown in Figure 3.17. In this case, the router itself is overburdened by the combined traffic. Another cause of congestion is when a more powerful computer system transmits data to a less powerful system that cannot keep up the pace. If these situations go unchecked, eventually the router and under-powered system will begin to discard packets, which in turn will cause TCP to retransmit them, thus making the situation worse. In this case, the router and smaller system simply emit a source quench message, which indicates to the sender that it should stop sending data. As a result, the router and smaller system have time to process any outstanding packets.

There is no direct way to reverse the effects of the ICMP source quench message. However, any destination that receives a source quench lowers the rate at which it transmits packets to the destination. After no additional source quench messages are received, the remote system begins to gradually increase the rate of transmission, and eventually normal traffic resumes.

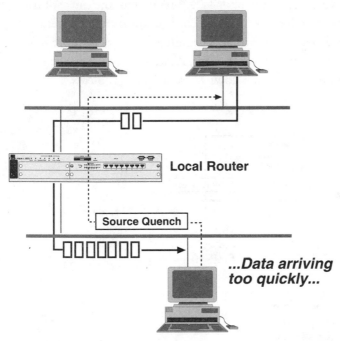

...Data arriving
too quickly...

Figure 3.17 *ICMP source quench redirect.*

Redirect

The ICMP redirect message informs routers of changes to the routing information within the network. One of the basic assumptions with TCP/IP is that routers know the routing topology within a network and this information is shared among participating routers. When a router detects a host using a non-optimal route, it emits a redirect message informing the host that a better route is available. It is up to the host to incorporate this new information within its routing configuration. In some cases, this is not automatic and must be done by the network administrator. Figure 3.18 shows an example of where a router will send an ICMP redirect message. Assume that Node A wants to talk to Node D. In this case, two paths exist between Node A and Node D, namely R1 and R2. The R1 path is shorter and contains fewer hops between Node A and Node D. The R2 path contains a few extra links, because it also provides connectivity to other networks that include Node B and Node

C. Should `Node A` attempt to communicate with `Node D` via `R2`, then `R2` will send the redirect message back to `Node A` telling it to use `R1`, which has a shorter path to `Node D`. Many times the cause of using the incorrect router rests with the configuration on the system itself or incorrect routing information emitted from one or more misconfigured routers. In either event, ICMP redirects help the network administrator track down these sorts of problems.

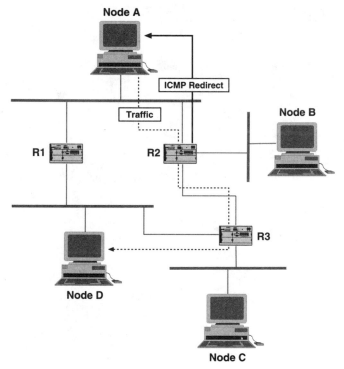

Figure 3.18 *ICMP redirect.*

Redirect messages do not provide a common mechanism for distributing routing information because they are limited to interaction between hosts and routers. Instead, routing protocols such as Routing Information Protocol (RIP) are used to propagate routing information within a network.

Time Exceeded
Each IP packet contains a time-to-live field, which controls how long a packet may exist within the network. When a router pro-

cesses the packet, it decrements this field before forwarding it. Whenever a router discards a packet because its time-to-live field is zero or because some other timeout occurred with the packet, the router emits an ICMP *time exceeded* message back to the source of the packet. This is the primary mechanism used to detect routing loops or excessively long routes within a network. The **traceroute** command, for example, uses the time-to-live field to trace the path an IP packet may take between two points and also measures the amount of time required to traverse each router along the path to the destination.

Address Resolution Protocol

As we previously discussed, IP imposes a certain structure and format on the addresses used by networking devices. In version 4 of IP, the address is 32 bits in length and is expressed in dotted decimal notation. In version 6, the address is even larger—128 bits. As with any higher-level network protocol such as IP, the requirement exists for a mechanism to translate these addresses into addresses used by such protocols as Ethernet, FDDI, or TokenRing. Known as datalink protocols, they each have their own addressing structure and format, which is quite different from IP. For example, Ethernet uses 48-bit addresses and is expressed using the colon hexadecimal notation. Thus, `8:0:20:4:cf:2c` represents a valid Ethernet address. In this case, this datalink address doesn't always map easily with addresses used by IP. This is true for many other datalink protocols as well. This creates a dilemma because, without a way to map IP addresses to physical interfaces, communication between nodes would not be possible.

It is desirable and very necessary that a simple, flexible, and yet powerful way to map between IP and datalink (physical) addresses be available. The Address Resolution Protocol (ARP) has been proven to be a very elegant and robust way to solve the address mapping problem. In particular, ARP was designed to handle address resolution of any network layer protocol to datalink protocol, not just between IP and Ethernet.

The basic operation of ARP is simple: When `Node A` wants to determine the physical address for `Node B`, `Node A` will send a spe-

cial broadcast message requesting the address of Node B to all
devices on the network, as shown in Figure 3.19. All hosts receive
the message, including Node B and Node C, but only Node B will
respond with the correct physical address, as shown in Figure 3.20.
The reason only Node B responds is because it examines the ARP
packet and determines that its own IP address matches the target IP
address that the requester is seeking.

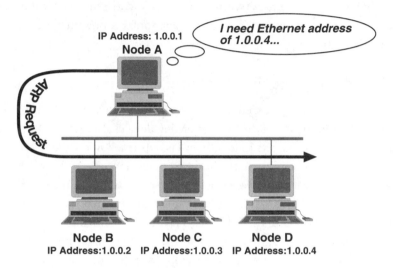

Figure 3.19 *ARP request.*

A sister function of ARP known as Reverse Address Resolution
Protocol, or RARP, does the inverse; given a datalink address, it
finds the corresponding IP address. RARP is primarily used when
diskless workstations need to determine their IP addresses during
system startup.

The term *broadcast* in the above example indicates a locally
directed packet to all network devices on a particular LAN segment. Certain datalink protocols such as Ethernet provide the
facility to transmit broadcast packets to all attached stations using
a special destination address. With Ethernet, all 1s (or FFs in hexadecimal) in the destination address is considered a broadcast. ARP
assumes that the details of getting messages to each station will be
handled directly by the datalink protocol.

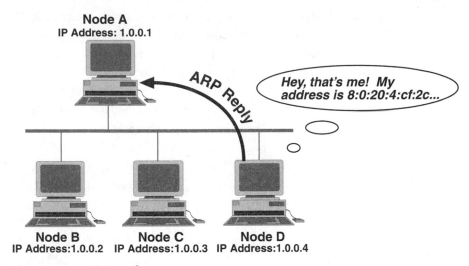

Figure 3.20 *ARP reply.*

As you can see, the ARP protocol is very simple. Yet, despite its simplicity, it has a few profound advantages. First, ARP is dynamic in nature, which obviates the need to statically track and store IP to physical addresses. This dynamic resolution behavior frees the network manager from constantly maintaining and ensuring correct information every time a device is added or removed from the network. With today's networks, it would be impossible to accomplish such a task given the size and growth rate of many internets. Second, ARP is a standard and is available on every device that supports TCP/IP, regardless of datalink protocol. That is why, for example, IP can operate on FDDI and TokenRing. This makes building heterogeneous networks much easier because ARP hides the datalink addressing details, and the network designer need not be concerned about physical address resolution when combining different datalink protocols. Third, ARP can be used in IP subnets to provide a very simple way for devices to communicate within a routed Internet.

Packet Format

Unlike other networking protocols, ARP packet fields are not all fixed-format but rather rely on certain fixed fields near the beginning of the packet. ARP and RARP share the same basic packet format. To make the ARP useful for other datalink protocols, the length of the fields will depend on the type of network. Figure 3.21 shows the standard ARP and RARP message format.

The *hardware type* field defines the hardware interface type for which the sender requires an answer. Standard values include 1 for Ethernet and 2 for FDDI. The *protocol* field specifies the high-level protocol type the sender is using, which for IP is 0800 in hexadecimal (decimal is 2048). The *operation* field notes if the message is an ARP request (1), ARP response (2), RARP request (3), or RARP response (4). The *Hlen* and *Plen* fields define the hardware and high-level protocol address field lengths. The *Hlen* and *Plen* fields permit ARP to work with any arbitrary datalink protocol because the sizes of the *hardware type* and *protocol* fields can be determined by inspecting the ARP packet directly. The sending entity will supply, if possible, the *Sender HA* and/or *Sender IP* field information when issuing the request. The *Sender HA* is used with the ARP request, while the *Sender IP* is used with an RARP request. The *Target HA* is used when responding to the ARP message; otherwise, the *Target IP* is used when responding to RARP.

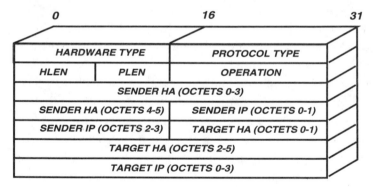

Figure 3.21 *ARP/RARP Message Format.*

ARP Cache

At first glance, the ARP service may seem inefficient because it will send a broadcast packet each time a device wishes to communicate with another. However, ARP implementations, on many systems, include the use of an ARP cache to temporarily store address bindings from previous ARP requests. In fact, before an ARP request is made, the higher-level software scans the ARP cache to see if the required datalink address mapping already exists in the cache. If it does, the existing binding is used; otherwise the ARP request is sent. As a result of the cache, network traffic is reduced because ARP requests are only made when devices are not known. Also, application performance is improved because the sender's ARP request can be satisfied by using the cache instead of transmitting a packet on the network. Finally, the cache provides the administrator with a way to view connectivity between the higher-level protocols and the network hardware. As we will see later in this book, inspecting the ARP cache can be a powerful way to troubleshoot network and system problems.

Here is one interesting question regarding the ARP cache: When should the bindings be discarded from the cache? The answer is not simple. If we presume to keep the ARP cache populated with entries forever (or until the system is restarted), the possibility exists that the cache will contain invalid information. Consider, for example, a network that contains systems monet and rembrandt, which are in the midst of communicating when the network interface card (NIC) fails on rembrandt and is subsequently replaced. The new NIC will contain a new datalink address unless the administrator has changed it after the interface was installed. As a result, monet can't talk to rembrandt any longer because the cache on monet contains an invalid datalink address for rembrandt. On the other hand, we can take the approach that bindings in the ARP cache should expire in a relatively short period of time, say every 30 seconds. Unfortunately, this will adversely affect network performance because more network broadcasts will be needed because the ARP cache will be very small. However, it will address the problem of the incorrect bindings for NIC that have recently been replaced because the old entry would have been purged in a reasonable period of time after the new NIC was operational.

Perhaps the best solution to this problem can be described by taking *the middle of the road* approach. That is to say, the binding expiration shouldn't be too small to be ineffective but also not too long to address changes in the network. In general, most UNIX systems will delete ARP entries in approximately 20 minutes. Some versions of UNIX also permit the administrators to change the ARP cache timeout to suit their:

- Datalink Address Format

- individual network requirements and, when necessary, alter it to address other network-related problems

Datalink Address Format

As indicated, datalink addresses are expressed in 48 bits (six bytes) and separated by colons. This colon notation is used as the primary method to represent these hardware addresses. Some UNIX network management tools, such as the **ifconfig** and **arp** commands, use this format. Datalink protocol addresses for FDDI, Ethernet, and TokenRing contain a vendor code identification number and serial number. This information can be used in node identification for inventory purposes. The IEEE registry authority assigns the vendor portion to those organizations that produce networking hardware and have requested a vendor code. These codes are also referred to as Organization Unique Identifiers (OUI). The first three bytes of the address represent the manufacturer or vendor of the device, and the remaining three bytes represent the serial number of the unit, as depicted in Figure 3.22.

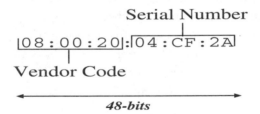

Figure 3.22 *Datalink address format.*

Often on a multi-homed system, the datalink addresses will be shared among all the defined interfaces. This may even be true for systems that contain different network interface types (i.e., Ethernet and FDDI). Table 3.7 shows some of the most common vendor codes. Notice that more than one vendor code might be associated with the same vendor. This may be true, for example, when one company purchases another company and their products. In this case, the vendor code of the company that was purchased now falls under the other company. This is why Table 3.7 contains multiple entries for both 3Com and Cisco. Knowing a few of these addresses can be very handy during network debugging to help identify the type of device and vendor to which a particular packet belongsIf you are interested in finding a vendor not listed in the Table 3.7, access the IEEE Web site at *http://standards.ieee.org/ regauth/oui/oui.txt.*

Table 3.7 *Sample vendor OUI codes*

Vendor Code	Vendor
00:20:AF 00-80-3E 00-C0-D4 (many more)	3Com Corporation Formerly Synernetics, Inc. Formerly AXON, Inc.
08-00-2B AA-00-00 AA-00-03 AA-00-04	Formerly Digital Equipment Corporation (DEC), now owned by Cabletron Systems
00:00:0C 00-E0-B0 00-E0-F7 00-E0-F9 00-E0-FE 00-06-7C 00-06-C1 00-10-07 (many more)	Cisco Systems, Inc. (Includes a large list of former companies)
00-60-69	Brocade Corporation
00-00-81 00-00-A2 00-80-E3	Formerly Bay Network, Inc. Formerly Coral Networks
00-E0-B1	Packet Engines, Inc.
08:00:5A	IBM Corporation
08:00:20	Sun Microsystems, Inc.
08-00-09	HP Corporation
00-10-E3	Compaq Corporation

Accessing this Universal Resource Locator (URL) will display the entire OUI file. Please note: This file is quite large (over 900K) and is growing! If you're not interested in seeing the entire contents of the OUI file, then search for the specific vendor codes you are looking for by accessing *http://standards.ieee.org/regauth/oui/index.html*.

Accessing this URL will display the page shown in Figure 3.23.

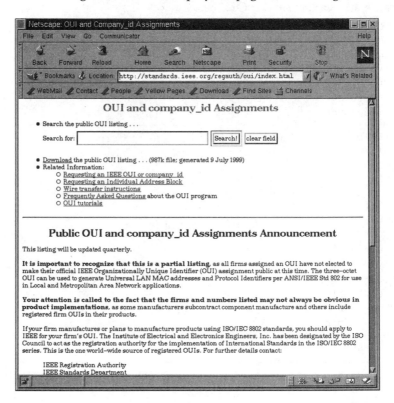

Figure 3.23 *IEEE OUI search page.*

Should you wish to search for a vendor, enter the name of the company in the search text box field. Also, if you know the OUI, but want the vendor, enter the address instead. Next, click the Search! button. Figure 3.24 shows the result obtained when the Brocade company was searched.

Figure 3.24 *OUI search results.*

Core System Utilities and Tools

This chapter provides a detailed overview of the commands and utilities that are available with the Linux operating system. Many of the tools discussed are part of a common set of tools and available on many other different UNIX platforms. For instance, the **arp** command operates in a similar fashion and has many of the same command-line options across Solaris, HPUX, and AIX systems.

The software discussed in this section includes tools that can assist the network manager or administrator in handling network-related tasks and address specific network problems. This chapter covers the following tools:

Command	Page
arp	106
ifconfig	115
netstat	125
ping	143
tcpdump	153
traceroute	171

ARP Tool

General Description

The **arp** command displays and manipulates the network address table on a local UNIX system. The address resolution protocol table, also known as the *ARP cache*, contains a complete list of all datalink protocol to IP address mappings for the local network. Recall from Chapter 3 that the ARP protocol is a dynamic facility that maps datalink addresses such as Ethernet to IP addresses. Whenever a system wants to transmit a message, it must first know the low-level (i.e., datalink) address for the target system. Many networking tools, such as `telnet`, `ftp`, and others, indirectly use the ARP table.

The **arp** command provides the ability to view and modify the ARP cache. Note that the terms ARP table and ARP cache can be used interchangeably and reference the same thing. Also, the terms *binding* and *mapping* refer to an ARP entry as well. Regular UNIX (non-root) users may display the ARP cache but cannot make any changes. The reason for this should be obvious; users could make alternations to the cache that would affect connectivity for all users.

With the **arp** command, the superuser can:

- display the ARP cache

- delete an ARP entry

- add an ARP entry

The ARP tool provides a number of command-line options. However, only the most important ones are listed in Table 4.1 and fully described below. Each of these options supports either a single command character or keyword, along with two dashes at the beginning. For instance, the -v option has an associated **--verbose** keyword. These are equivalent and can be used interchangeably on the command line. Table 4.1 shows both forms. The reason to choose one over the other is merely a matter of style. However, the keyword format may make it easier to remember individual options in the future.

Displaying the ARP Cache

Table 4.1 *Important* **arp** *command-line options*

Option	Keyword	Description
-a	**--display**	Displays the current ARP entry for a specific host
-d	**--delete**	Deletes an ARP entry
-f	**--file**	Loads a file that contains entries to place in the cache
-i	**--device**	Displays only those entries for specified interface
-n	**--numeric**	Shows numerical addresses instead of hostnames
-s	**--set**	Creates an ARP entry
-v	**--verbose**	Displays ARP cache using verbose mode

To display the contents of the ARP table, use the **arp -v** (**--verbose**) command. When the table is displayed, it includes the device name, hardware type, physical address, mask flag, and network interface. A sample is shown:

```
# arp -v
Address                HWtype    HWaddress         Flags Mask Iface
durer.home.com         ether     00:60:97:0E:A3:06    C        eth0
switch.home.com        ether     00:00:1D:0A:5D:01    C        eth0
probe.home.com         ether     00:C0:D4:00:09:40    C        eth0
rembrandt.home.comether           08:00.20:02:bc:05    C        eth0
rubens.home.com                     (incomplete)                eth0
monet.home.com         ether     08:00:20:04:cf:2c    C        eth0
Entries: 6 Skipped: 0            Found: 6
```

The `Address` field shows either the hostname or IP address that corresponds to the ARP entry. This is the address that is used to search the ARP table to determine if the desired entry exists. When an IP address (instead of a hostname) is displayed, this indicates that either the IP address couldn't be correctly resolved to a hostname or the `-n` option was used. This could be the result of an invalid or non-existing entry within the DNS server or /etc/hosts file, a misconfiguration in either of these, or connectivity problems to the DNS server.

The `HWType` field represents the network interface for which the ARP entry was obtained. As you can see, the keyword **ether** represents entries that were derived from an Ethernet network. Additional network types are supported, including ARCnet (`arcnet`), PROnet (`pronet`), AX.25 (`ax25`), and NET/ROM (`netrom`).

The `Flags Mask` field provides additional details regarding the ARP entry. Table 4.2 shows the available flags and their associated meanings.

Table 4.2 *ARP entry flags*

ARP Flag	Meaning
C	completed ARP entry
M	permanent (static) ARP entry
P	publish this ARP entry

The `HWaddress` (physical address) field contains the low-level address for each node on the local network and is expressed in six hexadecimal numbers in colon notation. Recall that colon notation uses the hexadecimal number separated by colons, as in

00:10:5a:28:5d:7c

The iface field corresponds to the network interface that is
attached to the local network, for which the ARP entry was
obtained. In the previous example, two separate interfaces are
shown with their own listings. In practice, most systems contain
only a single interface. The eth stands for Ethernet, which is the
name of the Ethernet hardware device driver. The zero on the end
indicates that this is the first interface defined within the system.

ARP entries that are marked P are permanent (or static) and
have been defined outside the normal ARP protocol (e.g., manually
entered with the **arp –s** command). Static entries are also used to
support networked systems that don't support the ARP protocol.
Therefore, the address binding must be manually entered in the
ARP table. One problem with this approach is that if the IP address
or hardware address of any of these system mappings is changed,
the ARP information must be manually updated to affect the
change. The C flag indicates a normal and complete entry, and most
if not all ARP entries should be marked with this flag.

Only the IP addresses associated with genuine interfaces are
advertised with ARP. It is interesting to note that ARP information
obtained from other network devices is not normally published by
third-party systems. It is usually the responsibility of each device to
respond to ARP requests with its own information. There is one
special case when a system will respond to ARP requests on behalf
of others. This is known as *proxy ARP*, which is used with routed
subnets or other special network configurations.

Mapped ARP entries include a timer, which controls how long
the entry will remain in the ARP cache. By default, most UNIX systems hold the entry for approximately 20 minutes before removing
it. Some systems permit the administrator to alter this timing value.

The incomplete string indicates that an ARP request is still
pending and the mapping is unresolved for the associated host. In
the ARP example above, the system rubens lacks a physical address
because the ARP request didn't obtain a reply. This is known as an
incomplete ARP entry. Many reasons could cause this condition:
hardware trouble with the device, network wiring problems, or
software configuration problems on the host. The bottom line is
that the ARP software wasn't able to communicate with the device

to obtain the desired information. The final string that is displayed shows a count of the number of entries in the cache.

In situations where there are many ARP entries, you can use -a followed by a valid hostname to list a specific system. For instance, the following command will list the ARP mapping for the host called socrates:

```
# arp -a socrates
socrates.home.com (10.0.2.201) at 00:60:97:0E:A3:03 [ether] on eth0
```

Also, you could have used the IP address instead of the hostname. Thus, the command **arp -a 10.0.2.201** would yield the same output.

Note

With the standard Linux 6.0 release, the manual page for the **arp** command incorrectly states that the --display option can be used instead of the -a option. Unfortunately, the ARP program doesn't support this, and the user will get an error when attempting to use the --display option. Thus, the **arp --display socrates** command will produce:

```
arp: unrecognized option `--display'
```

The **arp** command also accepts hostnames or IP addresses without the -a option. Without this command option, each of the field labels are displayed along with the ARP entry. Thus, the command

```
# arp socrates
Address              HWtype  HWaddress          Flags Mask   Iface
socrates.home.com    ether   00:60:97:0E:A3:03    C          eth0
```

provides more information than when using the -a option. Another option that ARP supports is -n. This option displays either hostnames or IP addresses within the listings. One reason for choosing to display the ARP entries using IP addresses is that it will be a little faster. Mapping between IP addresses and hostnames is usually done with Domain Name Server (DNS) and, as a result, may take some time to complete. In practice, the delay is negligible in most situations. However, if the name resolution facility (NIS or DNS, for instance) experiences delays or some other operational problem, then listing the ARP cache with the -n option will be much faster. The command **arp -n** will return the output quicker if

name resolution is completely non-functional given a fairly large
ARP cache. The format of the ARP listings using the first example
given in this section will display the following:

```
# arp -n -v
Address      HWtype   HWaddress           Flags Mask      Iface
10.0.2.10    ether    00:60:97:0E:A3:06      C             eth0
10.0.2.60    ether    00:00:1D:0A:5D:01      C             eth0
10.0.2.50    ether    00:C0:D4:00:09:40      C             eth0
10.0.2.127   ether    08:00:20:82:be:05      C             eth0
10.0.2.220            (incomplete)                         eth0
10.0.2.126   ether    08:00:20:04:cf:2c      C             eth0
Entries: 6 Skipped: 0      Found: 6
```

As you can see, the IP address of each host has been displayed
instead of the actual hostnames.

As previously mentioned, the **arp** command displays the interface name for which the entry was obtained. Given the output
above, all the mapping was from the eth0 interface. Sometimes, a
system may contain more than one interface. This is known as
multi-homing. When the ARP cache is displayed on these systems,
the output contains entries for each of the interfaces, as in the following example:

```
Address            HWtype   HWaddress           Flags Mask Iface
durer.home.com     ether    00:60:97:0E:A3:06      C        eth0
moster.home.com    ether    00:60:97:0A:B3:09      C        eth1
probe2.home.com    ether    00:80:96:0B:C1:01      C        eth1
switch.home.com    ether    00:00:1D:0A:5D:01      C        eth0
probe.home.com     ether    00:C0:D4:00:09:40      C        eth0
```

We can see that mapping exists for two interfaces for this system.
In this case, eth0 and eth1 are listed within the output. Since ARP
tracks entries by interface, we can use the -i option to display just
mappings from a particular interface.The following command,

```
#arp -i eth1
```

will display all ARP listings for the eth1 interface:

```
Address            Wtype    HWaddress           Flags Mask Iface
moster.home.com    ether    00:60:97:0A:B3:09       C       eth1
probe2.home.com    ether    00:80:96:0B:C1:01       C       eth1
```

Deleting an ARP Cache

It might become necessary to delete one or more entries from the ARP table. For example, should a hardware failure result in the replacement of a network interface card, the network hardware address of the system will change. In this case, the existing ARP entry won't reflect that the low-level address has changed. As a result, messages sent to this host from other devices will not be picked up because the hardware address used will not match that of the interface.

To address this problem, the -d option should be used to delete an ARP entry, as shown below. Because removing ARP bindings can cause network problems, only the superuser is permitted to remove them. The **arp** command expects the -d option to be used with a valid host or IP address. In this example, the host durer is removed from the ARP table:

```
# arp -d durer
```

If the ARP table were now displayed, the durer entry would be listed as shown here:

```
Address          HWtype     HWaddress        Flags Mask  Iface
durer.home.com              (incomplete)
```

If a non-root user attempted to remove this host from the table, an error message would be displayed:

```
% arp -d durer
SIOCDARP(priv): Operation not permitted
```

Adding an ARP Cache Entry

Several conditions may warrant manually adding entries to the ARP table. One such situation occurs when communication with a device is needed, but the device, for some reason, doesn't support ARP, or the implementation is non-functional. This might be the case with a very old system that is still in service. Further, should a NIC address change, the table must be manually updated to ensure connectivity. Finally, it may be necessary to add entries to support proxy ARP services.

To add an ARP entry, use the -s option followed by the host-name (or address) and the associated physical datalink address. For example, let's say we would like to add a system called bruegel to the ARP table. The format of the physical datalink is represented as x:x:x:x:x:x, where each x is a hexadecimal number between 0 and FF. To illustrate the example, the following command would be used:

```
# arp -s bruegel 08:00:20:82:be:05
```

If no error message is displayed, it can be assumed that the command was successful. Alternatively, you could list the ARP cache to see if bruegel was in fact added:

```
# arp bruegel
Address           HWtype  HWaddress          Flags Mask  Iface
bruegel.home.com  ether   08:00:20:82:be:05        CM      eth
```

Please note that this ARP binding is labeled with the M flag, which indicates it is a permanent entry because it was added on the command line. Since permanent mappings are statically defined, they don't timeout. Unfortunately, permanent entries are not saved across system reboots.

To understand why modifying the ARP table is restricted only to the superuser, consider that when static ARP entries are defined, no direct linkage exists between this information and the actual devices attached to the network. For example, the entry for bruegel was added manually, but no mechanism is available to ARP to ensure that the physical address is indeed correct. The **arp** command assumes the information provided is accurate and that the device is actually attached to the network. Therefore, if normal users had the ability to modify the ARP table, more errors would likely be introduced that would lead to loss of network connectivity. Should the physical address of a critical network resource (like a server) be incorrectly changed, all communication between the local system and the critical system would stop.

Loading ARP Bindings Using a File

The **arp** command also supports the ability to add bindings that are defined within a regular file instead of specifying the information on the command line. This method is used, for example, to load a list of ARP entries together in one step. It is not uncommon, for example, for a series of ARP bindings to be loaded during normal system startup procedures—especially if the system doesn't support distributed database lookup schemes such as NIS. The format of a file used for this purpose includes the following fields:

```
hostname datalink address [ temp ] [ pub ] [netmask]
```

Using a text editor, you can create a list of ARP bindings in the format above and save it to a text file—for example, /etc/arp-list. A sample file listing is shown:

```
bruegel 08:00:20:82:be:05 temp
rubens 08:00:20:81:ce:01 temp
rembrandt 08:00:20:86:fe:02
cezanne 08:00:20:81:bb:01
michelangelo 08:00:20:84:ee:02
```

Notice that both bruegel and rubens contain the **temp** keyword, which indicates that these entries will be deleted from the ARP table after they expire. In practice, the temp option is not commonly used because it might be undesirable for these bindings to expire and be removed from the cache. The **pub** keyword publishes the ARP binding to the network.

The **arp** command can be used to support proxy ARP services. Proxy ARP is a way to respond to ARP requests on behalf of another network device. Typically this configuration is used to support devices behind a router or a specialized configuration, such as those required for remote dial-up access strategies. The netmask option is primarily used to enable proxy ARP services for one or more systems on a subnet. Since proxy services are not normally implemented using a static ARP configuration, the netmask option is considered obsolete.

The file contains the desired entries. Use the -f option of the **arp** command to load the contents of the file into the ARP table:

```
# arp -f /etc/arp-list
```

If you want to load this table automatically, edit one of the system startup files (/etc/rc.d/init.d/network, for example) and include:

Listing 4.1 *ARP startup script*

```
1  #!/bin/bash
2  # Load custom ARP table
3  #
```

```
4   echo -n "Loading local arp table..."
5   if [ -f /etc/arp-list ]; then
6      /sbin/arp -f /etc/arp-list
7      echo "done."
8   else
9      echo "ARP file not found!"
10  exit -1
11  fi
```

When this script is added to a network startup script, it will load the ARP mappings contained within the /etc/arp-list file. The script checks to see if the /etc/arp-list file is present and is a regular file (line 5). If so, it will invoke the **arp** command with the -f option. If not, it displays an error message and then exits with an error.

Ifconfig Tool

General Description

The **ifconfig** command is short for *interface configuration* and is used to configure local network interfaces. This command is normally invoked during system startup to set up each interface with a predefined configuration. The **ifconfig** command can also be used to change the network interface parameters after the system has been booted. This command is often used for debugging and/or system tuning activities. This command performs the following:

- lists the configuration of each defined network interface

- disables/enables any defined network interface

- modifies network interface configuration parameters

- creates pseudo-interfaces

The **ifconfig** command provides a large number of options and keywords that are used to configure one or more interfaces. Table 4.3 lists the most important of these options and keywords, which are used as modifiers with other command-line options.

Listing Available Interfaces

To display all system interfaces, use the **ifconfig -a** command.

Table 4.3 **ifconfig** *options and keywords*

Option	Description
-a	Applies to all interfaces presently installed on the system
arp -arp	Enables the use of the Address Resolution Protocol (ARP) on this interface; disables the use of ARP with the -arp option
promisc -promisc	Enables promiscuous (i.e., listen for all traffic) mode on this interface. The -promisc option disables it
allmulti -allmulti	Enables all multicast traffic to be received by the interface. The -allmulti option will disable the reception of multicast packets
broadcast -broadcast	With the argument given, sets or clears the broadcast address for this interface. This is a network-layer broadcast address
pointtopoint -pointtopoint	Enables a point-to-point mode for this interface. The basic assumption is that this is a dedicated link between two devices. If the address argument is provided, it sets the protocol address for the other side of the link. Disables the point-to-point mode with the **pointtopoint** keyword
up	Causes the interface to be brought up or activated
down	Causes the interface to be shut down or deactivated
netmask	Sets the IP network mask for this interface. The specified argument can be in the form 255.0.0.0 (dotted decimal) or 0xff00000 (hexadecimal)
broadcast	Sets the IP broadcast for this interface. The specified argument can be expressed in the same format as the **netmask** keyword
address	Sets the IP address for this interface. This must be a unique IP address not previously assigned to another system

```
#ifconfig -a
eth0       Link encap:Ethernet  HWaddr 00:10:5A:28:5D:7C
           inet addr:10.0.2.201  Bcast:10.0.2.255
           Mask:255.255.255.0

UP BROADCAST RUNNING PROMISC MULTICAST  MTU:1500  Metric:1
           RX packets:822 errors:1 dropped:0 overruns:0 frame:1
           TX packets:108 errors:0 dropped:0 overruns:0 carrier:0
           collisions:0 txqueuelen:100
           Interrupt:10 Base address:0xfc00

lo         Link encap:Local Loopback
           inet addr:127.0.0.1  Mask:255.0.0.0
           UP LOOPBACK RUNNING  MTU:3924  Metric:1
           RX packets:92 errors:0 dropped:0 overruns:0 frame:0
           TX packets:92 errors:0 dropped:0 overruns:0 carrier:0
           collisions:0 txqueuelen:0

ppp0       Link encap:Point-to-Point Protocol
           POINTOPOINT NOARP MULTICAST  MTU:1500  Metric:1
           RX packets:0 errors:0 dropped:0 overruns:0 frame:0
           TX packets:0 errors:0 dropped:0 overruns:0 carrier:0
           collisions:0 txqueuelen:10
```

The -a option indicates that **ifconfig** should display all interfaces installed within the system regardless of their present configuration or operational state.

The example displayed above indicates that three interfaces are defined. The first, eth0, represents the physical hardware interfaces for 10Mbs Ethernet using the 3Com Ethernet driver. The second, lo, is the loopback interface, primarily used for internal communication and diagnostics. The loopback interface can be used to determine if the TCP/IP software is operating correctly on a local level. For instance, it is possible to **ping** the loopback address to determine valid responses. The final (ppp0) interface represents a point-to-point dial-up link for connectivity to a local Internet Service Provider (ISP).

For each interface, the display includes the following fields:

Link encap   This specifies the link encapsulation protocol that the interface will use when transmitting datalink frames. Supported types include Ethernet, Local Loopback, and Point-to-Point Protocol.

HWaddr   This is the datalink address for the encapsulation
                protocol. For instance, Ethernet uses the hexa-
                decimal notation, such as in the entry for the eth0
                interface: 00:10:5A:28:5D:7C.

inet addr   This is the IP address associated with this inter-
                face.

Bcast   This represents the network-layer broadcast
                address.

Mask   This represents the subnet mask address.

   In addition, the display includes the operational parameters for
the interface. These include UP, BROADCAST, RUNNING, PROMISC, and
MULTICAST. These options show the mode and current state of the
interface.

   Next, the display includes fields that represent the statistical
counters, such as received packets (RX packets), transmitted packets (TX packets), number of collisions (collisions), and so forth.
These provide a relatively easy way to benchmark the performance
of the interface. Finally, the remaining fields show the interrupt
number and I/O Base address of the interface hardware. Notice,
too, that not all interfaces have an associated interrupt number and
I/O address. The loopback interface lacks these fields because it
uses no specific hardware within the system.

Controlling Administration State

   With **ifconfig** it is possible to disable an active interface or enable
a disabled interface while the system is running. In the disabled
state, no packets will be permitted across an interface. This is
equivalent to disconnecting the interface from the network. When
an interface is disabled, it is considered down from an administrative standpoint. To place an interface in the down state, invoke the
ifconfig command with the appropriate interface and the **down** keyword option as shown:

```
# ifconfig eth0 down
```

   We can use the **ifconfig** command with the interface name instead
of the -a option to list an individual interface. The following com-

mand displays the configuration of the interface that we shut down
with the previous command.

```
# arp eth0
eth0      Link encap:Ethernet   HWaddr 08:00:20:04:CF:2C
          inet addr:10.0.3.127   Bcast:10.0.3.255
Mask:255.255.255.0
BROADCAST MULTICAST  MTU:1500  Metric:1
RX packets:3452 errors:0 dropped:0 overruns:0 frame:0
TX packets:3212 errors:1 dropped:0 overruns:0 carrier:1
          collisions:0 txqueuelen:100
          Interrupt:38 Base address:0x3200
```

Notice the keywords **up** and **running** are now missing from the
output. This is how **ifconfig** indicates that an interface has been disabled and is not available for use. To enable or activate this interface, we simply use the **up** command option:

```
# ifconfig eth0 up
```

When the interface is up, it is available on the network and
receiving network information. Without the indication of the **up**
flag, the interface is operational and perhaps connected to the network, but no information is flowing to or from the network.

Modifying Interface Parameters

Three methods can be used to modify network interface parameters. First, using **ifconfig** directly, changes can be made on the command line and will take effect immediately. The second approach
involves modifying the system startup and/or system files that **ifconfig** uses to configure the interface. This approach ensures that interface changes are made permanently and won't disappear across
system reboots. Sometimes both approaches are used. Often, a configuration change must be implemented quickly before the system
can be rebooted at a convenient time. As a result, **ifconfig** can be used
to make the immediate changes. Normally, when a new interface is
installed on a system, this configuration may be handled by the
installation procedure. The third method involves using the standard Linux control panel application, `control-panel`, to make the
changes. Chapter 9, "Web-enabled Tools," describes this application in more detail.

Using **ifconfig**, the following important information can be changed for an interface:

- IP address

- network mask

- broadcast address

- datalink address

- MTU

The IP address is specified in the normal dotted decimal notation and represents the unique address for the host on the network to which the system is attached. The network subnet mask (or netmask) specifies the filter used to calculate the network and host portions for the subnet. The broadcast address specifies the IP address to which broadcast packets should be directed. The datalink address represents the unique low-level hardware address used by Ethernet or FDDI, and is associated with the hardware itself. The maximum transfer unit (MTU) denotes the maximum message size that the interface can handle. The standard message size for Ethernet is 1500, for FDDI is 4096, and for TokenRing is 2048. The MTU is rarely modified and, when it is, can't be configured to support values higher than what the hardware will support; only lower values may be used.

Let's suppose that the IP address of a system must be changed because the system is moved to a different subnet. In this case, the netmask and broadcast information remains the same. The move to the new network involves changing the IP address of the interface only. The old IP address is 128.197.9.10 and the new IP address is 128.197.10.1. The following command would be used to change the network information on-the-fly:

```
# ifconfig eth0 128.197.10.1
```

To make this change permanent, we must modify the /etc/hosts file. This file contains the mapping between hostname and the associated IP address. On system startup, the IP address is derived from the file and applied to the interface. The netmask and broadcast information is the same; we can use the existing values.

The hostname could also be specified on the command line instead of the IP address. Thus, the command

```
# ifconfig eth0 fred
```

accomplishes the same result, assuming that fred has been assigned the IP address of 128.197.10.1. either in the /etc/hosts file, DNS, or the NIS hosts database.

As you can see, changing the IP address for an interface is relatively straightforward. However, changing other interface characteristics requires a bit more work. To extend the preceding example, let us now assume that we must change the netmask and broadcast information. To change the interface on-the-fly, we would use:

```
# ifconfig eth0 128.197.10.1 netmask 255.255.0.0 broadcast\
128.197.255.255
```

In the example above, the **netmask** and **broadcast** keywords must be used to identify the information that follows each keyword. The netmask contains 1s in the bit positions of the 32-bit address that are to be used for the network and subnet (if applicable) part, and 0s for the host portion. The netmask/subnet portion must occupy at least as many bits as is standard for the particular network class. If no subnets are defined, the standard netmask is used. As described in Chapter 2, "TCP/IP Protocol Suite," the use of subnets mandates that more bits than what is normally the host portion of the address are reserved to identify the subnet. A netmask can be specified in two different ways: dotted decimal notation and hexadecimal notation.

The dotted decimal notation is expressed in four single-byte numbers separated by dots (e.g., 255.255.255.0). The hexadecimal format includes using the 0x prefix followed by a hexadecimal string value. For example, the hexadecimal value for 255.255.255.0 is 0xffffff00. Since **ifconfig** supports both formats, they can be used interchangeably. Each of the standard IP class addresses has associated default netmask addresses, as shown in Table 4.4. Please note that these addresses are just the standard ones used if no subnetting is implemented. The specific subnet mask addresses used in many sites will differ from these because the subnets defined use more bits than the standard for that class.

Table 4.4 *Standard IP netmask addresses*

Class	Dotted Decimal Notation	Hexadecimal Notation
A	255.0.0.0	0xff000000
B	255.255.0.0	0xffff0000
C	255.255.255.0	0xffffff00

The broadcast address can be specified in the same ways as the netmask address. However, the broadcast address is usually formed by turning all the bits in the host portion of an address to 1s. For example, the broadcast address for the 128.197.0.0 network is 128.197.255.255.

Special Configurations Parameters

The **ifconfig** command supports additional parameters. These include:

- ARP

- multicast

- promiscuous mode

- media type

- point-to-point

The **arp** keyword specifies that the interface should support an ARP style IP address resolution. When an interface is created with **ifconfig**, the default is to support ARP. To disable ARP on an interface, use the -**arp** keyword. On most networks, ARP must be turned on.

The **allmulti** keyword enables or disables (-**allmulti**) all multicast traffic modes. If enabled, multicast packets (i.e., packets with Class D network addresses) will be received by the interface. Despite the fact that multicast traffic is available on the interface, an application that supports multicast traffic will need to be running to make use of this type of traffic. Multicast is used by multimedia applications to transport packets that contain real-time video and audio data.

The **promisc** keyword will enable the interface to receive all network traffic. It is known as *promiscuous mode* when all network traffic is read, not just the normal traffic sent to it by other systems on the network. Use the -**promisc** command to disable this mode. Certain networking tools such as **tcpdump** will enable this mode automatically when in operation.

The **media** keyword changes the physical connectivity type for the interface. Not all interfaces support the ability to dynamically change interface media types. For those that do, many of the most common types may be used, such as 10base2 for thin Ethernet, 10baseT for twisted pair Ethernet, and AUI for external Ethernet associated with 10base5 Ethernet.

The **pointtopoint** keyword enables the use of a *point-to-point* link layer encapsulation protocol, which generally means that direct connectivity will exist between two systems. The commonly supported protocols such as PPP or SLIP can be used.

Logical Interfaces

The **ifconfig** command creates and configures logical (also known as virtual or pseudo-) interfaces. These interfaces behave like physical interfaces and can be used to assign multiple IP addresses to the same system. From a configuration standpoint, logical interfaces are configured independently but share the same physical address and interface characteristics as the real physical interface.

To configure a pseudo-interface, combine the physical interface with a logical interface reference number, separated by a colon. For example, to configure the first logical interface for eth0, use the following command:

```
# ifconfig eth1:1 10.0.2.128 netmask 0xffffff00 broadcast 10.0.2.255
```

Logical interfaces are displayed just like the physical ones using the **ifconfig -a** command. The following output shows one logical interface defined from the physical interface eth1.

```
eth0      Link encap:Ethernet  HWaddr 08:00:20:04:CF:2C
          inet addr:10.0.3.127  Bcast:255.255.255.255
          Mask:255.255.0.0
          UP BROADCAST RUNNING MULTICAST  MTU:1500  Metric:1
          RX packets:0 errors:0 dropped:0 overruns:0 frame:0
          TX packets:0 errors:2 dropped:0 overruns:0 carrier:2
          collisions:0 txqueuelen:100
          Interrupt:38 Base address:0x3200

eth1      Link encap:Ethernet  HWaddr 08:00:20:04:CF:2C
          inet addr:10.0.2.127  Bcast:10.0.2.255
          Mask:255.255.255.0
          UP BROADCAST RUNNING MULTICAST  MTU:1500  Metric:1
          RX packets:1810 errors:0 dropped:0 overruns:0 frame:0
           TX packets:1173 errors:0 dropped:0 overruns:0 carrier:0
          collisions:0 txqueuelen:100
          Interrupt:55 Base address:0x3000

eth1:1    Link encap:Ethernet  HWaddr 08:00:20:04:CF:2C
          inet addr:10.0.2.128  Bcast:10.0.2.255
          Mask:255.255.255.0
          UP BROADCAST RUNNING MULTICAST  MTU:1500  Metric:1
          Interrupt:55 Base address:0x3000

lo        Link encap:Local Loopback
          inet addr:127.0.0.1  Mask:255.0.0.0
          UP LOOPBACK RUNNING  MTU:3924  Metric:1
          RX packets:360 errors:0 dropped:0 overruns:0 frame:0
           TX packets:360 errors:0 dropped:0 overruns:0 carrier:0
          collisions:0 txqueuelen:0
```

Notice the pseudo-interface, eth1:1 contains the same Ethernet hardware address (08:00:20:04:CF:2C) and the same interrupt level (55) as the real interface. These are additional clues that indicate that this interface is the same as the eth1 interface.

To remove a logical interface, use the **down** keyword. Thus, the command

```
ifconfig -a eth1:1 down
```

will remove the eth1:1 interface from the system. If this logical interface was created during system startup, then the interface will be configured again when the system is restarted.

Netstat Tool

General Description

The **netstat** command provides a wealth of information regarding the present status of network connections, routing information, and other important network-related data. This tool, short for *network status*, is strictly for monitoring and is one of the most popular debugging aids available on UNIX. Different command-line options control the display behavior of **netstat**. Given this, the functionality can be divided into a number of categories and used to accomplish the following:

- list active network sessions

- show interface information and statistics

- display routing table information

- show network data structures

This tool also provides specific keywords that control the operation and output formatting. Table 4.5 contains the major keywords that control which data structures are displayed. Some of the command options/keywords have a single-character option and a mnemonic string. For instance, the `-h` and `--help` options, which display command-line summary help, can be used interchangeably.

Table 4.5 netstat *keywords*

Option	Mnemonic	Description
`-i`	`--interface`	Shows network interface parameters and statistical information
`-g`	`--groups`	Displays multicast group membership information
`-M`	`--masquerade`	Lists all sessions that use the masqueraded capabilities within FTP
`-N`	`--netlink`	Shows netlink interfaces and activity

Table 4.5 netstat *keywords (continued)*

Option	Mnemonic	Description
-r	--route	Shows the network routing tables
-t	-tcp	Displays active TCP socket connections. The -tcp option will continuously display these connections until interrupted by the user

Table 4.6 contains command-line modifiers that either provide additional information or modify the output when used with the keyword options.

Table 4.6 netstat *command options*

Option	Mnemonic	Description
-A	--af	Specifies a different address family. Specific keywords include **--unix, --ipx, --ax25, --netrom,** and **--ddp**
-c	--continue	Causes the output to be continuously displayed until the user interrupts the output
-h	--help	Displays command-line summary information to the user
-n	--numeric	Displays numeric information (for example, IP addresses) instead of attempting to resolve to a host, port, or username
-p	--program	Shows the process name and identifier for each network socket listed
-v	--verbose	Prints additional information

One helpful feature of this tool is online help. Just invoke the command with the `-h` or `--help` option:

```
netstat --help
```

Listing 4.2 displays the results:

Listing 4.2 *Results of* **netstat --help**

```
usage: netstat [-veenNcCF] [<Af>] -r       netstat {-V|--version|-h|--help}
       netstat [-vnNcaeol] [<Socket> ...]
       netstat { [-veenNac] -i | [-cnNe] -M | -s }

        -r, --route            display routing table
        -i, --interfaces       display interface table
        -g, --groups           display multicast group memberships
        -s, --statistics       display networking statistics (like SNMP)
        -M, --masquerade       display masqueraded connections

        -v, --verbose          be verbose
        -n, --numeric          dont resolve names
        -N, --symbolic         resolve hardware names
        -e, --extend           display other/more informations
        -p, --programs         display PID/Program name for sockets
        -c, --continuous       continuous listing

        -l, --listening        display listening server sockets
        -a, --all, --listening display all sockets (default: connected)
        -o, --timers           display timers
        -F, --fib              display Forwarding Infomation Base
(default)
        -C, --cache            display routing cache instead of FIB

<Socket>={-t|--tcp} {-u|--udp} {-w|--raw} {-x|--unix} --ax25 --ipx --
netrom
<AF>=Use '-A <af>' or '--<af>' Default: inet
List of possible address families (which support routing):
    inet (DARPA Internet) ax25 (AMPR AX.25) netrom (AMPR NET/ROM)
```

Displaying Active Network Sessions

One of the significant services provided by **netstat** is the ability to view active connections between systems. Any TCP session between the local host and any other system can be monitored. Also, any stream sockets that have been created will be displayed as well. Streams are used as a program-to-program communication channel. To display the currently established connections, issue the **netstat** with the `-t` option as shown:

```
# netstat -t
Active Internet connections (w/o servers)
Proto Recv-Q Send-Q Local Address           Foreign Address         State
tcp       0      0 110.orlando-11-12r:1052 192.215.123.37:www      ESTABLISHED
tcp       1      0 110.orlando-11-12r:1051 192.215.123.37:www      CLOSE
tcp       0      6 110.orlando-11-12r:1050 postoffice.worldn:pop-3 ESTABLISHED
tcp       0      0 110.orlando-11-12r:1049 www3.yahoo.com:www      ESTABLISHED
tcp       0      0 socrates.home.co:telnet durer.home.com:1033     ESTABLISHED
tcp       0      0 socrates.home.co:telnet durer.home.com:1032     ESTABLISHED
```

Recall from Table 4.5 that the `-t` option will display TCP socket activity. As indicated, the output of the above command includes the connections on the local system. Each connection includes information regarding the local and remote addresses, statistical information, and connection status. The local and remote addresses are displayed to include hostname and port information in the format:

```
host.port
```

where `host` can either be an assigned hostname from `/etc/hosts` (or from another host resolution mechanism such as NIS or DNS) or a valid IP address. The `port` represents either a reserved port, as defined in `/etc/services`, or a socket allocated by the system. The local address is the source and the remote address is the destination. Recall that TCP uses four elements to make up a connection and uses a state machine model as part of TCP's overall transport mechanism. As a result, `monet.telnet` and `rembrandt.1036` are considered one connection. From the `State` field, we can see that this connection is in the `ESTABLISHED` state, which means it is passing data back and forth.

Recall that TCP uses a state machine to control each of the defined states, and that we can use the **netstat** command to track and display the state of each TCP connection. Table 4.7 shows the most common states and includes a general description of each.

The preceding **netstat** command only displayed connections that are or were in the `ESTABLISHED` state. Sometimes it is helpful to list all services that are available and active on a system. This can be accomplished by using **netstat** with the `-a` option, as shown below.

Table 4.7 *TCP States shown with* **netstat**

State	Description
ESTABLISHED	The connection is operational
LISTEN	A service or application is waiting for a client connection
SYN_SENT	Local system wants to open a remote connection
SYN_RCVD	Remote system wants to open a connection
FIN_WAIT_1	Local system is in the process of closing a connection
FIN_WAIT_2	Local system is in the process of closing a connection
CLOSE_WAIT	Remote system wants to close a connection
LAST_ACK	Final step to CLOSE_WAIT
TIMED_WAIT	Final step to FIN_WAIT_1 or FIN_WAIT_2
UNKNOWN	The state of the socket is unknown

Please note that the following output has been reduced to make it more readable. Executing this command on most systems will produce a larger list because it will include the stream interfaces as well. However, we can use the -t and -u options to further refine the output to only include TCP and UDP sockets. The following output provides a list of both UDP and TCP services, regardless of their connection states. This is useful because it is not always obvious which transport protocol a particular service uses.

```
#netstat -a -t -u
Active Internet connections (servers and established)
Proto Recv-Q Send-Q Local Address        Foreign Address      State
tcp        0      0 socrates.home.co:telnet durer.home.com:1033   ESTABLISHED
```

(continued)

```
tcp       0       0 110.orlando-11-1:domain *:*                     LISTEN
tcp       0       0 *:1048                  *:*                     LISTEN
tcp       0       0 *:1047                  *:*                     LISTEN
tcp       0       0 *:1046                  *:*                     LISTEN
tcp       0       0 *:1045                  *:*                     LISTEN
tcp       0       0 *:1044                  *:*                     LISTEN
tcp       0       0 *:1037                  *:*                     LISTEN
tcp       0     710 socrates.home.co:telnet durer.home.com:1032     ESTABLISHED
tcp       0       0 *:6000                  *:*                     LISTEN
tcp       0       0 *:nntp                  *:*                     LISTEN
tcp       0       0 *:www                   *:*                     LISTEN
tcp       0       0 *:smtp                  *:*                     LISTEN
tcp       0       0 *:713                   *:*                     LISTEN
tcp       0       0 *:1024                  *:*                     LISTEN
tcp       0       0 *:683                   *:*                     LISTEN
tcp       0       0 *:678                   *:*                     LISTEN
tcp       0       0 *:673                   *:*                     LISTEN
tcp       0       0 *:652                   *:*                     LISTEN
tcp       0       0 *:printer               *:*                     LISTEN
tcp       0       0 10.0.2.205:domain       *:*                     LISTEN
tcp       0       0 10.0.2.202:domain       *:*                     LISTEN
tcp       0       0 socrates.home.co:domain *:*                     LISTEN
tcp       0       0 localhost:domain        *:*                     LISTEN
tcp       0       0 *:linuxconf             *:*                     LISTEN
tcp       0       0 *:auth                  *:*                     LISTEN
tcp       0       0 *:finger                *:*                     LISTEN
tcp       0       0 *:login                 *:*                     LISTEN
tcp       0       0 *:shell                 *:*                     LISTEN
tcp       0       0 *:telnet                *:*                     LISTEN
tcp       0       0 *:ftp                   *:*                     LISTEN
tcp       0       0 *:sunrpc                *:*                     LISTEN
udp       0       0 110.orlando-11-1:domain *:*
udp       0       0 *:xdmcp                 *:*
udp       0       0 localhost:1119          *:*
udp       0       0 *:800                   *:*
udp       0       0 *:1022                  *:*
udp       0       0 *:714                   *:*
udp       0       0 *:1023                  *:*
udp       0       0 *:1026                  *:*
udp       0       0 *:2049                  *:*
udp       0       0 *:681                   *:*
udp       0       0 *:676                   *:*
udp       0       0 *:671                   *:*
udp       0       0 *:661                   *:*
udp       0       0 *:650                   *:*
udp       0       0 *:1024                  *:*
udp       0       0 10.0.2.205:domain       *:*
udp       0       0 10.0.2.202:domain       *:*
```

```
udp        0        0 socrates.home.co:domain *:*
udp        0        0 localhost:domain        *:*
udp        0        0 *:snmp                  *:*
udp        0        0 *:ntalk                 *:*
udp        0        0 *:talk                  *:*
udp        0        0 *:sunrpc                *:
```

Under the TCP heading, not only are the two TCP connections displayed from the previous example, but additional services are included as well. Any services listed in the LISTEN state are waiting for incoming connections and are usually known as server-based resources. When a service is waiting for requests from the network, it is free to access connections from any remote address. That is why *.* is listed under the foreign address field. Servers also generally place * in the local host portion to further indicate that the server is free to establish a connection if a client request is made. When a request from a client is sent to a server, the server makes a copy of itself to handle the request and continues listening for additional client requests. Thus when this occurs, **netstat** displays multiple instances of the same service, as shown:

```
netstat -a | grep ftp
tcp        0        0 socrates.home.:ftp-data durer.home.com:1034   TIME_WAIT
tcp        0        0 socrates.home.com:ftp   durer.home.com:1033   ESTABLISHED
tcp        0        0 *:ftp                   *:*                   LISTEN
```

The above command issues a **netstat** and pipes the output into the **grep** command, which scans the input for the ftp string. As a result, all lines with the ftp string are displayed. In the output above, the FTP server is still listening for incoming connection requests while an FTP session is established to socrates.

Under the UDP heading in the previous output example, only a local address and state field have been displayed; the foreign address is not specified. This is because UDP is a connectionless protocol and therefore doesn't require remote address information. Also, notice that no statistical information is available for UDP. This is another indication that UDP is fundamentally different by design and does not need this type of information.

Despite the rather large amount of information provided with the -a option, **netstat** can be used to provide a quick check to ensure that the correct services are running on a given system. By scanning the output of **netstat**, the network administrator can easily notice any service that shouldn't be running. For example, many organizations consider the finger facility to be a security risk because it can provide user account information to anyone requesting it. Once detected with **netstat**, the finger service can be disabled by modifying the /etc/inetd.conf network configuration file.

If you are interested in displaying the streams defined on the system, issue the **netstat** command with the --unix option. The output includes the UNIX streams socket interfaces. Since these connections are mainly used for interprocess communication, their specific use and function won't be described in great detail. Since the number of streams used on a UNIX system can be significant, the output from the **netstat** command can be rather long. As a result, the following output shows just a few lines versus what would typically be displayed:

```
unix  1        [ ]            STREAM    CONNECTED    2399    /dev/log
unix  1        [ ]            STREAM    CONNECTED    2384    /tmp/.ICE-unix/963
unix  1        [ N ]          STREAM    CONNECTED    2364    /tmp/.X11-unix/X0
unix  1        [ ]            STREAM    CONNECTED    2220    /tmp/orbit-root/orb-
      11931020341330722701
unix  1        [ ]            STREAM    CONNECTED    2217    /tmp/orbit-root/orb-
      2122911451756745208
unix  1        [ ]            STREAM    CONNECTED    2213    /tmp/orbit-root/orb-
      16956010373298973
unix  1        [ ]            STREAM    CONNECTED    2206    /tmp/.X11-unix/X0
unix  1        [ ]            STREAM    CONNECTED    2202    /tmp/orbit-root/orb-
      2122911451756745208
unix  1        [ ]            STREAM    CONNECTED    2196    /tmp/orbit-root/orb-
      16956010373298973
unix  1        [ ]            STREAM    CONNECTED    2197    /tmp/orbit-root/orb-
      13881122161642635705
unix  1        [ ]            STREAM    CONNECTED    2188    /tmp/.X11-unix/X0
unix  1        [ ]            STREAM    CONNECTED    2179    /tmp/orbit-root/orb-
      16956010373298973
```

These streams have been created by system programs and applications as a mechanism to communicate with themselves and other programs.

One extremely useful feature of **netstat** is the -p option, which will show the associated process or program name that has opened or is using a system. The command

```
# netstat -t -p -a
```

produces this output:

```
(Not all processes could be identified, non-owned process info
will not be shown, you would have to be root to see it all.)
Active Internet connections (servers and established)
Proto Recv-Q Send-Q Local Address          Foreign Address          State
PID/Program name
tcp       0    285 socrates.home.co:telnet durer.home.com:1032   ESTABLISHED
    906/in.telnetd
tcp       0      0 *:1036                  *:*                    LISTEN
    846/gnomepager_appl
tcp       0      0 *:1035                  *:*                    LISTEN
    843/gen_util_applet
tcp       0      0 *:1034                  *:*                    LISTEN 821/gmc
tcp       0      0 *:1033                  *:*                    LISTEN 823/gnome-
    name-serv
tcp       0      0 *:1032                  *:*                    LISTEN 812/panel
tcp       0      0 *:1025                  *:*                    LISTEN 766/gnome-
    session
tcp       0      0 *:6000                  *:*                    LISTEN 738/X
tcp       0      0 *:nntp                  *:*                    LISTEN 685/innd
tcp       0      0 *:www                   *:*                    LISTEN 602/httpd
tcp       0      0 *:smtp                  *:*                    LISTEN
    573/sendmail: accep
tcp       0      0 *:713                   *:*                    LISTEN 536/amd
tcp       0      0 *:1024                  *:*                    LISTEN -
tcp       0      0 *:683                   *:*                    LISTEN
    495/rpc.mountd
tcp       0      0 *:678                   *:*                    LISTEN
    495/rpc.mountd
tcp       0      0 *:673                   *:*                    LISTEN
    495/rpc.mountd
tcp       0      0 *:652                   *:*                    LISTEN
    473/rpc.statd
tcp       0      0 *:printer               *:*                    LISTEN 455/lpd
tcp       0      0 10.0.2.205:domain       *:*                    LISTEN 441/named
tcp       0      0 10.0.2.202:domain       *:*                    LISTEN 441/named
tcp       0      0 socrates.home.co:domain *:*                    LISTEN 441/named
tcp       0      0 localhost:domain        *:*                    LISTEN 441/named
tcp       0      0 *:linuxconf             *:*                    LISTEN 397/inetd
tcp       0      0 *:auth                  *:*                    LISTEN 397/inetd
tcp       0      0 *:finger                *:*                    LISTEN 397/inetd
tcp       0      0 *:login                 *:*                    LISTEN 397/inetd
tcp       0      0 *:shell                 *:*                    LISTEN 397/inetd
tcp       0      0 *:telnet                *:*                    LISTEN 397/inetd
tcp       0      0 *:ftp                   *:*                    LISTEN 397/inetd
tcp       0      0 *:sunrpc                *:*                    LISTEN 290/portmap
```

Once executed, additional columns are added to the normal output of **netstat**. They include the PID (process identification) and the `Program name` fields. As you can see, it is now very easy to track down sockets and find which process and/or program is using them. Note that this version of **netstat** warns the user that not all processes may be listed unless the user is running **netstat** as `root`. The output above was derived from executing the command as the root user, but the message is still displayed. From a practical stand-point, this message should be ignored.

Displaying Interface Information

The **netstat** command can obtain details on the configuration of the network interface and rudimentary packet counts as well. The `-i` command-line option obtains a list of each defined interface on the system, one interface per line:

```
#netstat -i
Kernel Interface table
Iface   MTU Met    RX-OK RX-ERR RX-DRP RX-OVR    TX-OK TX-ERR TX-DRP TX-OVR Flg
eth0   1500   0        0      0      0      0        0      1      0      0 BRU
eth0:  1500   0       - no statistics available -                         BRU
eth1   1500   0     3946      0      0      0      138      0      0      0 BRU
lo     3924   0      192      0      0      0      192      0      0      0 LRU
```

As you can see, **netstat** displays some of the same information that the **ifconfig** command provides, plus some basic statistics regarding operating characteristics of each interface—specifically, the name of the interface, the maximum transfer unit (MTU), the network or destination address, and the address of the interface. Also, it displays a count of the total number of input packets, input error packets, input dropped packets, and input overflow counter. It contains the same counters for transmitted packets as well. The `Flg` field contains a condensed listing of the interface configuration options as enabled and reported by the **ifconfig** command.

The `RX-OK` (received) and `TX-OK` (transmitted) fields represent the reception and transmission of valid traffic across the interface, respectively. The next fields, `RX-ERR` and `TX-ERR`, indicate any input and output error packets that have occurred on the interface; this includes, for example, any runt packets (those that are smaller than the standard size) and other errors. The `RX-DRP` and `TX-DRP` fields are counters that represent problems with the transmission of pack-ets on the interface. In the output above, note that the interface `eth0` reports a number of output packet errors. In this case, these errors are being generated because the interface is not physically attached to a network, yet the system is attempting to send out packets. Some UNIX systems can't detect when an interface is actually attached to a network. This is also the reason that the RX-OK and TX-OK fields are zero; this indicates that no traffic has been sent or received across this interface.

The TX-ERR field indicates the number of collisions (or other transmission errors) that have occurred as recorded by the system. A collision is when two or more devices attempt to transmit packets at nearly the same time. After this happens, a jam signal is sent to inform all devices on the network that a collision has occurred and that any transmission should stop briefly and then, after randomly determined intervals of time, be tried again. This is known as *back-off* and is the mechanism used by devices to resume normal operations. Collisions only occur on broadcast network technologies such as Ethernet. When the TX-ERR field is non-zero, it indicates that the interface has recorded collisions for which it was directly involved. It is important to note that this field does not represent all collisions that have occurred on the network because the system may not always count the number of jam messages transmitted as a result of a collision caused by other systems.

The RX-DRP and TX-DRP fields represent packets that were discarded before being received or transmitted. These fields are useful in situations when the system is performing routing functions where lost or discarded packets could cause connectivity problems between systems or networks. Another instance when it may be important to monitor these counters is when the system is a server, where the network traffic can be significant. In practice, the fields aren't that important for a system that may be used as a single-user workstation. The RX-OVR and TX-OVR fields provide counters for packets that caused overflow conditions for the networking software. Again, these are only critical when the system being monitored is considered critical.

When logical (or pseudo-) interfaces are defined on the system, **netstat** lists each interface as a separate entry. However, you will notice that given the example above, **netstat** doesn't collect statistical information for these interfaces. As a result, the message no statistics available is displayed. In all other respects, **netstat** shows logi-

cal interfaces with the same information as normal interfaces. This
includes, for example, the interface (Flg) field codes.

Some of the packet totals displayed from **netstat** closely match
the values obtained directly from the Linux SNMP agent known as
snmpd. The snmpd program is an agent that supports MIB objects
that correspond to objects reported by **netstat**. The MIB objects can
be mapped to the **netstat** packet counter fields and are listed in
Table 4.8. See Chapter 6, "Using SNMP Agents," for more details
regarding snmpd and the MIB objects listed.

Table 4.8 *Linux agent MIB objects that map to* **netstat** *output*

netstat Field	MIB Objects
RX-OK	IfInUcastPkts + ifInNUcastPkts
RX-ERR	IfInErrors
RX-DRP	IfInDiscards
TX-OK	IfOutUcastPkts + ifOutNUcastPkts
TX-ERR	IfOutErrors
TX-DRP	IfOutDiscards

If the system has a large number of interfaces and you are only
interested in a particular one, use the --interfaces command-line
option to specify the one you want. Note that the online manual
specifically describes this feature, but for some reason **netstat**
ignores any interface command options.

Display Routing Information

The system uses the routing table to determine the path that will
be used to send IP packets to particular hosts or networks. Normally systems are configured with a default router so that routing
decisions are straightforward and simple. However, there may be
instances when a machine has more than one interface, and each is
attached to a different IP network. In this case, the system might
also be forwarding IP packets (routing) between these networks.
As a result, the routing function becomes a bit more complex. As
part of the overall routing system, a routing table is defined that

can be displayed as the need arises. One of the primary ways to
examine this table is with the -r option:

```
# netstat -r
Kernel IP routing table
Destination     Gateway         Genmask         Flags  MSS Window  irtt Iface
199.70.195.41   *               255.255.255.255 UH       0 0          0 ppp0
10.0.2.201      *               255.255.255.255 UH       0 0          0 eth0
10.0.2.0        *               255.255.255.0   U        0 0          0 eth0
127.0.0.0       *               255.0.0.0       U        0 0          0 lo
default         199.70.195.41   0.0.0.0         UG       0 0          0 ppp0
```

The output above was from a server system that contains two
separate network interfaces. In this example, the routing table
includes a destination network, gateway (or router), network
mask, some status flags, two size fields, a metric value, and the
interface with which the route is associated. The destination field
specifies the network for which the route has been established. The
gateway field shows the IP address or hostname of the router that
forwards packets to the IP address listed in the Destination column. A * indicates that the router has not been configured for the
associated network. If an IP address or hostname is shown in this
field, then a router has been configured.

The Genmask field shows the network mask that has been configured for this interface. This mask is used like a subnet mask to calculate the network address specified in the Destination column.

The Flags field displays status information regarding the route.
The U flag indicates that the route is up and active. The H flag
shows that the route entry refers to a host system, not an actual
router. With UNIX, there is always a route to the local system,
which is used internally by the networking software. The G flag
indicates that the route is via an external gateway or router.

The terms route and gateway are used interchangeably.   **Note**

When we list the routing tables from a workstation that contains a single interface, we may see the following entries:

```
# netstat -r
```

(continued)

```
Kernel IP routing table
Destination     Gateway         Genmask          Flags Metric Ref     Use Iface
199.70.195.41   *               255.255.255.255  UH    0      0         0 ppp0
10.0.2.201      *               255.255.255.255  UH    0      0         0 eth0
10 0.2.0        *               255.255.255.0    U     0      0         0 eth0
127.0.0.0       *               255.0.0.0        U     0      0         0 lo
default         199.70.195.41   0.0.0.0          UG    0      0         0 ppp0
```

In this case, a default route has been set to `199.70.195.41`,
which happens to be a connection to a local ISP using the point-to-
point protocol (PPP). When a system contains a single interface, a
default route can be used as a shorthand method to specify the only
way out of the local network. Without the default entry, every network for which the system must connect will require a separate
routing entry. When the `ppp0` link is activated (either, manually or
automatically) the default route is installed automatically by the
PPP software.

The `MMS` field represents the Maximum Segment Size (MSS) for
a TCP session or connection. Normally with **netstat**, this field contains a zero value. The `Window` field controls the TCP window size
for a connection using this route; typically this is for certain WAN
protocols or other network drivers that have a hard time handling
back-to-back frames. Again, this field normally has a value of zero.

The `irtt` field shows the initial round-trip time (IRTT) for a
TCP session or connection; again used for WAN network protocols. The **netstat** command shows the value zero. The final field
(`Iface`) shows the network interface to which that route belongs. It
is important to note that within the routing tables many routes
could use the same interface. In fact, the previous example shows
no less than three routes using the same interface. This is normal
and proper because the routing function is concerned with forwarding IP packets from one network to another, regardless of
which physical network may be involved or the path that is traversed. This, albeit, in a small way, illustrates the modularity of the
TCP/IP protocols and networking software.

Additionally, the **netstat** command supports an alternative format when listing the routing tables. The UNIX **route** command
alters the system routing tables and can display the routing information as well. The **netstat** command can display routing information in the same format as the **route** command. Thus, the **netstat -r**

command will, when combined with the command-line option -e, and executed on the same system from which the previous output was obtained, display the system routing tables.

The command: **netstat -e -r** displays the following:

```
Kernel IP routing table
Destination     Gateway         Genmask         Flags Metric Ref Use Iface
199.70.195.41   *               255.255.255.255 UH    0      0   0 ppp0
10.0.2.201      *               255.255.255.255 UH    0      0   0 eth0
10.0.2.0        *               255.255.255.0   U     0      0   0 eth0
127.0.0.0       *               255.0.0.0       U     0      0   0 lo
default         199.70.195.41   0.0.0.0         UG    0      0   0 ppp0
```

The Metric field records the distance or hop count to the target network or host. The Ref is the total number of routes sharing the same datalink or physical address, and the Use field shows the number of packets transmitted since the interface was activated. Unfortunately, the **netstat** command doesn't seem to be able to obtain any valid values for the Ref and Use fields because they are always set to zero.

Display Multicast Information

Multicast is a mechanism that supports the delivery of high-volume traffic to a network and associated workstations in a very efficient manner. A multicast group is a defined collection of workstations and multicast routers that forward traffic using a special multicast IP address. The -g option displays multicast routing information that is related to the routing groups and interfaces that have been defined on the system. Using this option, the **netstat -g** command will show the currently configured multicast groups:

```
IPv4 Group Memberships
Interface       RefCnt Group
--------------- ------ --------------------
lo              1      224.0.0.1
eth0            1      224.0.0.1
eth1            1      224.0.0.1
```

In this example, each of the defined interfaces on this system is a member of the default multicast group known as 224.0.0.1 or ALL-SYSTEMS.MCAST.NET. This group, which is a standard multicast group, is used to send multicast traffic to all systems on a local network. So if any application uses the address of 224.0.0.1 to transmit traffic, this system would receive the information. When multicast is deployed using standard multicast applications, additional multicast groups may be defined to restrict the multicast traffic to only those systems for which the information is required.

Display Protocol Statistics

The **netstat** command can be used to display protocol statistics. The --statistics option, by itself, will display the supported protocols, including TCP, UDP, and RAW. RAW is a combination of both IP and ICMP packets and can be displayed separately using the keyword **raw**.

```
# netstat --statistics
Ip:
    3003 total packets received
    0 forwarded
    0 incoming packets discarded
    212 incoming packets delivered
    2847 requests sent out
Icmp:
    489 ICMP messages received
    0 input ICMP message failed.
    ICMP input histogram:
        destination unreachable: 486
        echo replies: 3
    487 ICMP messages sent
    0 ICMP messages failed
    ICMP output histogram:
        destination unreachable: 487
Tcp:
    0 active connections openings
    0 passive connection openings
    0 failed connection attempts
    0 connection resets received
    1 connections established
    2295 segments received
    1700 segments send out
    2 segments retransmited
    0 bad segments received.
    0 resets sent
Udp:
    171 packets received
    2 packets to unknown port received.
    0 packet receive errors
    657 packets sent:
```

Alternatively, you could just display one of the listed protocols instead of the entire list. In this situation, use one of the **--raw**, **--tcp**, or **--udp** keyword options. Then, only that protocol will be displayed. For instance, to display just IP and ICMP packets, use the following command:

```
netstat --statistics --raw
```

As a result of this command, the following would be displayed:

```
Ip:
    3360 total packets received
    0 forwarded
    0 incoming packets discarded
    213 incoming packets delivered
    3090 requests sent out
Icmp:
    489 ICMP messages received
    0 input ICMP message failed.
    ICMP input histogram:
        destination unreachable: 486
        echo replies: 3
    487 ICMP messages sent
    0 ICMP messages failed
    ICMP output histogram:
        destination unreachable: 487
```

Additional Command-line Options

Some additional options are available with the **netstat** command; these include the -t option, which is used to control the display of numeric addresses versus trying to determine symbolic hostname, port, or usernames. Use this option when name-resolution services such as DNS or NIS do not function correctly or are unavailable. The default behavior for **netstat** is to display hostname and other symbolic information. The **netstat** command will display the current TCP connections on the local system:

```
Proto Recv-Q Send-Q Local Address         Foreign Address      State
tcp        0    126 socrates.home.co:telnet durer.home.com:1035 ESTABLISHED
```

However, when the -t option is added, the following is displayed:

```
Proto Recv-Q Send-Q Local Address         Foreign Address      State
tcp        0    126 10.0.2.201:23         10.0.2.10:1035       ESTABLISHED
```

Notice also that not only was the IP address information displayed, but the port numbers were displayed as well. Normally **netstat** will examine the /etc/services file to determine mappings between port names and numbers and will show port names. The -t option suppressed these mappings for ports. Another useful option is the -c option, which toggles continuous displays of information. If we wanted to constantly monitor the information displayed in the previous example, we would use the following command:

```
# netstat -c -t
```

to generate the following output:

```
Active Internet connections (w/o servers)
Proto Recv-Q Send-Q Local Address          Foreign Address        State
tcp       0    126 socrates.home.co:telnet durer.home.com:1035    ESTABLISHED

Active Internet connections (w/o servers)
Proto Recv-Q Send-Q Local Address          Foreign Address        State
tcp       0    124 socrates.home.co:telnet durer.home.com:1035    ESTABLISHED

Active Internet connections (w/o servers)
Proto Recv-Q Send-Q Local Address          Foreign Address        State
tcp       0      0 socrates.home.com:ftp   durer.home.com:1036    ESTABLISHED
tcp       0    126 socrates.home.co:telnet durer.home.com:1035    ESTABLISHED

Active Internet connections (w/o servers)
Proto Recv-Q Send-Q Local Address          Foreign Address        State
tcp       0      0 socrates.home.com:ftp   durer.home.com:1036    ESTABLISHED
tcp       0    124 socrates.home.co:telnet durer.home.com:1035    ESTABLISHED

Active Internet connections (w/o servers)
Proto Recv-Q Send-Q Local Address          Foreign Address        State
tcp       0      0 socrates.home.:ftp-data durer.home.com:1037    ESTABLISHED
tcp       0      0 socrates.home.com:ftp   durer.home.com:1036    ESTABLISHED
tcp       0    124 socrates.home.co:telnet durer.home.com:1035    ESTABLISHED
```

From this output we can see that a single telnet connection is first established between socrates and durer. Then, an FTP session is started between these systems, as shown:

```
tcp       0      0 socrates.home.com:ftp   durer.home.com:1036    ESTABLISHED
```

Once the ftp session was set up, the user executed and/or transferred a file. This can be seen with the ftp-data connection using port 1037, which is created when a user issues an **ftp** command or transfers a file. To stop the continuous display of output, use a **^c** (**control +c**) sequence. As you can imagine, this is a very handy way to monitor network connectivity.

Ping Tool

General Description

The **ping** command provides two basic services. First, it can be used to determine whether a basic level of connectivity is available between one or more endpoints or systems. The ping tool can be used to determine if a remote device is reachable on a network from the local system and help debug connectivity problems among systems. Second, it can provide rudimentary network performance statistics, which can be used to diagnose traffic-related network problems. The term *ping* is derived from the phrase *packet internet groper*. The ping tool can be used in one of two ways: by specifying a valid hostname or IP address, or by using command-line options with a hostname or IP address. Using the first form, ping provides a handy way to determine that a remote device is available on the network.

Recall from Chapter 3, "TCP/IP Protocol Suite," that ping uses the Internet Control Message Protocol (ICMP) to emit ICMP requests and waits for valid ICMP replies. Because ICMP is a required protocol within the TCP/IP family, ping can generally be used with every device that supports TCP/IP and is available on many operating systems and other networking devices. For instance, a Cisco router provides the capability to ping other devices on the network. The ping tool is a client-side application only; no additional software is needed nor required for it to function and interact directly with the remote system's protocol layer to accomplish its task.

Determine System Availability

The ping tool can be used to determine general availability of any TCP/IP device even if it doesn't specifically have a general operating system. For example, to determine if the host rembrandt is reachable, issue the following **ping** command:

```
#ping durer
PING durer.home.com (10.0.2.10): 56 data bytes
64 bytes from 10.0.2.10: icmp_seq=0 ttl=128 time=0.9 ms
64 bytes from 10.0.2.10: icmp_seq=1 ttl=128 time=0.8 ms
64 bytes from 10.0.2.10: icmp_seq=2 ttl=128 time=0.8 ms
64 bytes from 10.0.2.10: icmp_seq=3 ttl=128 time=0.8 ms

--- durer.home.com ping statistics ---
4 packets transmitted, 4 packets received, 0% packet loss
round-trip min/avg/max = 0.8/0.8/0.9 ms
```

In this case, **ping** displays no packet loss to durer, which happens
to be a PostScript laser printer. This basically states that durer is
alive and operating normally from an IP perspective. The default
behavior of **ping** means that the user must type ^c (**control+c**) to stop
the output. This message generally means that the TCP/IP software
is operational. Although *alive* indicates that the system is visible on
the network, it is no guarantee that other network services, such as
FTP or Telnet, are available. This is an important distinction. The
ping tool can only be used to determine basic protocol connectivity—not the availability of higher-level applications or services. In
fact, some systems will answer a **ping** even before they are fully
booted. Keep in mind that no single piece of software can determine that every TCP/IP application or service is installed and operating on a system.

If the host durer is not reachable, **ping** will display the following
message after ^c is typed:

```
PING rubens.home.com (10.0.2.220): 56 data bytes
--- rubens.home.com ping statistics ---
2 packets transmitted, 0 packets received, 100% packet loss
```

Normally, **ping** issues ICMP requests forever and, if no reply is
received, generates the message shown above only after the user
has interrupted the command. This is somewhat unfortunate
because other versions of **ping** will eventually timeout without the
user having to manually interrupt the command. Luckily, a maximum number or count of the total number of requests can be specified, which has the effect of controlling **ping** so that the user
doesn't need to manually intervene. Using the -c command-line
option with an argument of 1, the **ping** command will issue a single
request to rubens:

```
# ping -c 1 rubens
```

and will generate the following output if this host is down:

```
PING rubens.home.com (10.0.2.220): 56 data bytes
--- rubens.home.com ping statistics ---
1 packets transmitted, 0 packets received, 100% packet loss
```

This is useful so that the user can quickly determine reachability of a host without wasting additional time or network bandwidth. Reducing the number of **ping** requests is generally a good thing for the network. Specifying the count in this manner is sometimes preferable when using **ping** within a shell script where issuing a ^c would be difficult or inconvenient. Using the count option is an ideal way to obtain a very good round-trip delay average and to determine performance over time.

It is interesting to note that if the host rubens isn't on the same subnet as the host issuing the **ping**, it is possible that the host is functioning correctly, but that an intermediate device, such as a network router, is responsible for the lack of connectivity. I term this problem *connectivity fussiness*. In this case, **ping** can't determine why rubens is not reachable. To further understand this problem, consider the sample network in Figure 4.1. This network diagram shows several devices attached to two different networks that are interconnected via Router A. When a **ping** request is issued from Node B on Network A to Node D on Network B, the request is passed via Router A. If Router A should stop functioning, the requests will never reach Node D. As a result, Node D becomes unreachable from the perspective of Node B.

Because **ping** can check reachability of any TCP/IP device, we can now issue a **ping** for Router A to further diagnose the problem. By probing the router closest to Node D, we will learn that the loss of connectivity is most likely being caused by Router A's network interface to Network B, and not Node D itself. Also, if we **ping** other devices on Network B, this would confirm that all devices are unreachable and lead us to conclude that there is a problem with Router A. This example demonstrates that network problems can be caused by devices other than those easily identified as sender and receiver. Tools such as **ping** help to isolate the sources of routing and many other network failures or problems.

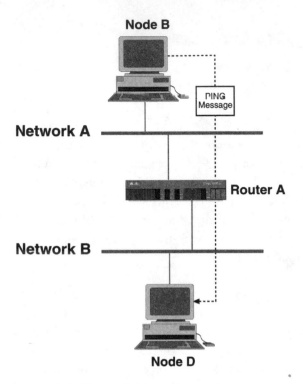

Figure 4.1 *Unreachable node problem.*

The second form of the **ping** command provides a number of options to control additional functionality. Table 4.9 provides a list of the most popular command-line options available.

Table 4.9 **ping** *command options*

Option	Description
-c	Send only a certain number of packets
-f	Flood the network with packets
-i	Delay the number of seconds between each request
-n	Show network addresses
-p	Specify up to 16 bytes to pad a packet with customized data

Table 4.9 **ping** *command options (continued)*

Option	Description
-q	Quiet mode
-R	Toggle record route option
-s	Specifies the number of bytes to be sent with each request

Determining Network Performance

The **ping** command can be used to measure the amount of time required to transmit a message to a remote destination and the time required to obtain a response. This use of the **ping** command in essence measures the relative performance of the path between the two devices at a given point in time. It does not, by any means, provide a detailed analysis of the devices or connectivity between them. Rather, it provides a glimpse of the general condition of the path at the point it is measured. It could be said that network performance is like the stock market. One day it is up and the next it is down. The primary difference with respect to volatility is whether we are talking in terms of days or milliseconds. A large number of factors can cause network performance to vary. These include users that are overly aggressive about using network resources, hardware problems, software configuration problems, and so forth.

The **ping** command provides a means of determining system response times as well, but it takes a little more work to determine if the observed performance problem is related to a specific slow system or a delay in some other network component. The ping tool shows output that can be used to measure and report round-trip time and provide packet-loss statistics. By default, **ping** issues an ICMP request every second to the destination supplied on the command line and reports the status of each ICMP reply. Sample output includes the following:

```
# ping didymus
PING didymus-gw2.home.com (10.0.2.127): 56 data bytes
```

(continued)

```
64 bytes from 10.0.2.127: icmp_seq=0 ttl=255 time=1.2 ms
64 bytes from 10.0.2.127: icmp_seq=1 ttl=255 time=1.1 ms
64 bytes from 10.0.2.127: icmp_seq=2 ttl=255 time=1.2 ms
64 bytes from 10.0.2.127: icmp_seq=3 ttl=255 time=1.2 ms

--- didymus gw2.home.com ping statistics ---
4 packets transmitted, 4 packets received, 0% packet loss
round-trip min/avg/max = 1.1/1.1/1.2 ms
```

This report provides the packet size, the hostname or IP address of the target device, a sequence number, round-trip time value, and a statistical summary. The time value shows the round-trip time in milliseconds (1000th of a second) for each reply received. The bottom of the report calculates the minimum, average, and maximum trip times for all replies, also displayed in milliseconds. The total length of the ICMP packet transmitted to didymus is 64 bytes. This is the default size, which is usually sufficient. However, it might be necessary to increase the packet size to get a better measure of throughput. In this case, a large packet size may be specified using the -s command-line option. For example, the command:

```
# ping -s 100 didymus
```

issues the ICMP requests with a packet size of 100 bytes to the target host didymus. This might be required to obtain a better picture of performance because network throughput may differ for larger packet sizes versus smaller values. When executed, this command shows the following:

```
PING didymus-gw2.home.com (10.0.2.127): 100 data bytes
108 bytes from 10.0.2.127: icmp_seq=0 ttl=255 time=2.7 ms
108 bytes from 10.0.2.127: icmp_seq=1 ttl=255 time=1.5 ms
108 bytes from 10.0.2.127: icmp_seq=2 ttl=255 time=1.3 ms
108 bytes from 10.0.2.127: icmp_seq=3 ttl=255 time=1.3 ms
108 bytes from 10.0.2.127: icmp_seq=4 ttl=255 time=1.3 ms
108 bytes from 10.0.2.127: icmp_seq=5 ttl=255 time=1.3 ms
108 bytes from 10.0.2.127: icmp_seq=6 ttl=255 time=1.3 ms
108 bytes from 10.0.2.127: icmp_seq=7 ttl=255 time=1.3 ms

--- didymus-gw2.home.com ping statistics ---
8 packets transmitted, 8 packets received, 0% packet loss
round-trip min/avg/max = 1.3/1.5/2.7 ms
```

As you can see from this output, **ping** adds eight bytes of overhead for each packet sent; this is determined by subtracting the 100 bytes specified with the -s option from the 108 bytes transmitted by **ping**. Notice that the response times didn't change much, despite the fact that we used a large data size. We would need to increase the size significantly to observe a larger delay in processing the packets.

> You may have noticed that the hostname didymus was used on the command line, but when **ping** echoed back the hostname, it showed a different name, like didymus-gw2.home.com. The reason for this is that didymus is an alias of didymus-gw2.home.com, and using the alias with many UNIX commands results in the official name being returned instead. The alias was created in the /etc/hosts file.

Note

The ping tool uses a sequence number to keep track of requests and replies. Each request is given the next number in sequence and is then matched with the corresponding reply. This sequencing is used to determine packet loss if any requests do not receive an appropriate reply. Generally speaking, packet loss on a small network should be very rare and, if it does occur, it might indicate a network- or system-related problem. However, on a large network or internet (internet with a lower case *i*) or on the Internet, packet loss is common and represents a normal state of affairs. Given a popular Internet site as shown below, a certain amount of packet loss may be observed:

```
ping -c 10 www.whitehouse.gov
PING www.whitehouse.com (209.67.27.247): 56 data bytes
64 bytes from 209.67.27.247: icmp_seq=7 ttl=244 time=240.1 ms
64 bytes from 209.67.27.247: icmp_seq=8 ttl=244 time=240.1 ms
64 bytes from 209.67.27.247: icmp_seq=9 ttl=244 time=240.1 ms

--- www.whitehouse.com ping statistics ---
10 packets transmitted, 3 packets received, 70% packet loss
round-trip min/avg/max = 240.1/240.1/240.1 ms
```

The report above indicates that 70% of the packets sent to the www.whitehouse.gov system did not have corresponding replies! They were lost. In other words, we sent ten packets, but only received three back; seven out of ten is 70%. One possible reason for this noticeable packet loss is that some of the critical Internet routers might be quite busy or even overloaded with network traffic. As a result, some of the ICMP requests might be discarded because the requests expired before they were delivered to the final destination. Also, the relative load of the target device can be a factor because these systems might not have the computing resources to answer all network requests as required. Because of the popularity of this site, it is not unreasonable to think that both the servers and the networks that connect them are all quite busy or even overloaded. An overloaded condition will occur when too many users are using resources from the system at the same time.

Sometimes it is desirable to provide additional time for acknowledging each **ping** request instead of using the default value of one second. If additional time is desired between successive ICMP requests, the `-i` option can be used, followed by the desired value. The interval should be long enough to provide the required amount of time for the remote system to respond. When we increase the timeout value as suggested, we will generally notice less packet loss. The command

```
ping -c 10 www.whitehouse.gov -i 5
```

adds a five-second delay to each request, thus providing additional time for the processing of the requests through the network and to the destination server. Using the command above, the following was produced:

```
PING www.whitehouse.com (209.67.27.247): 56 data bytes
64 bytes from 209.67.27.247: icmp_seq=1 ttl=244 time=240.1 ms
64 bytes from 209.67.27.247: icmp_seq=2 ttl=244 time=240.1 ms
64 bytes from 209.67.27.247: icmp_seq=3 ttl=244 time=240.1 ms
64 bytes from 209.67.27.247: icmp_seq=4 ttl=244 time=240.0 ms
64 bytes from 209.67.27.247: icmp_seq=5 ttl=244 time=250.1 ms
64 bytes from 209.67.27.247: icmp_seq=6 ttl=244 time=240.1 ms
64 bytes from 209.67.27.247: icmp_seq=7 ttl=244 time=240.1 ms
64 bytes from 209.67.27.247: icmp_seq=8 ttl=244 time=240.2 ms
64 bytes from 209.67.27.247: icmp_seq=9 ttl=244 time=250.1 ms

--- www.whitehouse.com ping statistics ---
10 packets transmitted, 9 packets received, 10% packet loss
round-trip min/avg/max = 240.0/242.3/250.1 ms
```

As noted from the output, the packet loss to this site was reduced to 10%. Bear in mind, that other factors could have also contributed to the reduction, such as users leaving the site or the network not being used. In general, increasing the amount of time for each request should reduce the overall load on the system. However, this is not guaranteed to always be the case because the system may be overloaded to the point that no additional amount of time would really help.

Miscellaneous Options

With the -n option, **ping** displays IP addresses rather than hostnames. This is useful, for example, when network problems involving DNS impact the use of **ping**. This option instructs **ping** not to invoke hostname resolution, thus permitting the tool to function while the name service is slow or temporarily disabled.

The -R option enables the record route option with the IP protocol. Toggling the record route informs each router along a path to place its IP address in the IP header. As a result, a list of routers that were used to reach the final destination can be obtained. This is the chief mechanism that the **traceroute** command utilizes. This tool is described later in this chapter. Another interesting option is flood mode using the -f option. This option tells **ping** to attempt to flood the network with ICMP requests approximately 100 times per second or as fast as the remote destination can process each request.

By the way, a note of caution is in order here; the -f option can be a dangerous thing. It can consume a significant amount of network bandwidth and cause systems to disappear from the network because they are too heavily loaded to respond to other network requests. It is not recommended that this option be used on a live network when loss of connectivity could impact the business operations of the individuals that use the network. Also, it is not reasonable to flood other networks that you are not associated with.

Having said all this, the command

```
ping -c 100 -f durer
```

displays the following output:

```
PING durer.home.com (10.0.2.10): 56 data bytes
................
--- durer.home.com ping statistics ---
1015 packets transmitted, 1000 packets received, 1% packet loss
round-trip min/avg/max = 1.0/14.3/121.0 ms
```

The first thing that is different from the standard output is that a series of dots (................) is shown. This indicates that **ping** has received responses back from the requests sent to durer. Second, notice that out of 1015 packets sent, only 1000 packets were received. Yet **ping** reported only a 1% packet loss. Actually, the packet loss is closer to 1.5%. The **ping** command reports only whole numbers, not numbers to the right of the decimal point. In this case, the problem isn't significant, since we can determine more accurate loss by hand if necessary. However, this is somewhat moot since the **ping** facility isn't really considered the most scientific and/or empirical approach to measuring data loss or throughput on a network.

Perhaps to many, the important question is, "Why use the flood capability anyway?" The reason is simple; attempt to produce a significant amount of traffic on the network and see what happens. You will find that in networking, determining how things work sometimes includes attempting to break things or do things in such a way as to exceed the practical limitations of a device or system. In the case of networking devices such as routers, industry experts and users want to know what will happen to the device if it is exposed to high-traffic patterns. Measuring performance and other networking characteristics when the network is under tremendous load will help the network manager truly understand the behavior of critical networking devices and systems when they are deployed in their networks. The flood option is one easy way to do this.

The final interesting **ping** option is quiet mode. This option -q is used to limit the amount of output that would normally be produced. The command

```
ping -c 100 didymus
```

would produce a large number of lines (over 100) that represented each request and associated reply. With the -q option, only a few lines are displayed; the beginning and the summary:

```
ping -q -c 100 didymus
PING didymus-gw2.home.com (10.0.2.127): 56 data bytes

--- didymus-gw2.home.com ping statistics ---
100 packets transmitted, 100 packets received, 0% packet loss
round-trip min/avg/max = 1.1/1.1/2.5 ms
```

Clearly, this option reduces the output, which may be just what is necessary when **ping** is used within a script.

Tcpdump Tool

General Description

The **tcpdump** command is a general-purpose network traffic monitor that can capture and display packets and their contents. This command can be used as a *protocol analyzer,* providing one of the best ways to investigate communication and/or connectivity problems among systems and networking devices. Most of the time, network troubleshooting focuses on network configuration problems and diagnosing hardware-related failures. Every now and then, however, you will be faced with a protocol-related problem and forced to delve into the heart of the particular protocol to resolve the problem. With **tcpdump,** the packets scanned will be displayed with information in either a short or long format, depending on the command-line options used. Also, **tcpdump** has a very powerful filtering mechanism that can search for packets that match a specific string or criteria.

Two primary capture modes are provided by **tcpdump:** *promiscuous* and *non-promiscuous.* In promiscuous mode, every packet transmitted on the network is captured, whether or not the packet was sent to the system on which **tcpdump** is executing. This is the mode, for instance, that RMON probes use when monitoring network traffic. Network probes listen on the network for traffic and collect protocol information and statistics. Because Local Area Network (LAN) protocols such as Ethernet are broadcast-based, every frame transmitted can be seen by any network interface attached to the LAN. Any device can read every frame transmitted if that device chooses and is configured to do so. When a device or interface reads every frame from the network, it is said to be in promiscuous mode. In practice, the interface must be configured

for promiscuous operation and is only used on special occasions
when network diagnosis is required. For this reason, only **root** may
enable promiscuous mode on an interface. This is the primary reason that non-root users are not permitted to invoke **tcpdump**. When
the attempt is made by a non-root user to execute the command,
the following message is displayed:

```
tcpdump: socket: Operation not permitted
```

If you want to give a regular user the ability to invoke the **tcpdump** command, you can *setuid* the program to run as **root** or
install and configure a program like **sudo**. The **sudo** utility gives specific users access to privileged programs as deemed appropriate by
the system administrator. Appendix C contains additional information regarding the **sudo** command.

With non-promiscuous mode, only broadcast frames and
frames addressed to the local system will be available to the interface. The term *broadcast* actually refers to both normal broadcast
(with all 1s in the destination field) and multicast traffic. Under
normal circumstances, the interface is in non-promiscuous mode.

When **tcpdump** is invoked without command-line options, it
opens the primary network interface and begins capturing frames
from the local network and displaying their contents. Because **tcpdump** can produce a significant amount of output, we will use the
quiet option (-q) to reduce the amount of output displayed. When
executed by **root**, the command

```
# tcpdump -q
```

will display all network frames in the single-line, non-verbose format. The format of the output will include a timestamp, source and
destination hosts (or address), the high-level network protocol,
some flags, additional protocol information, and a summary:

```
tcpdump: listening on eth0
15:41:58.055268 durer.home.com.1032 > socrates.home.com.telnet: tcp 0 (DF)
[tos0x50]
15:41:58.055446 socrates.home.com.telnet > durer.home.com.1032: tcp 28
(DF)
15:41:58.274933 durer.home.com.1032 > socrates.home.com.telnet: tcp 0 (DF)
[tos0x50]
15:41:58.275115 socrates.home.com.telnet > durer.home.com.1032: tcp 164
(DF)
```

```
15:41:58.494694 durer.home.com.1032 > socrates.home.com.telnet: tcp 0 (DF)
[tos0x50]
15:41:58.494880 socrates.home.com.telnet > durer.home.com.1032: tcp 165
(DF)
15:41:58.544828 socrates.home.com > didymus-gw2.home.com: icmp: echo
request
15:41:58.545719 didymus-gw2.home.com > socrates.home.com: icmp: echo
reply5:34:10.601950 socrates.home.com.telnet > durer.home.com.1032: tcp
165 (DF)

8 packets received by filter
0 packets dropped by kernel
```

The output includes the time, source/destination, protocol port, protocol contained with the frame, and additional protocol information. In this example, `durer`, the source host, and `socrates`, the destination host, have a Telnet session established. We can tell this by looking at the destination port, which is `telnet`. By default, **tcpdump** captures packets until the user interrupts the program by issuing **^c**. Also, `socrates` has issued a **ping** request to `didymus-gw2`, and it has responded with a reply. The `->` string indicates the direction of the communication. Note that **tcpdump** always orients the communication path to point to the right, as in the case of the ICMP Echo request above. To indicate communication in the other direction, **tcpdump** reverses the hosts (not the pointer), as shown with the ICMP Echo reply entry. The **tcpdump** command displays the higher-level protocols in lower case, as in `tcp` and `icmp`, followed by more specific information pertaining to the protocol, which might include ports, additional protocol information, and data. The output also includes a summary of the number of packets obtained before the user terminated the command.

The end of the output includes a count of the number of packets captured by **tcpdump** and the number of packets that were dropped. In this case, a total of eight packets were captured and zero packets were discarded.

The tcpdump tool provides a large number of command-line options to select capture modes, control output, specify filter specifications, and specify additional operating characteristics. These options are grouped according to their function and include the following categories:

- operating modes

- display options

- packet filter options

Operating Mode Options

These options are used to control how **tcpdump** will capture and display network traffic. The available options are summarized in Table 4.10 and described fully below.

Table 4.10 tcpdump *operating mode options*

Option	Description
-c	Captures specified number of packets
-F	Uses file as source for filter expression
-i	Captures packets using alternate network interface
-p	Disables capturing in promiscuous mode
-r	Reads capture file instead of network interface
-w	Saves raw packets to file

Normally, **tcpdump** will listen for traffic on the primary network interface. Usually the primary interface has the smallest numeric identifier if the system contains two or more interfaces of the same type. For example, eth0 is considered the primary when the system contains two Ethernet interfaces: eth0 and eth1. However, if you want to run **tcpdump** on a different interface, use the -i option and the device name to specify the alternate interface. For example, to select the point-to-point (ppp0) interface, use the following command:

```
# tcpdump -i ppp0
tcpdump: listening on ppp0
```

As previously indicated, **tcpdump** will capture packets until ^c is typed from the controlling terminal (or if placed in the background, until the process is terminated with the **kill** command). If you wish to specify the number of packets to be captured, use the -c option

followed by a packet count value. To capture ten packets from the
eth1 interface, use the following command:

```
tcpdump -t -q -i eth1 -c 10
tcpdump: listening on eth1
chips.home.com > didymus-gw2.home.com: icmp: echo request
didymus-gw2.home.com > chips.home.com: icmp: echo reply
chips.home.com > didymus-gw2.home.com: icmp: echo request
didymus-gw2.home.com > chips.home.com: icmp: echo reply
socrates.home.com.1032 > switch.home.com.snmp: udp 44
switch.home.com.snmp > socrates.home.com.1032: udp 111
socrates.home.com.1032 > switch.home.com.snmp: udp 51
switch.home.com.snmp > socrates.home.com.1032: udp 61
socrates.home.com.1032 > switch.com.snmp: udp 51
switch.com.snmp > socrates.home.com.1032: udp 54
socrates.home.com.1032 > switch.home.com.snmp: udp 51
```

In this case, **tcpdump** has captured a **ping** session between
socrates and didymus-gw2, as detected by the first four lines. Also,
socrates was querying a device called switch using SNMP, as
denoted by the SNMP port and the UDP protocol used (the
remaining lines). We can confirm the number of captured packets
by counting the number of lines displayed. Specifying the number
of packets to capture is useful when the intent is to monitor a critical network transaction that uses a fixed number of packet
exchanges. This option is also useful when monitoring packets
within a shell script because you don't have to be concerned about
stopping **tcpdump** after it has been started. The -t option, which
removes the packet timestamp information, was used in this example as well.

As previously indicated, **tcpdump**, by default, opens the network
interface in promiscuous mode to capture all network traffic. Promiscuous mode means that all network traffic, regardless of the
destination of the packet, will be capturd by **tcpdump**. Sometimes, it
is more effective to examine packets delivered to a specified host
than it is to read all packets on the network. If we want to capture
those packets addressed to the host that **tcpdump** is running on, the
-p option is used to disable promiscuous mode capture. You will
see later that we can tell **tcpdump** to capture packets coming from or
going to a particular host using filters.

```
# tcpdump -d le1 -p
tcpdump: listening on eth0
```

Unfortunately, the **tcpdump** command doesn't confirm the use of the -p option. As a result, the user has no way of knowing after the command was executed which mode it is capturing with, except to examine the output to see the destination addresses. In other words, any packet that isn't a broadcast or sent to a local address indicates that **tcpdump** is capturing with promiscuous mode enabled. Why would you disable promiscuous mode with this option anyway? Sometimes it becomes necessary to examine just the traffic that arrives normally at a particular system. With this option, we can see every packet that is destined by the local system, and nothing more. This can be used to easily detect (by monitoring the incoming packets), for example, whether a request for a particular service is reaching the system. Given a client/server environment, we can determine if requests from client systems are reaching the server (by running **tcpdump** on the server) or if a particular client is transmitting requests in the first place (by running **tcpdump** on the client). It is true that we can use filters to accomplish the same thing, but it is more efficient and easier to just reduce the number of packets in the first place.

On a very active network or a busy system, and when using certain command-line options, **tcpdump** can produce a large amount of output. To help manage this, the -w option can be used to redirect the captured information into a file. One reason to use a file is to save the captured data for later inspection and analysis. This could include manipulating the data in other ways, possibly using the data to build specialized reports, and the like.

To capture network traffic and save it to a file called traffic-data, use the following command:

```
# tcpdump -w traffic-data
tcpdump: listening on eth0
```

The file, traffic-data, is created in the local directory once the command above is invoked. However, the data captured isn't written to the file until the user interrupts the program or the -c option is used. Once the user does this, the following is displayed:

```
48 packets received by filter
0 packets dropped by kernel
```

Note that the file created is not an ordinary text file, but rather a specially formatted data file that only **tcpdump** and certain other programs understand. One such program, called **tcpslice**, can cut out or splice different **tcpdump** files together.

To learn a little bit more about the **tcpdump** file, use the UNIX file command. If this is run against the traffic-data file, it reports that it is associated with the **tcpdump** command, the version of the software, and that the data contains packets that are of type Ethernet, with a frame length of 68 bytes. It is not a human-readable text file. The UNIX command

```
# file traffic-data
```

shows the following:

```
traffic-data: tcpdump capture file (little-endian) - version 2.4
(Ethernet, capture length 68)
```

As previously mentioned, it is interesting that **tcpdump** labels the frame types that are contained with the datafiles. In the previous example, the label indicates that Ethernet frames are stored in this file. Additional types include raw IP, FDDI, and others. Thus, if a packet capture were done on a point-to-point link, as in the ppp0 interface, then the raw IP packet type would be displayed.

If you were trying to view the file, it would appear to be a long series of strange characters. However, this file can be read into the ethereal program, which provides a GUI-based approach to protocol capture and analysis. The next chapter discusses this tool.

The **tcpdump** command does a reasonable job of compressing data stored in files. For instance, over 3,000 packets consume approximately 260K worth of disk space. If you are going to save a significant amount of captured data, it may be necessary to compress the data further using either **compress** or **gzip**. The **compress** utility manages to reduce the size of this data file to a little over 33K, while the gzip program reduces the byte count down even more to just over 18K. Not bad from a byte size of over 260K!

To display the packets that have been saved in a data file, use the -v option followed by the name of the packet capture file. For instance, to replay the packets saved within the `traffic-data` file, issue the following command:

```
# tcpdump -r traffic-data
```

Display Options

These options control how **tcpdump** will display packets from the network. The list of the available options under this category is summarized in Table 4.11 and described fully below.

Table 4.11 *TCPDUMP display options*

Option	Description
-e	Prints link-level header information on each line
-v	Specifies verbose mode
-q	Specifies quick mode, displays short packet information
-t	Disables printing of the timestamp
-s	Limits the size of packets captured
-x	Displays both hexadecimal and ASCII format

Sometimes it is useful to determine the length of datalink frames. This can be helpful, for example, when investigating performance problems related to higher-level applications. The **tcpdump** tool provides a way to obtain the size of each frame, including both the header and data portion, with the -e command-line option. The following sample command and output show a file transfer session using FTP and ARP broadcasts:

```
# tcpdump -t -e
0:10:5a:28:5d:7c Broadcast arp 42: arp who-has didymus-gw2.home.com
    tell socrates.home.com
0:10:5a:28:5d:7c Broadcast arp 42: arp who-has didymus-gw2.home.com
    tell socrates.home.com
0:10:5a:28:5d:7c Broadcast arp 42: arp who-has didymus-gw2.home.com
    tell socrates.home.com
0:10:5a:28:5d:7c 0:60:97:e:a3:6 1514: socrates.home.com.ftp-data
durer.home.com.1036: tcp 1448 (DF) [tos 0x8]
```

```
0:10:5a:28:5d:7c 0:60:97:e:a3:6 1514: socrates.home.com.ftp-data
durer.home.com.1036: tcp 1448 (DF) [tos 0x8]
```

As you can see, the length field is displayed next to the protocol, or if no protocol is shown, after the destination address. It shows the total size of the frame in bytes. The reason the packets from socrates to durer are greater than 1500 bytes is because FTP fills the packet with as much data as it can hold. Ethernet has a data capacity of approximately 1500 bytes, not including the header portion of the frame.

The -x option provides a way to display a hexadecimal dump of network frames. It displays link-level header information such as source and destination address. Consider the series of packet exchanges when the host rembrandt attempts to open an FTP session to a system called durer. The **tcpdump** command:

```
tcpdump -d le1 -x 0 tcp and port 21
```

will capture any FTP activity on the network. When this command is executed and a FTP session is started, the packets will be captured and displayed as follows.

```
0:60:97:e:a3:6 0:10:5a:28:5d:7c ip 78: durer.home.com.1044 >
socrates.home.com.f
tp: S 9262138:9262138(0) win 8192 <mss 1460,nop,wscale
0,nop,nop,timestamp[|tcp]
(DF) [tos 0x1d] (ttl 128, id 19970)
                        451d 0040 4e02 4000 8006 93c6 0a00 020a
                        0a00 02c9 0414 0015 008d 543a 0000 0000
                        b002 2000 a43e 0000 0204 05b4 0103 0300
                        0101 080a 0000
0:10:5a:28:5d:7c 0:60:97:e:a3:6 ip 74: socrates.home.com.ftp
durer.home.com.1044: S 1087677057:1087677057(0) ack 9262139 win 32120 <mss
1460,sackOK,timestamp> 1106589[|tcp]> (DF) (ttl 64, id 490)
                        4500 003c 01ea 4000 4006 2000 0a00 02c9
                        0a00 020a 0015 0414 40d4 a281 008d 543b
                        a012 7d78 92b7 0000 0204 05b4 0402 080a
                        0010 e29d 0000
0:60:97:e:a3:6 0:10:5a:28:5d:7c ip 66: durer.home.com.1044 >
socrates.home.com.ftp: .ack 1 win 8760 <nop,nop,timestamp 84320 1106589> (DF)
[tos 0x1d] (ttl 128,id 20226)
                        451d 0034 4f02 4000 8006 92d2 0a00 020a
                        0a00 02c9 0414 0015 008d 543b 40d4 a282
```

(continued)

```
                        8010 2238 d35b 0000 0101 080a 0001 4960
                        0010 e29d
0:10:5a:28:5d:7c 0:60:97:e:a3:6 ip 163: socrates.home.com.ftp
durer.home.com.1044: P 1:98(97) ack 1 win 32120 <nop,nop,timestamp 1106595
84320> (DF) [tos 0x10] (ttl 64, id 493)
                        4510 0095 01ed 4000 4006 1f94 0a00 02c9
                        0a00 020a 0015 0414 40d4 a282 008d 543b
                        8018 7d78 b4a1 0000 0101 080a 0010 e2a3
                        0001 4960 3232
0:60:97:e:a3:6 0:10:5a:28:5d:7c ip 66: durer.home.com.1044
socrates.home.com.ftp: . ack 98 win 8663 <nop,nop,timestamp 84323 1106595> (DF)
[tos 0x1d] (ttl 128, id 20994)
                        451d 0034 5202 4000 8006 8fd2 0a00 020a
                        0a00 02c9 0414 0015 008d 543b 40d4 a2e3
                        8010 21d7 d352 0000 0101 080a 0001 4963
                        0010 e2a3
```

Please note that some unwanted information has been manually removed from the output to make it more readable.

As you can see, the output shows a summary line that contains the following information (we are using the first packet in the preceding example):

Datalink Source Address:	`0:60:97:e:a3:6`
Datalink Destination Address:	`0:10:5a:28:5d:7c`
Highlevel Protocol:	`ip`
Frame Size:	`78`
IP Source Host:	`durer.home.com`
TCP Source Port:	`1044`
IP Destination Host:	`socrates.home.com`
TCP Destination Port:	`ftp`

After the TCP destination port, we see the TCP packet flags. These map to the standard TCP packet types listed in Table 3.5 of Chapter 3, "TCP/IP Protocol Suite." The S indicates that the packet is a SYN, or start of a TCP connection, while the P means it is a push of data. The ack indicates an acknowledgment. The next part of the listing shows the entire frame in hexadecimal. Unfortunately, it doesn't do a good job of showing us the ASCII version of the frame where appropriate. For instance, when a user starts an FTP session to a host, some valuable information is displayed along with a login prompt:

```
# ftp socrates
220 socrates.home.com FTP server (Version wu-2.4.2-VR17(1) Mon Apr
19 09:21:53 E
DT 1999) ready.
Name (socrates:root):
```

This information is contained within the frames shown above, but **tcpdump** doesn't show us this information in ASCII.

Using Packet Filters

One very important aspect of network protocol debugging involves the use of packet filters. A packet filter is a predefined pattern that is compared to incoming packets and consists of a series of one or more primitives that may be combined with operators such as and, or, and not. When the pattern is matched, that packet is captured and displayed, or else the packet is discarded and not displayed. Packet filters are useful in searching for a particular protocol type or any other specific information available within the packet. We first used a packet filter in the previous example by telling **tcpdump** that we were interested in displaying packets that were related to a file transfer.

The **tcpdump** command supports user-defined packet filters. A filter is installed by **tcpdump** when a filter expression is given on the command line. This filter is placed in memory and will filter according to the rules that have been defined using the keywords and primitives. Every packet is compared to the filter, and when a match is found, the packet is displayed. Otherwise, the packet is discarded. Figure 4.2 shows a high-level overview of a packet filter.

Normally, network packets are read from the network interface by the associated driver on behalf of the kernel. Next, **tcpdump** requests the information from the kernel using system calls. The **tcpdump** tool provides a large number of predefined expressions or primitives that can build very powerful packet filters. These expressions can be divided into three groups. The first group, called *address primitives*, operates on packets using address information such as IP or datalink addresses; the second group, known

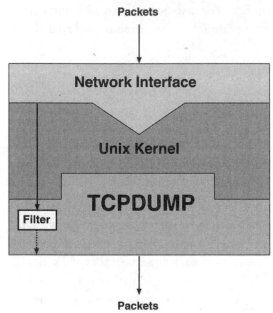

Figure 4.2 tcpdump *packet filter diagram.*

as *protocol primitives*, operates on packets that use different protocols including IP, AppleTalk, and others. The final group includes *Boolean* and *arithmetic primitives* (or operators) that can be used with the first two expression types to produce compound filters. Compound filters include more than one expression type separated by reserve words such as and, not, and or. These filters can also include arithmetic operators such as +, -, *, and others. These expressions are evaluated to be either true or false, and the result will determine what action **tcpdump** will take. A description of the primitives follows.

Address Primitives

Expressions that operate on the addressing portions of a packet are listed in Table 4.12 and described in more detail below.

The gateway primitive selects packets that have been forwarded by a router. This indicates that the datalink address of the packet (either source or destination) matches that of the router, while the IP address matches that of the host. Normally, a router will not change the IP address information when forwarding packets, but

Table 4.12 *Address-related Primitives*

Primitive	Description
gateway	Selects packets that have been used by a specified host acting as a gateway
host	Selects packets from a specified host
ipaddr etheraddr	Selects packets from either IP or datalink addresses
broadcast	Selects broadcast packets that contain all 1s or Fs in either source or destination fields
multicast	Selects packets that are sent to multicast addresses
net	Selects packets that contain specified network portions used with the IP protocol
port	Selects packets that contain specified port addresses used with the IP protocol

the datalink address will match the device that forwards the packet.

The host primitive followed by a valid hostname can select packets that are either sent to or received from the specified hostname. The **host** keyword is mainly used to avoid ambiguity that might arise if you were to specify a hostname that just happens to be the same as one of the **tcpdump** existing keywords. For example, when monitoring the host called gateway, the **host** keyword must be used because the **gateway** keyword will be interpreted as a keyword rather than as a valid hostname. Thus the **tcpdump** command listed produces an error because the gateway string is assumed to specify a local gateway:

```
# tcpdump gateway
tcpdump: hostname required:
```

The way to specify the capture of packets from a host called cisco-gw2 would be the following:

```
# tcpdump host cisco-gw2
```

The ipaddr and etheraddr options specify actual IP addresses and datalink addresses in dotted and colon formats, respectively. For example, to capture all packets from the IP address 10.0.2.100, the following command would be used:

```
# tcpdump ipaddr 10.0.2.100
```

The ipaddr and etheraddr primitives will match either the source or destination address. Some datalink addresses begin with a letter and will cause **tcpdump** to misinterpret these as hostnames rather than true addresses. To avoid this problem, insert a zero in front when specifying these types of addresses.

To capture broadcast packets, use the broadcast primitive. A *broadcast* is a special address that designates that all devices should receive the message. Several network protocols and services such as ARP, NIS, and RIP use broadcasts to propagate information across the network. Using broadcast will result in the capture of broadcast packets from the datalink level. This means that any address that contains 255 or FF values within the source or destination field will be captured. This includes datalink packets that contain broadcasts (such as ARP requests) and high-level protocol broadcasts (such as an IP broadcast). This primitive could be used to capture routing data from the routing information protocol (RIP) because routers periodically broadcast routing updates.

Also, to obtain multicast traffic such as Internet radio, use the multicast primitive. The standard multicast address of 224.0.0.1 supports this type of traffic as defined by the multicast standard. Additional addresses (both physical or IP) can be used at your site. It may be necessary to determine the exact multicast addresses before you start filtering these types of packets.

Protocol Primitives

The **tcpdump** application provides protocol primitives as a shorthand way to select specific network traffic, without requiring or knowing the low-level protocol information. For example, the ip primitive can be used to capture all IP traffic. Without this keyword, you would need to use the IP type of x0800, which is harder to remember. These primitives support the TCP/IP, AppleTalk, and

DECnet family of protocols. Table 4.13 lists and describes these protocol keywords.

Table 4.13 *Protocol Primitives*

Primitive	Description
apple	AppleTalk protocol family
arp	Address Resolution Protocol—includes both request and reply
fddi	FDDI datalink protocol
ethertype	Another protocol type (used with a type code)
decnet	DECnet protocol family
ip	Internet Protocol
icmp	Internet Control Message Protocol—includes both echo and reply
rarp	Reverse Address Resolution Protocol—includes both request and reply
tcp	Transmission Control Protocol
udp	User Datagram Protocol

To select a protocol family or type that isn't provided directly by **tcpdump,** use the ethertype primitive along with the type code for the desired protocol. For example, to monitor Novell NetWare packets, which have a type code of 0x8137, use the following command:

```
# tcpdump ethertype 0x8137
```

Please note that because **tcpdump** doesn't support the Novell protocol family directly, no packet information can be displayed beyond the datalink layer. If **tcpdump** finds packets that contain a Novell header, it will list the datalink information only. However, despite this disadvantage, **tcpdump** is still useful for identifying certain packet types and providing rudimentary packet count information.

Operators

The **tcpdump** command supports several expression (or operator) types and can be combined with primitives and qualifiers to produce compound filters. These expressions include the arithmetic and Boolean operators listed in Table 4.14. Operators can build powerful expressions to search for specific packets. Expressions can be composed of numbers, packet field selections, length primitives, and arithmetic operators. To use the value of a field in an expression within a packet, use the following syntax:

```
primitive [offset [: size] ]
```

where the word `primitive` is replaced with `ether`, `ip`, `udp`, `tcp`, or `icmp`. The `offset` is used in the base of the protocol primitive, and the `size` specifies the length of the field. If not supplied, they default to `1`.

Packet field sections can be used in a variety of ways. Consider the following examples:

```
tcpdump "ether[1:4]&0xffffffff = 0xffffffff"
```

In this example, **tcpdump** will display all broadcast packets transmitted on the local network—this means all frames with a destination address of all 1s (`255` in decimal, `0xff` in hexadecimal). The 1 in `ether[1:4]` indicates the first addressable byte of the frame (the destination address), and the 4 value specifies the length of this field. Despite the fact that Ethernet addresses are six bytes, we can examine the first four bytes to determine if it is a broadcast address.

Table 4.14 *Arithmetic and Boolean operators*

Arithmetic Operators	Description
>	Greater than
<	Less than
>=	Greater than or equal
<=	Less than or equal
=	Equal to

Table 4.14 *Arithmetic and Boolean operators (continued)*

Arithmetic Operators	Description
!=	Not equal
+	Plus
-	Minus
*	Multiply
/	Divide
&	Bitwise AND
|	Bitwise inclusive OR
^	Bitwise exclusive OR
Boolean Operators	
and or &&	Concatenation
or or ||	Alternation
not or !	Negation

To display all packets that originate from a particular Sun system, for example, use this command:

```
tcpdump "ether[6:4]&0xffffffff = 0x08002004"
```

This tells **tcpdump** to examine the sixth byte of the frame (the source frame address) and compare it to the 0x08002004 addresses using the & (and) operator. This datalink address represents the address of a local system called monet. Recall that Ethernet addresses are six bytes in length and we can use the first four bytes to identify the system desired. As a result, all packets transmitted from monet will be displayed. To identify another system, obtain the datalink address of the system, convert it to hexadecimal, and place it on the right side of the preceding command.

Miscellaneous Primitives

A few additional primitives are also available from **tcpdump** that can't be classified as either address or protocol primitives. These include the following:

- `greater`
- `less`
- `length`

The `greater` and `less` primitives are used in conjunction with other **tcpdump** commands to filter, based on the total length of the packet. For example, to display all packets that are greater than 56 bytes, invoke the following command:

```
# tcpdump greater 56
```

To display all packets that are less than 60 bytes, use the `less` primitive:

```
# tcpdump -x less 60
```

This command will display all frames that are less than 60 bytes. For instance, ARP (Address Resolution Protocol) request frames are smaller than 60 bytes. Executing this command will display any ARP messages, as shown here:

```
tcpdump: listening on eth0
23:45:29.240364 arp who-has durer.home.com tell socrates.home.com
0001 0800 0604 0001 0010 5a28 5d7c 0a00
02c9 0000 0000 0000 0a00 020a
```

Why would you use the **greater** or **less** commands? The primary reason is to search for packets based on size, rather than content. Another primitive, `length`, can also be used to handle capturing packets based on their exact size. The `length` can be used when the need to capture packets is based on some calculation. For example, the command below will display any packet that is not equal to 56:

```
# tcpdump length != 56
```

Qualifiers

Three qualifiers may be used in conjunction with the primitives listed in the preceding tables. A qualifier can further define search characteristics to pinpoint specific network traffic. These qualifiers include the following:

- `from` **or** `src`

- `to` **or** `dst`

- `ether`

The `from` and `src` qualifiers are used with the `host`, `net`, `ipaddr`, `etheraddr`, `port`, or `rpc` primitives to filter based on a specific destination address or port. The qualifiers `to` or `dst` modify the primitives just mentioned, but will result in the captured packets going to a particular address or port. The `ether` modifier resolves a name to a datalink address when used with the `host` primitive. To illustrate the use of the **host** keyword, let's suppose we want to capture traffic from a particular host only. The following **tcpdump** command could be used:

```
# tcpdump from host monet
```

Contrast the command above with the following:

```
# tcpdump host monet
```

In the latter example, all the traffic involving `monet`, which includes packets being sent to and received from `monet`, will be displayed. In the former example, only traffic received from `monet` will be displayed. As you can see, this can make a big difference when attempting to isolate a network problem.

Tcpdump Examples

Table 4.15 contains a list of command examples and associated description of each one. It is hoped that these commands will provide a quick reference on using the **tcpdump** in real-world situations.

Traceroute Tool

General Description

The **traceroute** command examines and records the path to a specified network destination. Within a traditional IP network, one or more routers are used to provide connectivity between different IP networks. IP routers come in different shapes and sizes,

Table 4.15 tcpdump *command examples*

Command	Description
tcpdump host barney	Will capture and display traffic sent from or delivered to the system called barney. This command examines both the source and destination address fields of the IP header
tcpdump host not barney	Will capture and display traffic from all hosts on the network, except the system called barney
tcpdump host barney and host fred and \ (not pebbles\)	Will capture and display traffic from hosts barney and fred, but not from the system called pebbles. The parentheses were added to make the command more readable. However, each of the **tcpdump** arithmetical and Boolean operators have precedence and the parentheses can be used to define command interpretation ordering. Note: since the parentheses are special to some shells, they must be escaped using the backslash (\)
tcpdump arp	Will capture and display all Address Resolution Protocol (ARP) packets. This includes both requests and replies
tcpdump host durer and tcp	Will capture and display all Transmission Control Protocol (TCP) packets from/to the host durer
tcpdump host vectra and port 23	Will capture and display all packets using port 23 from or to host vectra. This amounts to inspecting all Telnet packets going to this system from others on the network. Recall, that port 23 is the Telnet service port for all incoming packets
tcpdump ether multicast	Will capture and display multicast packets. See next command for alternative

Table 4.15 tcpdump *command examples (continued)*

Command	Description
tcpdump 'ip[16] >= 224'	Will capture and display all packets that use the multicast address. This command compares the sixteenth byte (which is the destination address) of the IP packet to the 224 value. This prefix for the standard multicast address of 224.0.0.1 which means all hosts within the default multicast group
tcpdump 'ether[0] & 1 = 1'	Will capture and display all broadcast packets. The sequence ether[0] provides access to the first field of the Ethernet datalink destination field and is compared to the value of 1. If the destination fields contain all 1s (which will be true if broadcast address, when expressed in binary) and when the and (&) operator is applied to a positive value, it will yield a value of 1. In this case, the expression is true and the packets are displayed
tcpdump 'ip[2:2] > 512'	Will capture and display all IP packets that are larger than 512 bytes. The sequence ip[2:2] identifies the second byte of the IP header (which is the size of the packet) and compares this value of ⁻12. The 2: indicates the offset of the IP packet while the remaining 2 is the number of bytes within that field

from a simple multi-homed UNIX system with two interfaces to an industrial-strength Cisco router series that contains a large number of interfaces. In each of these cases, the routing function is primarily the same; it forwards IP packets from one interface to another based on established routing information. The **traceroute** command uses the Time-To-Live (TTL) field contained within an IP packet and attempts to obtain an ICMP TIME_EXCEEDED message from each host along the route to the destination. Coupled with an attempt to attach to the destination at an unreachable port, it will cause a systematic response from every router along the path to the ultimate destination. It accomplishes this task by sending out requests (or probes) with a TTL of 1 and increases the TTL by 1 until it either reaches the desired host or exceeds the maximum TTL value. By default, the TTL is set to 30 hops, but this can be changed.

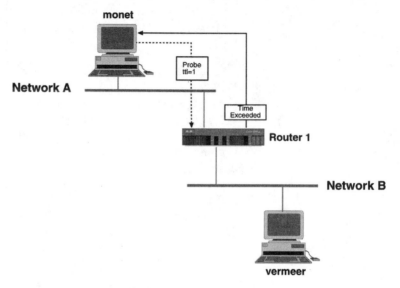

Figure 4.3 **traceroute** *with one hop.*

This command has a large number of command-line options, but the only required argument is either a hostname or an IP address of the destination. For example, to display the IP path between the local system running **traceroute** and the destination system called vermeer, issue the following command:

```
# traceroute vermeer
```

Figures 4.3 and 4.4 show a sample network that consists of one router and two network nodes. When the above **traceroute** command is executed on monet, the following output will be displayed:

```
# traceroute vermeer
traceroute to vermeer (128.197.2.200), 30 hops max, 40 byte packets
```

```
1  router-1 (10.0.2.129)  4.256 ms  *  2.899 ms
2  vermeer (128.197.2.200)  7.340 ms  7.433 ms  7.526 ms
```

By default, **traceroute** sends a total of three probes, each with a different TTL value, to every hop. The first line of the output includes the destination along with the IP address, the default number of hops **traceroute** used, and the size of the packets being sent. The second line (with a 1) displays the first hop encountered by **traceroute** (see Figure 4.3).

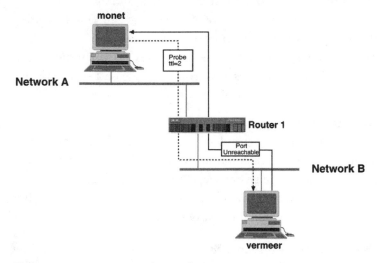

Figure 4.4 **traceroute** *with two hops.*

Because `vermeer` is on a different physical network than `monet`, a router must be used to reach this system. Because the default router in this example is `router-1`, the first packet is sent there. The first packet sent is an ICMP request packet with the TTL field set to 1. With IP, any packet that reaches the router decrements the TTL by 1, which makes it zero. When a router gets a packet and the TTL is zero, it is supposed to discard the packet and notify the sender. This forces the router to respond with a `TIME_EXCEEDED` message back to `monet`. After this happens, **traceroute** measures the amount of time between when it sent the packet and when it obtained the reply. This is known as the *round-trip time* or *RTT* and is displayed in milliseconds (1000th of a second) as shown after the hostname and IP address information. This implies that the RTT of the first series of probe packets took 4.25 milliseconds (or .004 seconds), and the third series took 2.89 milliseconds (or .028 seconds).

The second line details the second routing hop and shows that **traceroute** reached the destination system vermeer with slower RTT times than the first (see Figure 4.4). When the second probe was sent, the router decremented the TTL, and then passed this packet to vermeer. Because the **traceroute** is attempting to access an unused port, vermeer responds with the PORT UNREACHABLE error. In fact, as a general rule on large (and sometimes small) internets, performance between systems and networks will and can vary a significant amount even from one moment to the next.

There is no restriction on what constitutes a destination; it can be any kind of device that ranges from a simple host system to an Internet router. The only requirement is that it must support IP.

Reading traceroute Output

Due to variations and problems with router devices along certain paths, the general fluctuations of network routes can lead to unpredictable and strange **traceroute** output. As a result, certain codes might appear after the timing information is displayed. Table 4.16 lists these codes and their associated meanings.

Table 4.16 **traceroute** *display codes*

Code	Meaning
*	No response to probe packets
!	TTL in the received packet is set to 1
!H	Destination host is unreachable
!N	Destination network is unreachable
!P	Destination protocol is unreachable
!S	The source route option has failed. In practice, this shouldn't happen, and if it does, it indicates a bug or problem with the router that generated the error

Table 4.16 **traceroute** *display codes (continued)*

Code	Meaning
!F	Fragmentation was needed for a probe packet. In practice, this shouldn't happen, and if it does, it indicates a bug or problem with the router that generated the error
!X	The path is blocked due to communication being administratedly-disabled. In other words, the path is shut down or blocked from a software standpoint
!N>	An ICMP error code where N is that number

Some of these display codes come in handy when you debug network problems. For example, if a destination is not reachable (like *www.whitehouse.gov*) by the system that is running the **traceroute** command, executing

```
monet# traceroute www.whitehouse.gov
```

will produce

```
traceroute to www.whitehouse.gov (198.137.240.91), 30 hops max, 40
    byte packets
1   monet (10.0.2.126)  4.281 ms !N *  1.896 ms !N
```

In this example, the network 198.137.240 can't be reached from the local system, and **traceroute** displays the error string !N to indicate this problem. In this particular case, monet can't send any packets to 198.137.240 because no route to that network exists. The * means that the particular probe packet never received a response; the * is used as a timeout indicator. To further verify these results, use the **ping** command with the same destination. Thus the command

```
monet# ping www.whitehouse.gov
```

will show the same problem, except the error is a little more descriptive:

```
ICMP Net Unreachable from gateway monet (10.0.2.126)
for icmp from monet (10.0.2.126) to www.whitehouse.gov
```

In the same way, both !H and !P error codes are also used to debug general network problems. However, in these two cases, !H reports when a host is unreachable and the !P reports when the protocol is unreachable. The host unreachable message will be displayed, for example, when the network is also unreachable.

Given the fact that at any point in time, the performance or RTT between networks and systems can change significantly, a trace to the Web site of the Louvre Museum first reveals the following:

```
# traceroute 198.137.240.91
traceroute to 198.137.240.91 (198.137.240.91), 30 hops max, 40 byte
    packets
 1  10.0.2.76 (10.0.2.76)  19.906 ms   9.801 ms   8.174 ms
 2  199.70.195.38 (199.70.195.38)  197.460 ms  188.000 ms  181.029 ms
 3  12.77.194.1 (12.77.194.1)  166.802 ms  184.713 ms  185.857 ms
 4  12.127.12.205 (12.127.12.205)  245.026 ms  270.253 ms  266.718 ms
 5  12.127.15.145 (12.127.15.145)  215.191 ms  211.920 ms  208.979 ms
 6  192.205.31.165 (192.205.31.165)  217.875 ms  232.610 ms  222.274 ms
 7  204.6.117.65 (204.6.117.65)  266.797 ms  239.000 ms  215.671 ms
 8  38.1.4.69 (38.1.4.69)  235.431 ms  225.447 ms  301.119 ms
 9  38.1.25.5 (38.1.25.5)  235.369 ms  236.134 ms  263.557 ms
10  38.1.25.5 (38.1.25.5)  252.172 ms  238.984 ms  263.013 ms
11  38.146.148.45 (38.146.148.45)  241.956 ms  248.091 ms  243.300 ms
12  198.137.240.33 (198.137.240.33)  249.361 ms  228.717 ms  252.927 ms
13  198.137.240.91 (198.137.240.91)  238.799 ms  259.967 ms  236.384 ms
```

When the trace is repeated later, it shows the following:

```
# traceroute 198.137.240.91
traceroute to 198.137.240.91 (198.137.240.91), 30 hops max, 40 byte
    packets
 1  10.0.2.76 (10.0.2.76)  7.619 ms   5.863 ms   6.206 ms
 2  199.70.195.42 (199.70.195.42)  177.685 ms  177.691 ms  177.842 ms
 3  12.77.242.129 (12.77.242.129)  170.712 ms  177.096 ms  173.517 ms
 4  12.127.12.205 (12.127.12.205)  260.239 ms  248.072 ms  252.829 ms
 5  12.127.15.145 (12.127.15.145)  219.767 ms  215.645 ms  232.399 ms
 6  192.205.31.165 (192.205.31.165)  232.259 ms  225.243 ms  219.236 ms
 7  204.6.117.65 (204.6.117.65)  228.997 ms  218.067 ms  219.365 ms
 8  38.1.4.69 (38.1.4.69)  445.758 ms  232.797 ms  276.249 ms
 9  38.1.25.5 (38.1.25.5)  245.674 ms  443.611 ms  577.309 ms
10  38.1.25.5 (38.1.25.5)  432.994 ms  222.527 ms  242.844 ms
11  38.146.148.45 (38.146.148.45)  257.668 ms  249.923 ms  263.074 ms
12  198.137.240.33 (198.137.240.33)  276.658 ms  242.361 ms  *
13  198.137.240.91 (198.137.240.91)  248.266 ms  245.006 ms  251.071 ms
```

As you can see, most of the response times are very close. However, significant delays can be observed with hops 8, 9, and 10. In these cases, the RTT is almost doubled, which further indicates that performance on a large routed network (such as the Internet) can and does vary over time.

Changing Operational Characteristics

The **traceroute** command contains a number of operational parameters that can be modified to affect how it traces a path to the specified destination. Each of these parameters has an associated command-line option that can alter its default values. Table 4.17 lists these options.

Table 4.17 **traceroute** *operational options*

Option	Description
-i	Specifies an alternate interface
-p	Sets the alternate port to send probe packets
-g	Specifies a router for loose source routing
-f	Sets the initial TTL value to be used
-s	Uses the specified address as the source address in transmitting probe packets
-q	Sets the number of probe queries
-m	Sets the maximum hops
-d	Enables debug flag (SO_DEBUG)
-F	Specifies not to fragment
-t	Sets the type of service (TOS) flag
-w	Sets the wait time for probe packets
-x	Specifies not to calculate checksums

When **traceroute** is executed on a system that is multi-homed (i.e., a system that contains more than one network interface), it selects the first interface it encounters. Unfortunately, this might not be what you want because the destination you are after can only be accessed from another interface. To address this issue, the -i option can be used to force **traceroute** to send probe packets using the interface specified with this option. Thus the command

```
traceoute -i hem0
traceroute: Warning: Multiple interfaces found; using 10.0.2.126 @
    hme0
```

will cause **traceroute** to use the Fast Ethernet interface instead of the FDDI interface that it would normally use.

In certain situations, the default TTL value of 30 is not enough to reach a destination that might contain a larger number of routes. When this occurs, **traceroute** will never reach the destination. In this situation, use the -m option to increase the hop count.

When you do a **traceroute** to certain devices, it might sometimes fail, despite the fact that the path to the device is operational. Further, using the **ping** command against the device will indicate that it is working correctly as well. Why? Before we answer this question, let's look at an example:

```
monet# traceroute -m 5 128.197.2.200
traceroute to 128.197.2.200 (128.197.2.200), 5 hops max, 40 byte packets
1   rodin (10.0.2.129)   10.193 ms *   2.158 ms
2   * * *
3   * * *
4   * * *
5   * * *
```

This **traceroute** produces no response to the probe packets. Note the use of the -m option to keep the number of probe packets small.

The answer to this problem lies in the fact that, by default, **traceroute** sends probe packets based on the UDP protocol. It is most likely that the destination in question does not support this protocol directly or can't handle the UDP destination port used. From a TCP/IP standpoint, not all devices are required to support UDP, and if they do support UDP, they do not necessarily support the port number used by **traceroute**.

When **traceroute** sends out probe packets, it uses, by default, the UDP port of 33434 and assumes that this port isn't being used by any other application or network service. It uses this high port number in hopes that the destination will respond with a port unreachable message, thus terminating the route tracing. On the other hand, if that port is being used, it will cause problems for **traceroute**. If this happens, use the `-p` option followed by another port number, and **traceroute** will use that port instead of the default.

```
monet# traceroute -p 10 -m 5 128.197.2.200
traceroute to 128.197.2.200 (128.197.2.200), 5 hops max, 40 byte
    packets
1  rodin (10.0.2.129)  10.193 ms *  2.158 ms
2  * * *
3  * * *
4  * * *
5  * * *
```

If this still doesn't do the trick, attempt to use the `-I` option, which will instruct **traceroute** to use the ICMP protocol instead of UDP when sending probe packets. So the command

```
monet# traceroute -m 5 -I 128.197.2.200
```

with the `-I` option produces the correct results:

```
traceroute to 128.197.2.200 (128.197.2.200), 5 hops max, 40 byte
    packets
1  rodin (10.0.2.129)  4.412 ms *  2.235 ms
2  vermeer (128.197.2.200)  6.875 ms  6.955 ms  6.935 ms
```

As you can see, this took a bit of trial and error to obtain the desired result. However, this is not a contrived example; rather, vermeer represents an actual device: a laser printer. The real point here is that, when tracing the route to a particular destination, there can be many reasons why **traceroute** fails to reach a destination. Failure might not mean that the device is down or disconnected from the network.

Display Options

Two options are available to modify the output of **traceroute**. The first, `-v`, displays for each hop, the size and destination of the response packets. The following shows an example:

```
traceroute -v vermeer
# traceroute -i le1 -v rembrandt
traceroute to rembrandt (10.0.2.75), 30 hops max, 40 byte packets
1  rembrandt (10.0.2.75) 56 bytes to 10.0.2.1 3.450 ms 2.085 ms
2.094 ms
```

The second option, -n, displays addresses in numerical form rather than using the symbolic name. This removes the added task from **traceroute** of having to resolve each router's hostname.

Additional System Utilities and Tools

The tools in this chapter will be welcome additions to the collection of the software utilities and tools discussed thus far.

The major reason for including these tools in a separate chapter is this: The commands and programs discussed in the previous chapter are available on a number of different UNIX systems but are usually part of the standard core set of debugging aids. On the other hand, the tools in this chapter are not as widely known as the tools described in Chapter 4. Despite this, these tools provide very important services and will have a significant impact on diagnosing networking issues and problems. They include:

Command	Page
arpwatch	184
ethereal	188
fping	210
nmap	218
xtraceroute	239

Arpwatch Tool

General Description

The **arpwatch** command keeps track of and reports on changes observed in the datalink addresses on the local network. It also tracks Datalink/IP address pairs, i.e., Ethernet to Internet Protocol (IP) addresses. Due to the significant growth of the number of systems attached to most networks, it has become paramount that a mechanism be available to record additions and device changes. When **arpwatch** notices a discrepancy, it logs the information to a file and sends electronic mail.

Table 5.1 lists the small number of command-line options that this tool supports.

One of the most useful options is the -i, which controls the interface that **arpwatch** will use when monitoring the network. By default, the lowest primary network interface on system startup is selected to be monitored by **arpwatch**. For a system with more than one interface, it may be eth0, for example. When **arpwatch** detects

Table 5.1 arpwatch *command-line options*

Option	Description
-d	Enables debugging mode
-f	Specifies an alternate file to be used to store the database
-i	Specifies another network interface that overrides the default interface defined on the system
-r	Parses a file containing **tcpdump**-formatted data to read instead of monitoring the network.

changes in datalink addresses, it emits specific message reports. The types of messages generated include:

- new station

- changed Ethernet address

- flip flop

- new activity

New Station

This message is used when a new system is seen on the network for the first time. The **arpwatch** software will Email the root account on the local system with a message like the one below:

```
From root Mon Dec 27 13:05:09 1999
Date: Mon, 27 Dec 1999 13:05:09 -0400
From: arpwatch@socrates.home.com (Arpwatch)
To: root@socrates.home.com
Subject: new station

            hostname: probe
          ip address: 10.0.2.50
     ethernet address: 0:c0:d4:0:9:40
      ethernet vendor: Axon Networks Inc
            timestamp: Monday, Dec 27, 1999 13:05:08 -0400
```

The Email includes the hostname (if available), the IP address, Ethernet Address, Ethernet Vendor, and date/time stamp of the event. In this case, a RMON probe was installed on the local network and **arpwatch** detected this new device. Also, a message is sent to the syslog process that will find its way into the /var/log/messages file. The format of the syslog message is different than the format of the Email shown here:

```
Dec 27 13:05:09 probe arpwatch: new station 10.0.2.50
0:c0:d4:0:9:40
```

Clearly, being informed regarding this type of change on the network could really come in handy. New station messages will only be generated once when the device is first installed and powered up. Once this event has been logged for the first time, no additional messages will be generated, even if the device is booted multiple times or is disconnected from the network and re-attached at a later time. As long as the **arpwatch** database is maintained and preserved, a new station message will truly indicate that a new device has been added to the network. This is an excellent way to be informed when users add devices to the network without your explicit knowledge.

Changed Ethernet Address

This message is generated because **arpwatch** has detected that the datalink address of a device has changed, but the IP address has remained the same. This could happen when a new interface card is installed to replace a defective unit or the datalink addresses are changed for some other reason, perhaps even on purpose. The associated Email message that is generated includes the following:

```
From root  Fri Dec 24 23:07:43 1999
Date: Fri, 24 Dec 1999 23:07:43 -0400
From: arpwatch@socrates.home.com (Arpwatch)
To: root@socrates.home.com
Subject: changed ethernet address (switch.home.com)

           hostname: switch.home.com
         ip address: 10.0.2.60
   ethernet address: 0:0:1d:a:5d:1
    ethernet vendor: Cabletron
old ethernet address: 0:0:1d:a:5c:ff
```

```
old ethernet vendor: Cabletron
            timestamp: Friday, December 24, 1999 23:07:42 -0400
   previous timestamp: Thursday, December 23, 1999 21:25:30 -0400
                delta: 1 day
```

Actually, this message was not the result of a new interface being installed in a device. Rather, because this device is a multiple port Cabletron Ethernet switch, it contains a large number of network interfaces. Because the connection to the network for this device was moved from one port to another, **arpwatch** detected the change. The original interface had an address of 0:0:1d:a:5c:ff, while the new port had the address of 0:0:1d:a:5d:1. Note that in both cases, the vendor was identified as Cabletron, which was the correct vendor of the hardware. To make this report a little more useful, the delta of elapsed time is shown. This represents the amount of time that has passed when **arpwatch** first recorded the datalink/IP pair and when the port change first happened.

Flip Flop

This message type indicates that the host mentioned was the most recently monitored address, but now has become the second most-monitored address. For instance, the message

```
From root  Sat Jul 31 14:07:15 1999
Date: Sat, 31 Jul 1999 14:07:15 -0400
From: arpwatch@socrates.home.com (Arpwatch)
To: root@socrates.home.com
Subject: flip flop (durer.home.com)

             hostname: durer.home.com
           ip address: 10.0.2.10
     ethernet address: 0:60:97:e:a3:6
      ethernet vendor: 3Com
 old ethernet address: 0:0:1d:a:5c:ff
  old ethernet vendor: Cabletron
            timestamp: Saturday, July 31, 1999 14:07:15 -0400
   previous timestamp: Saturday, July 31, 1999 14:06:29 -0400
                delta: 46 seconds
```

indicates that the most recently seen host is called durer.home.com, which contains the datalink address of 0:60:97:e:a3:6 and uses a 3Com interface card. The second most-seen address was the Cabletron device with the datalink address of 0:0:1d:a:5c:ff.

Before this message was issued, the Cabletron device was the most active on the network.

New Activity

The new Activity message is generated when an Ethernet/IP address pair has been seen for the first time within a six month (or more) period of time. This will be useful for tracking devices that for some reason have been out of service or disconnected from the network for quite a while, and now have been placed back in service or reattached to the network. In practice, however, this may not be a very meaningful message because of the duration of time. Rather, it would be better if the interval of time could be customized by the user to be shorter. However, in the current version of the tool, this feature isn't supported.

One of the more interesting capabilities of the tool includes the parsing of **tcpdump** output. Using the -r option, **arpwatch** will parse these specially formatted files, build a database, and report the history of the network with monitoring messages previously discussed. This may come in handy when **arpwatch** reports are needed, but for some reason **arpwatch** can't be executed in real -time to monitor the network.

Ethereal Tool

General Description

The **ethereal** command is a powerful Ethernet network monitoring solution that can be used to capture and analyze network traffic in real-time or off-line modes. This tool picks up where **tcpdump** ends by providing full packet-level protocol decoding that boasts support for many popular network protocols and an easy-to-use packet capture interface. Additionally, **ethereal** supports many other commercial package capture formats, so you can continue to use your existing software and process these datafiles with **ethereal**.

This tool provides a robust GUI interface that streamlines the capturing of network data and subsequent browsing of network traffic. The main window contains a set of menu items, three panels, plus three status or input boxes on the bottom, as shown in Figure 5.1. Many of the menu items are self explanatory and won't be covered in detail. The first panel contains a summary of all the packets captured. This panel contains a packet number, timestamp, source, destination, protocol, and information fields. As you will see later in this section, these fields are customizable, and the user can remove or include additional packet field information.

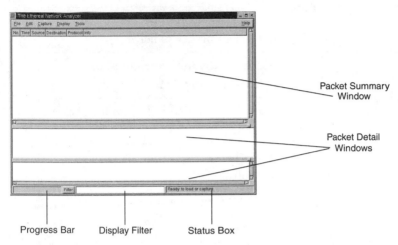

Figure 5.1 *Main* **ethereal** *window.*

The next panel shows a hierarchical view (packet detail) that contains all the higher-layer protocols displayed in a tree format. The remaining panel includes a hexadecimal display of the entire packet. As the user moves through the second panel via the tree view, the bottom panel highlights where the cursor is positioned within the packet. A progress area on the left-hand side of the main window shows the status of tasks, and a filter text box has been provided to accept filtering of displayed packets within the first panel. Finally, an information box on the right-hand side of the main window indicates the name of the data file and the number of dropped packets.

The software supports a number of important command-line options that can be divided into two categories: display mode and function mode options. Display mode options can control such items as the size of individual display panels and the type and size of font used. Table 5.2 lists the display options.

Table 5.2 ethereal *display options*

Option	Description
-B	Controls the initial height of the bottom hexadecimal panel
-P	Controls the initial height of the packet summary panel
-T	Controls the initial height of the packet tree view panel
-b	Uses the specified bold font for packet field display
-m	Uses the specified font instead of default
-t	Sets the format of the packet timestamp when displayed in the summary packet panel

The functional mode options control such items as which network interface will be used to read captured traffic, the maximum size of packets that should be read during a packet capture, etc. Table 5.3 lists these command options.

Table 5.3 ethereal *functional options*

Option	Description
-c	Capture the number of packets as specified with this option
-h	Show version and information
-i	Specifies the network interface to capture packets
-n	Disable hostname resolution and TCP/UDP port name mappings

Table 5.3 **ethereal** *functional options (continued)*

Option	Description
-r	Obtain network traffic data from specified file
-s	Specifies the default packet length when capturing live network traffic
-w	Specifies the capture file to use when saving data to disk

Many of the functional options are the same as those for the **tcp-dump** command, which was covered in the previous chapter. As such, many of the options at this point should be familiar to the reader. Nevertheless, the -s option bears a little more explanation. By default, **ethereal** attempts to read the entire packet while capturing traffic on the network. However, it is possible with this option to limit the actual number of bytes **ethereal** will read for each packet. The default length of bytes it reads is 65535, which should be large enough to handle most, if not all, packets that **ethereal** may encounter. Controlling the size of the packet has an impact on performance, data storage, and packet analysis.

Low-layer networking datalink protocols such as Ethernet and FDDI have fixed-size frames that represent the maximum amount of data that can be carried in each frame. The frames can be smaller than the maximum, too. Table 5.4 shows these sizes. As you can see, the sizes vary among the protocols, but the important thing to remember is that regardless of the size of the upper-level protocols, such as IP, what defines the size of the physical frame is the datalink protocol, not the high-level ones. Also, many higher protocols such as TCP and others have the ability to specify the length of their packets. In many of these instances, there is usually a ceiling or maximum size allowed. For IP, the maximum is 65535 and happens to be the same as the **ethereal** limit.

Armed with this information, we can arbitrarily adjust the amount of data read during capture instead of reading the entire frame. Why do this? Well, for starters if you are only interested in a few packet fields, such as source, destination, and frame type, there is little reason to process the frame to include additional fields. From a performance standpoint, it is much easier to process a smaller number of bytes per frame. Also, when filtering and/or saving the data to a UNIX file, this too will be much faster. Finally, there is a *gotcha*! In an effort to improve capture processing or reduce the amount of data to manage, we sacrifice functionality. When an artificial limit is placed on the frame size, it affects how much of the high-level protocols will be available for review and analysis. For instance,whe executed, the command

```
# ethereal -s 64
```

will start **ethereal** and change the default packet size to 64 bytes. This is the minimum size of the Ethernet frame, as shown in Table 5.4. This table includes additional datalink protocol sizes as well. If you are interested in examining TCP data, possibly from an FTP session, using this size will not permit you do to so; it will truncate the frames so that the FTP information will be lost. The best approach is to use the default size unless you are capturing a lot of packets and must reduce the overall amount of the data saved. The general rule is that if you are going to capture less than the default, you will limit what high-level protocols can be ultimately decoded from the captured packets.

Table 5.4 *Datalink frame sizes*

Datalink Protocol	Minimum	Maximum
ATM	6	53
Ethernet	64	1518
FDDI	64	4500
Fiber Channel	0	2112
TokenRing	48	2048

Capturing Network Traffic

To begin capturing network information, click on the Capture menu, and then select the Start... Ctl+k sub-menu item. Alternatively, you could issue a **^k** (**Control k**) from the keyboard. Once this is done, the **ethereal** Capture Preferences window will be displayed, as shown in Figure 5.2.

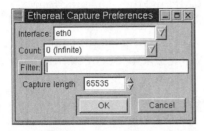

Figure 5.2 ethereal *Capture Preferences window.*

This window allows the user to change the network interface, packet count, and frame length before a capture session is started. Also, the user may define a filter in the text box. Recall from the previous chapter that a filter can be used to sort through the network traffic and pick out specific types of frames or any information that can be matched against a numeric and/or character pattern. The **ethereal** tool supports the **tcpdump** filtering protocol primitives and keywords. As a result, powerful filters may be defined very quickly and easily.

Clicking the OK button will start the capture. Doing so will cause the **ethereal** Capture Preferences window to disappear and the **ethereal** Capture/Playback window to be displayed, as shown in Figure 5.3.

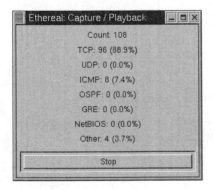

Figure 5.3 ethereal *Capture/Playback window.*

This window shows a running count of frames obtained by **ethereal**, sorted by protocol type and percentage of the total number of frames received. Figure 5.2 shows a total of 108 packets captured, with 96 of them being TCP, four ICMP, and the remaining four considered of type *other*. Other means packets captured from the network that didn't match the packet types listed in the count window. This provides visual feedback on the activities of **ethereal** and a quick snapshot of which types of frames have been seen on the network. If you want to stop the capture, click the Stop button. Sometimes a certain amount of delay can be seen from the time the user clicks the STOP button to the time the application actually stops capturing traffic. This in part will depend on the load of the network or other processes running on the system. Also, if filters are defined, this may make **ethereal** a little slower when responding to key and/or mouse control.

Once **ethereal** has stopped capturing data, it displays all the frames in the first packet summary panel. Figure 5.4 shows a representative sample of what the main window will resemble after capturing network traffic.

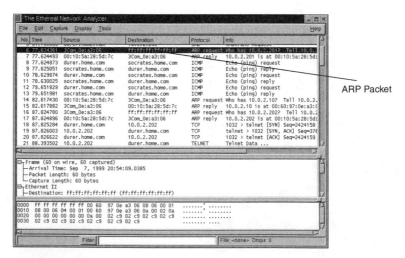

Figure 5.4 *Selected ARP packet with detail.*

In this example, we have several different packet types, as denoted by the Protocol field. We can see ARP, ICMP, TCP, and TELNET packets. If we want to examine a single packet in greater detail, we

simply click on it. In Figure 5.4, the first ARP packet was highlighted with the mouse causing the two lower panels to display
additional packet information. As previously stated, the middle
panel contains a tree view of each of the major sections of the
frame. The entire contents of the panel are shown below without
the hierarchical tick marks shown in the middle panel:

```
Frame (60 on wire, 60 captured)
    Arrival Time: Dec 27, 1999 20:54:09.0385
    Packet Length: 60 bytes
    Capture Length: 60 bytes
Ethernet II
    Destination: ff:ff:ff:ff:ff:ff (ff:ff:ff:ff:ff:ff)
    Source: 00:60:97:0e:a3:06 (3Com_0e:a3:06)
    Type: ARP (0x0806)
ARP request
    Hardware type: Ethernet
    Protocol type: IP
    Hardware size: 6
    Protocol size: 4
    Opcode: 0x0001 (ARP request)
    Sender hardware address: 00:60:97:0e:a3:06
    Sender protocol address: 10.0.2.10
    Target hardware address: 00:00:00:00:00:00
    Target protocol address: 10.0.2.201
```

The listing above includes just a single packet! This represents
the ICMP Echo request sent from network interface 3Com_0e:a3:06
(which is the interface card from the system durer). Note how **ethereal** replaces the first three bytes of the hardware address with a
string that clearly denotes the manufacturer of the interface.

Each packet contains at least three sections. These include
Frame, Ethernet II, and ARP. The Frame section represents the
frame number, which indicates the count or position within the list
of packets captured. This packet is the 60th frame read from the
network. Also shown are the Arrival Time field, Packet Length
field, and Capture Length field. Unless the sizes of frames were specifically limited on the command line or using the capture dialog,
the packet length and captured lengths should be equal.

The Ethernet II field represents the datalink frame, which is
formatted according to the Ethernet specification. Recall that each
Ethernet frame contains a fixed-length header that includes pream-

ble, destination, source, type, data, and checksum information. However, **ethereal** only reports the Destination field, Source field, and Type fields. The other fields are not displayed because the low-level Ethernet driver doesn't make the information available.

The remaining section includes the ARP portion, which in general denotes the higher-level protocols that have been encapsulated within the data portion of the Ethernet frame. As previously indicated, many higher-level protocols—like TCP, IP, and IPX—can be encapsulated in a frame just like ARP. In this case, the ARP packet includes information specific to the ARP protocol—hardware type, hardware address information, ARP packet type, sender's hardware address information, and target (desired) hardware address. We can determine that this packet is a ARP request because the opcode field is set to 1 (or 0x0001) and the Target hardware address is null (or 00:00:00:00:00:00).

The bottom panel contains the hexadecimal format of the packet displayed in rows and columns. As the user accesses each of the fields in the middle panel, the bytes that represent this data are highlighted in this bottom panel. For instance, when the user selects the Ethernet Source field of the packet, the following will be displayed:

```
0000   ff ff ff ff ff 00 60   97 0e a3 06 08 06 00 01
.......  ........
0010   08 00 06 04 00 01 00 60   97 0e a3 06 0a 00 02 0a
.......  ........
0020   00 00 00 00 00 00 0a 00   02 c9 02 c9 02 c9 02 c9
.......  ........
0030   02 c9 02 c9 02 c9 02 c9   02 c9 02 c9
.......  ...
```

As indicated, the set of values 00 60 97 0e a3 06 is shown in bold to represent the sender's datalink address of this packet. The data in this panel is very useful because it provides a quick conversion to the low-level format, which can be used to identify network traffic patterns. The hexadecimal format is nearly universal when representing packets at this level. In the last chapter, we showed how to use **tcpdump** to scan for a specific string within a packet. The data represented in the hexadecimal format provides a quick reference should we need to filter any specific patterns.

Since **ethereal** supports files specifically formatted by **tcpdump**, any file generated in this format (as produced with the **tcpdump** -w option) can be read into and processed by **ethereal**. In fact, both programs are completely compatible; output generated by **ethereal** can be processed by **tcpdump** as well.

Using Filters

The **ethereal** software provides two kinds of filters: the packet capture filter and the display filter. As indicated, **ethereal** supports the filter keywords, operations, and syntax similar to the **tcpdump** command that was discussed in the previous chapter. Capture filters can be set up before a capture session has begun by specifying one in the filter text box, as shown in Figure 5.5. For instance, the figure shows a filter that will capture only TCP packets by using the filter string tcp. This filter is known as an *ad-hoc* or temporary filter because once the application has terminated, the filter definition is lost. The TCP string is a keyword used by **ethereal**, which will filter out all packets that use TCP.

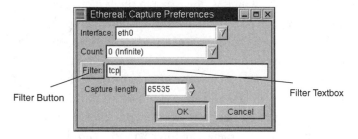

Figure 5.5 *TCP packet filter window.*

Permanent filters may be created as well. These will be available across packet capture sessions. To create this type of filter, click the filter button. When this is done, the Ethereal:Preferences dialog box will be displayed, as shown in Figure 5.6. As it turns out, this is the same window that is displayed when the user accesses the **ethereal** options.

By default, **ethereal** provides no existing filter definitions. Instead, the user must create them using this dialog box and save them for future use.

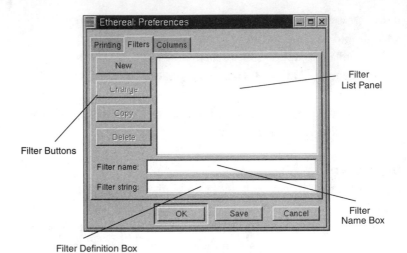

Figure 5.6 ethereal *filter window.*

This is the reason the filter definition panel is empty. If existing filters had been defined by the user, they would be displayed.

The filter window contains a set of buttons, input text boxes, and a filter definition panel. To build a new filter, type the name of the filter in the Filter name: text box. In this example, let's use the name ip-broadcast, which is described in the last chapter. Recall that this filter will inspect the IP header of the IP protocol to determine if the packet uses an IP broadcast address. Next, enter the filter definition in the Filter string text box; use the string: ip[19]&0xff = 0xff. Then click the New button. At this point, the ip-broadcast filter will be added to the filter list panel. Finally, click the Save button to permanently save the filter for future use. After these steps are complete, the filter window should contain the filter definition just created, as depicted in Figure 5.7.

The window also contains two additional filter definitions that were previously created. These include the snmp-p and host-durer. The first filter, called snmp-p, will search for the string p in the header of an SNMP packet, which can help track down which systems are polling SNMP devices. The second filter, host-durer, will display all traffic sent to the host named durer. As you can see, using the other buttons, filters may be modified, copied, and deleted very easily and quickly.

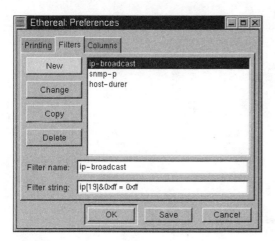

Figure 5.7 *IP Broadcast Filter Selection.*

If you want to use a filter while capturing network traffic, select the filter and then click the OK button. Assuming we select the ip-broadcast filter, **ethereal** places the filter definition into the filter text box of the capture window, as displayed in Figure 5.8.

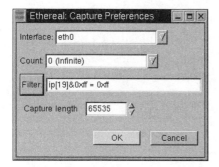

Figure 5.8 ethereal *filter displayed.*

Selecting the OK button in this window will activate the filter and begin the network traffic capture.

The display filter previously mentioned can also be used to select a subset of packets that have already been captured. For example, observe that in Figure 5.9 we have obtained FTP, TCP, and Telnet packets.

What if you would like to examine only the FTP packets? In this case, enter the filter string of FTP into the Filter box on the main

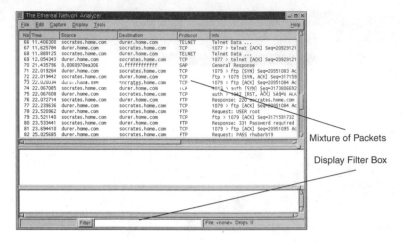

Figure 5.9 *Large list of packets sorted by protocol type.*

ethereal window, followed by the Enter key. Figure 5.10 shows the result of this action. As shown, the number of packets have been reduced significantly. What is interesting about display filters is that you can bring back the packets that were deleted from the summary panel. Just remove in this case the TCP filter and hit the Enter key. Once you do this, the complete list of packets will be restored. Packet selection is a powerful feature of this software and provides a very good way to narrow down the list when you're interested in reviewing only a few specific packets.

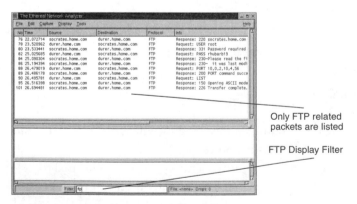

Figure 5.10 *FTP display filter.*

Bear in mind that FTP uses the TCP transport protocol and that additional FTP packets can be seen as TCP. The reason is that **ethe-**

real is sorting the packets by the port that the protocol uses. As a result, if we filter just FTP packets using the display filter, we end up getting all packets that used the FTP port. This has the unfortunate effect of not displaying other packets that may contain FTP information.

A useful feature of **ethereal** is that we can save the captured data in a regular UNIX file and also read capture files created by other software tools, such as **tcpdump** or **snoop**. The **snoop** tool provides the same basic capabilities and features as **tcpdump**, but is only available for the Sun Solaris platform. In contrast, **tcpdump** is available for many UNIX systems.

To save data from a capture, just select the Save item from the File menu. When this is done, a dialog box is displayed, as shown in Figure 5.11. If you will be doing a fair amount of capturing, it is recommended that a special directory be created to contain all the files. Also, it may be necessary to label the files with important information about the captured data so that, later on, they can be easily identified. Without complete and appropriate labeling of the files, the only way to know for sure what each capture file contains is to read it into the **ethereal** software and review it.

When the dialog box first appears, it contains the directory and any associated files from the location where the **ethereal** program was started. You can specify the destination file explicitly in the Selection: text box, or navigate using the drop-down menu. In this example, the path and filename

```
/home/capture/ftp-traffic-12-10-99.data
```

has been entered in the Selection: text box. As suggested, the filename contains both the type of packets and the date on which the capture took place. In most instances, this should be sufficient; however, additional information such as the name of the system the capture was from, additional protocol information, or other associated information could prove useful in the future. Note also that in the dialog window, three buttons are provided as a convenience to the user. These include Create Dir, Delete File, and Rename File buttons. Clicking the Create Dir button displays a small dialog box that requests the name of a directory to be created. Entering the directory name and clicking the Create button

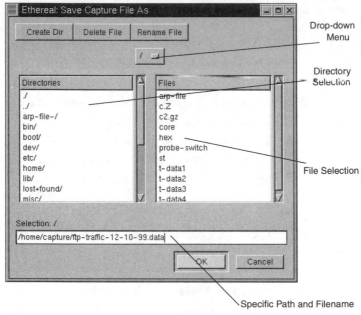

Figure 5.11 ethereal *save window.*

will create the directory, unless an error has occurred. The remaining two buttons function by operating on the files that have been
selected. Once a file is selected, each button will promptly carry
out the intended action as described by the button label.

Setting Preferences and Options

The **ethereal** tool provides some basic control over the look of the
main packet summary panel, the definition and maintenance of filters, and printing options. We have already discussed the operation
of filters, so we will concentrate on the summary panel options and
printing. To access the preferences, select the Preferences... item
from the Edit menu. Three tabs are shown that control access to
each of the associated screens. Selecting the Columns tab will display the packet summary panel options. Figure 5.12 shows the
window that will be displayed when this tab is selected.

By default, the summary panel of the main window displays the
packet number, timestamp, source address, destination address,
protocol, and additional packet information. One especially useful
feature of **ethereal** is that these fields are customizable. The user can

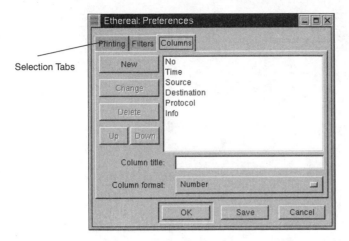

Selection Tabs

Figure 5.12 ethereal *preferences window.*

control which fields are displayed on the panel and in what order. This is very useful should the user need to view packet information in one or more specialized formats. One of the continuous complaints about some existing monitoring tools is the inability to produce reports; with these customizable features generating custom reports is a snap.

To access the printing options, click the Printing tab in the **ethereal** Preferences dialog box. Figure 5.13 shows the dialog box that will be displayed as a result.

The **ethereal** tool can print packets to either a printer or a regular UNIX file. The user can define a default printer and/or file to be used in subsequent sessions. In Figure 5.13, the UNIX **a2ps** command has been added to the Command: text box. This command converts ASCII data (regular text) to the Postscript language format for output to a Postscript-compatible printer. The command has a large number of options that can control the output, but by default it displays data in two side-by-side pages in landscape mode. This format, coupled with a smaller font size, means you can get a large amount of data within a relatively small number of pages. As shown in Figure 5.13, a default text file, ethereal.out, has been defined. However, with the current version of the software, this file isn't used when printing to a file. Rather, the user must enter another file name when printing to a file. Figure 5.14

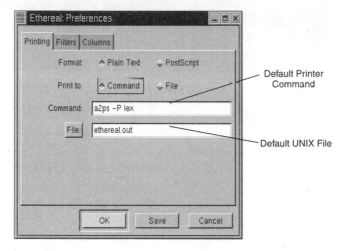

Figure 5.13 ethereal *printing preferences.*

contains a screen snapshot of the **a2ps** output as seen from a Post-script viewer application called **ghostview.** This is what you would expect to see when the file was printed. As you can see, using the **a2ps** program is an excellent way to output packet information.

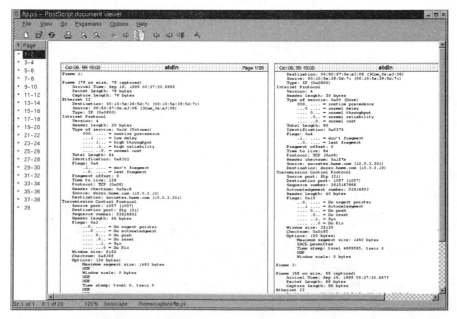

Figure 5.14 *Preview of the* **a2ps** *output.*

Because not all of the pages are visible in Figure 5.14, the user must use the scroll bars to examine the hidden portions of the output.

The **ethereal** software contains a display options window that can be used to alter the formatting of the time field contained within the summary panel. Selecting the Options... submenu from the Display menu will display the window shown in Figure 5.15.

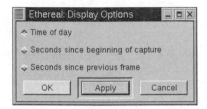

Figure 5.15 ethereal *time field display options window.*

One of the most useful display options is to display the time at which the packets arrived at the system. Selecting the Time of day option will display the exact time each packet was read by **ethereal**. This is very useful in tracking down network problems that happened during a specific period of time. The second option displays time as an offset from when the capture of packets first started. The final option shows time as an offset from each previous frame. Since the options are mutually exclusive, you can only select one of them. The Apply button may be used to alter the times within the summary panel without dismissing or deleting the options window. This will permit the user to view each time option in the summary panel. Figure 5.16 shows the summary packets with the Time of day option selected.

Additional Features

The Tools menu offers two additional menu commands that most users will find useful. First, **ethereal** provides a way to review all the printable ASCII values and certain protocol information that are contained within a TCP connection. Using the Follow TCP Stream menu item, the user can track all the data that transpired between systems.

Figure 5.17 shows the TCP stream after an FTP login session was captured from the system called socrates. In this example,

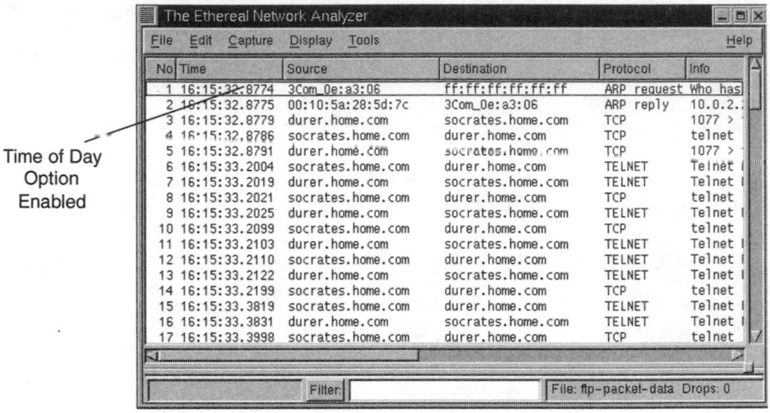

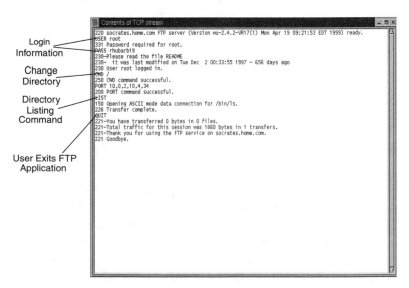

Figure 5.16 *Packets shown with Time of Day option.*

socrates permitted the user to login as root, change to the / directory, and execute a directory listing using the FTP **dir** command.

The window shown in Figure 5.17 only contains the data of the login sequence, transmission of the **CWD** and **LIST** commands, and the termination handshake information. You will note that the directory listing information is not displayed. The reason for this is simple: FTP uses an alternate TCP connection to transfer directory information. As a result, **ethereal** only shows the data from the first

Figure 5.17 *TCP login session information.*

connection. One interesting aspect of using the TCP stream feature
is that it secretly uses a special display filter when displaying TCP
session information. This reduces the packets in the summary
panel to only those packets involved within the given connection.
To cancel the effect of showing a single TCP connection, hit the
Enter key within the display filter text box that is shown on the
main **ethereal** window.

To examine the FTP directory listing resulting from the **LIST** command, the user must select a packet from that second connection.
To find out which packets are associated with a given TCP connection, the user must examine the destination ports. All data that
flows from an FTP connection, such as a directory listing or transfer of files, uses port 20. All FTP commands use port 21, which is
the same port on which the connection started. Once the user
selects a specific packet that is part of the second connection contained within the summary window, the directory information will
be displayed, as shown in Figure 5.18.

Since FTP uses a new TCP connection to handle every file transfer or directory listing, the user will need to select the appropriate
packets with those connections to obtain the data transferred. The
ability to see a complete TCP transaction using this method is significant. It permits the user to see the internal operation of many of
the TCP/IP protocols and services. This can have a profound
impact on network debugging and troubleshooting.

The other option under the Tools menu provides a summary of
the information about the capture. Selecting the Summary... submenu will display both generic and specific information about the
packets displayed within the packet summary panel. Figure 5.19
shows the **ethereal** summary window from the FTP session just discussed.

The summary window contains three sections; File, Data, and
Capture. The File section includes the name of the file (in the Name
field) to which the packets have been saved. The Length field shows
the size in bytes of this file. The Format field shows which file format was used to store the captured packets. The pcap format is
ethereal's native format. The Snapshot length field is the maximum
packet size used when capturing network traffic and, as previously
mentioned, is the default value.

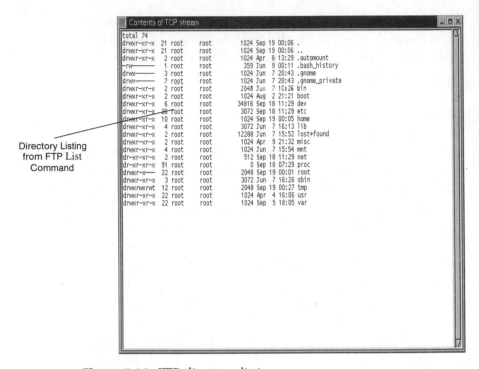

Figure 5.18 *FTP directory listing.*

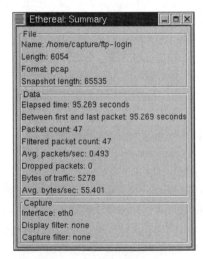

Figure 5.19 **ethereal** *packet summary window.*

The Data section includes the Elapsed time field, which indicates the total amount of time (in seconds) elapsed since receiving the last packet, i.e., the duration of the entire packet capture session. The next field, Between first and last packet, is the same as the Elapsed time field. The Packet count field shows the total number of packets received from the network or the number contained within the UNIX file. The Filtered Packet count field indicates the total number of packets that were accepted by the active filter. In this case, the default filter accepted all packets, and that is why it contains the same value as the Packet count field. The next field, Avg. packets/sec, contains the average number of packets coming into the network interface over a one second interval. The Dropped packets field indicates the number of packets that were dropped during the capture session. Figure 5.19 indicates that no packets were dropped. A number greater than zero indicates that the tool had to drop packets because they couldn't be processed quickly enough.

The Bytes of traffic field represents that amount of data that was transmitted within the packets, excluding any header portion from the low-level frames. The final field, Avg. bytes/sec, shows the transmission rate that measures the bytes per second during the capture period.

The Capture section specifies the Interface field, which shows the interface on the system from which the packets were obtained. In this situation, since the packet came from a UNIX file rather than a network interface, the field is marked as Unknown. The next field, Display filter, shows the name of the active display filter. In this case, it is not defined, and as a result, None is listed. The final field, Capture filter, lists the active capture filter. No active capture filter is defined, so None is displayed instead.

The **ethereal** software provides additional features that are not fully described in this text. These include:

- match selected

- colorize display

The Match Selected... option from the Display menu will scan each packet to search for a certain pattern or criteria. This is very useful if you are looking for a specific string or value after capturing a large number of packets. In these cases, manual inspection is not accurate or efficient and, therefore, an automated approach is necessary. The `Color Display...` option from the Display menu permits the user to change the foreground and background colors of certain packet types. This makes packet inspection and review much easier.

FpingTool

General Description

The **fping** command is very similar to the **ping** command previously discussed in this chapter. However, the **fping** software provides a few special functions that normal **ping** does not. Like its counterpart, **fping** uses the ICMP Echo Request and Reply to determine system reachability. However, unlike in regular **ping**, a list of hostnames or IP addresses may be specified on the command line. Also, **fping** will process a file that contains a list of hostnames or IP addresses. Instead of sending a request to a single target (like **ping** does), **fping** will send out an ICMP request to each target using a round-robin mechanism. Another important distinction is that **fping** was primarily intended to be used in script programming, not as a user command like normal **ping**. Still, when used on the command line, **fping** can effectively address some common IP address-related problems.

The command-line options available with **fping** can be divided into two sections. The first controls the various display options that can be used to customize the output. The second includes operational parameters that control the way **fping** obtains reachability information from devices and processes that information.

By default, when a target replies to an ICMP request, it is noted and removed from the list of targets that should be checked. If a target does not respond within the set time or retry limit, it is considered unreachable. The **fping** command can be made to loop indefinitely (like the normal **ping**) or send a user-defined number of ICMP requests to a target.

Display Options

Table 5.5 lists the many display options available with **fping**. Some of these options are self-evident and need no explanation beyond the description associated with that particular option. Others require additional detail and are described below.

Table 5.5 **fping** *display options list*

Option	Description
-A	Shows addresses of targets rather than hostnames
-Q	Like the -q option, but shows summary results information every n seconds. Unfortunately, this command doesn't seem to work
-a	Shows systems that are alive and reachable, given a list of targets on the command line
-d	Shows hostnames of targets instead of addresses. This is the reverse of the -A option
-e	Shows round-trip times from when packet was sent to receipt of reply
-q	Quiet mode. Don't display any results, but set the exit return status
-u	Shows systems are not alive, given a list of targets on the command line
-v	Displays command version information and Email address for sending comments and bug reports

One of the especially useful features of **fping** is that, given a list of targets following the -a option, it will display the systems that are reachable. For example, consider the following command:

```
# fping -a vermeer monet rodin louvre
monet
rodin
louvre
```

The hosts monet, rodin, and louvre are displayed—indicating that they are alive—while vermeer was not displayed because it didn't respond.

Conversely, the opposite list can be displayed with the `-u` option. In this case, the hosts that don't respond are displayed:

```
# fping -u vermeer monet rodin louvre
vermeer
```

We can go a step further and place a list of targets inside a file for processing. Let's assume a file called `host-list` contains the following IP addresses:

```
10.0.2.75
10.0.2.100
10.0.2.150
10.0.2.151
10.0.2.152
10.0.2.153
10.0.2.200
10.0.2.201
```

By redirecting the input to the `host-list` file, **fping** can process a larger number of targets instead of requiring you to specify them one by one on the command line:

```
# fping < host-list
10.0.2.75 is alive
10.0.2.100 is alive
10.0.2.150 is alive
10.0.2.151 is alive
10.0.2.152 is alive
10.0.2.153 is alive
10.0.2.200 is alive
10.0.2.201 is alive
```

This is a more reasonable way to handle a large number of hosts.

If you prefer, the `-f` option can also be used instead of the file redirection above. Thus the commands

```
# fping < host-list
# fping -f host-list
```

are functionally equivalent and yield the same result. However, the -f option is restricted to the `root` user, while any system user can use the redirection option shown in the first example.

The `alive` and `not alive` options (`-u` and `-a`) are very handy and can be used in a variety of situations. For example, let's assume you want to be notified via Email when certain systems are down. A simple script, as shown in Listing 5.1, might accomplish this for you.

Listing 5.1 *Sample* **fping** *script to identify down systems*

```
 1  #!/usr/bin/ksh
 2
 3  #
 4  # Simple script to notify user when
 5  # systems are down
 6  #
 7
 8  FILE=$1
 9
10  FPINGCMD=`fping -u < $FILE`
11  MAIL=/bin/mailx
12  USER=root
13
14  if [ "$FPINGCMD" != "" ]; then
15          $MAIL -s "down system(s)" -u $USER $FPINGCMD"
16  fi
```

This script runs the **fping** command (line 10) against the hosts included in the specified file, and if any devices contained in the file can't be reached, the user root is sent mail, as shown on line 15. Obviously, a more robust and elaborate script could be written, but the point here is that **fping** can help automate some small network management tasks.

On special occasions, it might be necessary to manipulate IP addresses directly, rather than hostnames as in the previous examples. When given a list of hostnames, it would be nice to return IP addresses. The -A option directs **fping** to display IP address information instead of the hostname. So, in our example within Listing 5.1, we process a file that contains a list of IP addresses. In this case, we will process a list of valid hostnames. The file hostname-list contains the following:

```
monet
durer
vermeer
rembrandt
lex-mark
```

(continued)

```
gateway
rodin
louvre
```

By processing this file with the `-A` option, we get:

```
# fping -A < hostname-list
10.0.2.126 is alive
134.111.2.1 is alive
10.0.2.75 is alive
10.0.2.75 is alive
10.0.2.129 is alive
128.197.2.200 alive
10.0.2.200 is alive
10.0.2.101 is alive
```

The **fping** command not only provides a way to determine whether systems are operating on the network, but also can provide some amount of performance information. In particular, a few options are available that display various statistics regarding the performance from the source of the **fping** to each target. The `-e` option will show the round-trip or elapsed time from the moment the packet is sent until it returns a reply. The command

```
# fping -e rembrandt
rembrandt is alive (2.82 ms)
```

provides output very similar to what you get when you use **ping** command. Another useful option, `-s`, shows a more complete cumulative statistical profile of the target:

```
# fping -s rembrandt
rembrandt is alive
        1 targets
        1 alive
        0 unreachable
        0 unknown addresses
        0 timeouts (waiting for response)
        1 ICMP Echos sent
        1 ICMP Echo Replies received
        0 other ICMP received
 3.09 ms (min round trip time)
 3.09 ms (avg round trip time)
 3.09 ms (max round trip time)
        0.015 sec (elapsed real time)
```

This option provides a detailed breakdown that shows the overall number of targets and the number of targets found alive (in this case, 1). Other information is self-explanatory, and the actual elapsed time is measured in seconds. To determine the accuracy of this information, consider this example:

```
# date; fping -s rodin; date
Sat Oct  3 13:25:01 EDT 1998
rodin is unreachable
        1 targets
        0 alive
        1 unreachable
        0 unknown addresses
        4 timeouts (waiting for response)
        4 ICMP Echos sent
        0 ICMP Echo Replies received
        0 other ICMP received
 0.00 ms (min round trip time)
 0.00 ms (avg round trip time)
 0.00 ms (max round trip time)
        4.080 sec (elapsed real time)
Sat Oct  3 13:25:05 EDT 1998
```

Here, **fping** is surrounded by the UNIX **date** command. The **date** program is executed before the **fping** is started and after it finishes execution. Discounting any delays from the operating system, the elapsed time is fairly accurate. The elapsed time might not be 100% accurate due to several factors, but for most applications it should be sufficiently accurate. A non-reachable system was chosen for this example so that **fping** would be forced to send out additional packets and wait the maximum amount of time. This gives a larger amount of time to measure the requests without resorting to using additional options necessary when the target is a live system.

Operational Options

Table 5.6 lists the many operational options available with **fping**. Some of these options are self-evident and need no explanation beyond the description associated with that particular option. Other options require additional detail and are described below.

The **fping** command sends a number of requests to a target, waiting longer for a reply with each successive request. The value used is determined by a wait factor, which uses a multiplier for each

Table 5.6 **fping** *operational options list*

Option	Description
-b	The number of bytes of data to include in the **ping** request
-B	This option followed by a value is used to determine the delay time that **fping** uses when waiting for replies. The value is used as a multiplier and must be given in floating point format.
-c	Determines the number of requests sent to each target
-C	Similar to -c, but per-target statistics are displayed in a format that is easier to parse
-f	Obtains list of targets from specified file. This is restricted to the root user. Regular users should use file redirection instead of this option
-l	Sends an indefinite amount of requests to target; can be stopped by ^c (**control-c**)
-p	Sets the amount of time in milliseconds that **fping** will wait between successive packets for a target. This is only meaningful with -l, -c, or -C options.
-r	The number of attempts that will be made to **ping** a specified target. The default value is 3.
-t	The amount of time to wait for the first response to the initial packet request. The default is 500 milliseconds.

request that doesn't receive a reply. The value of 1.5 is the default multiplier. To change this value, use the -B option followed by a floating-point value. For example, using the default, we observe the following:

```
# fping -s rembrandt
rembrandt is unreachable
       1 targets
```

```
          0 alive
          1 unreachable
          0 unknown addresses
          4 timeouts (waiting for response)
          4 ICMP Echos sent
          0 ICMP Echo Replies received
          0 other ICMP received
    0.00 ms (min round trip time)
    0.00 ms (avg round trip time)
    0.00 ms (max round trip time)
          4.077 sec (elapsed real time)
```

By using the -B option, we can double the delay factor for each packet sent. As a result, we see a significant amount of time used for each of the packet requests:

```
# fping -B 3.0 -s rembrandt
rembrandt is unreachable
          1 targets
          0 alive
          1 unreachable
          0 unknown addresses
          4 timeouts (waiting for response)
          4 ICMP Echos sent
          0 ICMP Echo Replies received
          0 other ICMP received
    0.00 ms (min round trip time)
    0.00 ms (avg round trip time)
    0.00 ms (max round trip time)
          20.037 sec (elapsed real time)
```

Notice that the elapsed time has increased to approximately 20 seconds because the delay factor is multiplied by each packet sent.

To control the number of requests **fping** sends to each target, use the -c option. By default, four attempts are made before giving up on the specified system. The -c option can be used to change the number of attempts :

```
# fping -c 5 monet
monet : [0], 84 bytes, 3.55 ms (3.55 avg, 0% loss)
monet : [1], 84 bytes, 2.53 ms (3.04 avg, 0% loss)
monet : [2], 84 bytes, 1.63 ms (2.57 avg, 0% loss)
monet : [3], 84 bytes, 1.99 ms (2.42 avg, 0% loss)
monet : [4], 84 bytes, 1.64 ms (2.26 avg, 0% loss)
monet : xmt/rcv/%loss = 5/5/0%, min/avg/max = 1.63/2.26/3.55
```

Nmap Tool

The **nmap** tool is a utility that locates and identifies all available
TCP and UDP ports on a target host system. Also known as a port
scanner, **nmap** will scan TCP ports from 0 to 1024 (by default),
attempting to determine the service listening on ports that will
accept a connection. The software has been built to maximize network bandwidth while maintaining processing resources on the
host used to run **nmap**.

Traditionally, **nmap** is viewed more as a security monitoring tool
used to locate security weaknesses on a system rather than a network management tool. However, network managers will find this
tool very helpful in identifying network services on unknown systems. A word of caution is in order: The tool has been implicated
in helping people to obtain illegal access to networks and associated systems all over the Internet. As a result, **nmap** has received
some negative publicity. If you use this tool on your own networks,
you may be OK, but if you intend to use this tool on networks, systems, or sites that you do not control, you should seek permission
first. Remember, having respect for the privacy of others' networks
and systems means that the favor may be returned to you someday.

On occasion, devices that interfere with normal network operations may be added to the networks. Also, the origin or nature of
these systems may not be apparent and the SNMP agent may be
inactive due to being disabled or not configured for some reason. It
may become necessary to scan the devices to learn more about the
services they provide. For instance, let's assume a device added to
the network is believed to be the cause of a network performance
problem, but because the device doesn't seem to support services
like **telnet**, it is difficult to identify the device.

We can **ping** the device, but this doesn't really provide us with
much information:

```
# ping 10.0.2.10
PING 10.0.2.10 (10.0.2.10): 56 data bytes
64 bytes from 10.0.2.10: icmp_seq=0 ttl=128 time=0.7 ms
64 bytes from 10.0.2.10: icmp_seq=1 ttl=128 time=0.7 ms

--- 10.0.2.10 ping statistics ---
```

```
2 packets transmitted, 2 packets received, 0% packet loss
round-trip min/avg/max = 0.7/0.7/0.7 ms
```

We can also **telnet** the device, but the connection never makes it because the device refuses this type of access:

```
# telnet 10.0.2.10
Trying 10.0.2.10...
telnet: Unable to connect to remote host: Connection
refused
```

However, we can let **nmap** probe the device and help us determine something about it.

```
nmap -O 10.0.2.10
```

As it turns out, the output of the **nmap** command fits the profile of the Windows 95 workstation :

```
Starting nmap V. 2.12 by Fyodor (fyodor@dhp.com, www.insecure.org/nmap/)
Interesting ports on  (10.0.2.10):
Port    State      Protocol  Service
135     open       tcp        loc-srv
139     open       tcp        netbios-ssn
427     open       tcp        svrloc

TCP Sequence Prediction: Class=trivial time dependency
                         Difficulty=13 (Easy)
Remote operating system guess: Windows NT4 / Win95 / Win98
```

Normally it wouldn't be easy to determine that a troublesome device was a Windows workstation, but using **nmap**, most systems can be identified fairly quickly and easily.

The **nmap** tool can also examine the networking services running on known systems within the network. This is useful in determining which system services are available across a number of systems. For instance, the following output was produced by using **nmap** on a Linux workstation system call socrates:

```
# nmap -O socrates

Starting nmap V. 2.12 by Fyodor (fyodor@dhp.com,
www.insecure.org/nmap/)
Interesting ports on socrates.home.com (10.0.2.201):
Port    State      Protocol  Service
```

(continued)

```
21      open    tcp     ftp
22      open    tcp     ssh
23      open    tcp     telnet
25      open    tcp     smtp
80      opcn    tcp     http
111     open    tcp     sunrpc
512     open    tcp     exec
513     open    tcp     login
514     open    tcp     shell
515     open    tcp     printer
610     open    tcp     npmp-local
615     open    tcp     unknown
620     open    tcp     unknown
982     open    tcp     unknown
1013    open    tcp     unknown
1024    open    tcp     unknown
6000    open    tcp     X11

TCP Sequence Prediction: Class=random positive increments
                         Difficulty=5369390 (Good luck!)
Remote operating system guess: Linux 2.1.122 - 2.1.132;
2.2.0-pre1 - 2.2.2
```

The -O option used here tells **nmap** that we would like it to
attempt to identify the target system using what it calls TCP/IP *fin-
gerprinting*. What this basically means is that several different
techniques are used to detect differences within operating systems
or the running software contained within the target device. Using
the data obtained from the device, **nmap** compares this information
with the *fingerprints* of known devices and systems. Every device
that **nmap** attempts to identify is compared to the data stored in a
file called nmap-os-fingerprints, which is located in the directory
/usr/local/lib/nmap. This file contains a large number of fingerprints for systems and networking devices. If you encounter a
device that doesn't match the entries in the fingerprints file, you
may want to consider sending the scan to the author of **nmap**.

The **nmap** software supports a number of important functions
and a number of command-line options. Also, it provides a large
number of system scanning techniques, as shown in Table 5.7. This
table also includes the associated command option and a general
description of the process involved with each scanning method.

The **nmap** tool was designed to work very efficiently when probing a large number of hosts on many different networks. Also, it is

Table 5.7 **nmap** *scanning techniques*

Scan Method	Command Line Option	Description
UDP port	-sU	Scans available UDP ports in the range of 1 to 1024, plus ports listed within the /usr/local/lib/nmap/ nmap-services file
TCP connect	-sT	Scans available TCP ports in the range of 1 to 1024, plus ports listed within the /usr/local/lib/nmap/ nmap-services file; uses low-level connect system call in attempt to establish connection to target system
TCP SYN (half)	-sS	Scans TCP ports using *half-open* technique, which means only one side of a TCP connection is open and waiting for acknowledgment
FTP Proxy	-b	FTP bounce scan; uses proxy feature in FTP services to attempt connection
Reverse Indent	-I	Enables TCP reverse ident scanning, which requests that the ident server be running; when enabled, permits the identification of the owner of the process that uses a TCP port
Ping Sweep	-sP	Uses ICMP when scanning probing systems. This is equivalent to issuing a **ping** request.
FIN	-sF	Known as stealth FIN, this scanning option uses FIN TCP packet in an attempt to elicit a response

Table 5.7 nmap *scanning techniques (continued)*

Xmax Tree	-sX	Similar to FIN but turns on FIN, URG, and PUSH bits within the TCP packet
Null Scan	-sN	Similar to FIN but turns off all TCP flags

considered one of the fastest port scanners available within the public domain, and it even rivals some commercial products as well. The command-line options are divided into two categories; the first is *scanning options*, listed in Table 5.7. The second category is *additional options*, which refine or control the behavior of the tool. Table 5.8 lists these additional options.

Table 5.8 *Additional* **nmap** *options*

Option	Description
-F	Fast scan mode; only scans the ports found in the nmap-services file
-i	Obtains target information from a specified file versus using a command line
-m	Displays minimal output which includes hostname, port numbers, etc.
-o	Logs program results to specified file
-p	Uses specified port or range instead of defaults
-v	Enables verbose mode, which provides additional information on the program's activity

Since **nmap** supports a large number of command-line arguments and options, use the -h option to list a synopsis:

```
# nmap -h
nmap V. 2.12 usage: nmap [Scan Type(s)] [Options] <host or net #1 ... [#N]>
Scan types
    -sT tcp connect() port scan
    -sS tcp SYN stealth port scan (must be root)
```

    -sF,-sX,-sN Stealth FIN, Xmas, or Null scan (only works against UNIX).
    -sP ping "scan". Find which hosts on specified network(s) are up but
        don't port scan them
    -sU UDP port scan, must be r00t
    -b <ftp_relay_host> ftp "bounce attack" port scan
Options (none are required, most can be combined):
    -f use tiny fragmented packets for SYN, FIN, Xmas, or NULL scan
    -P0 Don't ping hosts (needed to scan www.microsoft.com and others)
    -PT Use "TCP Ping" to see what hosts are up (for normal and ping scans)
    -PT21 Use "TCP Ping" scan with probe destination port of 21 (or
        whatever)
    -PI Use ICMP ping packet to determines hosts that are up
    -PB Do BOTH TCP & ICMP scans in parallel (TCP dest port can be specified
        after the 'B')
    -PS Use TCP SYN sweep rather than the default ACK sweep used in "TCP
        ping"
    -O Use TCP/IP fingerprinting to guess what OS the remote host is running
    -p <range> ports: ex: '-p 23' will only try port 23 of the host(s)
        '-p 20-30,63000-' scans 20-30 and 63000-65535. default: 1-1024
  + /etc/services
    -Ddecoy_host1,decoy2,ME,decoy3[,...] Launch scans from decoy host(s)
        along with the real one. If you care about the order your real IP
        appears, stick "ME" somewhere in the list. Even if the target
        detects the scan, they are unlikely to know which IP is scanning
        them and which are decoys.
    -F fast scan. Only scans ports in /etc/services, a la strobe(1).
    -I Get identd (rfc 1413) info on listening TCP processes.
    -n Don't DNS resolve anything unless we have to (makes ping scans
        faster)
    -R Try to resolve all hosts, even down ones (can take a lot of time)
    -o <logfile> Output scan logs to <logfile> in human readable.
    -m <logfile> Output scan logs to <logfile> in machine parseable format.
    -i <inputfile> Grab IP numbers or hostnames from file. Use '-' for
        stdin
    -g <portnumber> Sets the source port used for scans. 20 and 53 are good
        choices.
    -S <your_IP> If you want to specify the source address of SYN or FYN
        scan.
    -v Verbose. Its use is recommended. Use twice for greater effect.
    -h help, print this junk. Also see http://www.insecure.org/nmap/
    -V Print version number and exit.
    -e <devicename>. Send packets on interface <devicename>
        (eth0,ppp0,etc.).
    -q quash argv to something benign, currently set to "pine". (deprecated)
Hostnames specified as internet hostname or IP address. Optional '/mask'
        specifies subnet. For example: cert.org/24 or 192.88.209.5/24 or

(continued)

```
      192.88.209.0-255 or '128.88.209.*' all scan CERT's Class C.
SEE THE MAN PAGE FOR MORE THOROUGH EXPLANATIONS AND EXAMPLES
```

One of the strengths of **nmap** is that it supports many different scanning methodologies. Some scanners only support TCP scanning, which is very useful but has limitations. For instance, some networking devices don't provide generic TCP networking services like traditional UNIX systems do; they may only support a limited set of UDP services. In this instance, using a port scanner that only supports TCP would be useless. Consider the following scan and associated output:

```
# nmap -sT probe.home.com

Starting nmap V. 2.12 by Fyodor (fyodor@dhp.com,
www.insecure.org/nmap/)
Interesting ports on probe.home.com (10.0.2.50):
(Not showing ports in state: filtered)
Port     State        Protocol  Service

Nmap run completed -- 1 IP address (1 host up) scanned in
66 seconds
```

As you can see in this output, **nmap** didn't detect any services on the target system. However, scanning using the -sU option instructs **nmap** to scan a range of UDP ports instead of the default TCP port range. Thus, interestingly enough,

```
# nmap -sU 10.0.2.50
```

yields the following output when executed:

```
WARNING: -sU is now UDP scan -- for TCP FIN scan use -sF

Starting nmap V. 2.12 by Fyodor (fyodor@dhp.com,
www.insecure.org/nmap/)
Interesting ports on probe.home.com (10.0.2.50):
Port     State        Protocol  Service
161      open         udp       snmp

Nmap run completed -- 1 IP address (1 host up) scanned in
12 seconds
```

We find an SNMP process listening on the standard 161 port. This tells us that this device only supports SNMP and nothing else. If we wanted, we could query the device further using SNMP-based tools to determine more information about the agent that resides within the device. See Chapter 8, "Using SNMP Tools," for additional information regarding tools used to accomplish this task.

The default behavior of **nmap** is to use the TCP port scanning method on the standard TCP ports that have been included within the associated services file. Normally the file nmap-services is located in the /usr/local/lib/nmap directory, and **nmap** will use these ports plus scan all ports with the range of 1 to 1024. Using just the default values, **nmap** can be very useful. Consider the following command:

```
# nmap sparky
```

It shows a large amount of information on the host known as sparky:

```
Starting nmap V. 2.12 by Fyodor (fyodor@dhp.com, www.inse-
cure.org/nmap/)
```

```
Interesting ports on sparky.home.com (10.0.2.12):
Port      State        Protocol    Service
21        open         tcp         ftp
23        open         tcp         telnet
25        open         tcp         smtp
53        open         tcp         domain
79        open         tcp         finger
80        open         tcp         http
98        open         tcp         linuxconf
111       open         tcp         sunrpc
113       open         tcp         auth
119       open         tcp         nntp
513       open         tcp         login
514       open         tcp         shell
515       open         tcp         printer
652       open         tcp         unknown
673       open         tcp         unknown
678       open         tcp         unknown
683       open         tcp         unknown
713       open         tcp         unknown
1024      open         tcp         unknown
6000      open         tcp         X11
```

```
Nmap run completed --1 IP address (1 host up) scanned in 1 second
```

The output above was derived from a scan of a Red Hat Linux 6.0 system. As you can see, this scan shows that many of the standard UNIX services are running. Only TCP services are listed because this is the default mode; this is equivalent to using the command-line option -sT. The services running the system includes ftp, Telnet, smtp, and others. Also, several ports were not identified, and these are marked as Unknown. These ports include such services as amd on port 713, which is an automounter service, and port 678, which is the rpc.mountd rpc service, but **nmap** didn't recognize them as such. Additional services can be detected by using the **netstat** command while connected to the system. This command was described in the previous chapter.

If we wanted to scan UDP and TCP ports at the same time, we need to use the -sU and -sT options together. If we don't combine them, **nmap** will only scan one or the other. The command

```
# nmap -sU -sT sparky
```

will yield the following:

```
WARNING:   -sU is now UDP scan -- for TCP FIN scan use -sF

Starting nmap V. 2.12 by Fyodor (fyodor@dhp.com,
www.insecure.org/nmap/)
Interesting ports on socrates.home.com (10.0.2.201):
Port    State      Protocol   Service
21      open       tcp        ftp
23      open       tcp        telnet
25      open       tcp        smtp
53      open       udp        domain
53      open       tcp        domain
79      open       tcp        finger
80      open       tcp        http
98      open       tcp        linuxconf
111     open       udp        sunrpc
111     open       tcp        sunrpc
113     open       tcp        auth
119     open       tcp        nntp
161     open       udp        snmp
177     open       udp        xdmcp
513     open       tcp        login
514     open       tcp        shell
515     open       tcp        printer
517     open       udp        talk
518     open       udp        ntalk
```

```
650      open     udp     bwnfs
652      open     tcp     unknown
661      open     udp     unknown
671      open     udp     unknown
673      open     tcp     unknown
676      open     udp     unknown
678      open     tcp     unknown
681      open     udp     unknown
683      open     tcp     unknown
713      open     tcp     unknown
714      open     udp     unknown
800      open     udp     mdbs_daemon
1022     open     udp     unknown
1023     open     udp     unknown
1024     open     udp     unknown
1024     open     tcp     unknown
1026     open     udp     unknown
2049     open     udp     nfs
6000     open     tcp     X11
```

```
Nmap run completed -- 1 IP address (1 host up) scanned in 5
seconds
```

Note that now both UDP and TCP ports are displayed, sorted by port number.

As with any good port scanner, the ability to scan a particular port is paramount. One good way to determine if all the systems on a network have a standard set of network services or a particular service is to scan the network with a specific port number in mind. For example, assume we would like to determine if all the systems on the 10.0.2.0 network support some sort of SNMP agent. The command:

```
# nmap -p 161 -sU -o results 10.0.2.0/24
```

tells **nmap** to scan port 161 (the SNMP port) on network 10.0.2.0 using UDP and then save the output information in a file called results. If we display this file, we find the following:

```
# Log of: nmap -p 161 -sU -o result 10.0.2.0/24
No ports open for host durer.home.com (10.0.2.10)
No ports open for host king.home.com (10.0.2.21)
No ports open for host derry.home.com (10.0.2.25)
Interesting ports on probe.home.com (10.0.2.50):
```

(continued)

```
Port    State      Protocol  Service
161     open       udp       snmp

Interesting ports on switch.home.com (10.0.2.60):
Port    State      Protocol  Service
161     open       udp       snmp
Interesting ports on tux.home.com (10.0.2.65 ):
Port    State      Protocol  Service
161     open       udp       snmp

Interesting ports on didymus-gw2.home.com (10.0.2.129):
Port    State      Protocol  Service
161     open       udp       snmp

Interesting ports on didymus-gw3.home.com (10.0.2.130):
Port    State      Protocol  Service
161     open       udp       snmp
```

```
Host  (10.0.2.255) seems to be a subnet broadcast address
(returned 2 extra pin
gs).  Skipping host.
```

As it turns out, this is a very reasonable mechanism to use to inventory service on a grand scale. Any TCP or UDP service can be queried using this approach.

This example demonstrates another powerful feature of this tool. Namely, we can specify the target systems or networks using a few different notations. First, we can specify an IP address using a list or ranges for each part of the address. Thus we can scan an entire IP class with the "*" character. For instance, 128.197.*.* permits the scanning of the whole B class network. Another way to express this is to use the dash character. Thus 128.197.1-255.1-255 is functionally the same as using the 128.197.*.* syntax. Second, we can use the mask notation as shown in the previous **nmap** command example. Namely, 128.197.0.0/16 will mask and is equivalent to the two examples using either the "*" or "-" characters. Finally, we can use a numbered sequence combined with the range syntax. Thus 128.197.90.1, 2, 3, 4, 5, 100-105 will scan the following addresses: 128.197.90.1, 128.197.90.2, 128.197.90.3, 128.197.90.4, and 128.197.90.5, as well as addresses 128.197.90.100 through 128.197.90.105. Using these IP formats greatly improves the ease of scanning entire subnets or networks.

When scanning networks, it is sometimes helpful to know exactly what **nmap** is doing at all times. For this reason, the -v option has been provided. Bear in mind that a fair amount of output may be generated as a result, so it might be important to use this option with caution. In the previous example, we scanned an entire subnet. If we added the -v option with this command and reduced the number of targets by half using an IP range, the command **nmap -v -p 161 10.0.2.1-127** would display the following:

```
No scantype specified, assuming vanilla tcp connect() scan.
   Use -sP if you reall
y don't want to portscan (and just want to see what hosts
   are up).

Starting nmap V. 2.12 by Fyodor (fyodor@dhp.com,
   www.insecure.org/nmap/)
Host  (10.0.2.0) appears to be down, skipping it.
Host  (10.0.2.1) appears to be down, skipping it.
Host  (10.0.2.2) appears to be down, skipping it.
Host  (10.0.2.3) appears to be down, skipping it.
Host  (10.0.2.4) appears to be down, skipping it.
Host  (10.0.2.5) appears to be down, skipping it.
Host  (10.0.2.6) appears to be down, skipping it.
Host  (10.0.2.7) appears to be down, skipping it.
Host  (10.0.2.8) appears to be down, skipping it.
Host  (10.0.2.9) appears to be down, skipping it.
Host durer.home.com (10.0.2.10) appears to be up ... good.
Initiating TCP connect() scan against durer.home.com
   (10.0.2.10)
The TCP connect scan took 0 seconds to scan 1 ports.
No ports open for host durer.home.com (10.0.2.10)
Host  (10.0.2.11) appears to be down, skipping it.
Host  (10.0.2.12) appears to be down, skipping it.
Host  (10.0.2.13) appears to be down, skipping it.
Host  (10.0.2.14) appears to be down, skipping it.
Host  (10.0.2.15) appears to be down, skipping it.
Host  (10.0.2.16) appears to be down, skipping it.
Host  (10.0.2.17) appears to be down, skipping it.
Host  (10.0.2.18) appears to be down, skipping it.
Host  (10.0.2.19) appears to be down, skipping it.
Host  (10.0.2.20) appears to be down, skipping it.
Host  (10.0.2.21) appears to be down, skipping it.
Host  (10.0.2.22) appears to be down, skipping it.
Host  (10.0.2.23) appears to be down, skipping it.
```

(continued)

```
Host (10.0.2.24) appears to be down, skipping it.
Host (10.0.2.25) appears to be down, skipping it.
Host (10.0.2.26) appears to be down, skipping it.
Host (10.0.2.27) appears to be down, skipping it.
Host (10.0.2.28) appears to be down, skipping it.
Host (10.0.2.29) appears to be down, skipping it.
Host (10.0.2.30) appears to be down, skipping it.
Host (10.0.2.31) appears to be down, skipping it.
Host (10.0.2.32) appears to be down, skipping it.
Host (10.0.2.33) appears to be down, skipping it.
Host (10.0.2.34) appears to be down, skipping it.
Host (10.0.2.35) appears to be down, skipping it.
Host (10.0.2.36) appears to be down, skipping it.
Host (10.0.2.37) appears to be down, skipping it.
Host (10.0.2.38) appears to be down, skipping it.
Host (10.0.2.39) appears to be down, skipping it.
Host (10.0.2.40) appears to be down, skipping it.
Host (10.0.2.41) appears to be down, skipping it.
Host (10.0.2.42) appears to be down, skipping it.
Host (10.0.2.43) appears to be down, skipping it.
Host (10.0.2.44) appears to be down, skipping it.
Host (10.0.2.45) appears to be down, skipping it.
Host (10.0.2.46) appears to be down, skipping it.
Host (10.0.2.47) appears to be down, skipping it.
Host (10.0.2.48) appears to be down, skipping it.
Host (10.0.2.49) appears to be down, skipping it.
Host probe.home.com (10.0.2.50) appears to be up ... good.
Initiating FIN,NULL, UDP, or Xmas stealth scan against
    probe.home.com (10.0.2.50)
The UDP or stealth FIN/NULL/XMAS scan took 0 seconds to
    scan 1 ports.
Interesting ports on probe.home.com (10.0.2.50):
Port    State       Protocol  Service
161     open        udp       snmp
Host (10.0.2.51) appears to be down, skipping it.
Host (10.0.2.52) appears to be down, skipping it.
Host (10.0.2.53) appears to be down, skipping it.
Host (10.0.2.54) appears to be down, skipping it.
Host (10.0.2.55) appears to be down, skipping it.
Host (10.0.2.56) appears to be down, skipping it.
Host (10.0.2.57) appears to be down, skipping it.
Host (10.0.2.58) appears to be down, skipping it.
Host (10.0.2.59) appears to be down, skipping it.
Host switch.home.com (10.0.2.60) appears to be up ... good.
IInitiating FIN,NULL, UDP, or Xmas stealth scan against
    switch.home.com (10.0.2.60)
The UDP or stealth FIN/NULL/XMAS scan took 0 seconds to
    scan 1 ports.
```

```
Interesting ports on switch.home.com (10.0.2.60):
Port    State        Protocol  Service
161     open         udp          snmp
Host (10.0.2.61) appears to be down, skipping it.
Host (10.0.2.62) appears to be down, skipping it.
Host (10.0.2.63) appears to be down, skipping it.
Host (10.0.2.64) appears to be down, skipping it.
Host tux.home.com (10.0.2.65) appears to be up ... good.
IInitiating FIN,NULL, UDP, or Xmas stealth scan against
   switch.home.com (10.0.2.65)
The UDP or stealth FIN/NULL/XMAS scan took 0 seconds to
   scan 1 ports.
Interesting ports on tux.home.com (10.0.2.65):
Port    State        Protocol  Service
161     open         udp          snmp
No ports open for host switch.home.com (10.0.2.60)
Host (10.0.2.66) appears to be down, skipping it.
Host (10.0.2.67) appears to be down, skipping it.
Host (10.0.2.68) appears to be down, skipping it.
Host (10.0.2.69) appears to be down, skipping it.
Host (10.0.2.70) appears to be down, skipping it.
Host (10.0.2.71) appears to be down, skipping it.
Host (10.0.2.72) appears to be down, skipping it.
Host (10.0.2.73) appears to be down, skipping it.
Host (10.0.2.74) appears to be down, skipping it.
Host (10.0.2.75) appears to be down, skipping it.
Host (10.0.2.76) appears to be down, skipping it.
Host (10.0.2.77) appears to be down, skipping it.
Host (10.0.2.78) appears to be down, skipping it.
Host (10.0.2.79) appears to be down, skipping it.
Host (10.0.2.80) appears to be down, skipping it.
Host (10.0.2.81) appears to be down, skipping it.
Host (10.0.2.82) appears to be down, skipping it.
Host (10.0.2.83) appears to be down, skipping it.
Host (10.0.2.84) appears to be down, skipping it.
Host (10.0.2.85) appears to be down, skipping it.
Host (10.0.2.86) appears to be down, skipping it.
Host (10.0.2.87) appears to be down, skipping it.
Host (10.0.2.88) appears to be down, skipping it.
Host (10.0.2.89) appears to be down, skipping it.
Host (10.0.2.90) appears to be down, skipping it.
Host (10.0.2.91) appears to be down, skipping it.
Host (10.0.2.92) appears to be down, skipping it.
Ilost (10.0.2.93) appears to be down, skipping it.
Host (10.0.2.94) appears to be down, skipping it.
Host (10.0.2.95) appears to be down, skipping it.
```

(continued)

```
Host  (10.0.2.96) appears to be down, skipping it.
Host  (10.0.2.97) appears to be down, skipping it.
Host  (10.0.2.98) appears to be down, skipping it.
Host  (10.0.2.99) appears to be down, skipping it.
Host  (10.0.2.100) appears to be down, skipping it.
Host  (10.0.2.101) appears to be down, skipping it.
Host  (10.0.2.102) appears to be down, skipping it.
Host  (10.0.2.103) appears to be down, skipping it.
Host  (10.0.2.104) appears to be down, skipping it.
Host  (10.0.2.105) appears to be down, skipping it.
Host  (10.0.2.106) appears to be down, skipping it.
Host  (10.0.2.107) appears to be down, skipping it.
Host  (10.0.2.108) appears to be down, skipping it.
Host  (10.0.2.109) appears to be down, skipping it.
Host  (10.0.2.110) appears to be down, skipping it.
Host  (10.0.2.111) appears to be down, skipping it.
Host  (10.0.2.112) appears to be down, skipping it.
Host  (10.0.2.113) appears to be down, skipping it.
Host  (10.0.2.114) appears to be down, skipping it.
Host  (10.0.2.115) appears to be down, skipping it.
Host  (10.0.2.116) appears to be down, skipping it.
Host  (10.0.2.117) appears to be down, skipping it.
Host  (10.0.2.118) appears to be down, skipping it.
Host  (10.0.2.119) appears to be down, skipping it.
Host  (10.0.2.120) appears to be down, skipping it.
Host  (10.0.2.121) appears to be down, skipping it.
Host  (10.0.2.122) appears to be down, skipping it.
Host  (10.0.2.123) appears to be down, skipping it.
Host  (10.0.2.124) appears to be down, skipping it.
Host  (10.0.2.125) appears to be down, skipping it.
Host  (10.0.2.126) appears to be down, skipping it.
Host didymus-gw2.home.com (10.0.2.127) appears to be up ...
    good.
Initiating FIN,NULL, UDP, or Xmas stealth scan against
    didymus-gw2.home.com (10.0.2.127)
The UDP or stealth FIN/NULL/XMAS scan took 0 seconds to
    scan 1 ports.
Interesting ports on didymus-gw2.home.com (10.0.2.127):
Port    State       Protocol  Service
161     open        udp       snmp

Nmap run completed -- 127 IP addresses (5 hosts up) scanned
    in 1 second
```

As you can see, a large amount of output was produced despite the fact that only half of the subnet was scanned. Also, **nmap** identified four devices that support SNMP agents, as noted by the lines containing the string: `Host switch.home.com (10.0.2.60) appears to be up ... good`. Note that the most important point with respect to this example is that **nmap** is very smart about probing non-existent or down systems; it didn't spend much time or resources probing nonresponsive systems. Before **nmap** attempts to scan a device, it first determines if it is reachable on the network by performing a **ping** on it. This not only reduces the amount of time required to perform the scan and lessens system resources needed, but it helps to preserve network bandwidth as well. It is important not to underestimate the impact that scanning can have on a network, and **nmap** does a good job to reduce the network requirements while probing.

Nmap Output Listing

The listing below shows some of the **nmap** output when it is used against a series of different computer systems and networking devices. Certainly your mileage may vary, but this tool is quite good at detecting different kinds of systems. This section includes both output and a general description of the systems and supported networking services. Since most of the systems support many of the same networking services and processes, the common ones are listed in Table 5.9.

Table 5.9 *Standard* **nmap** *network listings*

Port	Service Name	Description
7	echo	Echoes characters sent to this port; service provided by the `inetd` process; primarily used for testing
8	discard	Discards any data sent to it; acts like `/dev/null` for networking services and other networking applications; primarily used for testing
13	daytime	Provides time in human-readable format; primarily used for testing

Table 5.9 *Standard **nmap** network listings (continued)*

Port	Service Name	Description
19	chargen	Character generator; produces ASCII character set; primarily used for testing
21	ftp	Standard File Transfer Protocol Server
23	telnet	Telnet server; provides remote login services
25	smtp	Simple Mail Transfer Protocol; usually sendmail server is listening on this port
37	time	Provides machine-readable time
53	domain	Domain name server process
79	finger	Finger server process
80	http	Web server process
111	sunrpc	Sun Remote Procedure Calls services
199	smux	SNMP master agent
382	hp-managed-node	HP agent. This process provides network management services for HP network manager products.
512	exec	Remote execution server with authentication
513	login	Remote login with authentication
514	shell	Remote shell server with authentication
515	printer	Remote printer server

Table 5.9 *Standard* **nmap** *network listings (continued)*

Port	Service Name	Description
540	uucp	UUCP server
4045	lockd	Lock daemon

AIX System

Description

This report was generated from an RISC 6000 system running AIX 4.2. It includes some of the standard UNIX networking services and some specific ones as well.

Report Results

```
Starting nmap V. 2.12 by Fyodor (fyodor@dhp.com, www.inse-
cure.org/nmap/)
Interesting ports on lexis.home.com (10.0.2.240):
Port    State       Protocol  Service
7       open        tcp       echo
9       open        tcp       discard
13      open        tcp       daytime
19      open        tcp       chargen
21      open        tcp       ftp
23      open        tcp       telnet
25      open        tcp       smtp
37      open        tcp       time
111     open        tcp       sunrpc
199     open        tcp       smux
382     open        tcp       hp-managed-node
512     open        tcp       exec
513     open        tcp       login
514     open        tcp       shell
515     open        tcp       printer
543     open        tcp       klogin
544     open        tcp       kshell
651     open        tcp       unknown
652     open        tcp       unknown
777     open        tcp       unknown
2401    open        tcp       cvspserver

TCP Sequence Prediction: Class=truly random
                         Difficulty=9999999 (Good luck!)
Remote operating system guess: AIX 4.2

Nmap run completed -- 1 IP address (1 host up) scanned in 4 seconds
```

Solaris System

Description

This report identifies the system called chips as either a Solaris 2.6 or a Solaris 2.7 system. In this case, the system is actually 2.6, but since there are relatively few differences between 2.6 and 2.7, **nmap** indicates both. Two interesting and unique services detected by **nmap** include lotusnote and xaudio. The first process represents a Lotus Notes Domino server, and the other is an audio/video application that provides multicast support.

Report Results

```
Starting nmap V. 2.12 by Fyodor (fyodor@dhp.com, www.inse-
cure.org/nmap/)
Interesting ports on chips.home.com (10.0.2.199):
Port    State       Protocol  Service
7       open        tcp       echo
9       open        tcp       discard
13      open        tcp       daytime
19      open        tcp       chargen
21      open        tcp       ftp
23      open        tcp       telnet
25      open        tcp       smtp
37      open        tcp       time
79      open        tcp       finger
80      open        tcp       http
111     open        tcp       sunrpc
512     open        tcp       exec
513     open        tcp       login
514     open        tcp       shell
515     open        tcp       printer
540     open        tcp       uucp
1103    open        tcp       xaudio
1352    open        tcp       lotusnote
4045    open        tcp       lockd
6112    open        tcp       dtspc
7100    open        tcp       font-service

TCP Sequence Prediction: Class=random positive increments
                         Difficulty=48025 (Worthy challenge)
Remote operating system guess: Solaris 2.6 - 2.7

Nmap run completed -- 1 IP address (1 host up) scanned in 2 seconds
```

HP-UX System

Description

This system, called dip, provides many of the standard services and includes Klogin/Kshell for security login and remote shell execution on ports 543 and 544, respectively.

Report Results

```
Starting nmap V. 2.12 by Fyodor (fyodor@dhp.com, www.inse-
cure.org/nmap/)
Interesting ports on dip.home.com (10.0.2.198):
Port    State       Protocol    Service
7       open        tcp         echo
9       open        tcp         discard
13      open        tcp         daytime
19      open        tcp         chargen
21      open        tcp         ftp
23      open        tcp         telnet
25      open        tcp         smtp
37      open        tcp         time
53      open        tcp         domain
94      open        tcp         objcall
111     open        tcp         sunrpc
113     open        tcp         auth
135     open        tcp         loc-srv
382     open        tcp         hp-managed-node
512     open        tcp         exec
513     open        tcp         login
514     open        tcp         shell
515     open        tcp         printer
543     open        tcp         klogin
544     open        tcp         kshell
590     open        tcp         tns-cml
659     open        tcp         unknown
661     open        tcp         unknown
816     open        tcp         unknown
980     open        tcp         unknown
984     open        tcp         unknown
988     open        tcp         unknown
993     open        tcp         simap
996     open        tcp         xtreelic
1501    open        tcp         sas-3
5520    open        tcp         sdlog
6111    open        tcp         spc
6112    open        tcp         dtspc
```

```
TCP Sequence Prediction: Class=64K rule
                         Difficulty=1 (Trivial joke)
Remote operating system guess: HP-UX 10.20 E 9000/777 or A
712/60 with tcp_random_seq = 0

Nmap run completed -- 1 IP address (1 host up) scanned in ? seconds
```

Windows NT System

Description

This report was generated from an NT workstation. The services identified don't match any common UNIX services.

Report Results

```
Starting nmap V. 2.12 by Fyodor (fyodor@dhp.com, www.inse-
cure.org/nmap/)
Interesting ports on  (10.0.2.124):
Port    State       Protocol  Service
135     open        tcp       loc-srv
139     open        tcp       netbios-ssn
427     open        tcp       svrloc

TCP Sequence Prediction: Class=trivial time dependency
                         Difficulty=13 (Easy)
Remote operating system guess: Windows NT4 / Win95 / Win98

Nmap run completed -- 1 IP address (1 host up) scanned in 1 second
```

Cisco Router System

Description

This report show which services are available from a Cisco router.

Report Results

```
[root@didymus /root]# nmap -O 199.82.24.1

Starting nmap V. 2.12 by Fyodor (fyodor@dhp.com,
www.insecure.org/nmap/)
Interesting ports on  (10.0.2.1):
Port    State       Protocol  Service
7       open        tcp       echo
9       open        tcp       discard
13      open        tcp       daytime
19      open        tcp       chargen
```

```
23      open      tcp      telnet
79      open      tcp      finger
6001    open      tcp      X11:1

TCP Sequence Prediction: Class=random positive increments
                         Difficulty=659 (Medium)
Remote operating system guess: IOS Version 10.3(15) - 11.1(20)


Nmap run completed -- 1 IP address (1 host up) scanned in 4 seconds
```

Xtraceroute Tool

The **xtraceroute** tool is an XWindow application based on its command line counterpart, **traceroute**. It provides a GUI interface and features a rotating globe showing the path of an **xtraceroute** session. Recall that the **traceroute** command, described in the previous chapter, uses the Internet Protocol to record each destination or hop en route to a specific target host. The command-line version records each hop by displaying the IP address and general performance information. This version of the tool provides the same information but also displays hops on a three-dimensional globe that can be moved with the mouse to control the viewing angle.

The **xtraceroute** software maintains a database that contains destination information such as IP and hostname. It also contains latitude and longitude information so that, should **xtraceroute** visit that site, it may be displayed on the globe. The user also has the ability to enter additional destinations not already provided in the standard database.

Figure 5.20 shows what will be displayed when **xtraceroute** is used to trace the path from the East Coast (Orlando, FL) of the USA to the **xtraceroute** Web site that is located on the West Coast of Sweden. Note that a line is drawn from Florida over the Atlantic and to Europe.

The tool's main window contains two menus, two panels, and two buttons. The first menu, File, has two items: New... and Quit. The Info button displays specific information on the host entry. The other button, which is blank, is located on the main window and is a short cut to the New... submenu. The New... submenu item is used to enter a destination target. To determine the correct

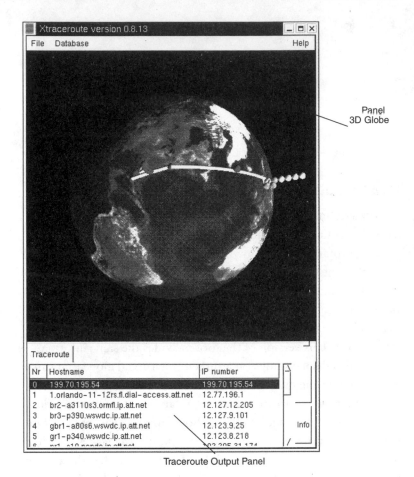

Figure 5.20 *TCP packet filter window.*

path, **xtraceroute** will use the destination addresses entered by the user. Selecting this submenu will display the dialog window shown in Figure 5.21. The user can enter either a fully qualified hostname or valid IP address. In the window shown in Figure 5.21, the Internet host location of where the **xtraceroute** software is available was entered.

The other submenu item is Quit, which is self-explanatory. The other menu item, Database, contains three submenu items. Each of these items accomplishes the same basic task— to add additional destination information so that **xtraceroute** can display the site on the globe. The most useful of the three is the Add Host... submenu

Figure 5.21 *New trace window.*

item. Selecting this option will display the dialog box shown in Figure 5.22.

Figure 5.22 *New host record dialog box.*

Clicking the Help button in this dialog box will provide additional information about adding global coordinates for the host entry being added.

When **xtraceroute** was first installed, the database didn't contain any information regarding the networks that covered the Orlando area. As a result, host information was added manually to the **xtraceroute** database. Some of this information is dependent on the user's Internet location. The user will use the New host record window to add new entries to the database. In Figure 5.22, the entry point for the Internet starts with a local ISP with the hostname of 1.orlando-11-12rs.fl.dial-access.att.net and an IP address of 12.77.196.1, which were entered in the Hostname and IP number fields, respectively. The Latitude and Longitude fields include the global coordinates of the location as shown on a world map or globe. Please keep in mind that both the latitude and longitude numbers were approximated for this example. Finally, the location including the city and state was entered into the Info field.

Clicking the OK button will add this entry to a local file called user_hosts.cache, which is stored in subdirectory .xt in the user's home directory. Unfortunately, the .xt directory must be manually created before **xtraceroute** will save any files to this location. This file is read when **xtraceroute** starts up and **xtraceroute** uses this database when updating the three-dimensional globe panel.

Like regular **traceroute**, the hop count. and hop hostname/IP are displayed in the bottom panel of the main window. Unlike normal **traceroute, xtraceroute** doesn't provide network round-trip performance information in the main panel. Instead, the user must select a hop destination and click the Info button located on the bottom of the main panel to get trip time data. Clicking this button displays a new window, as depicted in Figure 5.23.

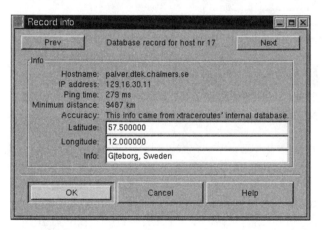

Figure 5.23 *Destination hop information.*

This window contains a few fields not shown in the window shown in Figure 5.22. These new fields include the Ping time, Minimum distance, and Accuracy fields. The Ping time field represents the round-trip time delay in microseconds for the originating site, and in this case, the destination target happens to be palver.dtek.chalmers.se. This particular host is located at the Chalmers University of Technology. The Minimum distance field helps define the length of the path to the remote destination. The final field, Accuracy, provides helpful information about the source of the destination information. The window also contains two buttons that make it easier to navigate the hops within the main window. The Next button moves closer to the destination target, while the Prev button moves further away from the destination target but closer to the source of the trace.

One of the powerful features of **xtraceroute** is its ability to manipulate the three-dimensional globe using the mouse. By default, when the application is first started, the entire continent of Africa is in view, with parts of Europe toward the top, and South America on the left. When a destination is entered and **xtraceroute** begins, it draws a starting point indicating the origin of the trace and one or more lines indicating each hop along the route to the final destination. Depending on which continent the user issues the trace from, the destination connecting point may not be in view. In this situation, use the mouse to bring the lines into view once the trace is complete. Use the left mouse button to drag the globe to the location desired. Sometimes, if the user holds the mouse too long or if the globe is dragged too far, the desired position is skipped. In time and with a little practice, controlling the position of the continents will be easy.

As previously mentioned, the **xtraceroute** database may not contain either the site where the user is located, any destination along the path of the target, or the target itself. As a result, the user must enter this information manually. Instead of using the GUI, the user may manually add entries to the default database located in his home directory. For instance, Listing 5.2 shows a few entries that were used to provide the path between the East Coast of the USA and West Coast of Sweden.

Listing 5.2 *User's personal database for xtraceroute*

```
1   199.70.195.54 199.70.195.54 30 0 0n 81 0 0w
2   12.77.196.1 1.orlando-11-12rs.fl.dial-access.att.net 30
      0 0n 81 0 0w
3   12.127.9.101 br3-p390.wswdc.ip.att.net 23 33 16n 81 33
      18w
4   204.70.10.150 core5-hssi5-0-0.Washington.cw.net 38 30 0n
      77 5 59w
```

The format of the personal database includes the IP address and hostname of the destination, followed by standard global coordinates. The interpretations of the coordinates included in the first entry are 30 degrees, zero minutes, zero seconds north of the equator by 81 degrees, zero minutes, zero seconds in the western hemisphere. When each hop destination is added to this file, **xtraceroute** will display a much more accurate mapping between the source of the trace and the final destination.

## 06

Overview of MIB-II

This chapter provides a detailed overview of SNMP MIB-II. Since MIB-II is a standard, the objects are available from a wide variety of sources, including 3Com, Brocade, Cisco, and many others. In fact, any device that claims to support SNMP standards, is required to support MIB-II. A significant amount of information about a particular device or group of devices can be obtained by querying specific MIB-II objects. The objects contained with MIB provide both system configuration and network performance information.

Overview of MIB-II

The SNMP standards define a collection of Management Information Base (MIB) objects that each SNMP agent supports. The first set of objects were known as MIB-I and were documented in RFC1156. Over time, these objects were expanded, and the collection of objects became known as MIB-II, described in RFC1213. The MIB-II objects provide generic information about the state of the networking aspect of the device. This MIB is divided into a collection of groups, described in Table 6.1.

Table 6.1 *List of MIB-II Groups*

Group	Description
system	Provides overall information about the device or system on which the agent is running
interfaces	Contains information about the operating network interfaces contained within the system
at	Address translation table for Internet IP addresses to datalink addresses. Note that this is a deprecated group
ip	Contains statistical information about the Internet Protocol (IP) of the device
icmp	Contains statistical information about the Internet Control Message Protocol (ICMP) of the device
tcp	Contains statistical information about the Transmission Control Protocol (TCP) of the device
udp	Contains statistical information about the User Datagram Protocol (UDP) of the device

Table 6.1 *List of MIB-II Groups (continued)*

Group	Description
egp	Contains statistical information about the Exterior Gateway Protocol (EGP) of the device
dot3	Provides information regarding the transmission and access protocols for each network interface
snmp	Contains statistical information about the Simple Network Management Protocol (SNMP) of the device

The collection of MIB-II groups can also be displayed graphically, as shown in Figure 6.1. The mib-2 group is shown as a tree structure with group members branching off to the right. The associated number or index for each object identifies the location within the tree hierarchy. Each of the associated mib-2 groups described in this chapter have additional subgroups or objects beneath them and are displayed in the tree view format. Recall from Chapter 2, "Simple Network Management Protocol," that the use of circles next to the object represents a subgroup (where additional subgroups or individual objects may be defined), while the square represents individual discrete objects. This makes it easy to distinguish a collection of objects from individual objects.

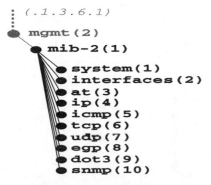

Figure 6.1 *The* mib-2 *group view.*

System Group

The system group consists of objects that provide generic information about the device or system on which the agent is running. Figure 6.2 presents the hierarchical view of the system group.

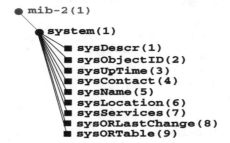

Figure 6.2 *The* system *group view.*

The objects in this group are mostly self-explanatory. The sysServices, sysUpTime, and sysOR prefixed objects require additional information. The sysServices object represents a seven-bit code that corresponds to the value of the combined services the device provides. Each bit within the code is associated with one of the layers of the OSI model and, if the device offers a service on a particular layer, then the bit for that layer is set. For example, consider a device that provides routing functions. The associated sysServices value for this device is 72. Table 6.2 contains a list of layers and associated services. The value of sysServices is the sum of the bit values, where the value of any particular bit is 2 raised to the power L-1 (where L is the layer). Thus, for a switch device that is a layer 1 and 2 device, we get

$$2^{1-1} + 2^{2-1} = 3$$

and/or an application server (layers 4 and 7), we get

$$2^{4-1} + 2^{7-1} = 72$$

We include layer 4 in this equation because an application server provides services on both layer 7 and layer 4.

Definitions for layers 5 and 6 do not currently exist. **Note**

Table 6.2 *Functional layers used to determine* sysServices

Layer	Device Functionality
1	Physical: A device that operates on this layer is known as a network repeater
2	Datalink and/or subnetwork layer: A device that operates on this layer includes a network bridge or switch
3	Internet/network: A device that operates on this layer is a gateway or router
4	End-to-end services, such as an IP host
7	Application services, such as mail relays, DNS server, etc.

The sysUpTime object indicates the amount of time that has transpired since the network management agent was last started. This doesn't necessarily mean that the device itself has been operating since that time. Take, for example, an agent running on top of an operating system. The agent can be restarted independent of the system and, therefore, may not represent the true amount of time the system has been in operation. However, with some devices, the agent can't be started or stopped independent of the system. In this case, the agent should be more accurate.

The system group also contains a few objects related to SNMPv2 devices acting in an agent role. These objects have names that begin with the prefix sysOR and are supported with SNMPv2 (or later) agents. The objects control the dynamic configuration of object resources. Because these objects were introduced with the SNMPv2 standards, SNMPv1 agents don't support them.

The system group contains the following set of objects:

Object Name: sysDescr

OID: system.1

Object Type: Display String [255]

Access Mode: read-only

Description: A description of the device or entity, such as the type of device, hardware characteristics, operating system information, etc.

Object Name: sysObjectID

OID: system.2

Object Type: Object Identifier

Access Mode: read-only

Description: The authoritative identification of the vendor of the device

Object Name: sysUpTime

OID: system.3

Object Type: TimeTick

Access Mode: read-only

Description: The amount of time since the network management portion of the system (agent) was last reinitialized

Object Name: sysContact

OID: system.4

Object Type: Display String [255]

Access Mode: read-write

Description: Information noting the contact person and/or other organization that provides support for this device

Object Name: sysName

OID: system.5

Object Type: Display String [255]

Access Mode: read-write

Description: The name of the device; may be the official hostname or another administratively assigned name

Object Name: sysLocation

OID: system.6

Object Type: Display String [255]

Access Mode: read-write

Description: The physical location where the device has been installed

Object Name: sysServices

OID: system.7

Object Type: Integer

Access Mode: read-only

Description: The services this device provides

Object Name: sysOrLastChange

OID: system.8

Object Type: TimeStamp

Access Mode: read-only

Description: The value of the sysUpTime object at the time of
                     the most recent change made in any instance of
                     the sysORID object

Object Name: sysORTable

OID: system.9

Object Type: Sequence of SysOREntry

Access Mode: read-only

Description: A table of dynamically configurable object
                     resources within an SNMPv2 system acting in
                     an agent role

Object Name: sysOREntry

OID: SysORTable.1

Object Type: Sequence

Access Mode: read-only

Description: Information on a specific configurable object

Object Name: sysORIndex

OID: sysOREntry.1

Object Type: Object Identifier

Access Mode: read-only

Description: Used as an index into the sysORTable

Object Name: sysORID

OID: sysOREntry.2

Object Type: Display String [255]

Access Mode: read-only

Description: The OID of this entry, analogous to the sysObjectID object

Object Name: sysORDescr

OID: sysOREntry.3

Object Type: Display String [255]

Access Mode: read-only

Description: A description of the object resource, analogous to the sysDescr object

Object Name: sysORUpTime

OID: sysOREntry.4

Object Type: TimeStamp

Access Mode: read-only

Description: Contains the value of the sysUpTime object at the time this instance (row) was last updated or instantiated

When the system group from a Linux system is queried, the following objects with their associated values are returned:

```
system.sysDescr.0 = "Linux socrates 2.2.5-15 #5 Mon Aug 2
   21:07:04 EDT 1999 i586"

system.sysObjectID.0 = OID: enterprises.ucdavis.ucdSn-
   mpAgent.linux

system.sysUpTime.0 = Timeticks: (160910) 0:26:49.10

system.sysContact.0 = "Steve Rossman"

system.sysName.0 = "socrates"

system.sysLocation.0 = "Media Lab - 10th Floor"

system.sysServices.0 = 72
```

In this example, the sysDescr object includes information about
the system on which the agent is running. The string provides the
same basic information that is obtained from the UNIX **uname**
command:

```
# uname -a
Linux socrates 2.2.5-15 #5 Mon Aug 2 21:07:04 EDT 1999 i586 unknown
```

The sysObject object contains an OID of the Linux branch
that identifies the agent. The sysContact shows that the agent has
been running for approximately 26 minutes and 49 seconds. The
sysContact, sysName, and sysLocation objects contain specific
information about the owner (Steve Rossman), name (socrates),
and location (Media Lab – 10th Floor) of the device. Chapter 7,
"Using SNMP Agents," will show how to update these fields to
include information specific to your system and environment.
Finally, the sysServices object shows that the device provides layer
4 and layer 7 services.

Interfaces Group

The interfaces group provides both configuration and statistical information regarding the network interfaces installed within
the device. As discussed in Chapter 2, "Simple Network Management Protocol," this group has an ifNumber object, which contains
the total number of network interfaces installed on the system,
regardless of the operating state of any particular interface. The
other object, ifTable, is a table that contains a row for each interface. The table is indexed by the ifIndex object and contains a
value between 1 and the value of the ifNumber object. The ifIndex
number can address each column or interface directly. The ifTable
contains 22 objects that provide the following:

- type, capacity, and other interface characteristics

- operational information

- performance and statistical information

Figure 6.3 shows a hierarchical representation of the interfaces
group. The figure shows different groups of objects that include
interface characteristics and incoming/outgoing traffic counters.

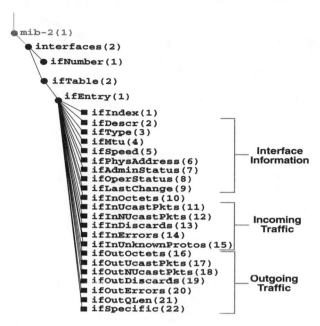

Figure 6.3 *The* interfaces *group view.*

Querying the interfaces table against a Linux system displays output similar to the following:

```
interfaces.ifNumber.0 = 2

interfaces.ifTable.ifEntry.ifIndex.1 = 1

interfaces.ifTable.ifEntry.ifIndex.2 = 2

interfaces.ifTable.ifEntry.ifDescr.1 = "lo0" Hex: 6C 6F 30

interfaces.ifTable.ifEntry.ifDescr.2 = "eth0" Hex: 65 74 68 30

interfaces.ifTable.ifEntry.ifType.1 = softwareLoopback(24)

interfaces.ifTable.ifEntry.ifType.2 = ethernet-csmacd(6)

interfaces.ifTable.ifEntry.ifMtu.1 = 3924

interfaces.ifTable.ifEntry.ifMtu.2 = 1500

interfaces.ifTable.ifEntry.ifSpeed.1 = Gauge: 10000000

interfaces.ifTable.ifEntry.ifSpeed.2 = Gauge: 10000000

interfaces.ifTable.ifEntry.ifPhysAddress.1 = ""

interfaces.ifTable.ifEntry.ifPhysAddress.2 = Hex: 00 10 5A 28 5D 7C
```

(continued)

```
interfaces.ifTable.ifEntry.ifAdminStatus.1 = up(1)

interfaces.ifTable.ifEntry.ifAdminStatus.2 = up(1)

interfaces.ifTable.ifEntry.ifOperStatus.1 = up(1)

interfaces.ifTable.ifEntry.ifOperStatus.2 = up(1)

interfaces.ifTable.ifEntry.ifLastChange.1 = Timeticks: (0) 0:00:00.00
interfaces.ifTable.ifEntry.ifLastChange.2 = Timeticks: (0) 0:00:00.00

interfaces.ifTable.ifEntry.ifInOctets.1 = 373912

interfaces.ifTable.ifEntry.ifInOctets.2 = 50204

interfaces.ifTable.ifEntry.ifInUcastPkts.1 = 1218

interfaces.ifTable.ifEntry.ifInUcastPkts.2 = 163

interfaces.ifTable.ifEntry.ifInNUcastPkts.1 = 0

interfaces.ifTable.ifEntry.ifInNUcastPkts.2 = 0

interfaces.ifTable.ifEntry.ifInDiscards.1 = 0

interfaces.ifTable.ifEntry.ifInDiscards.2 = 0

interfaces.ifTable.ifEntry.ifInErrors.1 = 0

interfaces.ifTable.ifEntry.ifInErrors.2 = 0

interfaces.ifTable.ifEntry.ifInUnknownProtos.1 = 0

interfaces.ifTable.ifEntry.ifInUnknownProtos.2 = 0

interfaces.ifTable.ifEntry.ifOutOctets.1 = 381304

interfaces.ifTable.ifEntry.ifOutOctets.2 = 174020

interfaces.ifTable.ifEntry.ifOutUcastPkts.1 = 1242

interfaces.ifTable.ifEntry.ifOutUcastPkts.2 = 565

interfaces.ifTable.ifEntry.ifOutNUcastPkts.1 = 0

interfaces.ifTable.ifEntry.ifOutNUcastPkts.2 = 0

interfaces.ifTable.ifEntry.ifOutDiscards.1 = 0

interfaces.ifTable.ifEntry.ifOutDiscards.2 = 0

interfaces.ifTable.ifEntry.ifOutErrors.1 = 0

interfaces.ifTable.ifEntry.ifOutErrors.2 = 0

interfaces.ifTable.ifEntry.ifOutQLen.1 = Gauge: 0

interfaces.ifTable.ifEntry.ifOutQLen.2 = Gauge: 0
```

```
interfaces.ifTable.ifEntry.ifSpecific.1 = OID: .ccitt.null0ID

interfaces.ifTable.ifEntry.ifSpecific.2 = OID: .ccitt.null0ID
```

Notice that the ifNumber object equals 2 because a total of two interfaces are defined on the system. As a result, the ifIndex.1 and ifIndex.2 objects are set to 1 and 2 respectively so that they can be used to index each interface separately. The ifDescr object contains the name of the interface as it is known by the agent running within the device. For instance, using the output above, the first Ethernet interface is known as eth0. As a result, the ifDescr object will contain this interface name, with each character converted to hexadecimal ("eth0" Hex: 65 74 68 30). Thus the hexadecimal value of eth0 is 65 74 68 30. The interface names provided by the agent are the same names displayed when using the **ifconfig** or **netstat** commands. See Chapter 4, "Core System Utilities and Tools," for additional information.

The ifType object records the type of the network interface using a single integer identifier. The number can be mapped to a keyword string that gives more descriptive information regarding the actual interface used. A large number of network interface types have been defined by the MIB-II standard. Table 6.3 lists some of the more popular interfaces. Consult RFC1213 for a complete list. Observe that the eth0 carries the interface type 6, which is ethernetCsmacd.

The ifMtu object, or the maximum transfer unit (MTU), identifies the maximum size of the protocol data unit PDU (or frame) that is allowed for the interface. Standard Ethernet is 1500, while the softwareLoopback is much higher at 3924. Different systems may implement the MTU for the software loopback with various values as deemed appropriate for each system. The ifSpeed object shows the maximum capacity of the interface. In the example, both interfaces contain the same speed of 10000000. This value represents the theoretical performance of an Ethernet LAN that is 10Mb per second. Other interfaces will show either higher or lower capacities depending on the interface type. Here is a case in point: A serial interface that supports PPP, contains an ifSpeed of 9600, which represents 9600 bits per second that can be supported, given the hardware characteristics of a serial RS-232 interface.

Table 6.3 *Popular interface types and descriptions*

Number	Type	Description
1	other	None of the following types
6	ethernetCsmacd	Ethernet network protocol
7	iso88023Csmacd	IEEE 802.3 Carrier Sense Multiple Access with Collision Detection (CSMA/CD) network protocol
9	iso88025TokenRing	IEE 802.5 TokenRing network protocol
15	fddi	ANSI Fiber Distributed Data Interface (FDDI) network protocol
20	basicISDN	Basic- rate Integrated Service Digital Network (ISDN)
21	primaryISDN	Primary-rate ISDN
23	ppp	The Point-to-Point Internet Protocol
23	softareLoopback	Internal interface used for communications between processes
30	ds3	Digital transmission line that uses DS-3 format
37	atm	Asynchronous transfer mode (ATM)
46	hssi	High-speed serial interface (HSSI)

The ifPhysAddress object identifies the datalink protocol address (where appropriate) for the interface. The eth0 interface has an ifPhysAddress of 00 10 5A 28 5D 7C, while the ifPhysAddress contains a null string value (""). The reason for this is that the software loopback doesn't use any hardware, and no datalink address is needed or required. The address contained within the ifPhysAddress is used for low-level network communications between systems. Every time a packet is emitted from this interface, this address is used as the source of the packet.

The ifAdminStatus and ifOperStatus objects show the administrative status and operational status of the interface. The network administrator uses the administrative status to control the interface. This object provides the ability to control when the interface is marked as up or down. Also, a third state, testing, can be set. The up state means that packets are permitted to flow across the interface, while the down state implies that no packets are to be received or sent from this interface. This is regardless of the state of the physical connection to the interface. In other words, a network interface may be connected to an operating network but if it is marked down, no network traffic will be read by the interface. The testing state enables internal interface diagnostics to validate the correct operation of the interface. The ifOperStatus object shows the current status of the interface, which is one of the defined states represented by the ifAdminStatus object. This object obtains the state of a particular interface.

> The access of the ifAdminStatus object is read-write; all of the other objects in the interface group can't be modified by a network manager because they have read-only access. The reason for this should seem quite natural and straightforward. It is reasonable that counters and descriptive information about an interface should not be changed because it is important to maintain interface type information to avoid networking configuration problems and maintain accurate performance metrics.

Note

The ifSpecific objects contain the value of ccitt.nullOID, which represents a valid but null OID string. The interfaces group contains the following set of objects.

Object Name: ifNumber

OID: interfaces.1

Object Type: Integer

Access Mode: read-only

Description: The total number of network interfaces con-
                     tained within the local system

Object Name: ifTable

OID: interfaces.2

Object Type: Sequence of ifEntry

Access Mode: na

Description: A list or row of the interface entries for this
                     table

Object Name: ifEntry

OID: interface.ifTable

Object Type: Sequence

Access Mode: not-accessible

Description: A specific interface entry that contains all the
                     objects defined below it

Object Name: ifIndex

OID: ifEntry.1

Object Type: Integer

Access Mode: read-only

Description: An MIB reference definition that is specific to a
                     particular media type that is used to access the
                     network interface

Object Name: ifDescr

OID: `ifEntry.2`

Object Type: `DisplayString [255]`

Access Mode: `read-only`

Description: A string description of the interface that includes the name of the interface from an operating system standpoint; possible values include: `eth0`, `ppp0`, and `lo0`

Object Name: `ifType`

OID: `ifEntry.3`

Object Type: `DisplayString [255]`

Access Mode: `read-only`

Description: The type of interface. Table 6.3 lists specific types

Object Name: `ifMtu`

OID: `ifEntry.4`

Object Type: `Integer`

Access Mode: `read-only`

Description: The maximum transmission unit of the interface. This represents the largest frame that can be sent and/or received on the interface

Object Name: `ifSpeed`

OID: `ifEntry.5`

Object Type: `Gauge`

Access Mode: `read-only`

Description: The data rate (capacity) of the interface

Object Name: `ifPhysAddress`

OID: `ifEntry.6`

Object Type: `PhysAddress`

Access Mode: `read-only`

Description: The datalink address of the interface

Object Name: `ifAdminStatus`

OID: `ifEntry.7`

Object Type: `Integer`

Access Mode: `read-only`

Description: The administrative status of the interface, which is one of the defined states listed in the `ifOperStatus` object. The owner of the device can control the interface with this object

Object Name: `ifOperStatus`

OID: `ifEntry.8`

Object Type: `Integer`

Access Mode: `read-only`

Description: The present operational state of the interface. The defined states include `up(1)`, `down(2)`, and `testing(3)`

Object Name: `ifLastChange`

OID: `ifEntry.9`

Object Type: `TimeTicks`

Access Mode: `read-only`

Description: The time when the interface was last updated to its present operating state

Object Name: `ifInOctets`

OID: `ifEntry.10`

Object Type: `Counter`

Access Mode: `read-only`

Description: The number of octets (bytes) received on the interface, including any datalink framing bytes

Object Name: `ifInUcastPkts`

OID: `ifEntry.11`

Object Type: `Counter`

Access Mode: `read-only`

Description: The number of unicast packets delivered via a higher-level protocol to a subnet

Object Name: `ifInNUcastPkts`

OID: `ifEntry.12`

Object Type: `Counter`

Access Mode: `read-only`

Description: The number of non-unicast packets that were delivered to a higher-level networking protocol

Object Name: `ifInDiscards`

OID: `ifEntry.13`

Object Type: `Counter`

Access Mode: `read-only`

Description: The number of inbound packets discarded
                     (despite no errors) and will not be delivered to a
                     higher-level networking protocol

Object Name: ifInErrors

OID: ifEntry.14

Object Type: Counter

Access Mode: read-only

Description: The number of inbound packets with errors that
                     caused them not to be delivered to a higher-level
                     networking protocol

Object Name: ifInUnknownProtos

OID: ifEntry.15

Object Type: Counter

Access Mode: read-only

Description: The number of inbound packets discarded due
                     to an unknown or unsupported networking pro-
                     tocol

Object Name: ifOutOctets

OID: ifEntry.16

Object Type: Counter

Access Mode: read-only

Description: The number of octets (bytes) transmitted on the
                     interface. This includes any datalink framing
                     bytes as well

Object Name: ifOutUcastPkts

OID: ifEntry.17

Object Type: Counter

Access Mode: read-only

Description: The number of packets that higher-level protocols (such as IP) requested be transmitted to a
network unicast address. This includes those
that were discarded or otherwise not sent

Object Name: ifOutNUcastPkts

OID: ifEntry.18

Object Type: Counter

Access Mode: read-only

Description: The number of packets that higher-level protocols (such as IP) requested to be transmitted to a
non-unicast address. This also includes packets
that were discarded or, for some other reason,
not sent.

Object Name: ifOutDiscards

OID: ifEntry.19

Object Type: Counter

Access Mode: read-only

Description: The number of packets that could not be transmitted due to some reason unrelated to a spe-
cific error condition. This could be caused, for
example, by the TTL of a packet expiring

Object Name: ifOutErrors

OID: ifEntry.20

Object Type: Counter

Access Mode: read-only

Description: The number of packets that could not be transmitted due to errors

Object Name: ifOutQLen

OID: ifEntry.21

Object Type: Gauge

Access Mode: read-only

Description: The length of the output packet queue on the device

Object Name: ifSpecific

OID: ifEntry.22

Object Type: Object Identifier

Access Mode: read-only

Description: The MIB reference definition that is specific to the particular media type used to realize the network interface

Address Translation Group

The at group consists of a single table that provides mapping from a network address to a physical address. Figure 6.4 shows a tree view of the address translation group. This group has been deprecated (which means that it was replaced by another group of MIB objects) but is provided for backward compatibility with the existing MIB-I standard. Many existing agents continue to support this group, including the Linux agent. Since this is the case, we have described the group here.

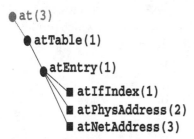

```
at(3)
  atTable(1)
    atEntry(1)
      atIfIndex(1)
      atPhysAddress(2)
      atNetAddress(3)
```

Figure 6.4 *The* at *group view.*

Each row of the at table provides a mapping between a network address and a physical address. Querying the at table against a Linux system displays output similar to the following :

```
at.atTable.atEntry.atIfIndex.1.1.10.0.2.10 = 1
at.atTable.atEntry.atIfIndex.1.1.10.0.2.50 = 1
at.atTable.atEntry.atIfIndex.1.1.10.0.?.127 = 1
at.atTable.atEntry.atPhysAddress.1.1.10.0.2.10 =  Hex: 00 00 00 00 00 00
at.atTable.atEntry.atPhysAddress.1.1.10.0.2.50 =  Hex: 00 C0 D4 00 09 40
at.atTable.atEntry.atPhysAddress.1.1.10.0.2.127 =  Hex: 00 60 97 0E A3 06
at.atTable.atEntry.atNetAddress.1.1.10.0.2.10 = IpAddress: 10.0.2.10
at.atTable.atEntry.atNetAddress.1.1.10.0.2.50 = IpAddress: 10.0.2.50
at.atTable.atEntry.atNetAddress.1.1.10.0.2.127 = IpAddress: 10.0.2.127
```

The network address is typically the IP address assigned to the interface. The physical address represents the datalink network address that is appropriate for that interface. The table is indexed by the atIfIndex object, which contains a mapping for the ifIndex object contained in the interface group. The network address object also indexes the at table. For instance, atIfIndex.1.1.10.0.2.50 is used as a pointer to the atPhysAddress and atNetAddress objects associated with that IP address. Note that the OID string contains the actual IP address of the interface and serves as an index key. The atPhysAddress object contains the physical address for the datalink protocol for that interface type. The example shows a valid Ethernet address in hexadecimal. The atNetAddress object contains the valid IP address for the interface expressed in normal dotted decimal notation.

The at table will change in size in concert with the ARP cache. Depending on network traffic, the ARP table will grow and shrink. The arp command can list the ARP table on a UNIX system. Chapter 4, "Core System Utilities and Tools," fully explains this utility. Also, since the at table represents ARP entries, this table

lists incomplete mappings as well. You can see this by examining
the atPhysAddress.1.1.10.0.2.10 = Hex: 00 00 00 00 00 00 listing. Notice that the hexadecimal value is all zeros, which implies
that no mapping was obtained for this IP address.

The at table contains the following objects:

Object Name: atTable **(Deprecated)**

OID: mib-2.at

Object Type: Sequence of AtEntry

Access Mode: read-only

Description: A mapping between network addresses and
                    physical (datalink) addresses

Object Name: ifEntry **(Deprecated)**

OID: mib-2.at

Object Type: Sequence

Access Mode: read-only

Description: A specific mapping that contains all the remain-
                    ing objects listed below

Object Name: atIfIndex **(Deprecated)**

OID: mib-2.at

Object Type: Integer

Access Mode: read-write

Description: References to each specific mapping

Object Name: atPhysAddress **(Deprecated)**

OID: ifEntry.22

Object Type: PhysAddress

Access Mode: read-write

Description: A media-dependent physical address (which is a valid IP address)

Object Name: atNetAddress **(Deprecated)**

OID: ifEntry.22

Object Type: NetworkAddress

Access Mode: read-write

Description: The IP address of the associated media-dependent physical address

Internet Protocol Group

The ip group contains network counters that measure the flow of IP traffic in and out of the system. The group also contains additional tables that provide network layer routing and datalink mapping information. Figure 6.5 shows the ip group in the tree view format.

The ip group contains the following set of objects:

Object Name: ipForwarding

OID: ip.1

Object Type: Integer

Access Mode: read-write

Description: Indicates whether the system is acting as an IP gateway (router) or just as a regular host providing no forwarding services. The valid values are Forwarding(1) and notForwarding(2)

Object Name: ipDefaultTTL

OID: ip.2

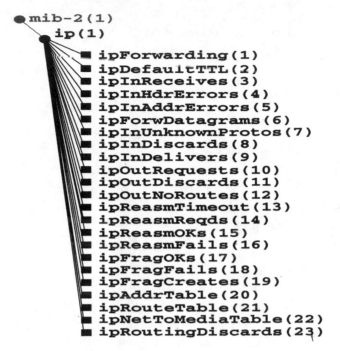

Figure 6.5 *The* ip *group view.*

Object Type: Integer

Access Mode: read-write

Description: The time-to-live (TTL) value that is placed into
                     the TTL field within an IP packet

Object Name: ipInReceives

OID: ip.3

Object Type: Counter

Access Mode: read-only

Description: The total number of input packets received from
                     all interfaces operating within the system

Object Name: `ipInHdrError`

OID: `ip.4`

Object Type: `Counter`

Access Mode: `read-only`

Description: The number of input packets that were discarded as a result of an error within the IP header

Object Name: `ipInaddrErrors`

OID: `ip.5`

Object Type: `Counter`

Access Mode: `read-only`

Description: The number of input packets that were discarded because the final IP destination address was invalid for this system

Object Name: `ipForwDatagrams`

OID: `ip.6`

Object Type: `Counter`

Access Mode: `read-only`

Description: The number of packets that the local system attempted to forward when acting as a gateway or router

Object Name: `ipInUnknownProtos`

OID: `ip.7`

Object Type: `NetworkAddress`

Access Mode: read-write

Description: The number of packets that were received from
                      the network successfully discarded because the
                      network layer protocol was unsupported or
                      unknown to the system

Object Name: ipInDiscards

OID: ip.8

Object Type: Counter

Access Mode: read-only

Description: The number of input packets that were dis-
                      carded due to lack of buffer space or another
                      condition unrelated to the packet itself

Object Name: ipInDelivers

OID: ip.9

Object Type: Counter

Access Mode: read-only

Description: The number of input packets that were delivered
                      to higher-level protocols successfully

Object Name: ipOutRequests

OID: ip.10

Object Type: Counter

Access Mode: read-only

Description: The number of IP packets that higher-level pro-
                      tocols delivered to the IP protocol for transmis-
                      sion

Object Name: `ipOutDiscards`

OID: `ip.11`

Object Type: `Counter`

Access Mode: `read-only`

Description: The number of output packets that were discarded due to lack of buffer space or another condition not relating to the packet itself

Object Name: `ipOutNoRoutes`

OID: `ip.12`

Object Type: `Counter`

Access Mode: `read-only`

Description: The number of packets that were discarded because no route to the required destination network was known

Object Name: `ipReasmTimout`

OID: `ip.13`

Object Type: `Counter`

Access Mode: `read-only`

Description: The interval in seconds that input IP fragment packets are held for before they are reassembled

Object Name: `ipReasmReqds`

OID: `ip.14`

Object Type: `Counter`

Access Mode: `read-only`

Description: The number of IP fragment packets received that must be reassembled

Object Name: `ipReasmOKs`

OID: `ip.15`

Object Type: `Counter`

Access Mode: `read-only`

Description: The number of IP fragment packets that were successfully reassembled

Object Name: `ipReasmFails`

OID: `ip.16`

Object Type: `Counter`

Access Mode: `read-only`

Description: The number of reassembly failures that were detected

Object Name: `ipFragOK`

OID: `ip.17`

Object Type: `Counter`

Access Mode: `read-only`

Description: The number of packets that have been fragmented successfully

Object Name: `ipFragsFails`

OID: `ip.18`

Object Type: `Counter`

Access Mode: `read-only`

Description: The number of packets that were not fragmented because the `don't-fragment` flag contained within the IP header was set

Object Name: `ipFragsCreates`

OID: `ip.19`

Object Type: `Counter`

Access Mode: `read-only`

Description: The number of IP packet fragments generated
on this system

Object Name: `ipAddrTable`

OID: `ip.20`

Object Type: `Sequence of IpAddrEntry`

Access Mode: `not-accessible`

Description: A table of addressing information that is related
to the system's IP addresses

Object Name: `ipRouteTable`

OID: `ip.21`

Object Type: `Sequence Of IpRouteEntry`

Access Mode: `not-accessible`

Description: A route to a particular destination

Object Name: `ipNetToMediaTable`

OID: `ip.22`

Object Type: `Sequence Of IpNetToMediaEntry`

Access Mode: `not-accessible`

Description: The mapping between IP addresses and datalink
                      addresses

Object Name: `ipRoutingDiscards`

OID: `ip.23`

Object Type: `Counter`

Access Mode: `read-only`

Description: The number of packets that were discarded
                      despite the fact that they were valid

Three tables are included within the `ip` group: `ipAddrTable`,
`ipRouteTable`, and `ipNetToMediaTable`. The `ipAddrTable` table stores
information related to the IP addresses that are used on the system. Figure 6.6 shows the tree view of this table.

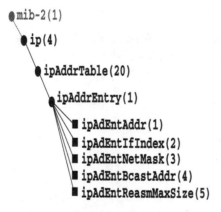

Figure 6.6 *The* `ipAddrTable` *view.*

Each row of the table, which is indexed by the object `ipAdEntIfIndex`
and includes a single IP address that corresponds to a physical network
interface, is assigned the interface number derived from the `ifIndex`
object from the `interfaces` group. For instance, the output listed
below includes the `ipAdEntIf-Index.12.77.195.141` object with a
value of 3. The 3 represents the third interface on the system that

happens to be a point-to-point link (ppp0). The IP address
12.77.195.141 is assigned to this interface. We can determine the
type of the third interface by examining the ifDescr object from the
interfaces table. The object ipAdEntNetMask identifies the network
mask or, if applicable, subnet mask for the IP address (ipAdEntAddr).
The ipAdEntBcastAddr object shows the value of the least significant
bit of the IP broadcast address used for sending packets on the logical
interface related to this IP address. The following is a sample listing
of the ipAddrTable table:

```
ip.ipAddrTable.ipAddrEntry.ipAdEntAddr.10.0.2.201 = IpAddress:
    10.0.2.201
ip.ipAddrTable.ipAddrEntry.ipAdEntAddr.12.77.195.141 = IpAddress:
    12.77.195.141
ip.ipAddrTable.ipAddrEntry.ipAdEntAddr.127.0.0.1 = IpAddress:
    127.0.0.1
ip.ipAddrTable.ipAddrEntry.ipAdEntIfIndex.10.0.2.201 = 2
ip.ipAddrTable.ipAddrEntry.ipAdEntIfIndex.12.77.195.141 = 3
ip.ipAddrTable.ipAddrEntry.ipAdEntIfIndex.127.0.0.1 = 1
ip.ipAddrTable.ipAddrEntry.ipAdEntNetMask.10.0.2.201 = IpAddress:
    255.255.255.0
ip.ipAddrTable.ipAddrEntry.ipAdEntNetMask.12.77.195.141 =
    IpAddress: 255.255.255.255
ip.ipAddrTable.ipAddrEntry.ipAdEntNetMask.127.0.0.1 = IpAddress:
    255.0.0.0
ip.ipAddrTable.ipAddrEntry.ipAdEntBcastAddr.10.0.2.201 = 1
ip.ipAddrTable.ipAddrEntry.ipAdEntBcastAddr.12.77.195.141 = 0
ip.ipAddrTable.ipAddrEntry.ipAdEntBcastAddr.127.0.0.1 = 1
ip.ipAddrTable.ipAddrEntry.ipAdEntReasmMaxSize.10.0.2.201 = -1
ip.ipAddrTable.ipAddrEntry.ipAdEntReasmMaxSize.12.77.195.141 = -1
ip.ipAddrTable.ipAddrEntry.ipAdEntReasmMaxSize.127.0.0.1 = -1
```

The ipRouteTable table provides IP routing information for the
entity and is used to make routing decisions when necessary. For
each known route, there is a single table entry that is indexed by
the ipRouteDest object. For every route, a local interface for the
next hop to the destination is contained within the ipRouteIfIndex
object. This value matches the IfIndex object from the interfaces
group. The following listing includes routing information related
to the 199.70.195.0 network:

```
ip.ipRouteTable.ipRouteEntry.ipRouteIfIndex.199.70.195.41 = 3
ip.ipRouteTable.ipRouteEntry.ipRouteMetric1.199.70.195.41 = 0
ip.ipRouteTable.ipRouteEntry.ipRouteMetric2.199.70.195.41 = -1
```

(continued)

```
ip.ipRouteTable.ipRouteEntry.ipRouteMetric3.199.70.195.41 = -1
ip.ipRouteTable.ipRouteEntry.ipRouteMetric4.127.0.0.0 = -1
ip.ipRouteTable.ipRouteEntry.ipRouteMetric4.199.70.195.41 = -1
ip.ipRouteTable.ipRouteEntry.ipRouteNextHop.199.70.195.41 =
  IpAddress: 0 0.0.0
ip.ipRouteTable.ipRouteEntry.ipRouteType.199.70.195.41 = direct(3)
ip.ipRouteTable.ipRouteEntry.ipRouteProto.199.70.195.41 = local(2)
ip.ipRouteTable.ipRouteEntry.ipRouteAge.199.70.195.41 = 0
ip.ipRouteTable.ipRouteEntry.ipRouteMask.199.70.195.41 =
  IpAddress: 255.255.255.255
ip.ipRouteTable.ipRouteEntry.ipRouteMetric5.199.70.195.41 = -1
ip.ipRouteTable.ipRouteEntry.ipRouteInfo.199.70.195.41 = OID:
  .ccitt.null0ID
```

Bear in mind that this output was selected from a list of other entries and formatted manually; the routing information would not normally be shown in the order listed. Figure 6.7 shows the tree view of the `ipRouteTable` table. The `ipRouteMetric1` object as well as the other three metric objects are used to denote the routing metrics for this route. The actual definitions of the metrics are determined by the routing protocol specified by the `ipRouteProto` value. In this case, the value of zero indicates that this is the most direct route for this network. When a particular metric object is not used (for example, `ipRouteMetric4.199.70 .195.41`), the value is -1.

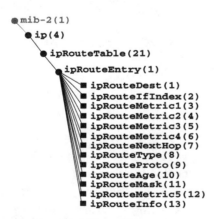

```
● mib-2(1)
  ● ip(4)
    ● ipRouteTable(21)
       ● ipRouteEntry(1)
           ■ ipRouteDest(1)
           ■ ipRouteIfIndex(2)
           ■ ipRouteMetric1(3)
           ■ ipRouteMetric2(4)
           ■ ipRouteMetric3(5)
           ■ ipRouteMetric4(6)
           ■ ipRouteNextHop(7)
           ■ ipRouteType(8)
           ■ ipRouteProto(9)
           ■ ipRouteAge(10)
           ■ ipRouteMask(11)
           ■ ipRouteMetric5(12)
           ■ ipRouteInfo(13)
```

Figure 6.7 *The* `ipRouteTable` *view.*

The `ipRouteNextHop` object identifies the next hop for the route. A value of `0.0.0.0` indicates the IP address that is bound to the interface. The `ipRouteType` object indicates the type of the route and includes the following values: `other(1)`, `invalid(2)`, `direct(3)`, and `indirect(4)`. The `ipRouteType` conveys the notion of direct and indirect routing. The `invalid` value invalidates the route, and `other` means that none of the other values list apply. The `direct` value means that the destination address is on a directly attached subnetwork, while `indirect` means the destination is not on an attached network but at least one additional route must be traversed before the destination can be reached. The `ipRouteProto` object indicates the mechanism used to learn the route. Table 6.4 lists the `ipRouteProto` values for an example in which the method used was `local`. This value means that the route was configured manually, without the aid of a routing protocol. This can be done, for instance when an interface is first initialized.

Table 6.4 *Defined* **IpRouteProto** *values*

ipRouteProto Value	Description
other	None of the following values
local	Routing information that is manually configured or derived from a nonrouting protocol source
netmgmt	Routing information obtained from a network management protocol
icmp	Feedback from hosts and other devices about a problem; provides a redirect message that gives specific routing information
egp	Exterior Gateway Protocol (EGP), which is described in RFC904; a simple router-to-router networking protocol
ggp	Gateway-to-Gateway Protocol; a routing protocol used by the early implementation of the Internet, but now obsolete

Table 6.4 *Defined* **IpRouteProto** *values (continued)*

hello	A simple routing protocol used between routes contained within the same autonomous system
rip	The Routing Information Protocol (RIP)— the de facto routing protocol for UNIX systems
is-is	Intermediate System-to-Intermediate System protocol
es-is	End System-to-Intermediate System protocol
ciscoIgrp	A Cisco proprietary interior gateway protocol
bbnSpfIgp	BBN's shortest-path first-interior gateway protocol
ospf	RFC1583, Open Shortest Path First (OSPF) autonomous gateway routing protocol
bgp	RFC1771, Border Gateway Protocol (BGP) autonomous gateway routing protocol

The ipRouteAge object represents the number of seconds since this route was last updated or determined to be a correct route. The ipRouteMask object indicates the mask to be logically and (&) with the destination address before being compared to the value in the ipRouteDest object. The ipRouteMetric5 object is an alternate routing metric for this route and, like the others, the value is -1 when not used. The final object, ipRouteInfo, is used as a reference to an MIB OID string that is specific to the particular routing protocol responsible for this route. If the information is not available, a valid object identifier of 00 should be used.

The ipRouteTable table has the following objects:

Object Name: ipRouteEntry

OID: ipRouteTable.1

Object Type: Sequence

Access Mode: na

Description: A route to a particular destination

Object Name: ipRouteDest

OID: ipRouteEntry.1

Object Type: IpAddress

Access Mode: read-write

Description: The IP address destination for this route definition

Object Name: ipRouteIfIndex

OID: ipRouteEntry.2

Object Type: Integer

Access Mode: read-write

Description: An index that identifies the local interface through which the next routing hop for this route can be reached

Object Name: ipRouteMetric1

OID: ipRouteEntry.3

Object Type: Integer

Access Mode: read-write

Description: The primary routing metric for this route

Object Name: ipRouteMetric2

OID: ipRouteEntry.4

Object Type: Integer

Access Mode: read-write

Description: An alternate routing metric for this route

Object Name: ipRouteMetric3

OID: ipRouteEntry.5

Object Type: Integer

Access Mode: read-write

Description: An alternate routing metric for this route

Object Name: ipRouteMetric4

OID: ipRouteEntry.6

Object Type: Integer

Access Mode: read-write

Description: An alternate routing metric for this route

Object Name: ipRouteNextHop

OID: ipRouteEntry.7

Object Type: IpAddress

Access Mode: read-write

Description: The IP address of the next hop for this route

Object Name: ipRouteType

OID: ipRouteEntry.8

Object Type: Integer

Access Mode: read-write

Description: A type identifier of this route. Valid types include other(1), invalid(2), direct(3), and indirect(4)

Object Name: ipRouteProto

OID: ipRouteEntry.9

Object Type: Integer

Access Mode: read-only

Description: The routing mechanism used to learn this route

Object Name: ipRouteAge

OID: ipRouteEntry.10

Object Type: IpAddress

Access Mode: read-write

Description: The time elapsed (seconds) since the route was updated or verified

Object Name: ipRouteMask

OID: ipRouteEntry.11

Object Type: IpAddress

Access Mode: read-write

Description: The mask address that is used (anded) with the destination address

Object Name: ipRouteMetric5

OID: ipRouteEntry.12

Object Type: Integer

Access Mode: read-write

Description: An alternate routing metric for this route

Object Name: ipRouteInfo

OID: ipRouteEntry.13

Object Type: Object Identifier

Access Mode: read-only

Description: The MIB definition reference to the routing
                      protocol responsible for this route

The ipNetToMediaTable table is an address translation table
that contains entries that correspond to IP addresses and physical
addresses. Figure 6.8 shows the tree view of this table.

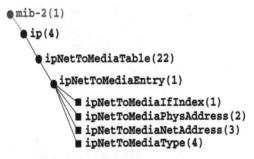

Figure 6.8 *The* ipNetToMediaTable *table view.*

The information contained within this table is basically the same
as that of the at table. The only difference is the ipNetToMediaType
object, which lists the type of mapping used.

Object Name: ipNetToMediaIfIndex

OID: ipNetToMediaEntry.1

Object Type: Integer

Access Mode: read-write

Description: The number of packets that were discarded despite the fact that they were valid

The `ipNetToMediaTable` table contains the following set of objects:

Object Name: `ipNetToMediaPhysAddress`

OID: `ipNetToMediaEntry.2`

Object Type: `PhysAddress`

Access Mode: read-write

Description: Media-dependent physical address; for example, Ethernet address

Object Name: `ipNetToMediaNetAddress`

OID: `ipNetToMediaEntry.3`

Object Type: `IpAddress`

Access Mode: read-write

Description: IP address that corresponds to the media-dependent physical address

Object Name: `ipNetToMediaType`

OID: `ipNetToMediaEntry.4`

Object Type: `Counter`

Access Mode: read-write

Description: The type of mapping that generated the address. Types include `other(1)`, `invalid(2)`, `dynamic(3)`, and `static(4)`

A sample listing of the `ipNetToMediaTable` table is shown here:

```
ip.ipNetToMediaTable.ipNetToMediaEntry.ipNetToMediaIfIndex.1.10.0.2.127 =
   1
ip.ipNetToMediaTable.ipNetToMediaEntry.ipNetToMediaPhysAddress.1.10.0.2.12
   7 = 0:60:97:e:a3:6
ip.ipNetToMediaTable.ipNetToMediaEntry.ipNetToMediaNetAddress.1.10.0.2.127
   = IpAddress: 10.0.2.127
ip.ipNetToMediaTable.ipNetToMediaEntry.ipNetToMediaType.1.10.0.2.127 =
   dynamic(3)
```

The `ipNetToMediaType` object is assigned the value of `dynamic(3)`, and additional values may include: `other(1)`, `invalid(2)`, and `static(4)`. The `dynamic` assignment implies that the entry was created by some automatic means, perhaps using Dynamic Host Configuration Protocol (DHCP) or some other mechanism.

IP Forwarding Group

The IP Forwarding table was added to MIB-II because of problems with the `ipRouteTable` table. With the IP Forwarding table, multiple routes to a single destination can appear, but access to these entries is dependent on the mechanism implemented to access this table. Unfortunately no way to obtain this routing information has been standardized within SNMP. The `IPForward` group was introduced for this purpose and has been placed at the end of the IP table and is shown in Figure 6.9.

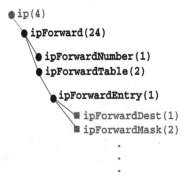

Figure 6.9 *The* `ipForward` *view.*

Most of the objects in the IPForwardTable table correspond to the objects within the IPRouteTable table and have the same syntax and meanings. As a result, a detailed listing of these objects is not listed. The chief difference is that each of the object prefixes has been changed from ipRoute to ipForward. Also, two new objects have been added: ipForwardPolicy and ipForwardNexHopAs. The ipForwardPolicy object indicates the policy of the route to a particular destination. With IP routing, the policy is based on the IP type-of-service field contained with the IP header. This field defines one of eight different levels of precedence and a binary value of delay. The ipForwardNextHopAs object helps those administering regional networks by providing the system number of the next hop within an autonomous routing domain.

The ipRouteDest object is used as the index in the ipRouteTable table. The ipForwardTable table can be indexed by ipForwardDest, ipForwardProto, ipForwardPolicy, and ipForwardNextHop.

ICMP Group

The icmp group contains counters that record the Internet Control Message Protocol operation. ICMP diagnoses connectivity problems and other network-layer problems. The famous ping utility uses this protocol. A list of icmp group objects are shown in Figure 6.10.

The icmp group contains the following set of objects:

Object Name:	icmpInMsgs
OID:	icmp.1
Object Type:	Counter
Access Mode:	read-only
Description:	The number of ICMP messages received

Object Name:	icmpInErrors
OID:	icmp.2

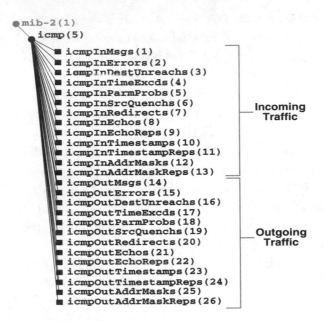

Figure 6.10 *The* icmp *group view.*

Object Type:	Counter
Access Mode:	read-only
Description:	The number of ICMP messages received that contained some ICMP-specific error

Object Name:	icmpInDestUnreachs
OID:	icmp.3
Object Type:	Counter
Access Mode:	read-only
Description:	The number of ICMP destination-unreachable messages received

Object Name:	icmpInTimeExcds
OID:	icmp.4

Object Type: Counter

Access Mode: read-only

Description: The number of ICMP time-exceeded messages received

Object Name: icmpInParmProbs

OID: icmp.5

Object Type: Counter

Access Mode: read-only

Description: The number of ICMP parameter problem messages received

Object Name: icmpInSrcQuenchs

OID: icmp.6

Object Type: Counter

Access Mode: read-only

Description: The number of ICMP source quench messages received

Object Name: icmpInRedirects

OID: icmp.7

Object Type: Counter

Access Mode: read-only

Description: The number of ICMP redirect messages received

Object Name: icmpInEchos

OID: icmp.8

Object Type: Counter

Access Mode: read-only

Description: The number of ICMP echo request messages
                     received

Object Name: icmpEchoReps

OID: icmp.9

Object Type: Counter

Access Mode: read-only

Description: The number of ICMP echo reply messages
                     received

Object Name: icmpTimestamps

OID: icmp.10

Object Type: Counter

Access Mode: read-only

Description: The number of ICMP timestamp request mes-
                     sages received

Object Name: icmpInTimestampReps

OID: icmp.11

Object Type: Counter

Access Mode: read-only

Description: The number of ICMP timestamp reply messages
                     received

Object Name: icmpAddrMasks

OID: icmp.12

Object Type: Counter

Access Mode: read-only

Description: The numberof ICMP address mask requests received

Object Name: icmpAddrMasksReps

OID: icmp.13

Object Type: Counter

Access Mode: read-only

Description: The number of ICMP address mask reply messages received

Object Name: icmpOutMsgs

OID: icmp.14

Object Type: Counter

Access Mode: read-only

Description: The number of ICMP messages that the system attempted to send

Object Name: icmpOutErrors

OID: icmp.15

Object Type: Counter

Access Mode: read-only

Description: The number of ICMP messages that the system couldn't send because of ICMP problems

Object Name: icmpOutDestUnreachs

OID: icmp.16

Object Type: Counter

Access Mode: read-only

Description: The number of ICMP destination unreachable
                      messages sent.

Object Name: icmpOutTimeExcds

OID: icmp.17

Object Type: Counter

Access Mode: read-only

Description: The number of ICMP time-exceeded messages
                      sent

Object Name: icmpOutParmProbs

OID: icmp.18

Object Type: Counter

Access Mode: read-only

Description: The number of ICMP parameter problem
                      messages sent

Object Name: icmpOutSrcQuenchs

OID: icmp.19

Object Type: Counter

Access Mode: read-only

Description: The number of ICMP source quench messages
                      sent

Object Name: icmpOutRedirects

OID: icmp.20

Object Type: Counter

Access Mode: read-only

Description: The number of ICMP redirect messages sent

Object Name: icmpOutEchos

OID: icmp.21

Object Type: Counter

Access Mode: read-only

Description: The number of packets that were discarded despite the fact that they were valid

Object Name: icmpOutEchoReps

OID: icmp.22

Object Type: Counter

Access Mode: read-only

Description: The number of ICMP echo request messages sent

Object Name: icmpOutTimestamps

OID: icmp.23

Object Type: Counter

Access Mode: read-only

Description: The number of ICMP echo reply messages sent

Object Name: icmpOutTimestampReps

OID: icmp.24

Object Type: Counter

Access Mode: read-only

Description: The number of ICMP timestamp request
                     messages sent

Object Name: icmpOutAddrMasks

OID: icmp.25

Object Type: Counter

Access Mode: read-only

Description: The number of ICMP timestamp reply messages
                     sent

Object Name: icmpOutAddrMaskReps

OID: icmp.26

Object Type: Counter

Access Mode: read-only

Description: The number of ICMP address mask request
                     messages sent

Sample output from querying the icmp group from a Linux
agent includes the following:

```
icmp.icmpInMsgs.0 = 27
icmp.icmpInErrors.0 = 0
icmp.icmpInDestUnreachs.0 = 7
icmp.icmpInTimeExcds.0 = 0
icmp.icmpInParmProbs.0 = 0
icmp.icmpInSrcQuenchs.0 = 0
icmp.icmpInRedirects.0 = 0
icmp.icmpInEchos.0 = 8
icmp.icmpInEchoReps.0 = 12
icmp.icmpInTimestamps.0 = 0
icmp.icmpInTimestampReps.0 = 0
icmp.icmpInaddrMasks.0 = 0
icmp.icmpInaddrMaskReps.0 = 0
```

```
icmp.icmpOutMsgs.0 = 10
icmp.icmpOutErrors.0 = 0
icmp.icmpOutDestUnreachs.0 = 2
icmp.icmpOutTimeExcds.0 = 0
icmp.icmpOutParmProbs.0 = 0
icmp.icmpOutSrcQuenchs.0 = 0
icmp.icmpOutRedirects.0 = 0
icmp.icmpOutEchos.0 = 0
icmp.icmpOutEchoReps.0 = 8
icmp.icmpOutTimestamps.0 = 0
icmp.icmpOutTimestampReps.0 = 0
icmp.icmpOutAddrMasks.0 = 0
icmp.icmpOutAddrMaskReps.0 = 0
```

As you can see from the output, many of the counters are quite low. This is as it should be. High counts for certain objects such as `icmpInTimeExcds` indicate a configuration problem or other operational problem.

TCP Group

The `tcp` group stores statistical and operational information about the Transmission Control Protocol (TCP) on a system. This group contains a single table that stores information regarding each TCP connection on the system. Figure 6.11 shows the tree view of this group.

The `tcp` group has the following objects:

Object Name:	`tcpRtoAlgorithm`
OID:	`tcp.1`
Object Type:	`Counter`
Access Mode:	`read-only`
Description:	The retransmission time algorithm; possible values include `other(1)`, `constant(2)`, `rsre(3)`, and `vanj(4)`

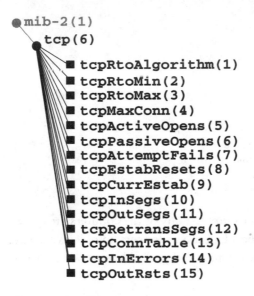

Figure 6.11 *The* tcp *group view.*

Object Name:	tcpRtoMin
OID:	tcp.2
Object Type:	Counter
Access Mode:	read-only
Description:	The minimum value for the retransmission timer

Object Name:	tcpRtoMax
OID:	tcp.3
Object Type:	Counter
Access Mode:	read-only
Description:	The maximum value for the retransmission timer

Object Name:	tcpMaxConn
OID:	tcp.4

Object Type:	Counter
Access Mode:	read-only
Description:	The total number (or limit) of TCP connections that the system can support

Object Name:	tcpActiveOpens
OID:	tcp.5
Object Type:	Counter
Access Mode:	read-only
Description:	The number of active opens this system has supported

Object Name:	tcpPassiveOpens
OID:	tcp.6
Object Type:	Counter
Access Mode:	read-only
Description:	The number of passive opens this system has supported

Object Name:	tcpAttemptFails
OID:	tcp.7
Object Type:	Counter
Access Mode:	read-only
Description:	The number of failed connection attempts that occurred on this system

Object Name:	tcpEstabResets
OID:	tcp.8

Object Type: Counter

Access Mode: read-only

Description: The number of resets that have occurred on this system

Object Name: tcpCurrEstab

OID: tcp.9

Object Type: Counter

Access Mode: read-only

Description: The number of TCP connections that are in either ESTABLISHED or CLOSE-WAIT states

Object Name: tcpInSegs

OID: tcp.10

Object Type: Counter

Access Mode: read-only

Description: The number of segments received, including those received in error

Object Name: tcpOutSegs

OID: tcp.11

Object Type: Counter

Access Mode: read-only

Description: The number of segments sent, but excluding those that contained retransmitted bytes

Object Name: tcpRetransSegs

OID: tcp.12

Object Type: Counter

Access Mode: read-only

Description: The number of retransmitted segments

Object Name: tcpConnTable

OID: tcp.13

Object Type: Counter

Access Mode: read-only

Description: TCP connection information

Object Name: tcpInErrors

OID: tcp.14

Object Type: Counter

Access Mode: read-only

Description: The number of segments received in error

Object Name: tcpOutRsts

OID: tcp.15

Object Type: Counter

Access Mode: read-only

Description: The number of TCP segments sent that contained the RST flag

The following was obtained by polling a Linux system:

```
tcp.tcpRtoAlgorithm.0 = other(1)
tcp.tcpRtoMin.0 = 0
tcp.tcpRtoMax.0 = 0
tcp.tcpMaxConn.0 = 0
tcp.tcpActiveOpens.0 = 105422
```

(continued)

```
tcp.tcpPassiveOpens.0 = 0
tcp.tcpAttemptFails.0 = 2968
tcp.tcpEstabResets.0 = 0
tcp.tcpCurrEstab.0 = Gauge: 2
tcp.tcpInSegs.0 = 63591
tcp.tcpOutSegs.0 = 111130
tcp.tcpRetransSegs.0 = 1881
```

The tcpConnTable table stores specific information regarding TCP connections on the system. Figure 6.12 shows the tree view of this table. The tcpConnEntry object is used as an index in the table. The size of this table is determined by the number of connections recorded on the system. On a busy server, it can be quite large.

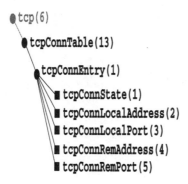

Figure 6.12 *The* tcpConnTable *view.*

The tcpConnState object identifies the current state of the connection. The valid values include the following: closed(1), listen(2), sysSent(3), sysReceived(4), established(5), finWait1(6), finWait2(7), closeWait(8), lastAck(9), closing(10), time-Wait(11), and deleteTCB(12). Excluding deleteTCB(12), the state values are representative of the TCP state machine model that was discussed in Chapter 2, "Simple Network Management Protocol." Recall that each connection will be in one of these defined states. The deleteTCB(12) state indicates that the TCP control block (TCB) for this connection has been deleted. The remaining objects store both the local and remote IP Addresses and port pair. For instance, consider the following output:

```
tcp.tcpConnTable.tcpConnEntry.tcpConnState.10.0.2.201.23.10.0.2.127.1033 =
    timeWait(11)
tcp.tcpConnTable.tcpConnEntry.tcpConnState.10.0.2.201.23.10.0.2.127.1035 =
    established(5)
tcp.tcpConnTable.tcpConnEntry.tcpConnState.10.0.2.201.53.0.0.0.0.0 = listen(2)
tcp.tcpConnTable.tcpConnEntry.tcpConnLocalAddress.10.0.2.201.23.10.0.2.127.1033=
    IpAddress: 10.0.2.201
tcp.tcpConnTable.tcpConnEntry.tcpConnLocalAddress.10.0.2.201.23.10.0.2.127.1035=
    IpAddress: 10.0.2.201
tcp.tcpConnTable.tcpConnEntry.tcpConnLocalAddress.10.0.2.201.53.0.0.0.0.0 =
    IpAddress: 10.0.2.201
tcp.tcpConnTable.tcpConnEntry.tcpConnLocalPort.10.0.2.201.23.10.0.2.127.1033 = 23
tcp.tcpConnTable.tcpConnEntry.tcpConnLocalPort.10.0.2.201.23.10.0.2.127.1035 = 23
tcp.tcpConnTable.tcpConnEntry.tcpConnLocalPort.10.0.2.201.53.0.0.0.0.0 = 53
tcp.tcpConnTable.tcpConnEntry.tcpConnRemAddress.10.0.2.201.23.10.0.2.127.1033
    =IpAddress: 10.0.2.127
tcp.tcpConnTable.tcpConnEntry.tcpConnRemAddress.10.0.2.201.23.10.0.2.127.1035
    =IpAddress: 10.0.2.127
tcp.tcpConnTable.tcpConnEntry.tcpConnRemAddress.10.0.2.201.53.0.0.0.0.0 =
    IpAddress: 0.0.0.0
tcp.tcpConnTable.tcpConnEntry.tcpConnRemPort.10.0.2.201.23.10.0.2.127.1033 = 1033
tcp.tcpConnTable.tcpConnEntry.tcpConnRemPort.10.0.2.201.23.10.0.2.127.1035 = 1035
tcp.tcpConnTable.tcpConnEntry.tcpConnRemPort.10.0.2.201.53.0.0.0.0.0 = 0
```

Given the connection

```
.tcpConnState.10.0.2.201.23.10.0.2.127.1035 = established(5)
```

which is the Established state, the `tcpConnLocalAddress` value is
`10.0.2.201` and the `tcpConnLocalPort` value is `23`, while the
remote information stored in the `tcpConnRemoteAddress` and
`tcpConnRemotePort` is `10.0.2.201` and `1035`, respectively.

UDP Group

The `udp` group contains objects that relate to the implementation and operation of the User Datagram Protocol (UDP) within
the system. A table called `udpTable` records the local address and
port information for UDP services listening for incoming requests.
The remaining objects are counters that record specific UDP traffic
statistics.

The `udp` group consists of the following objects:

Object Name: udpInDatagrams

OID: udp.1

Object Type: Counter

Access Mode: read-only

Description: The number of UDP datagrams delivered to
                      higher-level protocols and applications

Object Name: udpNoPorts

OID: udp.2

Object Type: Counter

Access Mode: read-only

Description: The number of received UDP datagrams for
                      which no specific application port was provided

Object Name: udpInErrors

OID: udp.3

Object Type: Counter

Access Mode: read-only

Description: The number of received UDP datagrams that
                      couldn't be delivered for reasons unrelated to
                      having an valid application or destination port

Object Name: udpOutDatagrams

OID: udp.4

Object Type: Counter

Access Mode: read-only

Description: The number of UDP datagrams sent from this
                      system

Object Name: udpTable

OID: udp.5

Object Type: Sequence of UdpEntry

Access Mode: not-accessible

Description: UDP listener address and port information

Object Name: udpEntry

OID: udpTable.1

Object Type: Sequence

Access Mode: not-accessible

Description: One udpTable for each UDP session

Object Name: udpLocalAddress

OID: udpEntry.1

Object Type: IpAddress

Access Mode: read-only

Description: Local IP address for this UDP listener, service, or application

Object Name: udpLocalPort

OID: udpEntry.2

Object Type: Integer

Access Mode: read-only

Description: Local port (socket) number for this UDP listener, service, or application

Figure 6.13 shows the tree view of the udp group.

Sample values were obtained by querying the Linux SNMP agent:

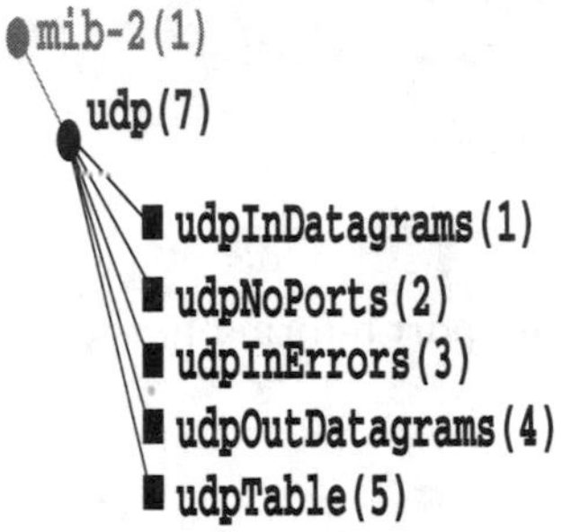

mib-2(1)

   udp(7)

      ■ udpInDatagrams(1)
      ■ udpNoPorts(2)
      ■ udpInErrors(3)
      ■ udpOutDatagrams(4)
      ■ udpTable(5)

Figure 6.13 *The* udp *group view.*

```
udp.udpInDatagrams.0 = 1867
udp.udpNoPorts.0 = 8
udp.udpInErrors.0 = 0
udp.udpOutDatagrams.0 = 1951
udp.udpTable.udpEntry.udpLocalAddress.0.0.0.0.111 = IpAddress: 0.0.0.0
udp.udpTable.udpEntry.udpLocalAddress.0.0.0.0.161 = IpAddress: 0.0.0.0
udp.udpTable.udpEntry.udpLocalAddress.0.0.0.0.177 = IpAddress: 0.0.0.0
udp.udpTable.udpEntry.udpLocalAddress.0.0.0.0.517 = IpAddress: 0.0.0.0
udp.udpTable.udpEntry.udpLocalAddress.0.0.0.0.518 = IpAddress: 0.0.0.0
udp.udpTable.udpEntry.udpLocalAddress.0.0.0.0.615 = IpAddress: 0.0.0.0
udp.udpTable.udpEntry.udpLocalAddress.0.0.0.0.626 = IpAddress: 0.0.0.0
udp.udpTable.udpEntry.udpLocalAddress.0.0.0.0.636 = IpAddress: 0.0.0.0
udp.udpTable.udpEntry.udpLocalAddress.0.0.0.0.641 = IpAddress: 0.0.0.0
udp.udpTable.udpEntry.udpLocalAddress.0.0.0.0.646 = IpAddress: 0.0.0.0
udp.udpTable.udpEntry.udpLocalAddress.0.0.0.0.679 = IpAddress: 0.0.0.0
udp.udpTable.udpEntry.udpLocalAddress.0.0.0.0.800 = IpAddress: 0.0.0.0
udp.udpTable.udpEntry.udpLocalAddress.0.0.0.0.1022 = IpAddress: 0.0.0.0
udp.udpTable.udpEntry.udpLocalAddress.0.0.0.0.1023 = IpAddress: 0.0.0.0
udp.udpTable.udpEntry.udpLocalAddress.0.0.0.0.1024 = IpAddress: 0.0.0.0
udp.udpTable.udpEntry.udpLocalAddress.0.0.0.0.1026 = IpAddress: 0.0.0.0
udp.udpTable.udpEntry.udpLocalAddress.0.0.0.0.1041 = IpAddress: 0.0.0.0
udp.udpTable.udpEntry.udpLocalAddress.0.0.0.0.2049 = IpAddress: 0.0.0.0
udp.udpTable.udpEntry.udpLocalAddress.10.0.2.201.53 = IpAddress: 10.0.2.201
udp.udpTable.udpEntry.udpLocalAddress.127.0.0.1.53 = IpAddress: 127.0.0.1
udp.udpTable.udpEntry.udpLocalAddress.127.0.0.1.1119 = IpAddress: 127.0.0.1
udp.udpTable.udpEntry.udpLocalPort.0.0.0.0.111 = 111
udp.udpTable.udpEntry.udpLocalPort.0.0.0.0.161 = 161
udp.udpTable.udpEntry.udpLocalPort.0.0.0.0.177 = 177
udp.udpTable.udpEntry.udpLocalPort.0.0.0.0.517 = 517
udp.udpTable.udpEntry.udpLocalPort.0.0.0.0.518 = 518
udp.udpTable.udpEntry.udpLocalPort.0.0.0.0.615 = 615
udp.udpTable.udpEntry.udpLocalPort.0.0.0.0.626 = 626
udp.udpTable.udpEntry.udpLocalPort.0.0.0.0.636 = 636
udp.udpTable.udpEntry.udpLocalPort.0.0.0.0.641 = 641
udp.udpTable.udpEntry.udpLocalPort.0.0.0.0.646 = 646
udp.udpTable.udpEntry.udpLocalPort.0.0.0.0.679 = 679
udp.udpTable.udpEntry.udpLocalPort.0.0.0.0.800 = 800
```

```
udp.udpTable.udpEntry.udpLocalPort.0.0.0.0.1022 = 1022
udp.udpTable.udpEntry.udpLocalPort.0.0.0.0.1023 = 1023
udp.udpTable.udpEntry.udpLocalPort.0.0.0.0.1024 = 1024
udp.udpTable.udpEntry.udpLocalPort.0.0.0.0.1026 = 1026
udp.udpTable.udpEntry.udpLocalPort.0.0.0.0.1041 = 1041
udp.udpTable.udpEntry.udpLocalPort.0.0.0.0.2049 = 2049
udp.udpTable.udpEntry.udpLocalPort.10.0.2.201.53 = 53
udp.udpTable.udpEntry.udpLocalPort.127.0.0.1.53 = 53
udp.udpTable.udpEntry.udpLocalPort.127.0.0.1.1119 = 1119
```

With most UNIX systems, a core set of networking services and applications use a standard address when binding to a local port. The standard address of 0.0.0.0 is used and means *this* host. For example, in the output above, the object

```
udpLocalAddress.0.0.0.0.161 = IpAddress: 0.0.0.0
```

demonstrates that a local address of 0.0.0.0 is used, which is bound to the UDP port of 161. The service that is associated with this port is the SNMP process (or snmpd), and the udpLocalPort.0.0.0.0.161 = 161 (which is of type Integer) holds this port information. As you can see, a large number of services are running the the udpEntry table, which contains one entry for each service.

If you would like to determine which process is associated with which port, you can look up the port number in the /etc/services file or run the **netstat** command. Consider the output from the **netstat** command:

```
# netstat -n -a -udp
(Not all processes could be identified, non-owned process info
 will not be shown, you would have to be root to see it all.)
Active Internet connections (servers and established)
Proto Recv-Q Send-Q Local Address      Foreign Address State
      PID/Program name
udp        0      0 0.0.0.0:177         0.0.0.0:*             699/
udp        0      0 127.0.0.1:1119      0.0.0.0:*             652/actived
udp        0      0 0.0.0.0:800         0.0.0.0:*             -
udp        0      0 0.0.0.0:1022        0.0.0.0:*             501/amd
udp        0      0 0.0.0.0:679         0.0.0.0:*             501/amd
udp        0      0 0.0.0.0:1023        0.0.0.0:*             501/amd
udp        0      0 0.0.0.0:1026        0.0.0.0:*             -
udp        0      0 0.0.0.0:2049        0.0.0.0:*             -
udp        0      0 0.0.0.0:646         0.0.0.0:*             460/rpc.mountd
udp        0      0 0.0.0.0:641         0.0.0.0:*             460/rpc.mountd
udp        0      0 0.0.0.0:636         0.0.0.0:*             460/rpc.mountd
udp        0      0 0.0.0.0:626         0.0.0.0:*             449/rpc.rquotad
udp        0      0 0.0.0.0:615         0.0.0.0:*             438/rpc.statd
udp        0      0 0.0.0.0:161         0.0.0.0:*             376/snmpd
```

(continued)

```
udp        0        0 0.0.0.0:1024      0.0.0.0:*              406/named
udp        0        0 10.0.2.201:53     0.0.0.0:*              406/named
udp        0        0 127.0.0.1:53      0.0.0.0:*              406/named
udp        0        0 0.0.0.0:518       0.0.0.0:*              362/inetd
udp        0        0 0.0.0.0.517       0.0.0.0:*              362/inetd
udp        0        0 0.0.0.0:111       0.0.0.0:*              255/portmap
```

The snmpd process, which is in bold, contains the same information as the udpTable. See Chapter 4, "Core System Utilities and Tools," for a complete description of the **netstat** command.

EGP Group

The egp group contains counters and objects related to the operation and implementation of the External Gateway Protocol within a system. Since most UNIX systems don't implement this group, the description has not been included. However, it is important to note that some networking devices, such as those that provide routing services, will support this MIB group.

Transmission (dot3) Group

The dot3 group contains objects that provide details about the low-level datalink medium for each of the defined interfaces on the system. Actually, the dot3 group isn't really a group at all, but rather a node under the MIB-II branch hierarchy. The primary purpose of this group is to provide interface-specific information in the form of an interface-specific MIB. Recall that the interfaces group provides generic information that applies to all the interfaces on a given system. The interface-specific MIBs under dot3 contain information that is related to a specific datalink protocol, such as Ethernet.

The Ethernet MIB, defined in RFC1643, defines a set of objects that represent attributes of an Ethernet-like communication medium. The EtherLike MIB contains three different access methods (or ifType) that include, ethernet-csmacd, iso88023-csmacd, and starlan. The ethernet-csmacd method is for the Ethernet standard of operation over 10Mbps using baseband coaxial cable medium. The iso88023-csmacd method covers all the standards developed by the IEEE 802.3 committee and the international standard ISO 8802-3. Included among the topology and cabling mediums is Fast Ethernet, which uses UTP and Fiber and Gigabit

Ethernet. The `starlan` method covers the obsolete 1Mbps LAN topology. Note that only networking technologies such as Ethernet use this MIB. Other networking media types, FDDI for example, do not have collisions. Devices that support these types of interfaces won't normally support this MIB group.

Figure 6.14 shows the four tables that the `dot3` group includes: `dot3StateTable`, `dot3SCollTable`, `dot3Tests`, and `dot3StateErrors`. The `do3StateTable` table contains statistics on the network traffic obtained at the interface between the agent software and the network medium. A table is required because a device may have a number of interfaces (e.g., a multi-protocol router).

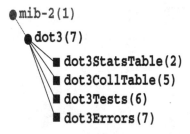

mib-2(1)

   dot3(7)

      ■ **dot3StatsTable(2)**
      ■ **dot3CollTable(5)**
      ■ **dot3Tests(6)**
      ■ **dot3Errors(7)**

Figure 6.14 *The* `dot3` *transmission group view.*

The `dot3StateTable` table records statistics regarding traffic observed between the agent and physical network medium. A table is needed instead of a set of specific counters because workstations, services, and other networking devices may contain more than one network interface. Thus, there is one table entry for each interface defined on the system. This table is indexed by the `dot3StateIndex` object. The `dot3StateTable` table objects are shown in Figure 6.15.

The `dot3StatTable` contains the following objects:

Object Name: `dot3StateEntry`

OID: `dot3StateTable.1`

Object Type: `Sequence`

Access Mode: `read-only`

Description: Statistics for an Ethernet-like network interface

Figure 6.15 *The* dot3StateTable *view.*

Object Name:	dot3StateIndex
OID:	dot3StateEntry.1
Object Type:	Integer
Access Mode:	read-only
Description:	Identifies an interface in the dot3StateTable table

Object Name:	dot3StateAlignmentErrors
OID:	dot3StateEntry.2
Object Type:	Counter
Access Mode:	read-only
Description:	Frames read from the network that is contained within the correct byte boundary

Object Name: `dot3StateFCSErrors`

OID: `dot3StateEntry.3`

Object Type: `Counter`

Access Mode: `read-only`

Description: Frames read from the network that did not pass the frame check sequence (FCS)

Object Name: `dot3StateSingleCollisionFrames`

OID: `dot3StateEntry.4`

Object Type: `Counter`

Access Mode: `read-only`

Description: Frames transmitted on the network that caused exactly one collision

Object Name: `dot3StateMulipleCollisionFrames`

OID: `dot3StateEntry.5`

Object Type: `Counter`

Access Mode: `read-only`

Description: Frames transmitted on the network that caused more than one collision

Object Name: `dot3StateSQETestErrors`

OID: `dot3StateEntry.6`

Object Type: `Counter`

Access Mode: `read-only`

Description: The frequency for the generation of the SQE test check

Object Name: dot3StateDeferredTransmission

OID: dot3StateEntry.7

Object Type: Counter

Access Mode: read-only

Description: The number of frames for which the first transmission attempt was delayed due to network
contention

Object Name: dot3StateLateCollisions

OID: dot3StateEntry.8

Object Type: Counter

Access Mode: read-only

Description: The number of times a collision was detected at
512-bit time intervals while transmitting

Object Name: dot3StateExcessiveCollisions

OID: dot3StateEntry.9

Object Type: Counter

Access Mode: read-only

Description: The number of transmitted frames that failed
due to excessive collisions

Object Name: dot3StateinternalMacTransmitErrors

OID: dot3StateEntry.10

Object Type: Counter

Access Mode: read-only

Description: The number of transmitted frames that failed due to internal media access control (MAC) errors

Object Name: `dot3StateCarrierSenseErrors`

OID: `dot3StateEntry.11`

Object Type: `Counter`

Access Mode: `read-only`

Description: The number of times that the carrier sense (CS) condition was lost or not asserted when transmitting a frame

Object Name: `dot3StateFrameTooLong`

OID: `dot3StateEntry.13`

Object Type: `Counter`

Access Mode: `read-only`

Description: The number of received frames that exceeded the maximum frame size

Object Name: `dot3StateInternalMacReceiveErrors`

OID: `dot3StateEntry.16`

Object Type: `Counter`

Access Mode: `read-only`

Description: The number of received frames that failed due to internal media access control (MAC) errors

Object Name: `dot3StateEtherChipSet`

OID: `dot3StateEntry.17`

Object Type: Counter

Access Mode: read-only

Description: The name of the chipset associated with this
                     interface

The dot3CollTable table contains a record of the collision activity observed on the network between the agent and the network medium. It stores a histogram for a set of interfaces defined on the system. The dot3CollCount object contains a single histogram point for each interface. The dot3CollFrequencies object stores the number of transmitted frames that experience exactly the number of collisions in the associated dot3CollCount object.

The dot3CollTable table has the following objects:

Object Name: dot3CollEntry

OID: dot3CollTable.1

Object Type: Sequence

Access Mode: read-only

Description: A group of collision histograms for a collection
                     of network interfaces

Object Name: dot3CollCount

OID: dot3StateEntry.1

Object Type: Counter

Access Mode: read-only

Description: One histogram point for a specific interface. The
                     total number of collisions for a specific interface

Object Name: dot3CollFrequencies

OID: dot3StateEntry.2

Object Type: Counter

Access Mode: read-only

Description: The number of frames on an interface that experienced exactly the number of collisions in the associated dot3CollCount object

The two remaining tables, dot3Tests and dot3Errors, are used when testing interfaces and reporting errors. The dot3Tests table contains two objects, dot3TestTdr and dot3TestLoopBack, that identify specific tests that can be invoked against the network media. The dot3TestTdr object invokes a time domain reflectometry (TDR) test, while the dot3TestLoopBack object provides a hardware loopback test. The dot3Errors table also contains two objects, dot3ErrorInitError and dot3ErrorLoopbackError, that store error information related to any tests that may have been executed from the dot3Tests table.

The dot3Tests and dot3Errors tables contains the following objects:

Object Name: dot3TestsTDR

OID: dot3Tests.1

Object Type: Counter

Access Mode: read-only

Description: TDR test

Object Name: dot3TestLoopBack

OID: dot3Tests.2

Object Type: Counter

Access Mode: read-only

Description: Loopback test

Object Name: dot3ErrorInitError

OID: dot3Errors.1

Object Type: Counter

Access Mode: read-only

Description: Identifies errors related to the chipset that failed
                     tests

Object Name: dot3StateIndex

OID: dot3StateEntry.1

Object Type: Counter

Access Mode: read-only

Description: Errors associated with running the loopback
                     tests

SNMP Group

The snmp group contains information related to the operation and implementation of SNMP. Some of the objects within this group are related to SNMP station management or agent functions. Hence, each SNMP implementation may use certain objects from the table. Those objects not supported by the agent contain a zero value.

With the exception of the snmpEnableAuthenTraps object, which is *read-write*, all the other objects are *read-only*. This object controls whether the agent is permitted to generate authentication-failure traps and is usually set by a network management application. Authentication failures are the result of a management entity attempting to execute some privileged function on the agent when it doesn't have the correct security permission or credentials to do so. Figure 6.16 shows the tree view of the snmp table.

Notice that both positions 7 and 8 are not listed because the MIB doesn't define any objects for these slots. As you can see in Figure 6.16, many of the SNMP objects are listed in gray, while a

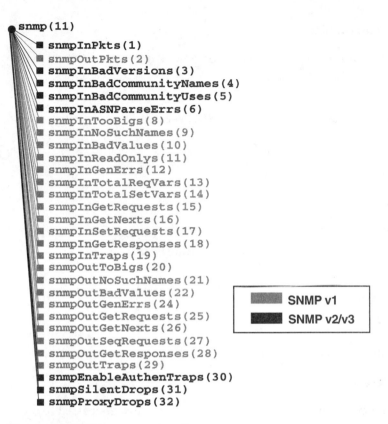

Figure 6.16 *The* snmp *group view.*

few are listed in black. This is because the original version of the
table included all the gray objects plus some of the others as well.
When the SNMPv2 specification was published, many of these
objects were deprecated. However, since many agents continued to
support SNMPv1, these objects are still in use. This is one example
of when newer MIB specifications have little effect on what was
implemented in the past. The older snmp group objects will be with
us for a long time. The snmp table contains the following objects:

Object Name: snmpInPkts

OID: snmp.1

Object Type: Counter

Access Mode: read-only

Description: The number of SNMP messages delivered to the agent

Object Name: snmpOutPkts **(Deprecated)**

OID: snmp.2

Object Type: Counter

Access Mode: read-only

Description: The number of SNMP messages passed from the agent to the transport layer

Object Name: snmpInBadVersions

OID: snmp.3

Object Type: Counter

Access Mode: read-only

Description: The number of SNMP messages passed to the agent that were unsupported

Object Name: snmpInBadCommunityNames

OID: snmp.4

Object Type: Counter

Access Mode: read-only

Description: The number of SNMP messages passed to the agent that contained an unknown community name

Object Name: snmpInBadCommunityUses

OID: snmp.5

Object Type: Counter

Access Mode: read-only

Description: The number of SNMP messages passed to the agent that contained an SNMP operation not allowed by the SNMP community name supplied

Object Name: snmpInASNParseErrs

OID: snmp.6

Object Type: Counter

Access Mode: read-only

Description: The number of BER and ASN errors encountered when decoding incoming SNMP messages

Object Name: snmpInTooBigs **(Deprecated)**

OID: snmp.8

Object Type: Counter

Access Mode: read-only

Description: The number of SNMP PDUs delivered to the agent for which the tooBig error occurred

Object Name: snmpInNoSuchName **(Deprecated)**

OID: snmp.9

Object Type: Counter

Access Mode: read-only

Description: The number of SNMP PDUs delivered to the agent for which the noSuchName error occurred

Object Name: snmpInBadValues **(Deprecated)**

OID: snmp.10

Object Type: Counter

Access Mode: read-only

Description: The number of SNMP PDUs delivered to the
agent for which the badValue error occurred

Object Name: snmpInReadOnlys **(Deprecated)**

OID: snmp.11

Object Type: Counter

Access Mode: read-only

Description: The number of SNMP PDUs delivered to the
agent for which the readOnly error occurred

Object Name: snmpInGenErrs **(Deprecated)**

OID: snmp.12

Object Type: Counter

Access Mode: read-only

Description: The number of SNMP PDUs delivered to the
agent for which the genErr error occurred

Object Name: snmpInTotalReqVars **(Deprecated)**

OID: snmp.13

Object Type: Counter

Access Mode: read-only

Description: The number of MIB objects retrieved successfully by the agent as a result of a valid SNMP
get-request and getnext-request

Object Name: snmpInTotalSetVars **(Deprecated)**

OID: snmp.14

Object Type: Counter

Access Mode: read-only

Description: The number of MIB objects retrieved success-fully by the agent as a result of a valid SNMP set-request

Object Name: snmpInGetRequests **(Depreciated)**

OID: snmp.15

Object Type: Counter

Access Mode: read-only

Description: The number of SNMP get-requests accepted and processed by the agent

Object Name: snmpInGetNexts **(Deprecated)**

OID: snmp.16

Object Type: Counter

Access Mode: read-only

Description: The number of SNMP getnext-requests accepted and processed by the agent

Object Name: snmpInSetRequests

OID: snmp.17

Object Type: Counter

Access Mode: read-only

Description: The number of SNMP set-requests accepted and processed by the agent

Object Name: snmpInGetResponses **(Deprecated)**

OID: snmp.18

Object Type: Counter

Access Mode: read-only

Description: The number of SNMP get-responses accepted
                     and processed by the agent

Object Name: snmpInTraps **(Deprecated)**

OID: snmp.19

Object Type: Counter

Access Mode: read-only

Description: The number of SNMP traps accepted and pro-
                     cessed by the agent

Object Name: snmpOutTooBig

OID: snmp.20

Object Type: Counter

Access Mode: read-only

Description: The number of SNMP PDUs generated by the
                     agent for which the tooBig error occurred

Object Name: snmpOutNoSuchNames **(Deprecated)**

OID: snmp.21

Object Type: Counter

Access Mode: read-only

Description: The number of SNMP PDUs generated by the
                     agent for which the noSuchName error occurred

Object Name: snmpOutBadValues **(Deprecated)**

OID: snmp.22

Object Type: Counter

Access Mode: read-only

Description: The number of SNMP PDUs generated by the agent for which the badValue error occurred

Object Name: snmpOutGenErrs **(Deprecated)**

OID: snmp.24

Object Type: Counter

Access Mode: read-only

Description: The number of SNMP PDUs generated by the agent for which the genErr error occurred

Object Name: snmpOutGetRequents **(Deprecated)**

OID: snmp.25

Object Type: Counter

Access Mode: read-only

Description: The number of SNMP get-request PDUs generated by the agent

Object Name: snmpOutGetNexts **(Deprecated)**

OID: snmp.26

Object Type: Counter

Access Mode: read-only

Description: The number of SNMP getnext-request PDUs generated by the agent

Object Name: snmpOutSetRequests **(Deprecated)**

OID: snmp.27

Object Type: Counter

Access Mode: read-only

Description: The number of SNMP set-request PDUs generated by the agent

Object Name: snmpOutGetResponses **(Deprecated)**

OID: snmp.28

Object Type: Counter

Access Mode: read-only

Description: The number of SNMP get-responses PDUs generated by the agent

Object Name: snmpOutTraps **(Deprecated)**

OID: snmp.29

Object Type: Counter

Access Mode: read-only

Description: The number of SNMP traps generated by the
agent

Object Name: snmpEnableAuthenTraps

OID: snmp.30

Object Type: Integer

Access Mode: read-write

Description: Whether authentication failure traps should be generated. Valid values are `enabled(1)` or `disabled(2)`. When an SNMP entity attempts to query the agent with an invalid community string or authentication token, the agent will emit an SNMP trap if enabled

Using SNMP Agents

This chapter provides a detailed overview of SNMP agents that are available specifically on Linux and Solaris systems. Red Hat Linux systems are shipped with the University of California at Davis (UCD) SNMP system agent that provides both MIB-II and UCD specific objects. The Sun agent, known as the Solstice Enterprise Agent (SEA), comes with the latest release of Solaris and includes Sun-specific MIB objects. The SEA package actually includes two agents: a master and a subagent. Because the term *Solstice* also refers to Sun's network management framework and mix of products, this book will use the terms *master agent* and *subagent* to describe these agents from Sun.

Overview of Agents

All three of the agents listed above provide some of the same fundamental services· namely, the retrieval and setting of MIB objects. Each of the agents supports the standard SNMP basic operations, including get, set, and trap. Additionally, each of the agents provides some specialized functions such as support for disk or memory management. Which agent to use depends on the environment and the types of problems you attempt to solve. It might, for example, be necessary to use all three agents because each provides services that are required.

The functionality of each of the agents can be summarized into several categories:

MIB-II Support: The agent supports either most of or the entire standard set of MIB-II objects. The MIB-II standard is described in the preceding chapter.

Process Management: Additional MIB objects are available to manage UNIX processes. Basic operations include listing and controlling these processes via the agent.

Remote Configuration: The agent can manipulate its own configuration file via the SNMP protocol. For example, the agent can be made to dynamically alter a predefined action when the monitored object reaches a critical threshold.

Extended MIB Support: The agent supports additional MIB objects, which provide information beyond the MIB-II standard. This might include either proprietary vendor-specific MIBs or standard MIBs such as the Host Resource MIB.

Flexible Configuration: The agent provides a flexible set of configuration options and keywords, which are primarily used to control the operating state and behavior of the agent.

Performance Objects: The agent supports additional MIB objects that provide additional performance information or statistical data.

Customizable Actions: The agent can execute external scripts or programs contained within the agent configuration file. These actions are usually the direct result of some specific condition or event that the agent has detected.

Memory/Disk Management: The agent provides additional MIB objects that provide additional memory or disk information or statistical data.

Master Agent Support: The agent provides the capability for subagents to register to receive SNMP messages. The master agent is responsible for handling outside communication on behalf of the subagents. The master agent uses SNMP port 161, while the subagents communicate with the master agent on another predefined port.

Extensible: The agent can be extended to support additional functionality and provide new features such as executing external UNIX shell scripts or other commands. This might also mean that the agent provides a development environment that includes interfaces that facilitate adding new features by recompiling (or linking) various components of the package.

SNMPv2/v3: The agent supports one or more elements of SNMPv2 and/or SNMPv3 protocol specifications.

Table 7.1 outlines the functionality of each agent and can be used as a quick reference when choosing an agent.

Table 7.1 *Functional overview of agents*

Category	Linux	Agent Sun Master	Sun
MIB-II objects	✓		✓
Process management objects	✓	✓	✓
Remote configuration	✓		
Additional system objects			✓
Flexible configuration	✓		✓
Additional performance objects	✓		✓
Customizable actions	✓		
Memory management objects	✓		
Disk management objects	✓		
Master agent		✓	
Subagent management		✓	
Extensible capabilities	✓		
SNMP v2/v3	✓		

The Linux SNMP Agent

The Linux agent, known as snmpd, provides a comprehensive list of SNMP-related services. The Linux agent is actually the agent from the University of California at Davis known as the UCD-agent and is available on a large number of operating systems, including Linux. This agent supports SNMPv1, SNMPv2, and SNMPv3 network management protocols. This means it supports not only the basic SNMP operations, but also those associated with SNMPv2, such as get-bulk, get-inform, and several others.

Also, it supports the User Security Model (USM) that is described within the SNMPv3 specifications. It supports MIB-II, the UCD MIB, and several other MIBs as well. The agent provides the capability to remotely execute UNIX commands that have been configured based on certain events or conditions. The agent can be used to monitor both system memory and process information.

The advantages of using the UCD package are significant. First, the software provides a very complete set of tools and features that are available within the public domain. The package includes user SNMP tools, plus a fully functional SNMP agent. Many SNMP packages are available on the Internet, but most don't compare to the stability, robustness, and features found within the UCD package. Second, despite the fact that the UCD software is in the public domain, it seems to have a loyal following and has seen continuous improvement over the years, even surpassing some well-established commercial products in terms of SNMP protocol support and features. The UCD tools are supported on a large number of computer platforms and operating systems. The package is included in certain Linux distributions, such as Red Hat. Finally, the UCD package is free, which means it can be deployed across the network enterprise without concern for licensing issues. This makes the agent very attractive to budget-constrained institutions and other organizations.

Sun's Master Agent

Sun provides a standard SNMP network management master agent that can be used as the basis for an enterprise management strategy. This agent, called `snmpdx`, provides a master/subagent facility for one or more subagents. Recall from Chapter 2, "Simple Network Management Protocol," that the main purpose and role of a master agent is to permit many SNMP agents to coexist. Because each SNMP agent must listen for requests on well-known SNMP port `161`, a mechanism must be provided so that all agents can share this port without conflict. Without special arbitration, the first agent to use the port would obtain an exclusive lock on the port, and all other agents would be denied access. With the `snmpdx` agent, many subagents can be installed on the same system without the traditional port contention problem. Also, this master agent

supports a collection of MIB objects that describe each of the subagents that have been configured with the master agent.

Sun's SNMP Agent

Sun also provides a standard SNMP network management system agent. This agent, known as `mibiisa`, supports SNMPv1 and
provides read-write access to both MIB-II and Sun enterprise specific objects. This agent works under Sun's master/slave agent
architecture, which means that it can operate in conjunction with a
master agent or in stand alone mode. It provides the ability to manage Sun workstations and servers from an operational and performance standpoint. It supports the standard MIB-II object groups
and some additional groups defined by Sun. Together, the features
of this agent can monitor some of the more critical network management problems that face network and system managers alike.

The advantages of using the UCD agent include integration into
the operating system and support by the vendor. Because the agent
is shipped with Solaris, the agent component can very easily be
loaded with the operating system software. On older versions of
the operating system that don't already have the agent, it is possible to install the agent in a straightforward manner by using Sun's
pkgadd utility. Additionally, because the agent was developed by
Sun, it will be supported should problems arise that require technical assistance. Finally, vendor support ensures that users can expect
enhancements and new functionality to be included in future
releases of the agent. This is important because SNMP will continue to change to meet the growing requirements of network and
system administrators.

Agent MIBs

Each of the agents described in this section implements either
standard or private (or both) MIBs. Because both the Sun and
UCD agents use private MIBs, access to these objects is at the
enterprise branch level. Figure 7.1 shows the path from root to
each of the vendor's private branches.

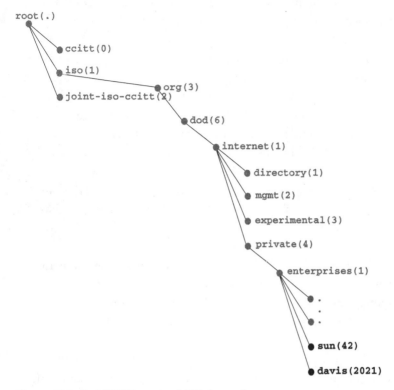

Figure 7.1 *Sun/UCD agent MIB branches.*

Security Considerations

These agents are very powerful and can have a profound impact on network management. Because they provide access to critical portions of the system, care should be taken when configuring and using them. For example, the configuration file for the Sun Agent provides the ability to set community strings for both read and write access to the MIB. Many network management systems and agents (including the ones listed here) are configured by default with the standard community strings public and private. It would be important to change these to nonstandard passwords when deploying these agents at a local site. Despite the fact that SNMP community string information can be obtained via a packet-capture device and decoded, community names should still be unique and hard-to-guess. In a large installation, it might be necessary to

use a set of community strings for a collection of devices either geo-
graphically co-located or of certain types, like Cisco or 3Com
devices

Failure to configure the agents correctly can be disastrous. For
example, with the Sun agent, a network interface can be disabled
with a simple SNMP `set` operation if the community string is
`public`. Someone with an MIB browser or **snmpset** command tool
could easily disable one or more system interfaces. If the disabled
interface is the only interface on that system, the system would
effectively become disconnected from the network. As a result, all
network-related processes would be affected by this action. In
some environments, this would be considered an outage and would
carry some significant consequences. To restore the system to its
original state, the administrator must log in to the system console,
if available, and enable the interface using the **ifconfig** command.
Alternately, if no system console exists, the system must be rebooted by removing power; this step also increases the likelihood
of data loss because there is no way to synchronize the file systems
beforehand.

The rule of thumb here is to be careful when setting up the agent
configuration files and don't use the standard SNMP community
names. As you will see, an access control list (ACL) and additional
security facilities available within agents will provide further pro-
tection.

The Linux SNMP Agent

General Description

The Linux Agent (`snmpd`) is a very powerful, extensible, fully
functional SNMP system agent that is available on a large number
of UNIX platforms. See the Installation section in Appendix B for a
list of specific platforms that are supported. As previously mentioned, the agent supports MIB-II (network statistics), SNMPv2
MIBs, SMUX MIB, the host resource MIB, and the UCD-SNMP
MIB. These MIBs are located by default in the
`/usr/local/share/snmp/mibs` directory. However, the agent will
still function correctly if it is unable to locate these files.

From a network management perspective, the agent can monitor critical system operating parameters (such as system load average) and provide alerts when these resources reach a critical threshold. The agent can do the following:

- monitor disk-space usage

- monitor system processes

- monitor system load

- invoke UNIX commands and shell scripts

- monitor agent information and status

- provide access to key MIB objects

The sections that follow explore each of these features in greater detail, including how to configure the agent to monitor these resources and how to proactively address system resource limitation problems.

Agent Configuration File

The agent requires a configuration file to operate. This file is located by default in the `/usr/local/share/snmp` directory. It contains one or more action directives, and each line has a single keyword with an associated number of arguments. The keyword can be divided into one of the following categories: *monitor*, *security*, *extensible*, and *informational*, as shown in Table 7.2. The monitoring directives (**proc, disk,** and **load**) include those used to track specific resources such as disk space or system load. Security keywords (**com2sec, group, view,** and **access**) are used to define various layers of security for access to the agent, which may include access control lists (ACL) and various views of MIB objects. The extensible keywords (**exec** and **pass**) define ways to add functionality to the agent without changing the agent software. Finally, the informational keywords (**syslocation** and **syscontact**) assign static information to MIB objects. Each of the keywords has a fixed number of required parameters and may have additional optional arguments as well.

Table 7.2 *UCD agent commands sorted by category*

Category	Keyword	Description
Monitor	proc	Checks whether specified processes are running
	disk	Determines available disk space of specified file system
	load	Monitors system load average
Security	com2sec	Specifies a mapping between source/community name and security name
	group	Defines a mapping between a model/security name and a group
	view	Defines one or more specific views into the agent's MIBs
	access	Security Configuration Parameter
Extensible	exec	Executes the specified command and makes the output available via the MIB
	pass	Passes an MIB tree to specified program that can manipulate the MIB objects
Informational	syslocation	Represents the physical location of the agent device
	syscontact	Represents the contact person for the agent device

To insert comments, place the character # at the beginning of a line.

When the agent first starts up, it reads the configuration file. If changes are made to the file after the agent has started, the agent can be instructed to re-read the configuration file in two ways. First, the MIB object versionUpdateConfig can be set to 1. For example, using the UCD snmpset tool, the following command would force the agent on system rodin to process the configuration file again:

```
snmpset rodin private .1.3.6.1.4.1.ucdavis.version.version-
UpdateConfig.0 i 1
```

Second, the -HUP signal can be sent to the agent process by using the **kill** command. Before issuing this command, we must obtain the process id of the agent. This can be done, for example, by issuing the **ps** command. Assuming that the process id was found to be 304, the following command would be functionally equivalent to the **snmpget** command:

```
# kill -HUP 304
```

Some of the agent keywords, when executed, monitor resources that modify certain MIB objects that indicate the return status or additional information. These objects are part of the agent's MIB and are accessed from the UCD (2021) private branch. The starting path of the MIB is:

```
iso.org.dod.internet.mgmt.enterprises.ucdavis
```

or

```
1.3.6.1.4.1.2021
```

Also, if you find that the agent must be restarted due to some other operational problem, such as a crash, then invoke the standard startup script: snmpd. For example, to restart the agent, you would issue the following command:

```
# /etc/rc.d/init.d/snmpd restart
Shutting down snmpd:
[  OK  ]
Starting snmpd:
[  OK  ]
```

If the agent started successfully, the [OK] string will be displayed; otherwise an error string will be shown.

Note

> The snmpd script supports additional commands. These include **stop, start,** and **status.** The **stop** option will kill the agent if it is already running, while the **start** option will start the agent if it is not already active. The final option, **status,** checks whether the agent is running.

Monitoring System Load

The UCD agent provides the ability to monitor the system load average via the **load** agent command. The system load average is the average number of jobs (or programs) in the run queue. The agent provides the same basic information as the UNIX **uptime** and **w** commands. The syntax of this command includes:

load [1 minute max] [5 minute max] [15 minute max]

The **load** command, followed by either 1 maximum, 5 maximum, or 15 maximum will instruct the agent to monitor the system load for these times. If the system load exceeds the maximum for one-minute, five-minute, or 15-minute running averages, then the agent will set the loadaveErrorFlag object to 1 and include a descriptive error message in the loadaveErrMessage object. If no maximum load string is specified, then the default value of 1 minute is used.

The **load** command is an excellent way to monitor system utilization across a large number of systems. Establishing the system load threshold can be a little tricky because certain systems might need different thresholds. For example, a workstation might experience high system load because the user just started a CPU-intensive application. On the other hand, a user starting the same application on a server with a large number of users could pose a significant problem. Also, some systems might always have a higher load than other systems but, because the system is expected to be used in this manner, it might not represent a problem.

For critical systems, a load average higher than 2 or 3 may indicate a severe problem that must be addressed in a timely manner. In the following example, the agent has been configured to monitor the one-minute load average with a threshold of 2:

```
load 2
```

Should this limit be reached, the agent's MIB will be updated appropriately:

```
enterprises.ucdavis.loadTable.laEntry.laErrorFlag.1 = 1
enterprises.ucdavis.loadTable.laEntry.laErrorFlag.2 = 1
enterprises.ucdavis.loadTable.laEntry.laErrorFlag.3 = 0
enterprises.ucdavis.loadTable.laEntry.laErrMessage.1 = "1
   min Load Average too high (= 2.50)"
enterprises.ucdavis.loadTable.laEntry.laErrMessage.2 = "5
   min Load Average too high (= 2.26)"
enterprises.ucdavis.loadTable.laEntry.laErrMessage.3 = ""
```

In this case, the MIB shows that both the one- and the five-minute load averages exceeded the 2 limit threshold. The MIB shows three instances of the laErrorFlag and laErrMessage because the load average is measured in terms of one-, five-, and 15-minute averages. Thus, three separate MIB object instances are created.

The agent also provides access to both the current system load averages and the parameters for the configuration of the **load** command itself. For example, the following was obtained from the agent when the load was above the 2 mark:

```
enterprises.ucdavis.loadTable.laEntry.laNames.1 = "Load-1"
enterprises.ucdavis.loadTable.laEntry.laNames.2 = "Load-5"
enterprises.ucdavis.loadTable.laEntry.laNames.3 = "Load-15"
enterprises.ucdavis.loadTable.laEntry.laLoad.1 = "2.50" Hex: 32 2E 35 30
enterprises.ucdavis.loadTable.'aEntry.laLoad.2 = "2.26" Hex: 32 2E 32 36
enterprises.ucdavis.loadTable.laEntry.laLoad.3 = "1.38" Hex: 31 2E 33 38
enterprises.ucdavis.loadTable.laEntry.laConfig.1 = "2.00" Hex: 32 2E 30 30
enterprises.ucdavis.loadTable.laEntry.laConfig.2 = "2.00" Hex: 32 2E 30 30
enterprises.ucdavis.loadTable.laEntry.laConfig.3 = "2.00" Hex: 32 2E 30 30
```

As you can see, the load averages for one and five minutes are above 2. Also, the laConfig object is set at 2.00 for each load average threshold level. The laNames object is simply a label used to describe each load average window. This information was obtained directly from the agent configuration file.

Monitoring Disk Space

The agent can monitor disk-space consumption of any mounted file systems with the **disk** keyword command, using the following syntax:

```
disk file-system [minimum]
```

The agent will monitor the specified file system and determine if the total disk space available is less than the minimum. If it is, the MIB object diskErrorFlag will be set to 1, and the MIB object diskErrorMsg will contain a descriptive message. If no minimum is provided, the agent uses the default value of 100K. The minimum value is stored in the dskMinimum object and set either to the specified minimum from the configuration file or to the default if no minimum value is found in the configuration file.

By way of example, consider the following agent commands:

```
disk /
disk  /usr   1000
```

The first **disk** command will monitor the / (root) file system and compare the minimum value of 100 megabytes (Mb). If no size argument were supplied, a value of 100 kilobytes (the default) would be used. This value is compared to the total disk space that is available. The default value can be overridden. The second command will monitor the /usr file system and compare available space to the minimum value of 1,000 Kb. Because the minimum is in Kb units, we must add three zeros to the end to get the value in bytes. In this case, we get 1,000,000 bytes. Querying the agent returns the following:

```
enterprises.ucdavis.diskTable.dskEntry.dskMinimum.1 =
    100000
enterprises.ucdavis.diskTable.dskEntry.dskMinimum.2 = 1000
enterprises.ucdavis.diskTable.dskEntry.dskAvail.1 = 56924
enterprises.ucdavis.diskTable.dskEntry.dskAvail.2 = 32545
enterprises.ucdavis.diskTable.dskEntry.dskErrorFlag.1 = 1
enterprises.ucdavis.diskTable.dskEntry.dskErrorFlag.2 = 0
enterprises.ucdavis.diskTable.dskEntry.dskErrorMsg.1 = "/:
    less than 100000 free (= 56924)"
enterprises.ucdavis.diskTable.dskEntry.dskErrorMsg.2 = ""
```

You will notice that two sets of MIB objects are defined. The first set corresponds to the root (/) file system because it appears first in the agent configuration file. The second set is for the /usr file system because it comes after the first entry within the configuration file.

As you can see, the dskMinimum objects are set accordingly; the dskMinimum.1 instance, which maps to the / file system, is set to 100Mb (100,000,000 bytes), while the second, diskMinimum.2, which maps to the /usr file system, is set to 1Mb (1,000,000 bytes). The agent also stores the available disk space of each monitored file system in the dskAvail object, one for each file system. In this case, the / file system is approximately 56Mb, while the /usr file system is approximately 32Mb. The dskErrorFlag.1 object for the file system is set because the root file system is less than 100Mb and the dskErrorMsg.1 contains more descriptive information. In this case, the dskErrorMsg.2 object does not contain any information. The dskErrorFlag.2 is not set because the /usr file system contains enough space to satisfy the disk-space test.

The MIB also contains other information that can be used when monitoring disk space. The information is comparable to the output of the UNIX **df** (disk free) command. For example, the **df-k** command includes a summary of the disk space of the mounted file systems. The output below includes a partial list of the file systems reported:

```
Filesystem          1k-blocks       Used Available Use%
Mounted on
/dev/hdb1             82303        25286     56935  31%     /
/dev/hdb2            232141       199364     32545  86%
/usr
```

When the agent is queried, we find the following:

```
enterprises.ucdavis.diskTable.dskEntry.dskPath.1 = "/" Hex: 2F
enterprises.ucdavis.diskTable.dskEntry.dskPath.2 = "/usr" Hex: 2F 75 73 72
enterprises.ucdavis.diskTable.dskEntry.dskDevice.1 = "/dev/hdb1"
enterprises.ucdavis.diskTable.dskEntry.dskDevice.2 = "/dev/hdb2"
enterprises.ucdavis.diskTable.dskEntry.dskTotal.1 = 82303
enterprises.ucdavis.diskTable.dskEntry.dskTotal.2 = 232141
enterprises.ucdavis.diskTable.dskEntry.dskAvail.1 = 56935
enterprises.ucdavis.diskTable.dskEntry.dskAvail.2 = 32545
enterprises.ucdavis.diskTable.dskEntry.dskUsed.1 = 25286
```

(continued)

```
enterprises.ucdavis.diskTable.dskEntry.dskUsed.2 = 199364
enterprises.ucdavis.diskTable.dskEntry.dskPercent.1 = 31
enterprises.ucdavis.diskTable.dskEntry.dskPercent.2 = 86
```

Notice that the MIB contains all the information that the **df** command provides. This includes the mount points, file systems, total disk space, available disk space, used disk space, and percent disk space used. This information can be extremely helpful because, for example, it is possible to monitor disk-space usage in percentages instead of raw bytes by using the dskPercent objects. Also, the remaining objects can be used as an automated mechanism for inventory of system storage capacities. The "Linux MIB" section includes more information on these and other agent MIB objects.

Monitoring System Processes

The **proc** command can monitor specific application services or standard UNIX processes. The command uses the following syntax:

```
proc process [maximum limit] [minimum limit]
```

This command is followed by a valid process name or command to be monitored by the agent. This directive is used to monitor a critical process or a set of processes that must be running continuously on the system. If the process is not found running on the local system by the agent, an error flag is set in the MIB object procTable.prEntry.prErrorFlag, and a descriptive message is placed in the MIB object procTable.prEntry.prErrMessage. The agent uses the UNIX **ps-e** command to search for running processes as specified with the **proc** command. For instance, the following command can be used to ensure that the mountd process is alive:

```
proc mountd
```

Additionally, a *maximum* and *minimum* value can be included to further refine the number of processes that should be running. The maximum indicates how many processes should be running concurrently, while the minimum determines the smallest number that must be running. For example, since it is customary to have multiple mountd processes on a system, the agent can be configured to monitor the exact number. For the sake of discussion, let's

assume that we have enabled the system to support four instances
of `mountd`:

```
proc mountd 4 4
```

If the agent detects that either less than four or greater than four
`mountd` processes are currently running, it updates the MIB appropriately.

If no maximum and minimum values are specified, the default
of zero is assumed. In practice, the use of both the maximum and
minimum options provides a flexible way to address specific monitoring requirements.

The command

```
proc ntalkd 4
```

directs the agent to monitor the `ntalkd` process and update the
MIB if more than four are currently running. Therefore, the maximum option provides a convenient way to ensure that only a certain number of processes are permitted to run currently. If we want
to go a step further, we can automate the agent to take an action
(for example, kill the process) when `ntalkd` processes are found.
Since no minimum was listed, the agent will take no action when
no `ntalkd` processes are found to be running.

The selection of which UNIX processes to monitor with the
`proc` keyword is largely a matter of determining which services are
critical to the operation of your environment. If the computing systems support publishing software, you might care more about
print spoolers and word processing applications, while systems
supporting online order-entry software might need to have database server processes monitored.

On the other hand, one might take the approach that everything
running on a system is critical and must be monitored. At first
glance, this might seem like a reasonable strategy. Unfortunately,
this can lead to other problems and may well be overkill in most
situations. If we want to monitor all system processes, do we monitor temporary processes like networking services as well? If so,
which ones? Also, maintaining the configuration file for the agent
of these processes can be a chore at best because it must be updated
whenever new applications and software are added or removed

from the system. The agent's performance will be affected as well. Monitoring a large number of processes might result in overtaxing the agent, which should be avoided.

Assume we have configured the agent to monitor the `mountd` process and four `ntalkd` processes. The following example shows the values of the MIB when the agent detects that none of the `mountd` or `ntalkd` processes are running:

```
enterprises.ucdavis.procTable.prEntry.prErrorFlag.1 = 1
enterprises.ucdavis.procTable.prEntry.prErrorFlag.2 = 1
enterprises.ucdavis.procTable.prEntry.prErrMessage.1 = "No
    mountd process running."
enterprises.ucdavis.procTable.prEntry.prErrMessage.2 = "Too
    few ntalkd running (# = 0)"
```

Agent Security

The UCD agent supports SNMPv1, SNMPv2, and SNMPv3 security methods and is configured using the security keywords listed in Table 7.2. The prevalent security model implemented by the agent includes the View-based Access Control Model (VACM); however, the older security models of SNMPv1 and SNMPv2 are also supported. This VACM model was introduced with the SNMPv3 specifications and, in a nutshell, provides security based on different views and user levels that control access to individual objects, groups, or an entire MIB.

The keyword **com2sec** specifies a mapping between a source/community name and security name, and has the following syntax:

```
com2sec security_name source community_string
```

where `security_name` can be any string and is used in subsequent security policy definitions. The `source` parameter can be a hostname, IP address, network, or the reserved keyword **default**. The **default** word is a wildcard and will match any source. When specifying a network, two different formats are supported: the address with the address mask and the network address with an active bits number. Thus,

```
134.111.82.0/255.255.255.0
```

and

```
134.111.82.0/24
```

are equivalent and can be used interchangeably. The
`community_string` represents the community password that will be
supplied by the managing entity. The following is an example of
the **com2sec** entry :

```
com2sec public-sec-name default public
```

This entry defines a security name of `public-sec-name`, and any
source using the community string `public` is permitted access. The
following example provides additional control:

```
com2sec priv-sec-name 134.111.80.0/24 private-80
```

In this case, a new security string of `priv-sec-name` is defined,
which limits access to any device with a source address of
`134.111.80.0` and has `private-80` as the community password.

The keyword **group** directive defines a mapping between a
model/security name and a group:

```
group group_name available_model security_name
```

The `group_name` is a string that can represent a collection of
users or any other group definition. The `available_model` is one of
the defined security models supported by the agent. They include
any, v1, v2c, and **usm.** The **any** keyword is a wildcard that indicates
any of the other models. The **v1** model is associated with the
SNMPv1 community string, where a single string name is used as the
authentication token. The **v2c** model employs the use of community-based authentication based on public and/or private security
keys. The **usm** model, known as the User Security Model (USM),
was introduced with SNMPv3 and contains specifications that dic-
tate that users be defined within an SNMP agent for authentication
purposes.

The major purpose of the **group** keyword is to further define levels of control over individual groups of users or other entities. For
instance, consider the following:

```
group anybody any public-sec-name
```

The entry in this example defines a group called `anybody` that
basically indicates that any access using all security models is per-

mitted provided that the community string associated with
`public-sec-name` is used. Thus, in the example

```
group admin1 usm priv-sec-name
```

a group called `admin1` is defined with fairly tight restrictions on
access because it uses the **usm** model with the `priv-sec-name` security name. At this point, the exact syntax and semantics of the **v2c**
and **usm** security models are undefined. However, for the purposes
of this discussion, it is assumed that whatever is needed, the associated network manager software is responsible for supplying the
appropriate or correct information to the agent.

The keyword **view** defines one or more specific views into the
agent's MIBs. This is a very powerful feature because it lets the network management function of network and associated devices be
partitioned in interesting and beneficial ways. For example, an ISP
may provide their customers access to their internal networking
devices or specific interfaces. By providing access to only those
interfaces and networks to which the customer needs management
access, network security and administration is preserved for the
ISP, but customers can conduct advanced troubleshooting and performance monitoring. This can all be accomplished using different
views of the agent's MIB contained within the networking devices.

The syntax of the **view** command is as follows:

```
view name type mib_tree [mask]
```

The next argument of the **view** command is the name of the specific view. The name can be any string value but should be a
description of the MIB objects or groups defined within the view.
The **name** is followed by the type of view: **included** or **excluded**. The
included keyword means that the `mib_tree` object is included within
the view, while **excluded** means that the `mib_tree` object is not
included within the view. The `mib_tree` represents the MIB definition within the agent to which the view will be permitted or denied
access. The `mib_tree` object can include a specific MIB object or
group. For instance, `.1`, `system`, and
`.iso.org.dod.internet.mgmt.mib-2.interfaces` are all valid MIB
object definitions. The following is an example of a valid view:

```
view system_group include system fe
```

This example defines a new view called `system_group`, which permits access to the entire MIB-II `system` group. The final argument is the `mask` option, which controls more precisely the objects that are applied to the view. The `mask` value masks a particular set of object identifier strings. The mask provides a simple way to enable or disable parts of (or the entire) MIB tree. Each bit of the mask is compared against the corresponding MIB object identifier. If the bit in the mask is set to 1, then the object is used. If the bit is 0, then any value may appear in the object identifier position. The 0 value is used as a wildcard. Given the preceding example, let's examine why the mask of `fe` will permit access to the `system` group. First, we must consider that the OID path of the `system` group can be expressed in dotted notation, as shown:

```
system = 1.3.6.1.4.1.1
```

Next, we need to convert the mask of `fe` to binary:

```
fe (hex) = 1 1 1 1 1 1 1 0 (binary)
```

Now we need to compare the OID string with the mask:

```
1 3 6 1 4 1 1      (OID value)
1 1 1 1 1 1 1 0    (Mask value)
```

Comparing these values, you can see that all objects up to the system group are masked. Therefore, access is permitted only from the system group down.

Extending the Agent

One of the most powerful features of the UCD agent is that it can be extended to include execution of external commands. These commands can either be shell scripts or binary programs, which can be specified in the agent configuration. The output, via standard output, is captured within the agent MIB so that the information can be made available via the SNMP operations *get-requests* and *getnext-requests*.

To invoke external UNIX commands or shell scripts from the agent, use the **exec** command, which has the following syntax:

```
exec label program [args]
exec MIB program [args]
```

In the first form, the **exec** command is used with a label, program, and optional arguments. The label is used as an identifier, which is helpful when perusing the agent's MIB. The program is the actual UNIX binary or shell script that the agent will invoke, with the specified command line arguments listed in the `args` field. When the agent executes this command, the output is placed in the agent's MIB under the `extEntry` table. In the next example, the **exec** command executes the **uptime** command to determine the run level of the local system:

```
exec uptime /usr/bin/uptime
```

The **uptime** command shows how long the system has been running since it was last booted and the system load average. The `uptime` string is the label, and when the agent invokes the **uptime** command, the output is placed in the MIB and is available for viewing. Using the `snmpwalk` tool, described in Chapter 8, "Using SNMP Tools," the following sample output was obtained from the agent:

```
enterprises.ucdavis.extTable.extEntry.extIndex.1 = 1
enterprises.ucdavis.extTable.extEntry.extNames.1 = "uptime"
enterprises.ucdavis.extTable.extEntry.extCommand.1 =
   "/usr/bin/uptime"
enterprises.ucdavis.extTable.extEntry.extResult.1 = 0
enterprises.ucdavis.extTable.extEntry.extOutput.1 = 10:47pm
    up  2:09,  3 users,  load average: 0.57, 0.37, 0.22."
enterprises.ucdavis.extTable.extEntry.extErrFix.1 = 0
```

Notice that the `extResult` object contains a 0. This is because the command completed successfully. Also, both the `uptime` label and command, **/usr/bin/uptime**, are stored in the `extNames` and `extCommand` objects, respectively.

One characteristic of this version of **exec** is that only a single line of output is saved to the MIB. As a result, any output after the first line will be discarded by the agent. This limits, in a small way, the usefulness of this command. Luckily, the second form of the **exec** command can be used to capture output when there is more than one line.

With the second form, the **exec** command includes an MIB definition that will be used to store the **exec** command information and the complete output of the command that was executed by the agent. For example, consider the following command:

```
exec .1.3.6.1.4.1.2021.51 ps /bin/ps -e
```

This **exec** command will run the **ps** command and assign the output to the MIB branch

```
.iso.org.dod.internet.private.ucdavis.51
```

The **ps** command displays system/application process information. The -e option is used to collect information regarding all processes running on the system.

To examine the output of **ps**, we simply do a walk (using snmpwalk, for instance) on the 2021.51 MIB branch. Please note that for readability purposes, the OID string before the enterprises string was dropped from the output below.

Thus the command

```
snmpwalk socrates public .iso.org.dod.internet.private.enterprises.ucdavis.51
```

will give us the following results:

```
enterprises.ucdavis.51.1.1 = 1
enterprises.ucdavis.51.2.1 = "ps" Hex: 70 73
enterprises.ucdavis.51.3.1 = "/bin/ps -e"
enterprises.ucdavis.51.100.1 = 0
enterprises.ucdavis.51.101.1 = "  PID TTY          TIME CMD."
enterprises.ucdavis.51.101.2 = "    1 ?        00:00:03 init."
enterprises.ucdavis.51.101.3 = "    2 ?        00:00:00 kflushd."
enterprises.ucdavis.51.101.4 = "    3 ?        00:00:00 kpiod."
enterprises.ucdavis.51.101.5 = "    4 ?        00:00:00 kswapd."
enterprises.ucdavis.51.101.6 = "    5 ?        00:00:00 mdrecoveryd."
enterprises.ucdavis.51.101.7 = "  107 ?        00:00:00 apmd."
enterprises.ucdavis.51.101.8 = "  257 ?        00:00:00 portmap."
enterprises.ucdavis.51.101.9 = "  307 ?        00:00:02 syslogd."
enterprises.ucdavis.51.101.10 = "  318 ?        00:00:00 klogd."
enterprises.ucdavis.51.101.11 = "  332 ?        00:00:00 atd."
enterprises.ucdavis.51.101.12 = "  346 ?        00:00:00 crond."
enterprises.ucdavis.51.101.13 = "  364 ?        00:00:00 inetd."
enterprises.ucdavis.51.101.14 = "  394 ?        00:00:00 arpwatch."
enterprises.ucdavis.51.101.15 = "  408 ?        00:00:00 named."
enterprises.ucdavis.51.101.16 = "  422 ?        00:00:00 lpd."
enterprises.ucdavis.51.101.17 = "  440 ?        00:00:00 rpc.statd."
enterprises.ucdavis.51.101.18 = "  451 ?        00:00:00 rpc.rquotad."
enterprises.ucdavis.51.101.19 = "  462 ?        00:00:00 rpc.mountd."
enterprises.ucdavis.51.101.20 = "  477 ?        00:00:00 nfsd."
enterprises.ucdavis.51.101.21 = "  478 ?        00:00:00 nfsd."
enterprises.ucdavis.51.101.22 = "  479 ?        00:00:00 nfsd."
```

(continued)

```
enterprises.ucdavis.51.101.23 = "  480 ?        00:00:00 nfsd."
enterprises.ucdavis.51.101.24 = "  481 ?        00:00:00 nfsd."
enterprises.ucdavis.51.101.25 = "  485 ?        00:00:00 lockd."
enterprises.ucdavis.51.101.26 = "  486 ?        00:00:00 rpciod."
enterprises.ucdavis.51.101.27 = "  503 ?        00:00:00 amd."
enterprises.ucdavis.51.101.28 = "  540 ?        00:00:00 sendmail."
enterprises.ucdavis.51.101.29 = "  555 ?        00:00:00 gpm."
enterprises.ucdavis.51.101.30 = "  599 ?        00:00:01 xfs."
enterprises.ucdavis.51.101.31 = "  651 ?        00:00:00 innd."
enterprises.ucdavis.51.101.32 = "  654 ?        00:00:00 actived."
enterprises.ucdavis.51.101.33 = "  695 tty1     00:00:00 mingetty."
enterprises.ucdavis.51.101.34 = "  696 tty2     00:00:00 mingetty."
enterprises.ucdavis.51.101.35 = "  697 tty3     00:00:00 mingetty."
enterprises.ucdavis.51.101.36 = "  698 tty4     00:00:00 mingetty."
enterprises.ucdavis.51.101.37 = "  699 tty5     00:00:00 mingetty."
enterprises.ucdavis.51.101.38 = "  700 tty6     00:00:00 mingetty."
enterprises.ucdavis.51.101.39 = "  701 ?        00:00:00 prefdm."
enterprises.ucdavis.51.101.40 = "  703 ?        00:00:00 update."
enterprises.ucdavis.51.101.41 = "  705 ?        00:05:07 X."
enterprises.ucdavis.51.101.42 = "  708 ?        00:00:00 prefdm."
enterprises.ucdavis.51.101.43 = "  713 ?        00:00:00 Default."
enterprises.ucdavis.51.101.44 = "  726 ?        00:00:00 gnome-
  session."
enterprises.ucdavis.51.101.45 = "  758 ?        00:01:55
  enlightenment."
enterprises.ucdavis.51.101.46 = "  773 ?        00:00:01 xscreensaver."
enterprises.ucdavis.51.101.47 = "  775 ?        00:00:01 panel."
enterprises.ucdavis.51.101.48 = "  777 ?        00:00:00 gnome-name-
  serv."
enterprises.ucdavis.51.101.49 = "  781 ?        00:00:00
  gen_util_applet."
enterprises.ucdavis.51.101.50 = "  784 ?        00:01:09
  gnomepager_appl."
enterprises.ucdavis.51.101.51 = "  789 ?        00:00:05 gnome-
  terminal."
enterprises.ucdavis.51.101.52 = "  791 ?        00:00:07 gnome-
  terminal."
enterprises.ucdavis.51.101.53 = "  793 ?        00:00:02 gmc."
enterprises.ucdavis.51.101.54 = "  795 ?        00:00:01 gtcd."
enterprises.ucdavis.51.101.55 = "  796 ?        00:00:00 gnome-pty-
  helpe."
enterprises.ucdavis.51.101.56 = "  797 ?        00:00:00 gnome-pty-
  helpe."
enterprises.ucdavis.51.101.57 = "  798 pts/0    00:00:00 bash."
enterprises.ucdavis.51.101.58 = "  799 pts/1    00:00:00 bash."
enterprises.ucdavis.51.101.59 = "  949 ?        00:00:00 in.telnetd."
enterprises.ucdavis.51.101.60 = "  950 pts/2    00:00:00 login."
enterprises.ucdavis.51.101.61 = "  951 pts/2    00:00:00 bash."
enterprises.ucdavis.51.101.62 = " 1569 pts/0    00:00:01 snmpd."
enterprises.ucdavis.51.101.63 = " 1605 pts/2    00:00:00 snmpwalk."
enterprises.ucdavis.51.101.64 = " 1606 pts/0    00:00:00 ps."
enterprises.ucdavis.51.102.1 = 0
```

We can use some of the MIB objects found in the `ucdavis.51` MIB group to help identify the **ps** command output. The `ucdavis.51.2.1` and `ucdavis.51.3.1` objects contain the command label and the command itself, as specified in the agent configuration file. The remaining MIB objects (`ucdavis.51.101.1` to `ucdavis.51.101.23`) represent the command output. Also, the MIB object `ucdavis.51.101.1` shows the return status of the **ps** command. In this example, a `0` indicates that the **ps** command was executed successfully. As you can see, the **exec** command can extend the agent-monitoring coverage to include additional operating system tools and application functions. This is perhaps one of the most powerful features of the Linux agent.

Using the `pass` Facility

Another powerful feature of the UCD agent is the **pass** command. This command can give control of an MIB tree to a program that the agent executes. This gives the agent the ability to dynamically alter MIB objects, without requiring custom agent development. Figure 7.2 displays a high-level flow. In general, the agent receives one or more SNMP requests that access part of the MIB tree associated with the **pass** command. As a result, the agent executes the last two arguments of the **pass** command— in this case, `/bin/sh` and `/usr/local/passtest`, respectively. When this script is run, the agent supplies additional parameters to the `passtest` script that contains the OID that is being accessed, the type, and associated value. The output from the script is captured by the agent and placed within the MIB.

To use the `pass` option, a simple program is created that displays the required MIB object information and does any work that is needed. For example, consider this command:

```
pass .1.3.6.1.4.1.2021.255 /bin/sh /usr/local/passtest
```

The `pass` option includes an MIB object tree and the command that will be executed when the MIB is accessed. In this case, the MIB object `1.3.6.1.4.1.2021.255` is actually passed to the `passtest` script.

More specifically, the agent will call the `passtest` script in one of three ways, depending on the mode of operation requested.

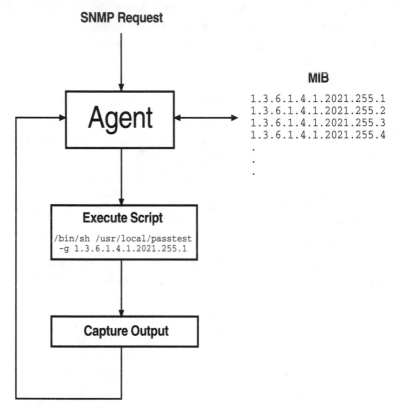

Figure 7.2 *Agent* pass *function.*

When an SNMP get-request is received by the agent, it calls the passtest script with the -g option, followed by the MIB OID. Thus, the agent will call the script:

```
/bin/sh /usr/local/passtest -g .1.3.6.1.4.1.2021.255
```

When the agent receives a getnext-request, the -n option is used instead of -g. With an SNMP set-request, the -s option plus the type and value of the MIB object will be supplied. These options are supplied to the script so that it can take the correct action based on the different requests.

The script is also responsible for generating the appropriate output to satisfy the SNMP request and the requirements of the agent. For instance, when an SNMP getnext-request is sent to the agent, the next OID after the supplied OID must be presented. The format of the output includes the OID string, type, and associated value. So if the script is to return a string value (e.g., `Hello World`) for the object `.1.3.6.1.4.1.2021.255.3`, then the script should return the following:

```
.1.3.6.1.4.1.2021.255.3
string
Hello World
```

Any data that the script wants to return must adhere to the requirements of the agent by specifying all three components; OID, type, and value. When the script is invoked, the agent incorporates its MIB into the data. The script can output any information but must use one of the existing predefined MIB object types. Table 7.3 lists these MIB object types, which inform the agent how to format the data from the script.

Table 7.3 *Supported agent MIB object types*

OID Type	Description
string	A data type representing zero or more octets, where each octet may take any value from 0 to 255
integer	A data type representing a cardinal number, where no limitation is made to the level of precision that might be required to represent the value
objectid	A data type representing an authoritatively named object that consists of a sequence of values that specify a MIB tree
timeticks	A data type that represents a non-negative integer that counts time in hundredths of a second since some established epoch. Timeticks is like a counter in every other aspect

Table 7.3 *Supported agent MIB object types (continued)*

OID Type	Description
ipaddress	A data type that represents an octet string that has a length of four bytes (32 bits), where each of the four octets relates to one of the four bytes of a standard IP address
counter	A data type that represents a non-negative integer that increases until it reaches a maximum value and then resets to zero. A counter is an integer that can take the value between 0 and 4294967295. A counter has no defined starting value
gauge	A data type that represents a non-negative integer that may increase or decrease and will trigger at a maximum value. A gauge is like a counter in every other aspect

To further understand the **pass** capabilities, consider the passtest script shown in Listing 7.1. This script comes with the standard release of Linux and can be found within the /usr/local directory. The script has been provided to serve as an example of how to write a shell script (module) to extend the Linux agent. As a result, it doesn't contain everything that should be included (like logging) in a more robust, production-quality script.

The first observation that can be made about this script is that each of the SNMP operations—set-request, getnext-request, and get-request—are specifically detected. That is to say, the script checks to ensure that the provided argument to the program has been supplied and is either -s or -n. Recall that the agent invokes the script with the appropriate command-line argument that corresponds to the appropriate SNMP operation. These are noted by the if statements found on lines 8 and 13. Both of these lines check to see if the first program argument ($1) is equal to -s or -n. If neither of these are provided, the script assumes that the -g was supplied.

Listing 7.1 *The* passtest *script*

```
 1  #!/bin/sh -f
 2
 3  PATH=$path:/bin:/usr/bin:/usr/ucb
 4
 5  PLACE=".1.3.6.1.4.1.2021.255"
 6  REQ="$2"
 7
 8  if [ "$1" = "-s" ]; then
 9    echo $* >> /tmp/passtest.log
10    exit 0
11  fi
12
13  if [ "$1" = "-n" ]; then
14    case "$REQ" in
15      $PLACE)        RET=$PLACE.1 ;;
16      $PLACE.1)      RET=$PLACE.2.1 ;;
17      $PLACE.2.1)    RET=$PLACE.2.2 ;;
18      $PLACE.2.2)    RET=$PLACE.3 ;;
19      $PLACE.3)      RET=$PLACE.4 ;;
20      $PLACE.4)      RET=$PLACE.5 ;;
21      $PLACE.5)      RET=$PLACE.6 ;;
22      *)             exit 0 ;;
23    esac
24  else
25    case "$REQ" in
26      $PLACE)    exit 0 ;;
27      *)         RET=$REQ ;;
28    esac
29  fi
30  echo "$RET"
31  case "$RET" in
32    $PLACE.1) echo "string"; echo "life the universe
         and everything"; exit 0 ;;
33    $PLACE.2.1) echo "integer"; echo "42"; exit 0 ;;
34    $PLACE.2.2) echo "objectid"; echo
         ".1.3.6.1.4.42.42.42"; exit 0 ;;
35    $PLACE.3) echo "timeticks"; echo "363136200";
         exit 0 ;;
36    $PLACE.4) echo "ipaddress"; echo "127.0.0.1" ;;
37    $PLACE.5) echo "counter"; echo "42"; exit 0 ;;
38    $PLACE.6) echo "gauge"; echo "42"; exit 0 ;;
39    *) echo "string"; echo "ack... $RET $REQ"; exit 0 ;;
40  esac
```

When the script detects that an SNMP `getnext-request` has been issued, it must retrieve the next OID object that is lexicographically larger than the previous one. As a result, the script uses a `case` statement to determine which object is being retrieved and advances the OID accordingly by placing the OID value in the `RET` variable. The `RET` variable will contain the return OID. Assume for the moment that the agent wants to retrieve the OID `.1.3.6.1.4.1.2021.255.3` object. Then, the case statement will assign the variable `PLACE.4` to `RET`. The `PLACE.4` variable contains the value `.1.3.6.1.4.1.2021.255.4`, which is then assigned to `RET`. After this, the program drops down to line 30, where it sends the contents of `RET` to standard out using the **echo** shell command. This line fulfills the first requirement of the script to send the OID string back to the agent. Next, the script detects which OID was just displayed by using another case statement. At this stage, the `RET` variable still contains the `.1.3.6.1.4.1.2021.255.4` object ,which is equal to `$PLACE.4` and forces the associated commands on line 36 to be executed. In this case, the script displays the string `ipaddress` and the value of `127.0.0.1`. The string of `ipaddress` satisfies the second requirement from the agent, which specifies the type of the OIB object. The final value of `127.0.0.1` that the script displays is the associated value of the `.1.3.6.1.4.1.2021.255.4` object.

To support the SNMP `get-request`, the `else` part of the code is executed starting on line 24. In this `case` statement, if the `REQ` argument (which is the OID string) is equal to the `PLACE` variable, then the script will exit with 0 status. This is done because the OID supplied by the agent for the `get-request` is the start of the OID table, and no value can be returned under this condition. Otherwise, any other OID value is assigned to the `RET` variable, and the script processes the request as stated above, starting on line 30.

Notice that on line 8, for the SNMP `set-request`, the arguments (using the `$*`) given to the script are directed to a log file called `/tmp/passtest.log`. That is, any SNMP `set-request` operation from the agent simply logs the information and returns a 0 exit code. This is due to the fact that the agent invokes the script every time the OID table is accessed. As a result, the script doesn't implement any mechanism to capture the set operations and apply them to the data that the script generates. If it were to implement the set feature, the script would need a way to alter any OID objects that were changed. Because it already uses the `passtest.log` file as temporary storage, it only needs to parse this file and alter the OID values contained within the script. Once it does this, the script should remove the previously parsed entries within the log file so that they are not mistakenly considered new when another set operation is requested. As you can see, the current version of the `passtest` script doesn't implement permanent `set-requests`. When an SNMP `getnext-request` operation is run against the agent using the OID supported by the `passtest` script, the following will be displayed:

```
enterprises.ucdavis.255.1 = "life the universe and everything"
enterprises.ucdavis.255.2.1 = 42
enterprises.ucdavis.255.2.2 = OID: 42.42.42
enterprises.ucdavis.255.3 = Timeticks: (363136200) 42 days,
   0:42:42.00
enterprises.ucdavis.255.4 = IpAddress: 1.0.0.127
enterprises.ucdavis.255.5 = 42
enterprises.ucdavis.255.6 = Gauge: 42
```

Listing 7.2 shows another example of the **pass** command. In this program, called `maintain-message.pl`, the SNMP *set-request* operation is used as a trigger to delete the contents of the system messages file. This script represents a functional example of how the `pass` facility can help to perform some useful system administration tasks. In this example, the script helps to maintain the `/var/log/messages` file across a number of systems.

Listing 7.2 *Perl script (`maintain-message.pl`) to maintain messages file*

```
1   #!/usr/bin/perl -w
2   ################################################################
3   #
4   # Extensible Agent Script Example - Maintenance of the
          /var/adm/messages file. It
5   # provides a way to delete the contents of the file to zero bytes
          and also shows the
6   # the last 50 lines of the file.
7   #
8   # Steve Maxwell
9   # December '99
10  #
11  ################################################################
```

(continued)

```
12  #
13  $MESSAGESFILE = "/var/log/messages";
14  $OID_PATHBASE = ".1.3.6.1.4.1.2021.255";
15  $SET_OID     = ".1.3.6.1.4.1.2021.255.51";
16  $SET_OID_OBJ = 51;
17  $DEF_LINES   = 50;
18  $LOG_NAME    = "agent-log";
19  $LOG_PATH    = "/etc/snmp/";
20  $DATE        = `/bin/date '+Date: %m/%d/%y Time: %H:%M:%S'`;
21  $TAIL        = "/usr/bin/tail -n";
22  $LOGGING     = 1;
23  ##
24  ## Creates logfile. On success, return 0, else 1.
25  ##
26  sub CreatLogFile {
27
28          $lf = sprintf("%s%s", $LOG_PATH, $LOG_NAME);
29          unless (open (LFP, ">> $lf" ) ) {
30                  print "Can't open log file: $lf\n";
31                  exit 1;
32          }
33          return 0;
34  }
35  ##
36  ## Logs any string passed to it.
37  ##
38  sub Log {
39          if ( $LOGGING ) {
40                  print LFP "$DATE $_[0]\n";
41          }
42  }
43  ##
44  ## Close open log file and exit program with supplied
45  ## error code.
46  ##
47  sub Leave {
48          close LFP;
49          exit $_[0];
50  }
51  ##
52  ## We need to purge the log file, but we need to make
53  ## sure the correct OID string is provided to us.
54  ##
55  sub SnmpSet {
56          ($oid, $type, $value) = @_;
57
58          ##
59          ## Make sure OID from agent matches are OID set object.
60          ## if so, then we know to execute the SET operation.
61          ##
62          if($oid eq $SET_OID) {
63                  Log "SnmpSet: oid...$oid, type...$type, and
                          value...$value\n";
```

```
64                $comm = sprintf("%s %s %s", "/bin/cp", "/dev/null",
                     $MESSAGESFILE);
65                Log "Executing... $comm";
66                $rc = system ($comm);
67                $stat = $rc/256;
68                if(! $stat ) {
69                     Log "SnmpSet: Command executes successfully";
70                     Leave 0;
71                }
72           }
73      Leave 1;
74 }
75 ##
76 ## Get the next OID and line from the messages
77 ## file.
78 ##
79 sub SnmpGetNext {
80      ($Reqoid, $master_oid) = @_;
81
82      @data = `$TAIL $DEF_LINES $MESSAGESFILE`;
83
84      if ($Reqoid eq $master_oid) {
85           Log "SnmpGetNext: OIDs are equal\n";
86           print "$Reqoid.0\n";
87           print "string\n";
88           print "$data[0]";
89           Log "SnmpGetNext: $Reqoid.0, string, $data[0]";
90           Leave 0;
91      } else {
92           $newstring = "";
93           $oidstring = $Reqoid;
94           (@oids) = split (/\./, $oidstring);
95           $count = $#oids-1;
96           for ( $i = 1; $i <= $count; $i++ ) {
97                $newstring = sprintf("%s.%s", $newstring,
                     $oids[$i]);
98           }
99           $lastoid = $oids[$#oids];
100          $oid_int = sprintf( "%i", $lastoid);
101          $oid_int++;
102          print "$newstring.$oid_int\n";
103          print "string\n";
104          print "$data[$oid_int]";
105          Log "SnmpGetNext: $newstring.$oid_int, string,
                 $data[$oid_int]";
106      }
107      Leave 0;
108 }
109 ##
110 ## Get an individual line of the messages file
111 ##
112 sub SnmpGet {
113      $Reqoid = $_[0];
```

(continued)

```
114
115          Log "SnmpGet: $Reqoid";
116          @lines = `$TAIL $DEF_LINES $MESSAGESFILE`;
117
118          (@oids) = split (/\./, $Reqoid);
119
120          $lastoid = $oids[$#oids];
121          if ( $lastoid == $SET_OID_OBJ ) {
122                  print "$Reqoid\n";
123                  print "integer\n";
124                  print "0";
125                  Leave 0;
126          }
127          if ( $lastoid > 0 && $lastoid < 50 ) {
128              print "$Reqoid\n";
129              print "string\n";
130              print "$lines[$lastoid]";
131              Log "SnmpGet: $Reqoid, string, $lines[$lastoid]";
132              Leave 0;
133          } else {
134              Leave 1;
135          }
136 }
137 ##
138 ## Main program starts here
139 ##
140
141 CreatLogFile;
142
143 ($arg1, $arg2, $arg3, $arg4)  = @ARGV;
144
145 if ($arg1 eq "-s") {
146         SnmpSet $arg2, $arg3, $arg4;
147 } elsif ($arg1 eq "-n") {
148         SnmpGetNext $arg2, $OID_PATHBASE;
149 } else {
150         SnmpGet $arg2;
151 }
```

This example may look somewhat complicated due to the number of lines, but actually the program is very straightforward and simple. Also, the sample program, called messages.pl, is written using the Perl language and was used with version 5.005_03 of the interpreter. The core part of the program is between lines 141 and 151, with the major portion being separated by several functions. As you can see, the program uses three functions that are modeled after the way the agent invokes the script. The functions include SnmpSet, starting on line 55; SnmpGetNext, which starts on line 79; and SnmpGet, which begins on line 112. Each of these are called by the agent depending on the SNMP operation that it receives. What is really new in this example as compared to the `passtest` script is that it supports the SNMP `set-request` operation. In this case, the set operation used against a specific OID (`1.3.6.1.4.1.2021.255.51`) will cause the contents of `/var/log/messages` file to be purged. The actual command is found on line 6. On this line, the **system** command is invoked with the `$comm` variable. In Perl, the **system** command will send the string directly to the operating system for execution. This variable is assigned the string `/bin/cp /dev/null /var/log/messages`. The rest of the function simply checks the return status of the **system** command and logs the script activity. If the command is successful, the script is terminated with a success value; otherwise, it returns an error status (line 73). A function called `Leave` is defined to close the log file and return the correct status condition before exiting the script. This function is defined on lines 47 and 50.

The `messages.pl` script also provides a way to view up to 50 lines from the messages file. The way to access the contents of this file is to do a `getnext-request` on the MIB object `1.3.6.1.4.1.2021.255.1`. Recall that the `getnext` operation will "walk" an MIB tree to retrieve the entire MIB or a group of MIB objects. Thus, we can obtain all of the objects under the `255` tree. As a result, the sample output will be produced as shown in Listing 7.3. The strings in quotes represent the actual lines from the `/var/log/messages` file.

Listing 7.3 *An SNMP "walk" of the* `/var/log/messages` *file*

```
enterprises.ucdavis.255.0 = "Sep  1 20:04:30 socrates chat[995]: expect (OK)"
enterprises.ucdavis.255.1 = "Sep  1 20:05:15 socrates pppd[993]: Connect script failed"
enterprises.ucdavis.255.2 = "Sep  1 20:05:15 socrates chat[995]: alarm"
enterprises.ucdavis.255.3 = "Sep  1 20:05:15 socrates chat[995]: Failed"
enterprises.ucdavis.255.4 = "Sep  1 20:05:16 socrates pppd[993]: Exit."
enterprises.ucdavis.255.5 = "Sep  1 20:05:16 socrates ifup-ppp: pppd started for ppp0 on /dev/modem
   at 115200"
enterprises.ucdavis.255.6 = "Sep  1 20:05:16 socrates pppd[1000]: pppd 2.3.7 started by root, uid 0"
enterprises.ucdavis.255.7 = "Sep  1 20:05:17 socrates chat[1002]: abort on (BUSY)
enterprises.ucdavis.255.8 = "Sep  1 20:05:17 socrates chat[1002]: abort on (ERROR)"
enterprises.ucdavis.255.9 = "Sep  1 20:05:17 socrates chat[1002]: abort on (NO CARRIER)"
enterprises.ucdavis.255.10 = "Sep  1 20:05:17 socrates chat[1002]: abort on (NODIALTONE)"
enterprises.ucdavis.255.11 = "Sep  1 20:05:17 socrates chat[1002]: abort on (Invalid Login)"
```

(continued)

enterprises.ucdavis.255.12 = "Sep 1 20:05:17 socrates chat[1002]: abort on (Login incorrect)"
enterprises.ucdavis.255.13 = "Sep 1 20:05:17 socrates chat[1002]: send (ATZ^M)"
enterprises.ucdavis.255.14 = "Sep 1 20:05:17 socrates chat[1002]: expect (OK)"
enterprises.ucdavis.255.15 = "Sep 1 20:06:02 socrates pppd[1000]: Connect script failed"
enterprises.ucdavis.255.16 = "Sep 1 20:06:02 socrates chat[1002]: alarm"
enterprises.ucdavis.255.17 = "Sep 1 20:06:02 socrates chat[1002]: Failed"
enterprises.ucdavis.255.18 = "Sep 1 20:06:03 socrates pppd[1000]: Exit."
enterprises.ucdavis.255.19 = "Sep 1 20:06:04 socrates pppd[1011]: pppd 2.3.7 st
arted by root, uid 0"
enterprises.ucdavis.255.20 = "Sep 1 20:06:04 socrates ifup-ppp: pppd started for ppp0 on /dev/modem
    at 115200"
enterprises.ucdavis.255.21 = "Sep 1 20:06:05 socrates chat[1012]: abort on (BUSY)"
enterprises.ucdavis.255.22 = "Sep 1 20:06:05 socrates chat[1012]: abort on (ERROR)"
enterprises.ucdavis.255.23 = "Sep 1 20:06:05 socrates chat[1012]: abort on (NOCARRIER)"
enterprises.ucdavis.255.24 = "Sep 1 20:06:05 socrates chat[1012]: abort on (NODIALTONE)"
enterprises.ucdavis.255.25 = "Sep 1 20:06:05 socrates chat[1012]: abort on (Invalid Login)"
enterprises.ucdavis.255.26 = "Sep 1 20:06:05 socrates chat[1012]: abort on (Login incorrect)"
enterprises.ucdavis.255.27 = "Sep 1 20:06:05 socrates chat[1012]: send (ATZ^M)"
enterprises.ucdavis.255.28 = "Sep 1 20:06:05 socrates chat[1012]: expect (OK)"
enterprises.ucdavis.255.29 = "Sep 1 20:06:50 socrates chat[1012]: alarm"
enterprises.ucdavis.255.30 = "Sep 1 20:06:50 socrates chat[1012]: Failed"
enterprises.ucdavis.255.31 = "Sep 1 20:06:50 socrates pppd[1011]: Connect scrip
t failed"
enterprises.ucdavis.255.32 = "Sep 1 20:06:51 socrates pppd[1011]: Exit."
enterprises.ucdavis.255.33 = "Sep 1 20:06:51 socrates pppd[1024]: pppd 2.3.7 st
arted by root, uid 0"
enterprises.ucdavis.255.34 = "Sep 1 20:06:51 socrates ifup-ppp: pppd started fo
r ppp0 on /dev/modem at 115200"
enterprises.ucdavis.255.35 = "Sep 1 20:06:52 socrates chat[1025]: abort on (BUSY)"
enterprises.ucdavis.255.36 = "Sep 1 20:06:52 socrates chat[1025]: abort on (ERROR)"
enterprises.ucdavis.255.37 = "Sep 1 20:06:52 socrates chat[1025]: abort on (NO CARRIER)"
enterprises.ucdavis.255.38 = "Sep 1 20:06:52 socrates chat[1025]: abort on (NO DIALTONE)"
enterprises.ucdavis.255.39 = "Sep 1 20:06:52 socrates chat[1025]: abort on (Invalid Login)"
enterprises.ucdavis.255.40 = "Sep 1 20:06:52 socrates chat[1025]: abort on (Login incorrect)"
enterprises.ucdavis.255.41 = "Sep 1 20:06:52 socrates chat[1025]: send (ATZ^M)"
enterprises.ucdavis.255.42 = "Sep 1 20:06:52 socrates chat[1025]: expect (OK)"
enterprises.ucdavis.255.43 = "Nov 2 20:01:02 socrates last message repeated 2 times"
enterprises.ucdavis.255.44 = "Nov 2 20:01:03 socrates PAM_pwdb[914]: (su) session opened for user
    news by (uid=0)"
enterprises.ucdavis.255.45 = "Nov 2 20:01:06 socrates PAM_pwdb[914]: (su) session closed for user
    news"
enterprises.ucdavis.255.46 = "Nov 2 20:01:15 socrates snmpd: Connection from 10.0.2.201"
enterprises.ucdavis.255.47 = "Nov 2 20:04:50 socrates last message repeated 2 times"
enterprises.ucdavis.255.48 = "Nov 2 20:06:16 socrates last message repeated 3 times"
enterprises.ucdavis.255.49 = "Nov 2 20:11:40 socrates last message repeated 102 times"

The output in Listing 7.3 corresponds to the last 50 lines of the system messages file. As you can see from the script, the lines from the `messages` file are obtained from the `SnmpGetNext` function starting on line79. Line 82 contains the UNIX **tail**command. Here, this command is invoked and the output is stored in an array (or list) variable called `data`. When this function is invoked, one of the lines within the array is displayed on standard out, it corresponds to the OID object that was referenced with the SNMP call. When an SNMP walk is issued, it calls this function multiple times with the OID of the next object in the tree. Lines between 92 and 105 examine the last number from the OID and increment it by one (line 101). Next, the function displays the new OID, the string type, and the output of one line from the **tail** command using the OID itself as the index into the array. The `SnmpGet` function operates basically the same way; it executes the UNIX **tail** command and returns one of the lines from the message file using the OID as an index in the `data` array.

A couple of observations can be made about this script. First, the `SnmpSet` function could be more robust regarding the purging of the `messages` file. It could, for example, define another object that would store the date and time information for when the purge took place. This certainly would be a useful feature in a large network environment. Next, since array elements within PERL start at zero, the output of the **tail** command does not exactly match up with the OID numbers. Notice in the output above that lines start at 1.3.6.1.4.1.2021.255.0 versus 1.3.6.1.4.1.2021.255.1. Finally, the script could be modified to handle hard-coded limits and other relevant data in a different way. For example, it checks to determine the range of the OID sent to it by the agent. This is shown starting on line 127. A sophisticated program would use a more dynamic approach when determining the OID range, etc.

Sample Agent Configuration File

Listing 7.4 shows a sample agent configuration file. This might be a good starting point for those who want to deploy the agent environment when monitoring some of the standard UNIX processes is critical. Also, the configuration includes call functions to automatically limit certain system processes so that the system doesn't become overloaded.

Listing 7.4 *Sample agent configuration*

```
#
# Sample Configuration
# Monitor these processes..
#
proc mountd
proc nfsd
proc lpsched
#
# Monitor load average above 2.0..
#
load 2
#
# Make sure we have a least 50 MB in root
# and 100 MB in /usr
#
disk /    50000
disk /usr 100000
#
# Execute the following programs to obtain
# output via the UCD mib...
#
exec .1.3.6.1.4.1.2021.255.1 top /usr/bin/top
exec .1.3.6.1.4.1.2021.255.2 ps /bin/ps -e
pass .1.3.6.1.4.1.2021.255.3 /usr/local/perl /etc/snmp/message.pl
```

Command-line Options

The agent provides a number of command-line options, as listed in Table 7.4. Because the agent in most instances will be started automatically when the system boots, some of these options should be changed in the startup file if they are to become permanent. However, some of the options only make sense when used on the command line.

By default, when snmpd is started, it uses well-known SNMP port 161. This must be changed if other agents are running on the same system or if you are using a master agent. The -p option has been provided for this purpose. The snmpd command will use this option, followed by the port number, to listen for incoming SNMP requests.

Several options can be used to assist in any debugging efforts that must be done with the agent. The -a option displays the IP address of any system that has been in communication with the agent, along with date and time information. This is useful for establishing that any configured ACLs are working properly. When an option is used, the agent will display messages like the following:

```
1999-11-21 16:04:17 Received SNMP packet(s) from 10.0.2.126
```

The -d option displays the UDP packets sent to and received from the agent and is used to help detect SNMP protocol-related problems or other operations issues. Also, this option can be used to examine the MIB object requested from SNMP client applications. A sample of the agent debugging output is shown here:

```
GET
    -- system.sysContact.0
    >> system.sysContact.0 = Steve Maxwell
sent 64 bytes to 10.0.2.126:
0000: 30 82 00 3C  02 01 00 04  06 70 75 62  6C 69 63 A2    0..<.....public.
0016: 82 00 2D 02  04 23 C1 E0  9F 02 01 00  02 01 00 30    ..-..#.........0
0032: 82 00 1D 30  82 00 19 06  08 2B 06 01  02 01 01 04    ...0.....+......
0048: 00 04 0D 53  74 65 76 65  20 4D 61 78  77 65 6C 6C    ...Steve Maxwell
```

In this sample, the agent obtains an SNMP get request from the system with IP address 10.0.2.126. The agent displays the string "--" to indicate what the remote SNMP entity requests (in this case, the sysContact object) and the ">>" string shows what the agent returns. The hexadecimal output corresponds to the entire UDP packet, which includes the community string information and any returned object(s). If you want just the protocol transaction and not the UDP packet trace, use the -V option. This option will display

```
GET
    -- system.sysLocation.0
    >> system.sysLocation.0 = Graphics Lab 11-B
```

as a result of a request for the sysLocation MIB object from an SNMP client application.

The -q option, according to the documentation in the UCD package, displays simpler formatting that can be used, for example, to automate parsing of the agent output. Unfortunately, this option doesn't seem to do anything in release 4 of the agent tested.

To further assist with agent debugging, the -f option instructs the agent not to fork from the shell. Without this option, the agent will detach by forking a new process from the current shell and return the shell prompt. The mibiisa agent, for example, behaves in this manner. When the -f option is used, the agent can be terminated by typing **^c** to the shell that was used to start the agent. Alternatively, if you want to stop the agent, you need to use the kill command with the appropriate process id of the agent.

If it becomes necessary to save the debugging information to a file, the -l option followed by a file name can be used. The output logged to this file includes both standard output (STDOUT) and standard error (STDERR). If the -l option is used without a file name, then the default /var/log/snmpd.log file is used. When conducting an SNMP trace (with the -V option), saving the output to a file will come in handy when dealing with a large number of transactions. If, however, you want to log information directed to standard output and standard error, then use the -L option. The -l and -L options are mutually exclusive and, therefore, should not be used together.

If you want the agent to use a specific configuration file, use the -c option followed by the complete path and filename. By default, the agent searches in preconfigured locations for one or more agent configuration files. If you don't want the agent to search for additional configuration files and, instead, want it to use only the one specified with the -c option, include the -C option as well. This forces the agent to use only the configuration file you provide and is one way of ensuring that any other configuration files are ignored.

UCD/Linux MIB

The agent implements MIB objects under the ucdavis (2021) enterprise number. The complete path to the UCD tree begins with iso.org.dod.internet.private.enterprises or 1.3.6.1.4.1. The UCD MIB provides the following important MIB objects and groups:

- procTable
- memory
- extTable
- disktable
- loadtable

- systemStats
- version
- snmperrors

This MIB definition can be found in the
/usr/local/share/snmp/mibs/UCD-SNMP-MIB.txt file after the UCD
package has been installed.

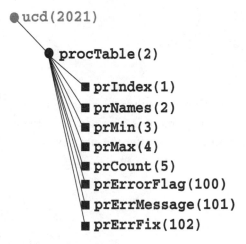

Figure 7.3 *The* procTable *view.*

UCD ProcTable

The procTable table consists of objects that obtain a list of system processes that are monitored by the agent and have been
placed in the agent configuration file. Figure 7.3 shows a hierarchical representation of these objects as they relate to the ucdavis
branch. The process information is accessed via the prEntry MIB
object. The procTable table contains the following set of objects:

Object Name: prIndex

OID: prEntry.1

Object Type: PRIndex (Integer)

Access Mode: read-only

Description: Reference index for each monitored system process. Because the `procTable` is in fact a table, the `prIndex` is used to access another instance of the table

Object Name: `prNames`

OID: `prEntry.2`

Object Type: `Display String [255]`

Access Mode: `read-only`

Description: The name of the process that the agent is monitoring. The process name is obtained from the agent configuration file after the **proc** keyword command

Object Name: `prMin`

OID: `prEntry.3`

Object Type: `Integer`

Access Mode: `read-only`

Description: The minimum number of processes that should be running on the system. If the number of processes is less than the minimum, an error flag is generated in the `prErrorFlag` and `prErr-Message` MIB objects. The minimum value is obtained from the agent configuration after the maximum value, if any, has been specified

Object Name: `prMax`

OID: `prEntry.4`

Object Type: `Integer`

Access Mode: read-only

Description: The maximum number of processes that should be running on the system. If the number of processes is greater than the maximum, an error flag is generated in other MIB objects. The maximum value is obtained from the agent configuration after the process name has been specified

Object Name: prCount

OID: prEntry.5

Object Type: integer

Access Mode: read-only

Description: The current number of processes actually running on the system that the agent is presently monitoring

Object Name: prErrorFlag

OID: prEntry.100

Object Type: integer

Access Mode: read-only

Description: This object is set to 1 if the agent detects trouble with the process and set to 0 if no problems are encountered. Possible problems include exceeding the maximum and minimum process count or the process not running at all

Object Name: prErrMessage

OID: prEntry.101

Object Type: DisplayString [255]

Access Mode: read-only

Description: If the agent has detected a problem with a process, this object will contain an error message
describing the problem in more detail

Object Name: prErrFix

OID: prEntry.102

Object Type: integer

Access Mode: read-only

Description: If the agent has been configured to support a
response to the trouble encountered with a pro-
cess, setting this object to 1 will instruct the
agent to attempt to fix the process problem
automatically by executing whatever script or
process the agent knows about

UCD Extensible Agent Table

The extTable table consists of objects that obtain a list of scripts
or programs that the agent will execute and whose results it will
store in UCD MIB. Figure 7.4 shows a hierarchical representation
of these objects as they relate to the ucdavis branch. This table
contains an MIB object called extEntry, which is used to access
each extTable element.

The extTable table contains the following set of objects:

Object Name: extIndex

OID: extEntry.1

Object Type: ExtIndex (Integer)

Access Mode: read-only

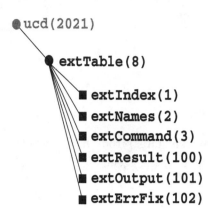

Figure 7.4 *The* extTable *view.*

Description:	Index into the extTable table for each config-ured extensible script
Object Name:	extNames
OID:	extIndex.2
Object Type:	DisplayString [255]
Access Mode:	read-only
Description:	A short (single-word) description of the extensi-ble command specified in the agent configura-tion file

Object Name:	extCommand
OID:	extIndex.3
Object Type:	DisplayString [255]
Access Mode:	read-only
Description:	The extensible command line specified in the agent configuration file

Object Name: extResult

OID: extIndex.100

Object Type: Integer

Access Mode: read-only

Description: The return code (exit status) from the extensible
                    command executed by the agent

Object Name: extOutput

OID: extIndex.101

Object Type: DisplayString [255]

Access Mode: read-only

Description: The first line of output from the extensible com-
                    mand executed by the agent

Object Name: extErrFix

OID: extIndex.102

Object Type: DisplayString [255]

Access Mode: read-only

Description: Flag to control whether the agent should
                    attempt a recovery from a problem encountered
                    when running the extensible command

UCD Disk Table

The diskTable table consists of objects that can be used to
obtain a list of all the file systems that the agent is monitoring and
any related objects. Figure 7.5 shows a hierarchical representation
of these objects as they relate to the ucdavis branch. This table

contains an MIB object called dskEntry, which is used to access
each diskTable element.

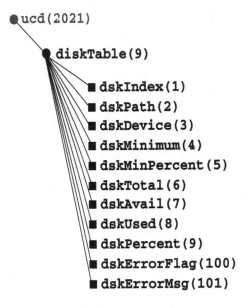

Figure 7.5 *The* diskTable *view.*

The diskTable table contains the following set of objects:

Object Name:	dskIndex
OID:	dskEntry.1
Object Type:	DiskIndex (Integer)
Access Mode:	read-only
Description:	Index into the DiskTable table for each file system that is being monitored by the agent

Object Name:	dskPath
OID:	dskEntry.2
Object Type:	DisplayString [255]

Access Mode: read-only

Description: The mount point of the file system being moni-
                    tored by the agent

Object Name: dskDevice

OID: dskEntry.3

Object Type: DisplayString [255]

Access Mode: read-only

Description: The actual device partition (slice) of the disk
                    mounted

Object Name: dskMinimum

OID: dskEntry.4

Object Type: integer

Access Mode: read-only

Description: The minimum amount of disk space required,
                    in kilobytes, before the agent triggers an event.
                    This value is specified with this object or the
                    dskMinPercent object from the agent
                    configuration file

Object Name: dskMinPercent

OID: dskEntry.5

Object Type: integer

Access Mode: read-only

Description: The minimum amount of disk space required, in kilobytes, before the agent triggers an event. This value is specified with this object or the dskMinimum object from the agent configuration file

Object Name: dskTotal

OID: dskEntry.6

Object Type: Integer

Access Mode: read-only

Description: Total size of the disk/partition, in kilobytes

Object Name: dskAvail

OID: dskEntry.7

Object Type: Integer

Access Mode: read-only

Description: The total amount of available disk space for the disk/partition, in kilobytes

Object Name: dskUsed

OID: dskEntry.8

Object Type: Integer

Access Mode: read-only

Description: The amount of used space on the disk/partition, in kilobytes

Object Name: dskPercent

OID: dskEntry.9

Object Type: Integer

Access Mode: read-only

Description: The amount of used space on the disk/partition,
                    as a percent

Object Name: dskErrorFlag

OID: dskEntry.100

Object Type: Integer

Access Mode: read-only

Description: Used to indicate that the disk/partition is under
                    the minimum amount of free disk space
                    specified by the agent configuration file

Object Name: dskErrorMsg

OID: dskEntry.101

Object Type: DisplayString [255]

Access Mode: read-only

Description: A descriptive warning message and free-space
                    summary pertaining to a monitored disk/
                    partition

UCD System Load Table

The loadTable table consists of objects that monitor the system
load. Figure 7.6 shows a hierarchical representation of these
objects as they relate to the ucdavis branch. This table contains an

MIB object called `laEntry`, which is used to access each `loadTable` element.

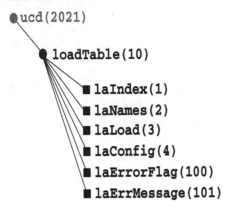

Figure 7.6 *The* `loadTable` *view.*

The `loadTable` contains the following set of objects:

Object Name: `laIndex`

OID: `laEntry.1`

Object Type: `Integer`

Access Mode: `read-only`

Description: Index into the `loadTable` table for each entry

.

Object Name: `laNames`

OID: `laEntry.2`

Object Type: `Display String [255]`

Access Mode: `read-only`

Description: The list of load average names that the agent is monitoring. This can be one of the three load average windows that the agent supports: one, five, and 15 minutes. These are represented by the strings Load-1, Load-5, and Load-15, respectively

Object Name: laLoad

OID: laEntry.3

Object Type: Display String [255]

Access Mode: read-only

Description: The actual system load averages for one, five, and 15 minutes, as recorded by the agent

Object Name: laConfig

OID: laEntry.4

Object Type: Display String [255]

Access Mode: read-only

Description: Contains the watch threshold for the load average to signal an error. This object obtains its value for the agent configuration file using the **load** command

Object Name: laErrorFlag

OID: laEntry.100

Object Type: Integer

Access Mode: read-only

Description: Used to indicate whether the load average threshold (contained in the `laConfig` object) has been exceeded. If the value is set to 1, then the threshold has been exceeded; otherwise, the value is 0.

Object Name: `laErrMessage`

OID: `laEntry.101`

Object Type: `Display String [255]`

Access Mode: `read-only`

Description: Descriptive error message indicating the load average and the threshold value that was exceeded

Sun's Master Agent

Master Agent Configuration/Configuring a Subagent

Before a subagent can be used, it must be registered with the master agent. This is accomplished by updating a small number of configuration files that are located in the `/etc/snmp/conf` directory. When the master agent starts, it parses any registration and resource files located in this directory. The master agent also ensures that messages from the network flow to the correct subagent and messages emitted from the subagents are also forwarded correctly. To register with the `snmpdx` master agent, the following files must contain entries for the subagent:

```
agent.reg
agent.rsrc
```

The `agent` prefix represents the name of the subagent that will be configured under the master agent. The `agent.reg` file registers the subagent with the master agent. The registration file consists of a keyword (or token) followed by a single value, separated by a new line. Comments are permitted in these files by using the hash character (#). A single collection of keywords and values are

enclosed in brackets and constitute a subagent entry. The keywords
that can be used in the registration file include **name, subtrees, timeout**, and **watch-dog-time**.

The **name** keyword is simply a label for naming the subagent
internally. The **subtrees** keyword specifies the MIB tree that the subagent supports when queried by another SNMP entity. The **timeout**
keyword controls how much time the master should wait for the
subagent to process an SNMP request. The timeout value is
expressed in microseconds. The **watch-dog-time** keyword is used by
the master agent to determine if the subagent is still functioning by
periodically checking the status of the subagent. The registration
file, shown in Listing 7.5, that is used by the mibiisa subagent further illustrates this.

Listing 7.5 *Agent registration file*

```
agents =
{
        {
                        name = "snmpd"
                        subtrees = { mib-2, sun }
                        timeout = 2000000
                        watch-dog-time = 86400
        }
}
```

In this case, the name of the mibiisa subagent is snmpd, which is
used internally to the master agent. The subtrees values denote
two macros that are shorthand for specific OID strings. The mib-2
value is defined as 1.3.6.1.2.1, and sun is 1.3.6.1.4.1.42. The
timeout value is two seconds (or 2,000,000 microseconds.); the
watch-dog-time value is expressed in seconds.

The resource file, agent.rsrc, is also needed when configuring a
subagent to work with a master agent. This file is primarily used to
indicate the registration file and the subagent program name. Listing 7.6 lists the resource file for the mibiisa subagent. This file
shares the same format as the registration file, with keywords followed by values. The resource file requires a **registration_file, policy,
type**, and **command** keyword and associated values. The
registration_file token assigns the subagent registration file that the
master agent will use. The **policy** token is used to indicate how the

master agent should execute the subagent. The **command** token represents the subagent program that the master agent will start after it completes parsing both the registration and resource files for each of the subagents. The SNMP port can also be specified in this file by using the **port** keyword. However, the subagent can also let the master agent assign a port to use by using the $PORT string. In Listing 7.6, the mibissa subagent uses the $PORT string instead of statically assigning a port.

Listing 7.6 *Agent resource file*

```
resource =
{
        {
                registration_file = "/etc/snmp/conf/mibiisa.reg"
                policy = "spawn"
                type = "legacy"
                command = "/usr/lib/snmp/mibiisa -p $PORT"
        }
}
```

The master agent requires the following files:

```
snmpdx.acl
snmpdx.reg
snmpdx.rsrc
```

The snmpdx.acl file can be used to specify the community string information that the master agent will use to control access to its MIB. The control mechanism is primarily used for the master agent MIB objects, not the subagent MIBs. This is an important distinction because the subagents (for example, the mibiisa agent) rely on the snmpd.conf file, not the snmpdx.acl file, for this purpose. The snmpdx.reg is the master agent registration file that serves the same purpose as the subagent file. The snmpdx.rsrc file is used to specify some timing parameters for the master agent. All these files are located in the /etc/snmp/conf directory.

Command-line Options

The snmpdx agent supports several command-line options, which are listed in Table 7.4 and described in following section.

The -a option specifies the path and filename for the access control file. The agent uses this file to control access to the MIB by external

Table 7.4 *Master agent command-line options*

Option	Description
-a	Specifies the path of the access control file used by the agent
-c	Changes the path on which to search for the agent configuration file
-d	Activates debugging level
-h	Prints online help
-i	Specifies the path of another status file that is used by an agent
-m	Instructs the agent to forward SNMP messages based on specified mode
-o	Specifies the path of the enterprise OID mapping file
-p	Specifies the port to use instead of the default of 161
-r	Specifies the path of the resource file
-y	Invokes recovery of the subagents

entities. The default file is /etc/snmp/conf/snmpdx.acl. The -i
option gives another full path for the master agent status file. This is
the file used by the master agent for recovery after a crash. It contains
the UNIX process id, port number, resource name, and agent name of
each subagent defined. The default location and name of the status
file is /var/snmp/snmpdx.st.

The -c option changes the default configuration path from
/etc/snmp/conf. The master agent searches for the agent configuration, resource file, and OID mapping files in this location. The -o
command-line option changes the default location and name of the
enterprise-name OID file. The master agent uses this file to map vendor names to enterprise numbers. This file is, by default,
/etc/snmp/conf/enterprises.oid. Trap processing by the master
agent requires this information to determine vendor-specific information. The -r option controls which resource file the master agent uses.

This file contains agent configuration information and the default path; the filename is /etc/snmp/conf/snmpdx.rsrc. Because the master agent is started at system boot time, these options should be changed in the /etc/init.d/init.snmpdx system startup file so that they may be permanent. However, it is recommended that any changes to the startup file be tested before the startup file is executed on a system reboot.

Why change the location of the files? Well, in some sites, the standard practice is to use a special file system location that has been previously set up and is commonly available across every system on the network. Further, this area might be archived more regularly than other file systems and, as a result, be used to store all configuration files for third-party tools. For this reason, using this area can be more beneficial than using the default location. Also, if you want to test new configurations that may exist in other locations and with different filenames, these options can help as well.

The -h option is useful because it displays the help summary of the master agent. Running the snmpdx master agent command with the -h option will display the available command-line options and their associated arguments:

```
# /usr/lib/snmp/snmpdx -h
Usage: snmpdx [-h]
        [-h]
        [-n relay_agent_name (default relay-agent)]
        [-p port (default 161)]
        [-r resource-file (default /etc/snmp/conf/snmpdx.rsrc)]
        [-a access-control-file (default /etc/snmp/conf/snmpdx.acl)]
        [-c config-dir (default /etc/snmp/conf)]
        [-i pid-file (default /var/snmp/snmpdx.st)]
        [-o enterprise-oid-file (default /etc/snmp/conf/enterprises.oid)]
        [-y]
        [-m GROUP | SPLIT (default GROUP)]
        [-d trace-level (range 0..4, default 0)]
```

The master agent provides the capability for messages to be displayed by using the -d option. This option can be very useful when debugging agent configurations or operational problems. Four debugging levels are supported that range from 0 (no debugging) to 4 (full debugging). The fourth level of debugging includes agent configuration information, decoding of each SNMP message PDU, session information, and complete packet contents displayed in hexadecimal. The third level includes the agent configuration, SNMP decoding, and session information, but not the packet display. The second level includes only the agent configuration and session information, and the first level includes agent configuration but little session information.

The -m option specifies the mode in which to forward SNMP requests to each subagent. Two modes are available with the master agent. The first, GROUP, indicates that multiple variables can be included with each request from the master agent. The second mode, SPLIT, ensures that each variable in the incoming request results in one send request to each subagent. The default forwarding mode is GROUP.

The -p option specifies an alternative port that the master agent will use when receiving or transmitting SNMP messages. The master agent uses the default SNMP port of 161 to send and receive SNMP messages. Using this option, the master agent will listen on another port specified after the -p argument. For example, the master agent will listen on port 200 if the command below is executed:

```
# /usr/lib/snmp/snmpdx -p 200 -y
```

Remember, if the default SNMP port is changed, any SNMP management software that will query the agent must also be configured to use this new port. Otherwise, SNMP queries made on the old port will never reach the agent and will, instead, timeout. One primary reason for using this option is to support more than one instance of the master agent on the same system. This configuration could be used during testing of a newer version of the master agent without affecting the operation of the current version.

The -y option is used when the master agent has crashed or restarted when one or more subagents are already running. This option is used when the master agent must recover its previous state before the crash to determine the configuration and status of each of the defined subagents. Further, you will notice that the -y option is included when the snmpdx command /etc/init.d/init.snmpdx (located in the system startup file) is executed. This startup script executes the master agent as shown here:

```
/usr/lib/snmp/snmpdx -y -c /etc/snmp/conf
```

When the agent is automatically started by the system, the master agent has no way of determining its previous state, and therefore uses the recovery option by default. Any subagent not found to be running when the master agent starts is restarted automatically by the master agent.

Master Agent MIB

The `snmpdx` agent implements a collection of MIB objects that provide information about the operational state and configuration of the master agent and any configured subagents. These objects are defined in the `/var/snmp/mib/snmpdx.mib` file under Sun's enterprise number (`42`) and are referenced from the `products` group (`enterprises.sun.products`) under the `sunMasterAgent` branch. Figure 7.7 shows the hierarchy of the `sunMasterAgent` group from the standard `enterprises` branch.

Because of the large number of these objects relating to the master agent, only the most important objects have been described and listed here. For those objects not presented, consult the `/var/snmp/mib/snmpdx.mib` file for additional information.

The `sunMasterAgent` group includes the following collection of MIB objects:

- global agent objects

- subagent configuration objects

Global Agent Objects

The global agent objects provide configuration information for the master agent and all registered subagents. This information is important because it might become necessary to poll the master agent directly to help debug both master agent and subagent operational issues and other problems. The objects are listed below:

Object Name: `sunMasterAgentStatusFile`

OID: `sunMasterAgent.1`

Object Type: `Display String`

Access Mode: `read-write`

Figure 7.7 *The* sunMasterAgent *view.*

Description:	This file contains a list of all the subagent process ids and is used by the master agent to recover after it unexpectedly stops or is killed

Object Name:	sunMasterAgentResourceConfigFile
OID:	sunMasterAgent.2
Object Type:	Display String
Access Mode:	read-write

Description: This file is used to contain subagent configuration information and is used by the master agent upon startup

Object Name: `sunMasterAgentConfigurationDir`

OID: `sunMasterAgent.3`

Object Type: `Display String`

Access Mode: `read-write`

Description: The directory that contains the configuration files for the master agent

Object Name: `sunMasterAgentTrapPort`

OID: `sunMasterAgent.4`

Object Type: `INTEGER`

Access Mode: `read-only`

Description: The port used by the master agent to receive SNMP traps from each of the subagents. These traps are then forwarded to one or more managers found in the master agent configuration file

Object Name: `sunCheckSubAgentName`

OID: `sunMasterAgent.5`

Object Type: `Display String`

Access Mode: `read-write`

Description: Used by the subagents to check that no duplicate subagent with the same name is running

Object Name: sunMasterAgentPollInterval

OID: sunMasterAgent.6

Object Type: INTEGER

Access Mode: read-only

Description: This variable contains the time interval when
                    the agent will perform housekeeping activities,
                    such as determining if the resource file has
                    changed, rediscovering each subagent, and
                    other related tasks

Object Name: sunMasterAgentMaxAgentTimeOut

OID: sunMasterAgent.7

Object Type: INTEGER

Access Mode: read-only

Description: This object is used to signify the maximum
                    allowed timeout that a subagent can set. This is
                    used by the master agent to wait when sending
                    requests to a subagent before the request is con-
                    sidered to have expired

Subagent Configuration Objects

Additional objects within the snmpdx.mib file provide information on each subagent operating under the master agent. This
information is available via a table and using index objects. The
table (sunSubAgentTable) lists all the subagents that have been registered with the master agent. Each entry in this table is described
as a sunSubAgentEntry object. Access to the sunSubAgentTable
table is via the sunSubAgentEntry object. Figure 7.8 shows the hierarchy of the sunSubAgentTable group from the standard
enterprises branch.

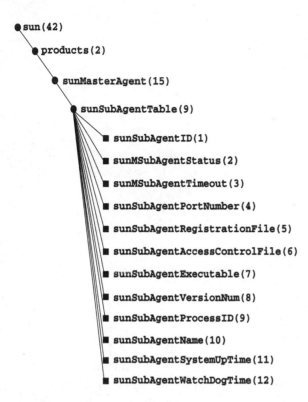

Figure 7.8 *The* sunSubAgentEntry *view.*

The sunSubAgentEntry table consists of the following subagent-related objects:

Object Name:	sunSubAgentID
OID:	sunSubAgentEntry.1
Object Type:	INTEGER
Access Mode:	read-only
Description:	This is the unique ID for each subagent running under the master agent

Object Name: `sunSubAgentStatus`

OID: `sunSubAgentEntry.2`

Object Type: `INTEGER`

Access Mode: `read-write`

Description: Indicates the state of the subagent. Possible states include `init(1)`, `load(2)`, `active(3)`, `inactive(4)`, and `destroy(5)`

Object Name: `sunSubAgentTimeout`

OID: `sunSubAgentEntry.3`

Object Type: `INTEGER`

Access Mode: `read-write`

Description: The maximum amount of time that the master agent will wait for a subagent to complete a request, expressed in microseconds

Object Name: `sunSubAgentPortNumber`

OID: `sunSubAgentEntry.4`

Object Type: `INTEGER`

Access Mode: `read-write`

Description: The port number used by the subagent to listen for requests from the master agent

Object Name: `sunSubAgentRegistrationFile`

OID: `sunSubAgentEntry.5`

Object Type: Display String

Access Mode: read-write

Description: Specifies the registration file used by the sub-agent. Each subagent must have its own file and contain the subagent name, MIB tree information, preferred SNMP port, etc

Object Name: sunSubAgentAccessControlFile

OID: sunSubAgentEntry.6

Object Type: Display String

Access Mode: read-write

Description: Specifies the access control file used by the sub-agent to store SNMP community information

Object Name: sunSubAgentExecutable

OID: sunSubAgentEntry.7

Object Type: Display String

Access Mode: read-write

Description: Contains the executable subagent program

Object Name: sunSubAgentVersionNum

OID: sunSubAgentEntry.8

Object Type: Display String

Access Mode: read-write

Description: The version information for the subagent

Object Name: sunSubAgentProcessID

OID: sunSubAgentEntry.9

Object Type: Display String

Access Mode: read-write

Description: The process ID of the subagent

Object Name: sunSubAgentName

OID: sunSubAgentEntry.10

Object Type: Display String

Access Mode: read-write

Description: The name of the subagent specified in the
                    registration file

Object Name: sunSubAgentSystemUpTime

OID: sunSubAgentEntry.11

Object Type: TimeTicks

Access Mode: read-write

Description: The system up time of the subagent

Object Name: sunSubAgentWatchDogTime

OID: sunSubAgentEntry.12

Object Type: INTEGER

Access Mode: read-write

Description: The amount of time that the master agent waits
                    before polling the subagent to ensure that it is
                    still operating correctly, expressed in seconds

Sun SNMP Agent

The Sun agent can provide the following services:

- obtain network statistics

- obtain system process information

- obtain system memory information

- send traps to specified systems

This system and network information will be available by polling the agent's MIB. The agent supports both MIB-II and portions of Sun's private MIB. The Sun MIB is described below. The *trap definition*, which must be done in the agent configuration file, is also described below.

Command-line Options

The `mibiisa` utility supports several command-line options, as outlined in Table 7.5. Perhaps one of the most important is the `-r` option, which can be used to disable write access to the agent's MIB. Because the `mibiisa` utility implements SNMPv1, the agent doesn't provide a very robust security model. It might be necessary to limit the access to the system objects supported by the agent. Using this option, all SNMP `set-requests` will be rejected, but read access will operate without being affected.

Any attempt to alter or set an MIB object after the `-r` option has been used will cause an error. More specifically, when using a MIB browser, for example, if an attempt is made to set MIB objects that are placed in read-only mode, the authentication trap message will be generated.

Table 7.5 *Master agent command options*

Option	Description
`-a`	Disable authentication traps
`-c`	Specify path to search for the configuration file
`-d`	Enable debugging output

Table 7.5 *Master agent command options (continued)*

Option	Description
`-p`	Use specified port instead of `161`
`-r`	Place the MIB in read-only mode

By default, the directory in which `mibiisa` searches for the required configuration file is `/etc/snmp/conf`. To specify an alternate directory, use the `-c` option followed by the directory name. This option can be used to help test new configuration files that might reside in other directory locations. The `mibiisa` agent requires a configuration file, and if it can't locate a valid configuration, it will exit with an error.

When an SNMP entity attempts to poll an agent with the incorrect community string, an authentication message is dispatched to the addresses configured in the `mibiisa` configuration file. If you would like to disable these trap messages, use the `-a` option.

To place the agent in debug mode, the `-d` option can be used when invoking the agent on the command line. Also, an optional debug level can be included that decreases levels of debugging from 3 (which is the highest) to 1 (which is the lowest).

Depending on the networking services presently running on the system, it might be necessary to use a different UDP port instead of the default of 161. This will be required if the `mibiisa` agent is running with a master agent. In this case, the agent will need to be started on a different port using the `-p` option. For example, to start the agent on port `32000`, use the following command:

```
# /usr/lib/snmp/mibiisa -p 32000
```

Configuring the Sun Agent

The `mibiisa` agent uses a configuration file called `snmpd.conf` and, by default, searches the `/etc/snmp/conf` directory for this file. This file contains configuration information that controls access to the agent's MIB and additional control information. Each entry contains a keyword followed by a string value, separated by one or more white spaces. Comments are also supported in this file by using the pound sign (#) and are ignored when processed by the agent. The keywords that can be used are outlined in Table 7.6 and described in more detail.

Table 7.6 *Agent configuration options*

Keyword	Description
sysdescr	System agent information
syscontact	System contact information
syslocation	Information on physical location of system
trap	Sends traps to specified hosts
system-group-read-community	Controls read access to MIB-II and Sun's system objects
system-group-write-community	Controls write access to MIB-II and Sun's system objects
read-community	Controls read access to the entire MIB
write-community	Controls write access to the entire MIB
trap-community	Trap community string
kernel-file	Symbol lookup file
managers	Hosts that are permitted to communicate with the agent

The **sysdescr** keyword maps to the MIB-II object `sysDescr`, and the associated value is used by the agent when responding to requests for this object. This describes the system on which the agent is running (e.g., `Utltra SPARC 2` or `SPARCclassic`). Values for this object might include any string, but should represent some information related to the type of system, and perhaps operating system information as well.

The `syscontact` keyword maps to the MIB-II object `sysContact`, and the associated value is used by the agent when responding to requests for this object. The sysContact object used to describe the contact group or name that is responsible for the system (e.g., Steve Rossman x3414).

The **syslocation** keyword maps to the MIB-II object sysLocation, and the associated value is used by the agent when responding to requests for this object. The sysLocation object is used to describe the physical location of the system (e.g., Building 2, Graphics Lab 11-B).

The **trap** keyword specifies one or more hosts that should receive traps from the agent. Up to five hosts may be included with this option. Either the IP addresses or hostnames may be used. Any additional hosts beyond the maximum will be ignored. One use of this keyword is to forward authentication traps when an SNMP entity attempts to poll the agent with an incorrect community string. This is the primary way to determine if another party is attempting to access a device without having the proper authorization.

An authorization trap may also indicate that the community string was changed on the agent side, and this change was not propagated to the manager side as well. Also, it may mean that a new SNMP management software package that uses the community strings of public or private was recently installed, and that these strings must be adjusted to the strings used at the local site.

The **system-group-read-community** and **system-group-write-community** keywords control read-write access to the agent MIB that includes only the system group within MIB-II and Sun's object groups. The **read-community** and **write-community** keywords control read-write access to the entire MIB. The **trap-community** keyword specifies the community string for trap messages. The **kernel-file** keyword specifies where the agent should search for symbols.

The **managers** keyword controls which hosts are permitted to communicate with the agent for either read or write access. It forms a basic access control list (ACL) for the agent. The ACL is one very good way to address some of the security flaws within the SNMP security model. However, bear in mind that this option provides a fundamental authentication mechanism, which is vulnerable to compromise given the right situation. For example, the ACL can be tricked if system chips was on the access list, but system dip assumed the identity of chip while it was down for repairs. Therefore, consider the **managers** option as only part of your overall security strategy.

Sample Configuration

Listing 7.7 further illustrates the agent configuration file options.

Listing 7.7 *Sample agent configuration file*

```
#
# System Information
#
sysdescr        SPARC Ultra 60
syscontact      Steve Rossman
syslocation     Science Center room 22B
#
# Community Strings (system group only)
#
system-group-read-community     louvrehasart
system-group-write-community    louvrehasart
#
# Community Strings (entire MIB)
#
read-community  louvrehasart_1834
write-community louvrehasart_1824
#
# Trap Information
#
trap            rembrandt
trap-community  louvrehasart
#
# Standard Unix kernel
#
kernel-file     /vmunix
#
# Which systems are permitted to talk to this agent
#
managers        rembrandt monet
```

The system information (`sysdescr`, `syscontact`, and `syslocation`) should be specific to each system on which the agent is running. In this example, the agent is running on a `SPARC ultra 60` workstation, the contact for the system is `Steve Rossman`, and the system is located in the `Science Center room 22B`. Note that any descriptive information could be included. Therefore, the `sysdescr` might not represent the actual type of system on which the agent is running. The system

MIB objects are accessed with the read and write community string of louvrehasart. Access to the rest of the MIB for both read and write access is set to the string louvrehasart_1824. The system community string is different from the entire MIB in case you want others to have access to system information (for inventory purposes, for example) without having access to the core of the other agent objects. All traps generated from this agent will be sent to the host rembrandt with a community string of louvrehasart. Using the **managers** keyword as the basic ACL, the agent is permitted to access SNMP requests from the hosts rembrandt and monet, and all other requests will be discarded by the agent.

Sun Agent MIB Objects

The mibiisa agent supports all of the objects defined within MIB-II, plus additional objects under the Sun enterprise-wide vendor number (42). The MIB-II objects have been previously described in Chapter 3, "TCP/IP Protocol Suite." However, Sun has changed some of the attributes relating to either the return values or access modes of the standard MIB-II definitions. This section describes these changes and the additional Sun objects.

Sun MIB Differences

The differences between mibiisa objects and the standard MIB-II objects include:

- Access to MIB objects has changed

- Certain MIB objects contain fixed values

Table 7.7 outlines these differences and contains a list of MIB objects, flags that indicate the object differences, the access method (either *read-write* or *read-only*), and the return value, if any. The object flags V and A refer to whether the object change is related to the value (V) of the object or the access mode (A) of the object. A check mark is placed in the column to indicate which object attribute is different from standard MIB-II definitions. For example, the access mode of the sysName object is read-write within MIB-II, while the Sun MIB provides only read-only access. As a result, a check mark is placed in column A. Most of the Sun objects in this table just return a fixed value. In many of these cases, a 1 is returned, which means that the agent doesn't support the object and it is provided only for compatibility purposes.

Table 7.7 *Comparison of MIB-II and Sun MIB objects*

MIB Object	V	A	Access within MIB-II	Access within mibiisa	Value within mibiisa
sysName		✓	read-write	read-only	
atIfIndex		✓	read-write	read-only	
ipDefaultTTL		✓	read-write	read-only	
ipRoutIfIndex	✓		read-write	read-write	(fixed)
IpRouteMetric1	✓		read-write	read-write	-1
IpRouteMetric2	✓		read-write	read-write	-1
IpRouteMetric3	✓		read-write	read-write	-1
IpRouteMetric4	✓		read-write	read-write	-1
IpRouteMetric5	✓		read-write	read-write	-1
IpRouteType	✓		read-write	read-write	(fixed)
IpRouteAge	✓		read-write	read-write	0
IpRouteMask	✓		read-write	read-write	(fixed)

Table 7.7 *Comparison of MIB-II and Sun MIB objects (continued)*

MIB Object	V	A	Access within MIB-II	Access within mibiisa	Value within mibiisa
icmpInDestUnreachs	✓		read-only	read-only	1
icmpInTimeExcds	✓		read-only	read-only	1
icmpInParmProbs	✓		read-only	read-only	1
icmpInSrcQuenchs	✓		read-only	read-only	1
icmpInRedirects	✓		read-only	read-only	1
icmpInEchos	✓		read-only	read-only	1
icmpInEchoReps	✓		read-only	read-only	1
icmpInTimestamps	✓		read-only	read-only	1
icmpInTimestamp-Reps	✓		read-only	read-only	1
icmpInAddrMasks	✓		read-only	read-only	1
icmpInAddrMaskReps	✓		read-only	read-only	1
icmpOutDestUn-reachs	✓		read-only	read-only	1
icmpOutTimeExcds	✓		read-only	read-only	1
icmpOutParmProbs	✓		read-only	read-only	1
icmpOutSrcQuenchs	✓		read-only	read-only	1
icmpOutRedirects	✓		read-only	read-only	1
icmpOutEchos	✓		read-only	read-only	1
icmpOutEchoReps	✓		read-only	read-only	1
icmpOutTimestamps	✓		read-only	read-only	1
icmpOutTimestamp-Reps	✓		read-only	read-only	1
icmpOutAddrMasks	✓		read-only	read-only	1
icmpOutAddrMask-Reps	✓		read-only	read-only	1
ifInUnknownProtos	✓		read-only	read-only	1

Table 7.7 *Comparison of MIB-II and Sun MIB objects (continued)*

MIB Object	V	A	Access within MIB-II	Access within mibiisa	Value within mibiisa
ipAdEntBcastAddr	✓		read-only	read-only	1
ipAdEntReasmMaxSiz	✓		read-only	read-only	65535
ipNetToMediaType	✓		read-only	read-only	Returns dynamic (3)
ipRoutingDiscards	✓		read-only	read-only	0

Sun Enterprise MIB Objects

The Sun enterprise objects supported by mibiisa include the following groups:

- sunSystem
- sunProcessTable
- sunHostPerf

The sunSystem group provides generic host information, such as agent and system information. The sunProcessTable group contains information regarding the presently running system processes found on the agent's system. The sunHostPerf group contains performance-related information. Each of these groups is described fully below. These groups are part of the Sun enterprise MIB, which contains additional groups. However, the agent only supports the three groups listed above. Figure 7.9 shows the hierarchical representation of all the groups under the Sun MIB from the enterprises branch.

The sunSystem group consists of objects that can be used to obtain system information such as the description of the system agent, the host identification string, part of the message-of-the-day file, and the system time. Figure 7.10 shows a hierarchical representation of the objects found in this group extending from the sun branch.

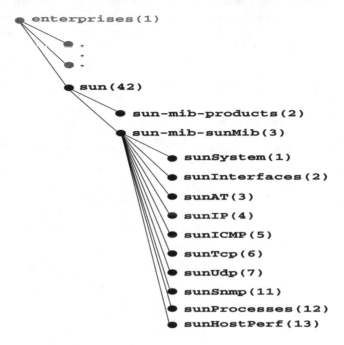

Figure 7.9 *Sun enterprise MIB.*

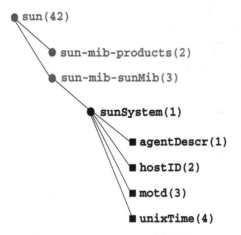

Figure 7.10 *The* sunSystem *view.*

A detailed description of these MIB objects appears below:

Object Name: agentDescr

OID: sunSystem.1

Object Type: Display String [255]

Access Mode: read-only

Description: A description of the SNMP agent, which is used
                    to identify itself to other entities, such as an
                    SNMP manager. The agent assigns the string
                    value of Sun Microsystems SNMP Agent

Object Name: hostID

OID: sunSystem.2

Object Type: Display String [255]

Access Mode: read-only

Description: A four-byte hardware identifier, which should be
                    unique for every Sun system. This value is equiv-
                    alent to executing the hostid utility on the
                    UNIX command line

Object Name: motd

OID: sunSystem.3

Object Type: Display String [4]

Access Mode: read-only

Description: The first line from the /etc/motd file. The
                     /etc/motd file is the message-of-the-day file in
                     which the file contents will be displayed every
                     time a user logs into the system. By default, the
                     first line will contain the operating system ver-
                     sion and related information, but it may also
                     contain any other information that the adminis-
                     trator wants to make available

Object Name: unixTime

OID: sunSystem.4

Object Type: Counter

Access Mode: read-only

Description: The UNIX system clock time, as measured in
                     seconds from 1/1/1970

Sun Process Table Group

The sunProcessTable table consists of objects that can be used
to obtain a list of system processes and related information. Figure
7.11 shows a hierarchical representation of these objects as they
relate to the main sun branch. The psEntry object is the index for
the sunProcessTable table and is used to access each member,
which represents a different UNIX process. Because each of the
objects listed below is a member of sunProcessTable, the OID is
represented as the index from the psEntry object's point of view.

The information available within this group can also be
obtained and compared to the operating system **ps** command. To
help you better understand how this group of objects is used, Figure 7.12 shows the objects that correspond to the fields from the **ps**
command.

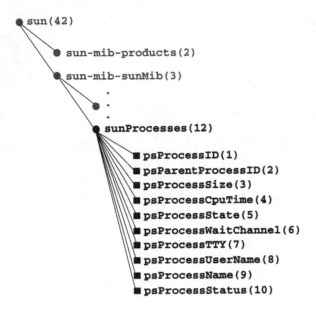

Figure 7.11 *The* sunProcessTable *view.*

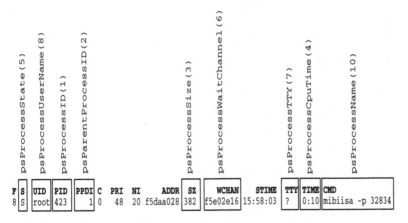

Figure 7.12 *Process status MIB mapping.*

The process table contains the following objects:

Object Name: psProcessID

OID: psEntry.1

Object Type: Counter

Access Mode: read-only

Description: Displays the process id

Object Name: psParentProcessID

OID: psEntry.2

Object Type: Counter

Access Mode: read-only

Description: Displays the process id's parent process

Object Name: psProcessSize

OID: psEntry.3

Object Type: Counter

Access Mode: read-only

Description: Displays the size of the memory that the process
                     is using, including stack and data segments

Object Name: psProcessCpuTime

OID: psEntry.4

Object Type: Counter

Access Mode: read-only

Description: Displays the amount of CPU time, including
                     both user and system time, that this process has
                     consumed at the time this value was retrieved

Object Name: psProcessState

OID: psEntry.5

Object Type: Display String [4]

Access Mode: read-only

Description: Displays the current running state of the process. This includes the use of the following flags:

R: runnable
T: stopped
P: in page wait
D: non-interruptible wait
S: sleeping (less than 20 seconds)
I: idle (more than 20 seconds)
Z: zombie

Object Name: psProcessWaitChannel

OID: psEntry.6

Object Type: Display String [16]

Access Mode: read-only

Description: Displays the reason that the process is in wait mode

Object Name: psProcessTTY

OID: psEntry.7

Object Type: Display String [16]

Access Mode: read-only

Description: Displays the controlling terminal of this process, if any

Object Name: psProcessUserName

OID: psEntry.8

Object Type: Display String [16]

Access Mode: read-only

Description: Displays the name of the user associated with
                      this process

Object Name: psProcessUserID

OID: psEntry.9

Object Type: counter

Access Mode: read-only

Description: Displays the numeric user id associated with the
                      psProcessUserName string

Object Name: psProcessName

OID: psEntry.10

Object Type: Display String [64]

Access Mode: read-only

Description: Displays the name of the command string for
                      this process

Object Name: psProcessStatus

OID: psEntry.11

Object Type: Counter

Access Mode: read-write

Description: Indicates the signal to send to this process

Sun Host Performance Group

The `sunHostPerf` group consists of a collection of system performance-related objects that range from the total number of timeticks used by a process to the total number of network collisions.
Due to the rather large number of these objects, only the most useful objects will be described. If you are looking for a complete list
of available objects within this group, consult the Sun MIB file
`/var/snmp/mib/sun.mib` for additional information.

Among the more useful objects within the `sunHostPerf` group
are objects relating to system swap, device interrupts, and network
traffic. Figure 7.13 shows a hierarchical representation of these
objects as they relate to the main `sun` branch. The traffic objects are
counters, which represent totals for the entire system regardless of
the number of network connections and are similar to the output
from the **netstat** command. For example, the `rsIfInPackets` object
provides the total number of input packets from the network for
all network interfaces defined on the system.

The `sunHostPerf` group includes the following objects:

Object Name:	`rsVpagesIn`
OID:	`sunHostPerf.9`
Object Type:	`Counter`
Access Mode:	`read-only`
Description:	Total number of pages read in from disk since last reboot

Object Name:	`rsVpagesOut`
OID:	`sunHostPerf.10`
Object Type:	`Counter`
Access Mode:	`read-only`
Description:	Total number of pages written to disk since last reboot

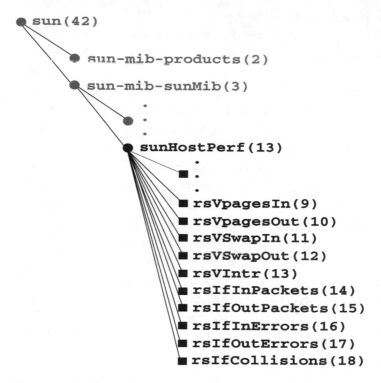

Figure 7.13 *The* sunHostPerf *view.*

Object Name:	rsVSwapIn
OID:	sunHostPerf.11
Object Type:	Counter
Access Mode:	read-only
Description:	Total number of pages swapped in since last reboot

Object Name:	rsVSwapOut
OID:	sunHostPerf.12
Object Type:	Counter

Access Mode: read-only

Description: Total number of pages read out from disk since last reboot

Object Name: rsVIntr

OID: sunHostPerf.13

Object Type: Counter

Access Mode: read-only

Description: Total number of device interrupts since last reboot; includes interrupts for all devices such as disks and other peripheral devices.

Object Name: rsIfInPackets

OID: sunHostPerf.14

Object Type: Counter

Access Mode: read-only

Description: Total number of input packets obtained from the network since last reboot

Object Name: rsIfOutPackets

OID: sunHostPerf.15

Object Type: Counter

Access Mode: read-only

Description: Total number of out packets transmitted to the network since last reboot

Object Name: rsIfInErrors

OID: sunHostPerf.16

Object Type: Counter

Access Mode: read-only

Description: Total number of input errors from the network
                     since last reboot

Object Name: rsIfOutErrors

OID: sunHostPerf.17

Object Type: Counter

Access Mode: read-only

Description: Total number of output errors encountered
                     while attempting to transmit to the network
                     since last reboot

Object Name: rsIfCollisions

OID: sunHostPerf.18

Object Type: Counter

Access Mode: read-only

Description: Total number of output collisions recorded on
                     the network since last reboot

SNMP Tools

Chapter 4, "Core System Utilities and Tools," and Chapter 5, "Additional System Utilities and Tools," discuss operating system tools and utilities. This chapter focuses more on network tools that can help manage both systems and networking elements such as switches, routers, probes, hubs, and other devices. All of them are based on SNMP and can be used to interrogate any SNMP-compliant agent for a wealth of information.

This chapter covers the following tools:

Command	Page
snmpdelta	422
snmpget	425
snmpgetnext	427
snmpnetstat	429
snmpset	434
snmpstatus	437
snmptable	440
snmptest	443
snmptranslate	443
snmptrap	445
snmptrapd	446
snmpwalk	450
snmpbulkwalk	451
snmpconf	454
tkmib	458

Monitoring/Administration Functions

The tools covered in this section provide access to a variety of agent information and are particularly useful in monitoring and administration. Some of the most important information that can be collected from devices include the following:

- SNMP system heartbeat

- system up/down messages

- protocol statistics

- interface performance measurements

- system process activity

- routing

- performance statistics

Some of the tools can also be used to configure network devices. The sections that follow describe each of these uses.

System Heartbeat

A system heartbeat is an SNMP `get-request` that a manager uses to determine the general reachability of the agent and the system. For example, the network manager may poll the system clock MIB variable of the agent to determine that each successive poll is more recent than the previous one. Each successive poll should indicate that time is moving forward. The MIB variable that the network manager may poll is the `unixTime` object, part of the `sun-System` group of the Sun system agent. As an alternative, the network manager may poll the `sysUpTime` object from the MIB-2 `system` group, which should be available from all SNMP agents.

System Up/Down Messages

Should the system be brought down and rebooted for any reason, a message will be sent to the designated network management system in the form of an SNMP `trap`. Recall that a `trap` is an unsolicited message emitted from the agent indicating some special condition or event. By receiving these messages, the manager is informed, for example, of system outages and can take appropriate action. The UCD agent configuration file and additional tools can be used to forward trap messages to one or more network management systems.

Protocol Statistics

Because many SNMP agents support the MIB-II standard, protocol performance monitoring and system monitoring are possible. This includes monitoring of IP, ICMP, TCP, SNMP, network interface counters, and additional agent system performance objects.

System Process Activity

With the Sun MIB extensions and the UCD agent, the monitoring of system processes is also possible. Objects can establish the overall health of the network or the condition of an individual system by monitoring critical processes.

Route Monitoring

The route monitoring agent can determine the routing configuration of a system and report any errors found. For example, if an organization has determined that each machine must have a default route, this can be verified by probing the SNMP agent within these devices.

Interface Performance

MIB-2 also provides objects that contain performance information for each of the interfaces installed within an SNMP device. It is possible to retrieve this information and monitor the performance of active interfaces.

Configuration Control

Many networking devices (e.g., routers and switches) must be configured before they can be effectively used on a network. Also, as network requirements change, so too the configurations within these devices must change. The tools listed here can be used to alter device configurations.

UCD Commands

General Description

The UCD package provides not only a robust and powerful SNMP agent, but it also provides a series of handy tools that can be used to manage SNMP-enabled networking devices. These tools support SNMPv1, SNMPv2, and SNMPv3. You can select which version is used with a command-line option. Further, these utilities can be used to build scripts or other programs to accomplish complex network management functions or customized tasks. For example, the **snmpget** command can monitor certain critical interfaces to determine if one or more of them becomes inoperable. In such a case, the appropriate support staff could be notified automatically.

Table 8.1 lists the tools and utilities that are supplied with the UCD package.

Table 8.1 *UCD SNMP tools*

UCD Tool	Description
snmpdelta	Monitors changes of SNMP variables
snmpget	Obtains one or more MIB objects
snmpgetnext	Continuously walks an SNMP MIB tree and obtains all supported MIB objects
snmpnetstat	Obtains agent interface configuration information
snmpset	Sets one or more MIB objects to specified value
snmpstatus	Obtains important MIB object information
snmptable	Obtains a complete SNMP table
snmptest	Communicates with an SNMP agent entity
snmptranslate	Converts MIB objects into more meaningful information
snmptrap	Sends SNMP trap messages to one or more managers
snmptrapd	Retrieves SNMP traps from the network
snmpwalk	Obtains a group of related MIB objects
snmpbulkwalk	Obtains an MIB object with SNMP bulk request
tkmib	Browses MIB objects. This tool is based on Tcl/Tk.

The basic syntax of the UCD tools is the following:

```
snmpcmd protocol_version [additional_options] hostname
community object [object]
```

The word `snmpcmd` is a placeholder and represents one of the UCD commands listed in the preceding table. All the UCD tools support this basic command syntax. The word `protocol_version` can be `1`, `2c`, or `3`. This string identifier specifies which SNMP version should be used when sending queries to the agent. Option `1` represents the standard SNMPv1 format. The `2c` option indicates differences within the supported SNMP protocol data units, but uses the same community-based approach as in SNMPv1. The `3` option indicates the use of the SNMPv3 security model.

The `additional_options` placeholder represents options that control both display attributes and operational behavior of the tools. The most commonly used command-line options are described below.

The word `hostname` can be replaced with the name of any host on the network that contains an SNMP agent that matches the `protocol_version` information specified on the command line. A valid IP address, expressed in dotted notation, may be used instead of a hostname.

The word `object` represents the MIB OID that should be retrieved (in the case of an SNMP `get-request`) or altered (in the case of an SNMP `set-request`). It may be expressed in either dotted numeric or dotted named notation. In the case of an SNMP `set-request` operation, additional object information will be required, as discussed in the upcoming "Snmpset Tool" section. Note that one or more objects may be specified on the command line.

Common Command-line Options

UCD tools share a number of common command-line arguments. Having a core set of options makes them easier to remember and use. The arguments supported by all the commands are divided into two categories: operational options and display options. The operational options control the behavior of each of the tools, while the display options control how the MIB objects, associated values, and other information are displayed.

Display Options

Table 8.2 lists the display arguments, which control some aspect of the output. Note that the table does not fully describe each of the eight available options. For instance, the -h option, which displays a help string of the command-line arguments, is not described because it is fairly intuitive.

Table 8.2 *Common display options*

Option	Description
-d	Dumps SNMP packets
-D	Displays debugging information
-h	Displays a help message
-f	Displays full object identifier path
-q	Makes it easier to parse for programs
-s	Displays only suffix identifiers
-S	Displays both suffix identifiers and MIB name
-V	Displays version information

Three of these options provide control over how MIB path information is formatted and displayed: -f, -s, and -S. The -f option displays the full object identifier path information. Thus, the -f option will display the object

```
system.sysContact.0
```

as shown:

```
.iso.org.dod.internet.mgmt.mib-2.system.sysContact.0
```

The -s option permits only the suffix of the OID to be printed; the last symbolic portion of the MIB object identifier will be shown. For example, the -s option will print

```
.iso.org.dod.internet.mgmt.mib-2.system.sysName.0
```

as shown:

```
sysName.0
```

Finally, the -S option requests that the MIB object be printed with both suffix and MIB name. Thus, the -S will display

```
.iso.org.dod.internet.mgmt.mib-2.system.sysUpTime.0
```

as shown:

```
SNMPv2-MIB:sysUpTime.0
```

Please note that, in this example, the sysUpTime object is found within the SNMPv2-MIB; this is true when you use the UCD tools. Traditionally, however, this object is found in the MIB-2 tree.

If you need to collect SNMP information from a device and use this information as input into another program, the -q option will come in handy. Normally, MIB object information is displayed as shown:

```
system.sysObjectID.0 = OID: enterprises.9.1.17
system.sysUpTime.0 = Timeticks: (139494644) 16 days, 3:29:06.44
system.sysContact.0 = Matthew Maxwell
system.sysName.0 = remote-gw5
system.sysLocation.0 = Remote Sales Office (San Jose))
system.sysServices.0 = 6
```

The -q option, which stands for *quick* format, causes the output above to be formatted differently. First, the equal sign (=) is removed; this makes it easier to parse because the data is now in column format. Second, notice that both the sysObjectID and sysUptime formats have been altered. The information for these two objects in the preceding example is interpreted, while, in the following example, only the raw data is displayed.

```
system.sysObjectID.0 enterprises.9.1.17
system.sysUpTime.0 16:3:24:11.44
system.sysContact.0 Matthew Maxwell
system.sysName.0 remote-gw5
system.sysLocation.0 Remote Sales Office (San Jose)
system.sysServices.0 6
```

To display debugging information, use the -d option. This shows the packet information, including the size and destination, and also provides a hexadecimal and ASCII dump of the packet. The output shown here is the result of an SNMP get-request of the system.sysContact MIB object:

```
sending 51 bytes to 10.0.2.220:161:
0000: 30 82 00 2F  02 01 00 04  06 70 75 62  6C 69 63 A0   0../.....public.
0016: 82 00 20 02  04 41 C9 4A  92 02 01 00  02 01 00 30   .. ..A.J.......0
0032: 82 00 10 30  82 00 0C 06  08 2B 06 01  02 01 01 04   ...0.....+......
0048: 00 05 00                                             ...

received 60 bytes from 10.0.2.220:161:
0000: 30 82 00 38  02 01 00 04  06 70 75 62  6C 69 63 A2   0..8.....public.
0016: 2B 02 04 41  C9 4A 92 02  01 00 02 01  00 30 1D 30   +..A.J.......0.0
0032: 1B 06 08 2B  06 01 02 01  01 04 00 04  0F 4D 61 74   ...+.........Mat
0048: 74 68 65 77  20 4D 61 78  77 65 6C 6C               thew Maxwell
system.sysContact.0 = Matthew Maxwell
```

The first part of the output is the request packet, as indicated by the string sending 51 bytes to 10.0.2.220:161 which includes the SNMP packet format. Note the visibility of the communication string public. The receiving packet is the response from the agent and it, too, uses the SNMP packet format. In this case, we see both the community string public and the sysContact object string. The second part is the response, which starts with the string received 60 bytes from 10.0.2.220:161.

Operational Options

Table 8.3 lists the eight available operational arguments but does not fully describe each of them. For instance, because the -c option's ability to define the clock values with SNMPv2 authentication messages is not a critical function for using the tools, it is not described.

Table 8.3 *Common operational options*

Option	Description
-c	Sets the clock values
-m	Specifies a list of MIB modules to load
-M	Specifies a list of directories to search for MIB files
-p	Uses the specified port to communicate with agent
-r	Specifies the number of retries
-R	Requests random access to the agent MIB table

Table 8.3 *Common operational options (continued)*

Option	Description
-t	Specifies the timeout between retry attempts
-v	Specifies the protocol version

By default, MIB objects are located in standard, well-known places within the MIB tree. Consider, for example, the system.sysContact.0 MIB object, which is normally found within the following tree:

.iso.org.dod.internet.mgmt.mib-2 tree

The UCD tools support a concept of random access MIBs. Using this approach, the system.sysContact MIB object may be entered as sysContact—without the system group name. To specify a single search of an MIB object, because it might appear more than once, specify the name of the MIB followed by the object, such as SNMPv2-MIB:sysContact.0. To enable random access, use the -R command-line option. This feature is most useful when searching for MIB objects that are not located in standard places and when more than one instance of the same object name exists within the agent.

As with any software tool that communicates with an SNMP agent, some method must be provided to convert the numeric dotted notation (such as .1.3.6.1) of the MIB object tree into the notation that uses names (such as .iso.org.dod.internet.mgmt.mib-2). Normally, without the MIB files, the UCD tools display MIB information using the numeric form. This is because these tools obtain only the numeric form from the agent; they don't know how to map these identifiers into the corresponding string names. For example, when an SNMP get-request is done against an agent with the MIB files not available, the following output snippet may be displayed:

```
.iso.3.6.1.2.1.1.1.0 = "Cisco Internetwork Operating Sys-
    tem Software ..IOS (tm) 4500 Software (C4500-J-M), Ver-
    sion 11.1(5), RELEASE SOFTWARE (fc1)..Copyright (c)
    1986-1996 by cisco Systems, Inc...Compiled Mon 05-Aug-96
    13:17 by mkamson"
.iso.3.6.1.2.1.1.2.0 = OID: .iso.3.6.1.4.1.9.1.50
.iso.3.6.1.2.1.1.3.0 = Timeticks: (99491814) 11 days,
```

```
  12:21:58.14
.iso.3.6.1.2.1.1.4.0 = "Neferelle Maxwell"
.iso.3.6.1.2.1.1.5.0 = "remote-gw"
.iso.3.6.1.2.1.1.6.0 = "Remote Sales Office (Florida)"
.iso.3.6.1.2.1.1.7.0 = 78
```

This output is from a query of a Cisco router, and, as you can see, the MIB object path information contains numeric strings only after the iso name. The iso string was included in the output because the UCD tools know only the starting point of the MIB tree. When it comes to nonstandard or vendor-specific MIBs, only the numeric form is available. To address this issue, the -m and -M options are provided. The -m option specifies a list of MIB modules that should be loaded before the UCD tool attempts any SNMP queries on an agent. When more than one MIB module is listed, the modules must be separated by a colon (:). An MIB module is just a file that contains the MIB definitions for an agent. Using the -m option, we can supply the correct MIB modules so that our snippet output above will contain all string names. The -M option helps because we can supply a list of directories in which to search for MIB files. Thus the command

```
# snmpwalk -M /var/mibs cisco-gw1 public system                    -
```

will search the directory /var/mibs. Assuming that it finds the standard MIB files, it will display the following:

```
system.sysDescr.0 = Cisco Internetwork Operating System Software
IOS (tm) 4500 Software (C4500-J-M), Version 11.1(5), RELEASE SOFTWARE
(fc1)
Copyright (c) 1986-1996 by cisco Systems, Inc.
Compiled Mon 05-Aug-96 13:17 by mkamson
system.sysObjectID.0 = OID: enterprises.9.1.50
system.sysUpTime.0 = Timeticks: (99487614) 11 days, 12:21:16.14
system.sysContact.0 = Neferelle Maxwell
system.sysName.0 = remote-gw
system.sysLocation.0 = Remote Sales Office (Florida)
system.sysServices.0 = 78
```

There is also a shorthand way to specify all MIB modules (as opposed to supplying a list)—by using the **all** command. This overrides the MIBS environment variable, which is discussed in the next section.

Environment Variables

Each of the UCD tools uses a small set of environment variables that helps establish global values for certain operating parameters and shortcuts for command-line options. These include the following:

- PREFIX
- MIBS
- MIBDIR
- SUFFIX

The PREFIX variable provides a standard way to define the prefix of MIB object identifiers. The default value is

.iso.org.dod.internet.mgmt.mib-2

If this variable is defined, the contents of the variable are added to the beginning of the MIB object being referenced when using one of the UCD tools. Defining this value will help in situations in which a nonstandard MIB is used.

The MIBS and MIBDIR variables provide a way to load in additional MIB modules. The variable MIBS functions the same way as the -m command-line option. The MIBDIR variable functions the same way as the -M option. Both are convenient because they work with all UCD applications.

The SUFFIX variable toggles the -s command-line option, which displays the suffix, or last component, of the MIB object path.

Snmpdelta Tool

The **snmpdelta** command collects changes in MIB integer values from an SNMP agent entity. This command monitors the specified integer objects and displays changes to the objects that occur over time. This is very useful in tracking networking errors. It might be necessary, for example, to determine the number of packets discarded from an interface; as with the ifInDiscards MIB-II object. To monitor this object from the device called remote-gw, the following command may be used:

```
# snmpdelta -R remote-gw public ifInDiscards.1
```

When invoked, this command will produce the following:

```
ifInDiscards.1 /1 sec: 0
ifInDiscards.1 /1 sec: 0
ifInDiscards.1 /1 sec: 0
ifInDiscards.1 /1 sec: 0
ifInDiscards.1 /1 sec: 0
ifInDiscards.1 /1 sec: 0
ifInDiscards.1 /1 sec: 0
ifInDiscards.1 /1 sec: 0
ifInDiscards.1 /1 sec: 0
```

Without user interaction, the above command continually polls the agent until a **control+c** (**^c**) is issued by the user. Note that in the command we have used, the -R option activates random access to the agent MIB. This makes it easy to obtain the desired MIB objects. A high discard rate may indicate trouble with the interface. This trouble could be caused by a hardware problem related to cabling or even a software configuration error. In the example above, the discard rate didn't change and is why the values are all zero. This command supports a number of additional command-line arguments over the common options previously discussed. Table 8.4 lists the available options.

Table 8.4 *Additional* snmpdelta *command-line options*

Option	Description
-f	Reads a configuration file
-k	Displays time information in output
-l	Writes the configuration to a file
-m	Displays the maximum value ever retrieved
-p	Specifies the polling period
-P	Specifies the reporting period as a number of polling requests
-s	Displays timestamp information
-S	Logs data to a log file
-t	Determines time interval
-T	Produces table output

With the -m option, **snmpdelta** will display the maximum value obtained from the MIB objects that are being polled. It displays the values of each poll and, when a new high value is received, includes it in the Max column. The command

```
# snmpdelta -R remote-gw public -m ifOutOctets.2
```

produces the following output:

```
ifOutOctets.2 /1 sec: 25784      (Max: 25784)
ifOutOctets.2 /1 sec: 21287      (Max: 25784)
ifOutOctets.2 /1 sec: 2743       (Max: 25784)
ifOutOctets.2 /1 sec: 8611       (Max: 25784)
ifOutOctets.2 /1 sec: 4473       (Max: 25784)
ifOutOctets.2 /1 sec: 10939      (Max: 25784)
ifOutOctets.2 /1 sec: 1882       (Max: 25784)
ifOutOctets.2 /1 sec: 9258       (Max: 25784)
ifOutOctets.2 /1 sec: 22751      (Max: 25784)
ifOutOctets.2 /1 sec: 28615      (Max: 28615)
ifOutOctets.2 /1 sec: 18599      (Max: 28615)
ifOutOctets.2 /1 sec: 28459      (Max: 28615)
ifOutOctets.2 /1 sec: 2662       (Max: 28615)
```

Notice that, when the new maximum value is obtained, it is updated in the Max column accordingly.

When monitoring a large number of MIB objects or data, you might find it helpful to save the information in a log file. The -1 option saves the data in a file in the following format:

```
{device}-{MIB object}
```

Thus, the command

```
# snmpdelta -R monet public -l ifOutOctets.12
```

will log ifOutOctets deltas in the file called monet-ifOut-Octets.2.

Inspection of this file will reveal the same format and data that are normally displayed.

If you need to display the output of **snmpdelta** in a more structured format, use the -T option. For instance, if it becomes necessary to monitor several MIB objects and add the data to a spreadsheet or other program, **snmpdelta** can display output in a tabular format:

```
snmpdelta -R remote-gw public -T ifInDiscards.1 ifInDiscards.2:
```

```
ifInDiscards.1  ifInDiscards.2
1592.00 9950.00
9136.00 2506.00
3338.00 5.00
6338.00 2624.00
8665.00 9971.00
5609.00 569.00
9282.00 7086.00
9153.00 8374.00
8653.00 8195.00
9877.00 3827.00
```

The output is a display of the number of discarded packets from two interfaces, presented in a columnar format.

Snmpget Tool

The **snmpget** command retrieves information from an SNMP agent entity. It uses the SNMP get-request with one or more MIB object names as arguments and returns their associated values. If an error occurs, a descriptive message will be shown to help pinpoint the problem. If a list of objects is specified on the command line, only those objects that are contained within the agent's MIB will be returned.

The command syntax is as follows:

```
snmpget [common arguments] MIB-object [MIB-object]
```

To retrieve the MIB objects sysDescr and sysContact from a Cisco router, the following command could be used:

```
# snmpget remote-gw public system.sysDescr.0 system.sysUpTime.0
```

Depending on the router model and configuration, this command would display output like the following:

```
system.sysDescr.0 = Cisco Internetwork Operating System Software
IOS (tm) 3000 Software (IGS-INR-L), Version 11.0(17), RELEASE
SOFTWARE (fc1) Copyright (c) 1986-1997 by cisco Systems, Inc.
Compiled Thu 04-Sep-97 14:17 by richv
system.sysUpTime.0 = Timeticks: (134381144) 15 days, 13:16:51.44
```

Notice that the Cisco router contains a rather long sysDescr string. This can be very useful when attempting to identify the model and current version of the internetwork operating system

(IOS) running on the system. The IOS is the Cisco system software that provides all the routing and processing functions for a large array of Cisco hardware devices. In this example, the system model is a 3000 series router running version 11.0 that has been up for the last 15 days.

Please note that sometimes when accessing objects from certain devices, we may encounter error messages that lead us to believe that the device in question does not support the objects specified with the SNMP command. For example, consider the following command that is executed against a Linux system called monet:

```
# snmpget monet private-write system.sysDescr.0
```

The command produces the following:

```
system.sysDescr.0 = "Linux monet 2.2.5-15 #5 Mon Aug 2
21:07:04 EDT 1999 i586
```

However, running the same command against the same system but using a different community string, as shown:

```
# snmpget monet bad-password system.sysDescr.0
```

displays the following message:

```
Error in packet
Reason: (noSuchName) There is no such variable name in this MIB.
This name doesn't exist: system.sysDescr.0
```

In the preceding example, the error message isn't clear about what is going on; the message suggests that the object being requested does not exist within the agent. Obviously, from the first example, the object (system.sysDescr.0) does exist and has an associated value. The reason for the disparity lies in the fact that the Linux agent supports different views of the MIB tree. In the last command, it simply attempted to search for the system.sys-Descr.0 object within the view that was associated with the bad-password community string. MIB views were introduced with SNMPv2, and the Linux agent supports these protocols. In actuality, since the bad-password command string is invalid, the agent issued the most appropriate response for the situation.

Further, when devices, such as SNMPv1 devices, that don't support MIB views are queried, and the same command is executed on a device called `dips`, we get the following:

```
Timeout: No Response from dips
```

This error message is displayed for the following reason: When the community string doesn't match the password configured within it, an SNMPv1 agent disregards the request. If authentication traps are enabled, it then sends the associated trap. The important thing to remember is that when polling for specific objects, don't assume that objects are not available despite the generation of error messages suggesting that they are unavailable. It might be helpful to execute an **snmpwalk** against the agent if questions come up regarding which objects are indeed supported by the agent.

Snmpgetnext Tool

The **snmpgetnext** command retrieves one or more MIB objects using SNMP `getnext-request`. For each object specified on the command line, **snmpgetnext** gets the next lexicographical MIB object found in the MIB tree. This tool is very useful for returning a series of objects when the exact structure of the MIB object that is being retrieved is unknown. Also, it permits the discovery of the structure of a MIB view dynamically. For example, the command:

```
# snmpgetnext probe public system.sysContact.0
```

will obtain the next MIB object after the `sysContact.0` object:

```
system.sysName.0 = "AXON" Hex: 41 58 4F 4E
```

The `sysName.0` object is displayed because it is *lexicographically next* to the `sysContract.0` object. How do we know this for sure? Well, the simplest approach is to display the entire `system` group. An **snmpwalk** of the group displays the following:

```
system.sysDescr.0 = "AXON LANServant - Ethernet (4.16)"
system.sysObjectID.0 = OID: enterprises.370.2.2
system.sysUpTime.0 = Timeticks: (868306) 2:24:43.06
system.sysContact.0 = "3Com Corporation"
system.sysName.0 = "AXON" Hex: 41 58 4F 4E
system.sysLocation.0 = ""
system.sysServices.0 = 15
```

The primary purpose of the **snmpwalk** command is to retrieve an agent table in a more effective manner. Consider the udp table, which contains information related to any open sockets using the User Datagram Protocol. Polling this table is polled on a Linux system, displays the partial output shown in Listing 8.1.

Listing 8.1 *UDP sample table*

```
 1  udp.udpInDatagrams.0 = 860
 2  udp.udpNoPorts.0 = 5
 3  udp.udpInErrors.0 = 0
 4  udp.udpOutDatagrams.0 = 911
 5  udp.udpTable.udpEntry.udpLocalAddress.0.0.0.0.111 =
      IpAddress: 0.0.0.0
 6  udp.udpTable.udpEntry.udpLocalAddress.0.0.0.0.161 =
      IpAddress: 0.0.0.0
 7  udp.udpTable.udpEntry.udpLocalAddress.0.0.0.0.162 =
      IpAddress: 0.0.0.0
 8  udp.udpTable.udpEntry.udpLocalAddress.0.0.0.0.177 =
      IpAddress: 0.0.0.0
 9  udp.udpTable.udpEntry.udpLocalAddress.0.0.0.0.517 =
      IpAddress: 0.0.0.0
10  udp.udpTable.udpEntry.udpLocalAddress.0.0.0.0.518 =
      IpAddress: 0.0.0.0
11  udp.udpTable.udpEntry.udpLocalAddress.0.0.0.0.624 =
      IpAddress: 0.0.0.0
12  udp.udpTable.udpEntry.udpLocalAddress.0.0.0.0.635 =
      IpAddress: 0.0.0.0
13  udp.udpTable.udpEntry.udpLocalPort.0.0.0.0.111 = 111
14  udp.udpTable.udpEntry.udpLocalPort.0.0.0.0.161 = 161
15  udp.udpTable.udpEntry.udpLocalPort.0.0.0.0.162 = 162
16  udp.udpTable.udpEntry.udpLocalPort.0.0.0.0.177 = 177
17  udp.udpTable.udpEntry.udpLocalPort.0.0.0.0.517 = 517
18  udp.udpTable.udpEntry.udpLocalPort.0.0.0.0.518 = 518
19  udp.udpTable.udpEntry.udpLocalPort.0.0.0.0.624 = 624
20  udp.udpTable.udpEntry.udpLocalPort.0.0.0.0.635 = 635
```

Listing 8.1 includes table objects that contain related information, but don't have an associated index to retrieve each object when needed. As you can see, the objects are referenced by the IP address (0.0.0.0) being used, as shown on line 5. This entry contains the local IP and port address for this socket. The IP is used as an index into the object listed in line 13, which contains the UDP

port information. The ability to retrieve MIB objects based on lexicographical order is the only way to discover each object in order.

Snmpnetstat Tool

The **snmpnetstat** command is similar to the UNIX netstat utility
and provides some of the same basic information about attached
device interfaces and routing. What is remarkable about this tool is
that it provides an easy way to obtain interface information from
any SNMP device. This includes, for example, devices such as routers, switches, network monitoring probes, and other devices that
support the MIB-II standard. This is a very powerful tool because
interface information can be collected without the use of complicated command sequences. Also, it removes the barrier requiring
the use of vendor-specific interfaces when a network consists of a
large number of different vendor products.

Like its UNIX counterpart, **snmpnetstat** supports a number of
command-line options that control basic operations and output.
Table 8.5 lists the available command options. As you can see,
many of these options are consistent with those of the **netstat** command.

Table 8.5 *The* snmpnetstat *command-line options*

Option	Description
-a	Shows the state of all socket connections
-i	Shows the state of all interfaces defined on the system
-I	Displays information on the specified network interface
-o	Displays an abbreviated status of interfaces
-n	Displays network addresses as numbers
-p	Shows statistics sorted by the network protocol
-r	Displays routing table information
-s	Shows per-protocol network statistics

Displaying Interface Information

To show the configuration of all network interfaces, use the -I option. In the example below, the **snmpnetstat** command queries a local Cisco router called `cisco-gw3`:

```
# snmpnetstat -i cisco-gw3 public
Name    Mtu   Network     Address       Ipkts Ierrs OpktsOerrs Queue
Ethern  1500  10.0.2      10.0.2.1      13377 315   132503501  15
Serial  1500  135.111.81  135.111.81.2  431375 127  462082816  50
Serial* 1500  none        none          1934  15446557336 998  150
```

The output should be familiar; it mirrors the UNIX `netstat` output. The only major differences are the names of the interfaces and the removal of the column that represents the total number of collisions on the interface. In general, the Cisco internal software uses the same type of interface and index number as the full interface name (such as `serial1`). However, in the example, the names are truncated (due to the column size) and derived from the interface type, not the actual Cisco interface name, when obtained from SNMP. Thus, when displayed with the **snmpnetstat** command, the entire interface name is not displayed nor are the index numbers shown.

To list the available interfaces in an abbreviated form, use the -s option. As you can see from the output below, only the columns of incoming and outgoing octets (bytes) are listed. Compare this to what is displayed with the -i option in the previous example.

```
# snmpnetstat -o cisco-gw4 public
Name    Network     Address       Ioctets   Ooctets
Ethern  10.0.2      10.0.2.1      487708    12778317
Serial  135.111.81  135.111.81.2  4331197   559999
```

The `cisco-gw4` device contains only two interfaces: one `Ethernet` and one `Serial`. Typically, Cisco routers and switches (and other vendor devices, too) may contain a large number of interfaces. For example, executing the above **snmpnetstat** command on a Cisco 7000 router will yield the following:

```
Name    Network Address    Ioctets    Ooctets
Fddi0/  10.10.1 10.10.1.1  3723440280 1783534532
Fddi1/  10.11.2 10.11.2.1  2560994642 2783361340
Ethern  10.0.2  10.0.2.254 2141819815 1555401237
```

```
Ethern* none    none                        0              0
Ethern* none    none                        0              0
Ethern* none    none                        0              0
Ethern* none    none                        0            ` 0
Ethern* none    none                        0              0
Fddi3/  10.14.1 10.14.1.1   2248945512 2083011069
Serial  10.250.10 10.250.10.11401691701 870256641
Serial* none    none        592331671  3226921185
Serial*none     none                        0              0
Serial* none    none                        0              0
FastEt  19.80.8 19.82.8.1   4086327200 421590301
FastEt  19.80.9 19.82.9.1   4017448469 3080615899
FastEt  19.80.10 19.82.10.1 269162560  1781784403
FastEt*none     none                        0              0
```

The actual number of interfaces will depend on the model of the
router and installed interface cards. In this example, 17 interfaces
have been listed. In the output, four different interface types have
been listed: Serial, Ethernet, FastEthernet, and FDDI. This output
was polled from a core backbone router, which explains the high
utilization on many of the interfaces.

To list an individual interface, use the -I option followed by the
interface name. This option is also used in conjunction with the
interval option. When **snmpnetstat** is invoked with the interval
argument, it shows a running count of network statistics relating
to the interface specified. The information displayed includes one
column for the specified interface and another column summariz-
ing information for all other interfaces. The first line of output presents a summary of information since the device was last rebooted.
All additional lines represent values that are changing over the
specified interval. The command

```
# snmpnetstat -I Ethernet cisco-gw4 public 10
```

will show the following:

```
input   (Ether)   output input  (Total)     output
packets errs  packets errs colls  packets errs  packets errs colls
68355   39800 131733   198   0499131392.46489457300
  178      62    93      68   0    376  255     236    220
   46      58   142      84   0    172  167     268    420
   93      63    67      60   0    210  134     359    140
  119      49   169      85   0    326  187     385     18    0
```

This display includes a running count of packet activity on the ethernet interface contained in the **cisco-gw3**. The command will continue displaying this output until a **control+c** (^c) is typed. The first two columns represent the number of input packets and input errors, while the next two represent the number of output packets and output errors. The fifth column provides the number of collisions. The remaining five columns are cumulative totals for all interfaces defined within the device.

Display Routing Information

To display the routing information from the same device, use the -r option, as in the following example:

```
# snmpnetstat -r cisco-gw3 public
```

The -r option will display the following:

```
Routing tables
Destination          Gateway      Flags    Interface
default              161.135.59.1 UG       if0
155.161.75/25        161.135.59.9 U        Serial0
155.161.114.128/26 rembrandt     U        Ethernet0
161.135              161.135.59.1 UG       if0
161.135.59/26        161.135.59.9 U        Serial0
161.135.59.64/26     161.135.59.8UG        if0
161.135.59.128/26  rembrandt     U         Ethernet0
170.5                161.135.59.1UG        if0
```

The statistics for each network protocol are supported with this command. Thus, the -s (shows statistics for each protocol) and -P (shows statistics sorted by each protocol) options can be used to show detailed protocol performance data. To see just the statistics for each protocol, use the following command:

```
# snmpnetstat -s monet public
```

This command will produce the following sample output:

```
udp:
 8606737 total datagrams received
 7727372 datagrams to invalid port
 1 datagram dropped due to errors
 851929 output datagram requests
tcp:
 0 active opens
```

```
8 passive opens
0 failed attempts
1 reset of established connections
0 current established connections
645 segments received
476 segments sent
0 segments retransmitted
icmp:
9741 total messages received
0 messages dropped due to errors
10042 ouput message requests
0 output messages discarded
Output Histogram:
Destination unreachable: 310
Echo Reply: 9732
Input Histogram:
Destination unreachable: 9
Echo Request: 9732
ip:
22222667 total datagrams received
0 datagrams with header errors
0 datagrams with an invalid destination address
0 datagrams forwarded
0 datagrams with unknown protocol
0 datagrams discarded
22222673 datagrams delivered
0 output datagram requests
0 output datagrams discarded
0 datagrams with no route
0 fragments received
0 datagrams reassembled
0 reassembly failures
0 datagrams fragmented
0 fragmentation failures
0 fragments created
```

This output provides a quick snapshot of the network performance and the activity of each of the networking protocols. Many of the counters appear to represent normal network usage. However, one metric value, `7727372 datagrams to invalid port`, may represent a significant problem. For some unknown reason, data is arriving into this system, from possibly several other systems, to one or more UDP ports that are invalid. One possible cause for this situation is that an application that should receive data from another source is not running, but the other end hasn't detected it yet. Another reason might be that a remote application is attempting to send information to this system but is misconfigured and attempting to send information to a nonexisting port.

One positive way to track down the cause of this problem is to capture traffic on the same network as this system and attempt to learn which remote device is sending the data. Once you get the identity of the remote system, investigating which application is causing this problem is simply a matter of notifying the owner of the system. It is easy to see why using the **snmpnetstat** command is a good way to determine potential network problems before they get out-of-hand.

Snmpset Tool

The **snmpset** command is one of the most useful and powerful commands within the UCD package. Many of the tools in this chapter focus on obtaining object values from an SNMP agent. However, this tool is used to alter modifiable MIB agent objects. The ability to alter an MIB object is profound in it implications because doing so changes the configuration or operating state of a managed agent.

This tool represents a power mechanism for controlling agents on a global scale. The ability to change the configuration of a large number of devices provides an important facility that every network manager or system administrator must have. Having the power to control many devices can represent a liability as well. Consider, for example, a router with several interfaces that serve as remote connection points between important distant office networks. A single **snmpset** command (with the appropriate security password) executed against one or more interfaces on this router could disable network connectivity between the local network and the remote office(s). Obviously, this could have disastrous consequence for business, to say nothing of your reputation.

Another liability is related to making a global change to a series of systems when the new configuration is incorrect or causes some service outage due to the nature of the change. Because the **snmpset** command is powerful, exercise caution when using this command on an active network. It can never be said too often that the first rule of thumb in networking is to review the proposed changes in a test environment first. That way, when the changes are deployed on the real network, failures and other nasty surprises are kept to a minimum.

The basic syntax of the **snmpset** command is as follows:

```
snmpset [common arguments] MIB-objectID type value [MIB-objectID type value]
```

The `MIB-objectID` is the MIB object that will be given a new value. The `type` argument represents the type of object that should be altered, and the `value` represents the new object value. The `type` is a single character that represents one of the object types listed in Table 8.6. Chapter 2, "Simple Network Management Protocol," discusses these object types.

Someone may ask, "What specific tasks can the **snmpset** command help with?" Listed below are some possible suggestions:

- disabling or enabling a network interface

- updating a device with new administration information (`sysContact`, for example)

- resetting certain network traffic counters

- restarting a device or agent

- modifying some configuration parameter

Table 8.6 `snmpset` *object types*

Character	Object Type
i	INTEGER
s	STRING
x	HEXADECIMAL STRING
d	DECIMAL STRING
n	NULL OBJECT
o	OBJECTID
t	TIMETICKS
a	IPADDRESS

You may recall an earlier scenario in which a disabled interface caused a network problem. There are also situations when not disabling an interface can cause additional network problems. For example, during a broadcast storm or when a cracker is attempting to penetrate the network, shutting down a network or interface might be the only way to prevent the problem from spreading to other parts of the network. However, before resorting to turning off interfaces, watch out for the *set of no return* syndrome. Consider the sample network shown in Figure 8.1.

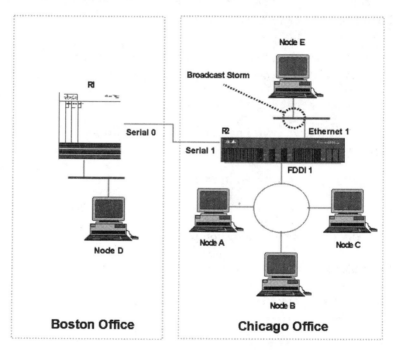

Figure 8.1 *Example of "set of no return."*

In this sample network, we have two routers, R1 and R2. Our only access to R2 is via router R1, using the serial1 interface. From device Node A, we issue an **snmpset** command to disable the serial0 interface from R2. This stops the broadcast storm but also causes a connectivity loss from the remote office. The problem is now: How do we enable the interface on R2 after the broadcast storm has been fixed? The *set of no return* means that the only means of access to the device has been cut off. Remote access to the router has been lost, unless some out-of-band management capability, such as dial-u, can be used. In this case, the port must be enabled from the local side, which could require instructing someone to enable the port or reboot the device to reset the port.

The best way to avoid the *set of no return* is to disable the local `serial1` interface on R1 or the remote `ethernet1` interface on R2. This way, the broadcast problem is contained, yet we still maintain access to the devices.

To disable a `serial0` interface on router R1, a modification of the `ifOperStatus` object must be made. This includes setting the object to zero (0) to disable the interface from an administrative perspective. Set this object using the following command:

```
# snmpset monet private interfaces.ifTable.ifEntry.ifAdminStatus.2 i 0\
interfaces.ifTable.ifEntry.ifAdminStatus.3 = 0
```

When executed, the command will disable the flow of traffic to and from this interface. With most agents, this object change is not permanent, meaning that a system reboot will reset this object back to the default (enabled) value. However, without a system reset, the only other way to restore network connectivity will be to enable the interface using the **snmpset** command.

The **snmpset** command can alter other MIB objects within the agent. For example, consider the `sysContact` and `sysLocation` objects. Let's assign new values to these objects using a single **snmpset** command:

```
# snmpset cisco-gw10 private system.sysContact.0 s "NCC Support"\
system.sysLocation.0 s "3rd Floor Closet"
```

When the command has been executed, it returns the following:

```
system.sysContact.0 = "NCC Support"
system.sysLocation.0 = "3rd Floor Closet"
```

Snmpstatus Tool

The **snmpstatus** command obtains important information from an SNMP network entity using the SNMP `get-request` operation. The syntax of the command is as follows:

```
snmpstatus host community
```

When the remote agent utilizes the generic community string of
`public`, the string may be dropped from the SNMP commands
because `public` is used by default. By the way, the use of the `public`
community string is highly discouraged.

When the **snmpstatus** command is used against a device, it displays the following information:

- IP Address of the device

- `sysDescr` MIB object

- `sysUpTime` MIB object

- number of packets received and transmitted on all active
  interfaces (i.e., the sum of `ifInUCastPkts.*` and
  `ifInNUCastPkts.*` objects)

- number of IP packets received and transmitted (i.e.,
  `ipInReceives.0` and `ipOutRequests.0`)

- number of active interfaces

- number of interfaces that have been disabled

  Thus, running the command

```
# snmpstatus switch-2200 private
```

on a device called switch-2200 displays the output shown in
Figure 8.2.

Using this command is a good way to obtain a quick snapshot
of a network device without knowing a lot about the node or some
of the specific MIB objects to poll. As you can see, the device is
`Linkswitch 2200` (made by 3Com), running version `7.1` of the
switching software. The device has been running for `90` hours and
`23` minutes. Notice that **snmpstatus** has detected eight interfaces
that are down. This isn't a problem in this case because the device
is an Ethernet switch where interfaces are attached to personal
computers or workstations.

Some users reboot their systems more often and power down
their systems when they leave the office each evening. This causes
the switch ports to be marked as down, and explains why they
show up in the **snmpstatus** output.

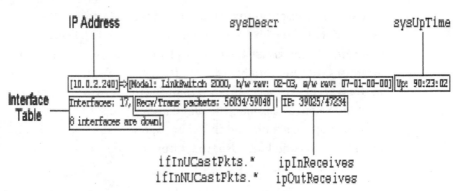

Figure 8.2 *Output of the* snmpstatus *command.*

This tool can do a quick inventory of a network by using the shell. For instance, consider the following command:

```
# foreach node (10.0.2.1 10.0.2.202 10.0.2.254 10.0.2.50)\
foreach? snmpstatus $node public; echo
"************************"
foreach? end
```

This command generates the following output:

```
[10.0.2.1]=>[Cisco Internetwork Operating System Software
IOS (tm) GS Software (RSP-JV-M), Version 11.1(16)CA, EARLY
  DEPLOYMENT RELEASE SO
FTWARE (fc1)
Synced to mainline version: 11.1(16)
Copyright (c) 1986-1997 by cisco Systems, Inc.
Compiled Sat 20-Dec-97 04:21 by] Up: 168 days, 3:23:39
Interfaces: 23, Recv/Trans packets: -1270803594/-666101155 | IP: -
  1516575442/102
937871
9 interfaces are down!
************************
[10.0.2.202]=>[Cisco Systems WS-C5000] Up: 167 days, 15:31:32
Interfaces: 100, Recv/Trans packets: 258062534/866645 | IP:
  22222133/0
32 interfaces are down!
************************
[10.0.2.254]->[Fibre Channel Switch.] Up: 1 day, 8:35:11
Interfaces: 2, Recv/Trans packets: 43996343/16638 | IP:
  20002011/7886
************************
[10.0.2.50]=>[AXON LANServant - Ethernet (4.16)] Up: 9:45:21
Interfaces: 3, Recv/Trans packets: 4027/1135 | IP: 0/0
```

Using the **foreach** built-in command of the `csh`, a list of IP addresses is assigned between the parentheses. When **foreach** is executed, it calls the **snmpstatus** command and replaces each of the IP addresses with the variable `node`. In the output above, it is obvious that it is very easy to use this tool to probe the network. In practice, it would be more reasonable to build a shell script to inventory these devices on a more continued basis, rather than interactively from the command line. Also, the output could be placed in a text file for later review.

Snmptable Tool

The **snmptable** command probes an agent and displays an MIB table using the SNMP `getnext-request` operation. The syntax of the command is as follows:

```
snmptable [common options ] [additional options] host community tableID
```

The minimum required arguments include `host`, `community`, and `tableID`. The `tableID` must be a real SNMP table, such as `interfaces.ifTable`. The `ifTable` table contains a series of MIB objects that contain performance information and other characteristics of the interfaces within a device. Within MIB-II, which is described in Chapter 6, "Overview of MIB-II," the following tables are defined and can be displayed with this command:

- interface table (`interfaces.ifTable`)

- IP address table (`ip.ipAddrTable`)

- IP routing table (`ip.ipRouteTable`)

- IP net media table (`ip.ipNetToMediaTable`)

- TCP connection table (`tcp.tcpConnTable`)

- UDP listener table (`udp.udpTable`)

Note that Chapter 6 describes the MIB-II tree. The basic purpose of this command is to give the user the ability to display SNMP tables and import the data into other programs for additional reporting and manipulation. For example, to display the TCP connection table, `tcpConnTable`, use the following command:

```
# snmptable 10.0.2.240 public tcp.tcpConnTable
SNMP table: tcp.tcpConnTable
tcpConnState tcpConnLocalAddress tcpConnLocalPort tcpConnRemAddress
tcpConnRemPort
listen      0.0.0.0     23          0.0.0.0            0
listen      0.0.0.0     111         0.0.0.0            0
listen      0.0.0.0     513         0.0.0.0            0
established 10.0.2.240  23          10.0.2.75          33441
```

If a non-table object is supplied, an error will be generated. Thus, the command

```
# snmptable 10.0.2.240 public system.sysContact.0
```

will return

```
Was that a table? system.sysContact.0.1.1
```

Here we provide the MIB object, `system.sysContact.0` (which is definitely not an MIB table), with the `snmptable` command. As you can see, an appropriate error is displayed that includes what should be the first element within the table (i.e. `.1.1`).

The **snmptable** command supports a few additional command-line arguments that can control the formatting of the output. Table 8.7 lists these additional options.

Table 8.7 *Additional* `snmptable` *command-line options*

Option	Description
-b	Displays a brief heading
-f	Specifies a character separator
-h	Prevents display of heading information
-H	Displays only table heading information
-w	Specifies the width of the table being displayed
-x	Adds the MIB index to the beginning of each entry listed

One of the most useful options is -f, which is used to specify an alternative column separator character. Thus, to use the colon (:) as the field separator when displaying the same TCP table above, use the following command sequence(shown with output):

```
# snmptable 10.0.2.240 public -f : tcp.tcpConnTable
SNMP table: tcp.tcpConnTable
tcpConnState:tcpConnLocalAddress:tcpConnLocalPort:tcpConnRe
mAddress:tcpConnRemPort
listen:0.0.0.0:23:0.0.0.0:0
listen:0.0.0.0:111:0.0.0.0:0
listen:0.0.0.0:513:0.0.0.0:0
established:10.0.2.240:23:10.0.2.75:33441
```

Each of the columns is now separated by the : character, making it very easy to parse this information as input into other programs. The -b option can be used to provide a more descriptive column label, as shown here. The at.atTable table contains the address translation mappings between IP addresses and physical addresses. In this case, three column labels are displayed: IfIndex, PhysAddress, and NetAddress. The ifIndex is the index in the interface table and shows from which interfaces these mappings originated. The PhysAddress is the datalink address (Ethernet in this case), and the NetAddress is the IP address associated with each device on the network. The command:

```
# snmptable cisco-gw5 public -b at.atTable
```

probes the MIB-II address translation group and provides the following sample output:

```
SNMP table: at.atTable
 IfIndex           PhysAddress           NetAddress
       2 "08 00 20 8D 81 82 "          10.0.1.100
       2 "00 60 47 1F 76 8A "          10.0.1.120
      14 "00 60 08 91 4A 64 "          10.0.2.110
      14 "00 60 95 AD F2 1F "          10.0.2.111
      14 "00 80 5F E2 8B 3D "          10.0.2.117
      14 "00 60 08 94 37 FC "          10.0.2.200
      14 "08 00 20 86 2F C2 "          10.0.2.221
      14 "00 60 08 62 C7 3E "          10.0.2.226
      14 "08 00 20 7A CA 49 "          10.0.2.234
      14 "08 00 20 25 70 E7 "          10.0.2.250
      14 "00 20 AF CA E6 99 "          10.0.2.251
      14 "00 60 08 1D FD 4D "          10.0.2.252
      14 "00 80 A3 03 4E 9B "          10.0.2.257
```

Snmptest Tool

The **snmptest** command provides a simple shell-like facility that makes it easy to communicate with a network entity using SNMP. Unlike most other SNMP tools, **snmptest** is interactive, prompting for information to accomplish one or more tasks.

The software supports three operating modes: snmp-get, snmp-getnext, and snmp-set. Issuing the **$N** command will place **snmptest** in snmp-getnext mode, while using the **$S** puts the command in snmp-set mode. To get back to snmp-get mode, use the **$G** command. By default, **snmptest** is placed in snmp-get mode, in which the user is prompted for an MIB object to retrieve from an SNMP device.

For example, the follow command sequence will obtain the sysUpTime object from a system called monet:

```
# snmptest monet stevewrite
Variable: system.sysUpTime.0
Variable:
Received Get Response from monet
requestid 0x4362F60A errstat 0x0 errindex 0x0
system.sysUpTime.0 = Timeticks: (379613) 1:03:16.13
Variable: ^c
```

Clearly, this is a rudimentary interface for issuing basic SNMP operations to network agents. It is somewhat useful if a large number of tasks must be performed against the same network target. Note that, to exit the program, you simply use the **^c** command sequence.

Snmptranslate Tool

The **snmptranslate** tool translates SNMP MIB objects into a more user-friendly and readable format. When this command is run with an MIB object, it will translate the object into either the SMI value or symbolic form. When no options are specified, it defaults to displaying the SMI value. Table 8.8 lists the command-line options supported with this tool. The primary use of the command is to help display the full characteristics of MIB objects, without resorting to reading the appropriate MIB definition files.

Table 8.8 snmptranslate *command-line options*

Option	Description
-d	Displays a description of the object
-p	Displays the symbol table from the loaded MIB files
-n	Displays objects in symbolic format
-s	Displays only the last symbolic part of the OID
-R	Uses random access when accessing the objects
-w	Displays warnings when symbol conflicts occur
-W	Displays more verbose warnings than -w displays

By default, **snmptranslate** displays the numeric dotted object notation. Thus, translation of the system.sysDescr MIB object can be accomplished with the command:

```
# snmptranslate system.sysDescr
```

which results in the following:

```
.1.3.6.1.2.1.1.1
```

To display a fairly complete description of an MIB object, use the -d option. For example, consider the following command:

```
# snmptranslate -d system.sysDescr
```

When executed, the command will produce the following:

```
.1.3.6.1.2.1.1.1
SYNTAX  OCTET STRING
DISPLAY-HINT    "255a"
MAX-ACCESS      read-only
STATUS  current
DESCRIPTION     "A textual description of the entity.
This value should include the full name and version
identification of the system's hardware type, software
operating-system, and networking software."
```

As shown, a complete reference of the MIB object can be obtained. This information is taken from the MIB definition files that the agent references. In this case, the file RFC1213-MIB.txt, which is located in the /usr/local/share/mibs directory, was used.

Snmptrap Tool

The **snmptrap** command will emit an SNMP trap to one or more designated SNMP managers. This tool is very useful when embedded in a shell script or other program for sending traps. One or more object identifiers can be specified on the command line, plus the type and value must accompany each object. The **snmptrap** supports both SNMPv1 and SNMPv2 formats. The basic syntax of the command is as follows:

```
snmptrap -v 1 [command arguments] enterprise-oid agent generic-
trap\ specific-trap uptime [object ID type value]
```

The enterprise-oid field identifies the network management subsystem that generated the trap. The agent is the host that emits the trap. The generic-trap corresponds to one of the predefined SNMP traps listed in Chapter 2, "Simple Network Management Protocol." The specific-trap value indicates more specifically the nature of the trap. The uptime field is used as a timestamp between the last initialization of the device and the issuance of the trap. The object ID, type, and value provide additional information relating to the trap. These additional fields are known as the variable binding and may contain any type of information that is related to the trap.

The enterprise-oid, agent, and uptime fields need not be specified on the command line. Instead, the empty character sequence ' ' may be used to specify the default values for these fields. The default agent value is the hostname of the machine running the **snmptrap** command. The uptime is obtained from the local system's MIB object system.sysUpTime.0.

Consider, for example, that we would like to emit a link-down trap to a network management system called rembrandt. Further, if we want to communicate that a particular port has gone down, we include the port within the variable bindings of the trap. We can use the following command:

```
# snmptrap -v 1 public '' monet 2 0 '' interfaces.iftable.ifentry.\
ifindex.1 i 1
```

In this example, we use the default values for the `enterprise-oid`
and `uptime` fields. Also, we specify the particular interface (`ifin-
dex.1`) and set the value to 1 (which indicates the second interface
with the device). The 2 represents the `link-down` trap, and 0 provides
a null value for the `specific-trap` value.

If we review the traps on `rembrandt`, we will see output like the
following:

```
Nov 24 17:51:27 monet snmptrapd[385]: 10.0.2.201: Link Down
Trap (0) Uptime:2:26:59, interfaces.ifTable.ifEntry.
  ifIndex.1 = 1
```

In practice, most `link-down` messages are not that meaningful or
interesting. However, when they come from critical devices, such as
core routers or switches, a disabled interface could spell disaster
for the network.

Care should be taken when configuring traps from network
devices because doing so can cause a *trap flood*. This condition
occurs when a large number of traps are sent in response to a particular recurring event. For example, within a LAN Ethernet
switch, a port's link state may bounce up and down many times per
second due to a hardware malfunction. This type of problem can
yield a large number of traps. In practice, trap notification should
be enabled only on critical devices and services. In this case, if possible, traps should be disabled for linkup/linkdown events from
generic network devices.

Snmptrapd Tool

The **snmptrapd** command will receive and log SNMP traps. Traps
that are sent on port 162 are either logged to the UNIX `syslog`
facility or displayed on the terminal. These messages are sent using
`LOG_WARNING` and the `LOG_LOCAL0` logging levels. The **snmptrapd** command must be run as superuser because it listens on a reserved system port. Executing the command without any options will cause
it to be placed in the background and detached from the calling
shell.

The **snmptrapd** command supports several command-line arguments: -P, -D, -d, and -q. The -P option will instruct **snmptrapd** to display any traps received on the standard output, and the -d option will display a dump of the trap packet. Thus, to show received traps and display the contents of trap packets, use the following command:

```
# snmptrapd -P -d
```

Executing this command, using the previous example on the host rembrandt, will display the following output:

```
1999-11-27 22:56:47 UCD-snmp version 4.0.1
received 69 bytes from 10.0.3.126:-32566:
0000: 30 82 00 41  02 01 00 04  06 70 75 62  6C 69 63 A4
   0..A.....public.
0016: 82 00 32 06  08 2B 06 01  04 01 03 01  01 40 04 0A
   ..2..+.......@..
0032: 00 03 7E 02  01 02 02 01  00 43 03 24  5C 96 30 82
   ..~......C.$\.0.
0048: 00 13 30 82  00 0F 06 0A  2B 06 01 02  01 02 02 01
   ..0.....+.......
0064: 01 01 02 01  01                                          .....
1999-11-27 22:56:51 monet [10.0.3.126] enterprises.3.1.1:
      Link Down Trap (0) Uptime: 6:37:09
      interfaces.ifTable.ifEntry.ifIndex.1 = 1
```

The first line shows the current version and when the **snmptrapd** process was run. Next, the output displays the number of bytes in the trap packet, the host the trap was sent from (monet), and the UDP port (32566, in this case). The contents of the trap include both hexadecimal and ASCII characters. Finally, the trap information, including the variable-binding information, is shown.

The -D option will display additional debugging information that includes the parsing of MIB files. The -q option provides a more verbose output, but it doesn't seem to be implemented in this version of the command.

The **snmptrapd** command can be used as a focal point for reception of traps for a large number of devices. However, it must be running continuously in order to receive traps from the network. By default, this tool is not started by the system on startup. To enable this command on system startup, you should add it to the existing UCD agent startup script called snmpd. This shell script can be found in the

/etc/rc.d/init.d directory. Listing 8.2 shows the startup script
with the **snmptrapd** command added on line number 21.

Listing 8.2 *UCD Startup Script with* snmptrapd *command*

```
 1  #!/bin/bash
 2
 3  # ucd-snmp init file for snmpd
 4  #
 5  # chkconfig: - 50 50
 6  # description: Simple Network Management Protocol (SNMP) Daemon
 7  #
 8  # processname: snmpd
 9  # config: /etc/snmp/snmpd.local.conf
10  # config: /etc/snmp/snmpd.conf
11  # config: /usr/share/snmp/snmpd.local.conf
12  # config: /usr/share/snmp/snmpd.conf
13
14  # source function library
15  . /etc/rc.d/init.d/functions
16
17  case "$1" in
18    start)
19            echo -n "Starting snmpd: "
20            daemon /usr/sbin/snmpd -l /etc/snmp/agent.log
21            daemon /usr/sbin/snmptrapd -s
22            touch /var/lock/subsys/snmpd
23            echo
24            ;;
25    stop)
26            echo -n "Shutting down snmpd: "
27            killproc snmpd
28            rm -f /var/lock/subsys/snmpd
29            echo
30            ;;
31    restart)
32            $0 stop
33            $0 start
34            ;;
35    status)
36            status snmpd
37            ;;
38    *)
39            echo "Usage: snmpd {start|stop|restart|status}"
40            exit 1
41  esac
42
43  exit 0
```

In this example, the script will be executed on system startu-
pand and the **snmptrap** command will be invoked with the -s option
(see line 21). This option enables the logging of messages to the
syslog facility. Before messages can be received by syslog, however, the /etc/syslog.conf configuration file must be updated to

include an entry for trap processing. Listing 8.3 shows the standard Linux `syslog.conf` with the appropriate trap entry added (see line 25).

Listing 8.3 *Standard* `syslog.conf` *file with* `trap` *entry*

```
 1   # Log all kernel messages to the console.
 2   # Logging much else clutters up the screen.
 3   #kern.*
     /dev/console
 4
 5   # Log anything (except mail) of level info or higher.
 6   # Don't log private authentication messages!
 7   *.info;mail.none;news.none;authpriv.none
     /var/log/messages
 8
 9   # The authpriv file has restricted access.
10   authpriv.*
     /var/log/secure
11
12   # Log all the mail messages in one place.
13   mail.*
     /var/log/maillog
14
15   # Everybody gets emergency messages, plus log them on
     another
16   # machine.
17   *.emerg*
18
19   # Save mail and news errors of level err and higher in a
20   # special file.
21   uucp,news.crit
     /var/log/spooler
22
23   # Save boot messages also to boot.log
24   local7.*
     /var/log/boot.log
25   local0.*
     /var/log/trapd.log
26
27   #
28   # INN
29   #
30   news.=crit
     /var/log/news/news.crit
31   news.=err
     /var/log/news/news.err
32   news.notice
     /var/log/news/news.notice
```

The new line defines the `syslog` entry that the **snmptrapd** uses when posting messages to the `syslogd` process. The entry indicates that all messages from the `local0` category will be collected. Note that all messages obtained will be saved to the `/var/log/trapd.log` file.

Snmpwalk Tool

The **snmpwalk** command will *walk* an agent MIB tree using the SNMP getnext-request. Why use this command instead of the **snmpget** tool? Well, the **snmpwalk** command can discover the entire MIB store contained within the agent automatically. With **snmpget**, you need to explicitly reference an object to obtain a value. With the **snmpwalk** command, you can start at a given point and move through the agent's MIB to the end. An object variable may be given on the command line to specify with which portion of the MIB space the search will begin. Without an MIB object argument, **snmpwalk** searches and starts with the MIB-II object store. Thus, the command

```
# snmpwalk monet public
```

will walk the entire system agent on the device monet. Since MIB-II contains a large number of objects, the command will produce a rather long listing. Instead of listing every object supported by the agent, we can limit the search and display only a single group of objects. Thus, we can list all the objects found within the MIB-II system group using the following command:

```
# snmpwalk cisco-gw5 public system
```

Executing this command on the Cisco router generates the following sample output:

```
system.sysDescr.0 = Cisco Internetwork Operating System Software
IOS (tm) GS Software (RSP-JV-M), Version 11.1(13a)CA1, EARLY
DEPLOYMENT RELEASE SOFTWARE (fc1)
Synced to mainline version: 11.1(13a)
Copyright (c) 1986-1997 by cisco Systems, Inc.
Compiled Wed 13-Aug-97 04:12 by richardd
system.sysObjectID.0 = OID: enterprises.9.1.46
system.sysUpTime.0 = Timeticks: (236153209) 27 days,
7:58:52.09
system.sysContact.0 = Susan Maxwell
system.sysName.0 = cisco-gw4
system.sysLocation.0 = Testing Lab
system.sysServices.0 = 78
```

To walk the entire MIB within a given agent and save the output to a file, use the following command:

```
# snmpwalk cisco-gw5 public .1 > walk.out
```

This command uses the .1 as the starting point to begin listing objects. Doing this will ensure that every object will be displayed because .1 is the root of the entire MIB tree and all objects are accessible from this point. Walking the entire MIB tree with an agent will help identify certain MIB objects or give you an idea of exactly how many objects a particular agent may support. To see the approximate number of objects the cisco-gw5 supports, count the number of lines in the file. Because the **snmpwalk** command displays each MIB object on its own line (unless the line is longer than the maximum number of characters for a line), we can then use the UNIX **wc** command to total the number of lines within the walk.out file. Thus, the command

```
# wc -l walk.out
```

produces the following output:

```
2242 walk.out
```

This command output shows that the agent contained within the cisco-gw5 device supports roughly 2242 MIB objects. When no object is specified with the **snmpwalk** command, it will search the MIB-II object tree by default. When the **snmpwalk** command reaches the end of the MIB within the agent, it will display the message End of MIB.

Note that the use of **snmpwalk** is a rather inefficient means to obtain a large number of MIB objects from an agent. This is because the command continuously queries a single MIB object to obtain an associated value. It is recommended that the **snmpbulkwalk** command be used whenever possible to reduce network traffic and load on the agent system. This command significantly reduces the work involved for a lower level to obtain a large amount of information from an agent. See the **snmpbulkwalk** section for additional information.

Snmpbulkwalk Tool

The **snmpbulkwalk** tool communicates with a network entity using SNMPv2 bulk-request. Like the **snmpwalk** tool, **snmpbulkwalk** will walk an MIB tree until the end of the MIB is reached or an error occurs. The `bulk-request` provides a more efficient mechanism to transfer a large amount of data than the regular SNMPv1 *get-request*. For example, assume we would like to retrieve the entire MIB-II `interface` group from a Linux server. We would issue the following command:

```
# snmpwalk monet public interfaces
```

This command will result in a series of SNMP `getnext-requests` to the `interfaces` MIB group against a network node called `monet`. The SNMPv1 `snmpwalk` (which uses a normal `get-request`) command will obtain the information using 136 packets. How do we know this? Just before the **snmpwalk** command was executed, a packet capture was started using the following command:

```
# tcpdump host monet -w output.file
```

The **tcpdump** command, which is described in Chapter 5, "Additional System Utilities and Tools," will capture all packets coming from or going to the host called `probe`. These packets are saved in the file called `output.file`. Once the **snmpwalk** command has finished, the **tcpdump** command is manually stopped. Next, we simply count the number of packets that were captured within the `output.file` file. Thus, with

```
# tcpdump -r output.file | wc -l
    136
```

we see that a total of 136 packets were captured. This is the number of packets needed to retrieve the `interfaces` table. Please note that depending on the number of interfaces defined within a device, more or fewer packets would be required. However, if we query the same device using the **snmpbulkwalk** command instead,

```
# snmpbulkwalk -v 2c monet public interfaces
```

we will poll the same interfaces group information but only use two packets!

This is a tremendous savings in terms of network bandwidth and increased SNMP performance for both the agent and manager. The SNMP *bulk-request* option is efficient because it attempts to place as many MIB OID values as possible within the variable-binding field of the SNMP response packet(s). The only limit to the amount of data that can be placed within the SNMP packet is the maximum packet size of the underling protocols. By the way, **tcp-dump** isn't the only command available to capture network traffic. The **ethereal** tool, which is described in Chapter 5, "Additional System Utilities and Tools," can also be used. Figure 8.3 contains output from the capture of the **snmpbulkwalk** operation using the Ethereal software. As you can see in the figure, only two packets were captured when the **snmpbulkwalk** command was executed: the SNMP *bulk-request* and the response. In the example, the response packet contains all the MIB objects from the `interfaces` table. This is the reason this packet is significantly larger than response packets from either an **snmpget** or **snmpgetnext** operation.

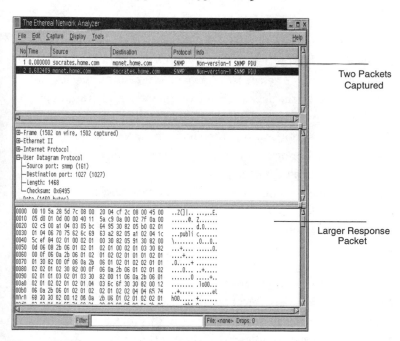

Figure 8.3 `snmpbulkwalk` *operation packet capture.*

To walk the entire MIB tree of the device called `cisco-gw1`, use the following command:

```
# snmpbulkwalk -v 2c cisco-gw1 public
```

The **snmpbulkwalk** command only works with SNMPv2 or SNMPv3 agents. This is because the bulk-request facility specification came after the widespread deployment of SNMPv1. Using this command on an SNMPv1 agent will, therefore, generate an error.

For instance, the following command attempts to walk the MIB tree of a device called remote-gw starting from the system group. In this example, remote-gw3 supports only the SNMPv1:

```
# snmpbulkwalk -v 2c remote-gw3 public system
```

Since this device doesn't understand the SNMP bulk-request, it eventually times out, and the following message is displayed following the **snmpbulkwalk** command:

```
Timeout: No Response from remote-gw3
```

A timeout error condition occurs because the requests are issued to the device, but the agent residing in the device doesn't understand the SNMP bulk-request format. As a result, the packet is not answered by the agent and the command simply times out. In practice, many networking devices have been upgraded to support the bulk-request operation. Therefore, this problem will diminish over time as older devices are replaced or upgraded.

Note that **snmpbulkwalk** requires that you use either the 2c or 2p security options. If you attempt to invoke **snmpbulkwalk** without specifying which version of the SNMP protocol is to be used, the following error will be displayed:

```
snmpbulkwalk: Cannot send V1 PDU on V2 session
```

By default, the **snmpbulkwalk** command will search the entire MIB-II tree if an MIB object or group isn't specified on the command line. From a practical standpoint, this makes the tool a little easier to use if the complete MIB-II objects store is desired.

Snmpconf Tool

The **snmpconf** command provides the ability to configure devices using the **snmpset** command according to MIB objects defined within a configuration file. The configuration file may contain a list of MIB objects and values that will be set on an SNMP device. This tool provides an automated mechanism to apply standard configuration information to a number of devices or even a single device that must be configured the same way more than once. Consider, for example, the installation of several router devices. It would be easy to create a configuration file that contains many of the commonly configured objects that the router devices share. Such a configuration could be used when each of the devices was first installed. Compared to manually configuring each router by hand, using the configuration file approach reduces the amount of time needed to install a device and decreases the likelihood of configuration errors.

The configuration file associated with **snmpconf** may contain MIB object entries, comments, and blank lines. You may add comments by using the hash mark (#). A valid configuration entry consists of a type, OID, value, and comment string. Listing 8.4 shows a sample configuration file.

Listing 8.4 *Sample* SNMPCONF *file*

```
#
# Setup standard system group information
#
S .1.3.6.1.2.1.1.4.0 Susan-Maxwell     system contact
S .1.3.6.1.2.1.1.5.0 host.dt.com       system name
S .1.3.6.1.2.1.1.6.0 Graphics_Lab      system location
```

In Listing 8.4, each of the three configuration entries contains the S character in the first field, which identifies the type of MIB object listed in the second field. The S means that the object is of type STRING. This field is interpreted as a string and, therefore, it must not contain any extra spaces. Thus, "Virginia-Maxwell" is acceptable, but "Virginia Maxwell" (with the space character) is not. Also, the use of double quotes is not permitted. If the string "Virginia Maxwell" is used, it will result in a configuration error. The **snmpconf** tool defines two additional types: I for INTEGER and A for IPADDRESS.

The second field is the MIB object that will be changed to the value contained within the third field. Note that only a fully qualified OID expressed in dotted notation is supported by **snmpconf**. Any other format, such as a dotted name format, e.g.,

```
iso.org.dod.internet.mgmt.mib-2.system.sysLocation.0
```

or abbreviated MIB strings will cause configuration errors.

As stated before, the third field is the value to which the MIB object will be set. As such, it must match the type character specified in the first field. Thus, in this example, each of the configuration lines expects a string in this field. The last or fourth field is for comments. It provides a comment that should be used to identify the MIB object and value. In this case, the MIB objects are the `contact` (`sysContact`), `name` (`sysName`), and `location` (`sysLocation`) objects from the MIB-II `system` group.

Once the configuration file contains the needed and/or required MIB objects and values, it can be used against an SNMP device. The basic syntax of the **snmpconf** command is as follows:

```
snmpconf hostname community configuration_file
```

Thus, assume that the above configuration is stored in a file called `config1` and we would like to apply this file to the device called `nicodemus`, which also has a community string of `private`. Given this information, the following command could be used:

```
# snmpconf nicodemus private config1
```

Executing this command executes displays the following output:

```
#
# Setup standard system group information
#
Set display string 'system contact' to Susan-Maxwell
Set display string 'system name' to host.dt.com
Set display string 'system location' to Graphics_Lab
Done.
```

Notice that defined comments are displayed along with a confirmation that each **set** command was successful. If you would like to verify this, simply execute an **snmpwalk** within the MIB-II `system` group. Thus, the command

```
# snmpwalk nicodemus public system
```

will produce the following output:

```
system.sysDescr.0 = unknown
system.sysObjectID.0 = OID:
enterprises.ucdavis.ucdSnmpAgent.linux
system.sysUpTime.0 = Timeticks: (260363) 0:43:23.63
system.sysContact.0 = Susan-Maxwell
system.sysName.0 = host.dt.com
```

```
system.sysLocation.0 = Graphics_Lab
system.sysServices.0 = 72
```

The host `nicodemus` is running the UCD SNMP agent, and the output above shows only part of the system group. In this example, we can confirm that the `sysContact`, `sysName`, and `sysLocation` objects have been updated according to the **snmpconf** configuration file.

The **snmpconf** software provides a couple of ways to specify the required configuration file. First, the name of the file may be given on the command line as in the preceding example; **snmpconf** will examine the current directory to find the file. Next, the file may be provided with a fully qualified pathname. Finally, if the environment variable `SNMPCONF_LIB` has been set, the software will search the directory specified in this variable.

The **snmpconf** tool provides some basic error-checking and, when problems occur, displays useful information. However, it is difficult to determine the cause of certain types of problems. For example, if an incorrect community string is given or the device given isn't currently on the network, the same error message is displayed. Thus, the commands

```
# snmpconf didymus private config1
# snmpconf monet public config1
```

produce the same errors as shown, but for different reasons:

```
#
# Setup standard system group information
#
UNABLE to set display string 'system contact' to Susan-
   Maxwell
UNABLE to set display string 'system name' to host.dl.com
UNABLE to set display string 'system location' to
   Graphics_Lab
Done.
3 errors encountered.
```

The first command attempts to set MIB objects on the system `didymus`, which isn't presently reachable on the network; that is, the device was powered down when this command was run. The second command uses the wrong community string. In this case, the correct community string is `private`, not `public`. As you can see, the tool doesn't respond differently to a down system and an incorrect community, making it difficult for you to determine the cause of the particular errors. However, with care, you can get around this problem by issuing the **ping** command before executing the **snmpconf**. In this way, you can avoid this kind of ambiguity and address the separate problems appropriately.

The **snmpconf** software provides two command-line options. The first, **-version**, displays version information for both the **snmpconf** tool itself and the CMU support library. The second, **-quiet**, instructs **snmpconf** to squelch messages when executing.

Tkmib Tool

The tkmib utility provides a GUI front end to many of the Linux SNMP tools, including **snmpget, snmpgetnext, snmpwalk**, and **snmptable**. This software is known as an "MIB browser," which can be used to interrogate an SNMP agent regarding the specific MIB objects and associated values. To invoke this tool, issue the **tkmib** command within a UNIX shell. When the software is started, it displays a rather large window that contains several menus, panels, and buttons, as shown in Figure 8.4.

The window contains four major panels: the MIB tree view panel, the MIB object definition panel, the MIB description panel, and the MIB value panel.

Using the software to query an agent is simple: Navigate to the desired OID string found in the top panel, enter a hostname or IP address in the target host text box, and click one of the appropriate SNMP operation buttons.

The functions of the buttons stop, get, getnext, and walk should be fairly easy to understand. Unfortunately, the graph function doesn't seem to work correctly; it produces a large number of error messages when invoked. The remaining button, table, bears a little more explanation. This button provides a great way to view SNMP tables. We have previously discussed the functions of the **snmptable** command, which displays MIB tables. One of the primary features of this tool is the ability to format the data as input to other applications and programs. It also shows the format of tables. The table button with tkmib is mainly used to review MIB tables and does a better job than the **snmptable** command of formatting the elements of a particular table.

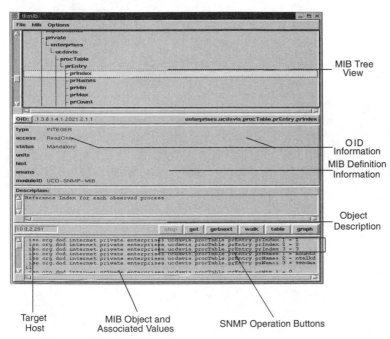

Figure 8.4 tkmib *main window.*

Consider the `tcpConnTable` table, where each index is constructed with an IP address and port pair. At first glance, it is a bit difficult to understand how this table is organized. However, with the help of the tkmib tool, the table is more understandable. Figure 8.5 shows the view of the `tcpConnTable`. that was retrieved from the device with the IP address of `10.0.2.201`. To obtain this listing, the `tcpConnTable` table (which is from the `tcp` MIB-II group) was selected and the `table` button was clicked.

The bottom panel shown in the figure contains a scroll bar that is used to list all of the columns of the table. These include `tcpConnState`, `tcpConnLocalAddress`, `tcpConnLocalPort`, etc. Also note the `Index` column, which contains the index for each of the rows within the table.

Menu Items

The `tkmib` tool provides three main menus: `File`, `Mib`, and `Options`. The `File` menu contains a single item, `Quit`, which is self-explanatory. The next menu, `Mib`, contains three items: `Find a mib node`, `Load a New Mib File`, and `Load a New Mib Module`. The subitem `Find a mib`

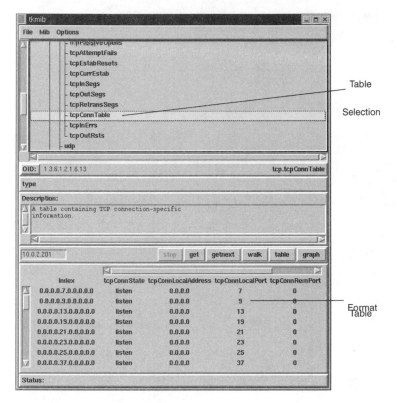

Figure 8.5 *Table button display.*

node can search the existing MIBs for a specific object or group. For instance, assume we are searching for the udpInDatagrams MIB object. First, select the Find a mib node submenu from the Mib menu to display the dialog window shown in Figure 8.6.

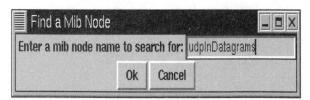

Figure 8.6 *Search Node dialog window.*

Enter the udpInDatagrams object name and click the OK button. If the object can be found, the MIB tree panel will be updated to display the desired object. Otherwise, an error dialog is displayed, stating that the object couldn't be found. The other menu items load additional MIB modules and files into tkmib.

New MIB files can be imported directly into the tkmib tool so that OID objects will be displayed using the standard name strings. To load a new MIB, select the Load a New Mib File menu item. A new dialog window will appear, as shown in Figure 8.7.

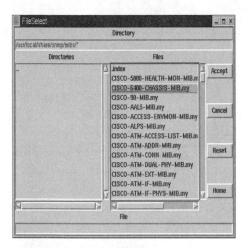

Figure 8.7 *Load MIB file dialog window.*

Enter the name in the bottom text box or select from the panel on the right the filename that represents the MIB that should be loaded. In this example, a Cisco MIB called CISCO-6400-CHASSIS-MIB.my will be imported. This MIB contains elements used to describe chassis-based Cisco switch and router products. Once a selection is made, the tree view panel will be redrawn and display the default tree items. To determine if the MIB file was imported as expected, navigate to where the MIB object should begin.

In this example, a series of Cisco-related groups from the enterprises branch have been created. Figure 8.8 shows a snapshot of the top tree view panel that contains just the MIB view displaying the new MIB groups defined under the Cisco branch. If different vendor-specific MIBs are loaded, the vendor-specific names should appear in this list as well.

The remaining menu contains four items: Display, Time between graph polls, Port number, and Community Name. The Display sub-menu controls each of the MIB object attributes that are displayed

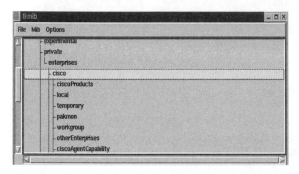

Figure 8.8 *Tree view for Cisco branch.*

within the object description panel. The submenu contains a number of check boxes, one for each MIB property. When one of the boxes is unchecked, the appropriate MIB attribute is removed from the object panel.

The `Time between graph polls` menu option controls the amount of time that will elapse for each retrieval of MIB objects used within a graph. By default it is five seconds. The `Port number` submenu item defines the TCP port used when querying the SNMP target agent. The default is the standard port of `161`. To change the default, select the `Port number` item and, when the new dialog box is displayed (shown in Figure 8.9), enter the desired port and click the `Ok` button.

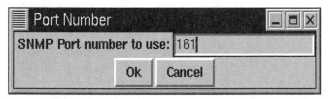

Figure 8.9 *Port number dialog window.*

The community string password can also be changed. The value of `public` is set by default. To change the default, select the `Community Name` sub-menu item and enter the new value in the new dialog window that is displayed, as shown in Figure 8.10.

Unfortunately, changes to any of the items within the `Options` menu are not permanently saved when the application is termi-

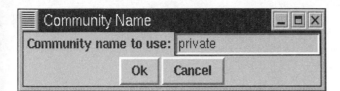

Figure 8.10 *Community string dialog window.*

nated. Therefore, any values altered will need to be changed every time the application is started.

## 09

Web-enabled Tools

As the previous chapter discusses network management tools and utilities for the UNIX command line and some specialized GUIs, this chapter focuses on network management tools that can be used from a Web browser. No one can discount the significant impact the Web has had on application development, common interfaces, and ease-of-use, specifically in the area of network management. Because of the immense popularity of Web-based computing, it is reasonable to include some tools that can be used via common Web browsers.

These tools include both SNMP-based and non-SNMP-based software. Non-SNMP tools have been selected for those sites that have yet to implement SNMP functionality or just need a system tool that can be implemented without a lot of fuss. For those who already use SNMP, the tools in this section will be a welcome addition to any existing suite of software.

This chapter discusses the MRTG and NTOP tools.

MRTG Tool

General Description

The Multi-router Traffic Grapher (MRTG) tool can monitor and graph network traffic obtained from networking devices that use SNMP. As the name implies, it displays traffic utilization and other statistical information gathered from routers and other networking devices. It generates HTML pages and GIF images, providing a visual representation of network performance via a Web browser. Network performance is one of the most important aspects of network management. This tool will make it easy to pinpoint both device and network performance problems.

For example, given the network topology shown in Figure 9.1, MRTG can monitor the network from the remote router called `remote-gw` and other important devices, such as the backbone switch/router and workgroup switch. Because this network is critical, it is important to monitor the network traffic going to and from the router. Specifically, it is important to monitor the serial interface and both Ethernet interfaces to ensure they do not become overloaded. Further, the backbone network and any attached subnetworks should also be monitored to ensure smooth operations.

Because MRTG can monitor any device that supports SNMP, it can be put to use monitoring both edge and backbone routers as well as other critical devices. An edge router (or other device) is closer to user workstations and servers, while the backbone devices are those at the heart or core of the network. The point here is that MRTG can be used to collect vital information from many devices on the network to gain a better performance picture.

The primary method MRTG uses to collect information is the **snmpget** command, which was discussed previously. However, you

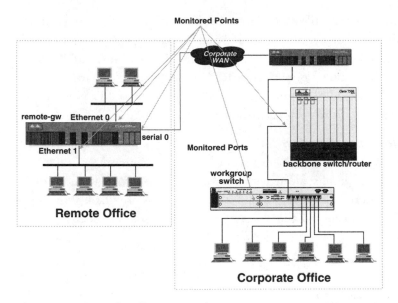

Figure 9.1 *Sample office network.*

can customize MRTG to display information derived through other means as well. For example, MRTG can display UNIX system load and disk space utilization. Further, because MRTG can poll any SNMP MIB object, many additional performance metrics and MIB objects can be retrieved. As a result of these capabilities, there are many practical uses for MRTG, including, but not limited to, the following:

- displaying network utilization on LAN and WAN links

- displaying system CPU load on networking devices

- displaying system memory utilization on network devices

- displaying modem usage on remote access servers

Conceptually, MRTG polls specific performance MIB objects from devices and displays the values in a graphical format using HTML. Figure 9.2 shows the high-level flow of MRTG. The basic operation includes collecting data from external devices and creating associated log files to store the data. Once the log files are created, HTML reports can be generated. Also, MRTG must have a configuration file that tells the program which devices to monitor and controls specific operating and formatting parameters. Unfortunately, each network is different, and the user must build this configuration file. Luckily, MRTG provides an automated tool that accomplishes much of the work needed to build a configuration specific to each network.

Web Page Overview

By default, MRTG displays the results of network polls in a series of graphs, along with additional device information for each monitored interface. A total of four graphs is provided, showing bytes transmitted and received per second in daily, weekly, monthly, and yearly averages.

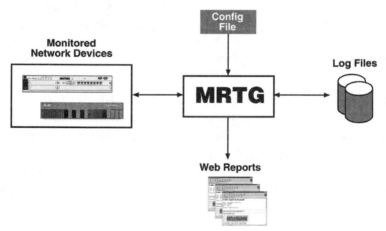

Figure 9.2 *Basic operation of MRTG.*

This report includes information that was obtained via SNMP from the MIB-II `system` and `interfaces` groups from the device `remote-gw`. Consult Chapter 6, "Overview of MIB-II," for additional information regarding these MIB groups. The `System` field is derived from the `sysName` and `sysLocation` objects, while the `Maintainer` field is obtained from the `sysContact` object. The `Interface` string represents the physical hardware interface contained within the device, and the number `(1)` indicates that this is the first interface. Notice in Figure 9.3 that the interface is labeled `Ethernet0`, which means that this is the first Ethernet interface on the device. It is labeled this way because Cisco routers always number their interfaces starting at zero. Figure 9.3 also shows only a partial MRTG report containing some device information plus the `Daily` usage graph.

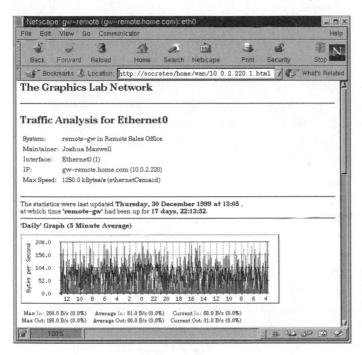

Figure 9.3 *MRTG Web report.*

The `IP` string indicates that no associated hostname was found for the IP address of this device. This is not really a problem, because, some of the time, access to many networking devices is via the IP address, not the hostname. To correct this, enter the valid hostname in the local `/etc/hosts` file, or, if running DNS, add the entry in the DNS server configuration file.

The `Max Speed` field is calculated from the `ifSpeed` object that was divided by eight. This represents the maximum number of bytes per second that the interface can theoretically support. The value of eight was selected because there are eight bits in a single byte. The `Max Speed` field also confirms that this interface is Ethernet by displaying the type as `ethernetCsmacd`, which is derived from the `ifType` object contained within the MIB-2 store. The report also displays the date and time that the report was updated and how long the device has been running since it was last booted or since the network management component of the device was last reset.

The daily graph shows bytes per second over an approximate 36-hour period using a five-minute average. This average is the difference between each successive poll of bytes transmitted or received, not cumulative totals or raw counts. In other words, the displayed value is the difference between the current and previous values and is divided by the time elapsed between these readings. The horizontal axis (*x*-axis) shows time in two-hour increments, while the vertical axis (*y*-axis) shows bytes that range from zero to a given maximum value. The graph displays bytes transmitted in and out of the interface, obtained from `ifOutOctets` and `ifInOctets` MIB objects, respectively.

The bottom of the report shows the legend; in this case, incoming traffic is displayed in green, while outgoing traffic is displayed in blue. However, because this book is in black and white, the green in the graph appears gray and the blue appears black. Later on, the section called "Customizing MRTG Reports" will show how to change the colors used in the graphs. Also, the bottom of the graph contains a short summary that lists the maximum, average, and current incoming and outgoing bytes per second. This can help you spot trouble quickly. Using the customization options available with MRTG, these colors, as well as many other report and graph attributes, may be changed.

An MRTG report also contains additional graphs for weekly, monthly, and yearly totals. The weekly graph contains weekly averages for the past seven days, with the current day displayed to the left of the graph by default. The monthly report shows the last five weeks, with the current week on the left and the previous weeks to the right. The data in this graph has been averaged over a two-hour period. The yearly graph spans the previous 12 months, with the current month shown on the left, and shows the data as a daily average. Figure 9.4 shows these three graphs.

As you can see, all the graphs grow from the left, which is the default. The graphs can be made to grow from the right by enabling one of the **MRTG** command options. Also, by default, the report pages are updated automatically every five minutes when new

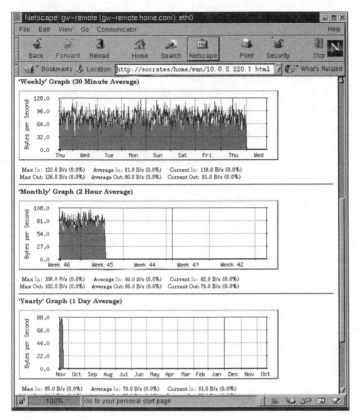

Figure 9.4 *MRTG weekly, monthly, and yearly reports.*

information is obtained for each of the monitored interfaces. You can customize this update interval (or refresh rate) as well.

Basic Configuration of MRTG

MRTG uses a configuration file to specify which devices are to be monitored. The MRTG package doesn't come with a predefined configuration because the devices listed wouldn't likely match those at your site. Instead, the package includes a utility program called **cfgmaker,** which is used to build a basic configuration so you don't have to create one from scratch. The purpose of this utility is to poll a network device for specific SNMP objects (e.g., interfaces table) and build a configuration file suitable for MRTG. The syntax of **cfgmaker** is as follows:

```
cfgmaker community@device
```

Two arguments are required: the device's community string and hostname (or IP address). Because **cfgmaker** writes to standard out, the output should be redirected to a file when you want to save the results. To illustrate the use of this utility, let's assume that we want to monitor a single router in a remote office. In this example, we have a Cisco 2500 series router, called `remote-gw`, with a community string of `louvre`. Thus the command:

```
# cfgmaker louvre@remote-gw > cisco.conf
```

probes the `remote-gw` device and builds the MRTG configuration file with the name of `cisco.conf`. Assuming the arguments provided to the **cfgmaker** are correct and the device responds to the SNMP requests, Listing 9.1 shows the configuration that would be generated (minus the comments added by **cfgmaker**) by the **cfgmaker** script:

Listing 9.1 *Sample* **cfgmaker** *configuration file*

```
Target[10.0.2.75.1]: 1:public@10.0.2.75
MaxBytes[10.0.2.75.1]: 1249994
Title[10.0.2.75.1]: remote-gw (No hostname defined for IP
address): Ethernet0
PageTop[10.0.2.75.1]: <H1>Traffic Analysis for Ethernet0
 </H1>
 <TABLE>
   <TR><TD>System:</TD><TD>remote-gw in Graphics Lab 11-
B</TD></TR>
   <TR><TD>Maintainer:</TD><TD>Steve Maxwell</TD></TR>
   <TR><TD>Interface:</TD><TD>Ethernet0 (1)</TD></TR>
   <TR><TD>IP:</TD><TD>No hostname defined for IP address
(161.135.59.129)</TD></TR>
   <TR><TD>Max Speed:</TD>
       <TD>1250.0 kBytes/s (ethernetCsmacd)</TD></TR>
  </TABLE>
#-------------------------------------------------------------------
Target[10.0.2.75.2]: 2:public@10.0.2.75
MaxBytes[10.0.2.75.2]: 6982
Title[10.0.2.75.2]: remote-gw (No hostname defined for IP
address): Serial0
PageTop[10.0.2.75.2]: <H1>Traffic Analysis for Serial0
 </H1>
 <TABLE>
   <TR><TD>System:</TD><TD>remote-gw in Graphics Lab 11-
B</TD></TR>
```

```
<TR><TD>Maintainer:</TD><TD>Steve Maxwell</TD></TR>
<TR><TD>Interface:</TD><TD>Serial0 (2)</TD></TR>
<TR><TD>IP:</TD><TD>No hostname defined for IP address
(161.135.59.9)</TD></TR>
<TR><TD>Max Speed:</TD>
    <TD>6982.0 Bytes/s (rfc877x25)</TD></TR>
</TABLE>
#-----------------------------------------------------------------
```

To support comments in the MRTG configuration file, use the hash (#) character at the beginning of each line. The file ignores blank lines. The configuration file includes one or more polling instances that contain tokens and associated values. These tokens collectively represent a single monitored element. Each element represents a polled entity that includes the SNMP objects to query from the device being monitored and additional display formatting for the resulting information. Each element is separated by a single hash (#) followed by a series of " - " characters (as shown in the last line of Listing 9.1). This particular router contains only a few network interfaces, and the keyword **target** corresponds to each router interface. This is a key observation; any data that is going to be monitored and displayed by MRTG requires a **target** entry.

This particular router contains three interfaces—one Ethernet and two serial—but **cfgmaker** only reports two interfaces. Because the third interface is administratively down, **cfgmaker** skipped this interface. Either this interface was not configured within the router or it was disabled for some other reason. In any event, **cfgmaker** includes the first two interfaces but inserts a comment character in front of the third interface in the cisco.conf file so that it will not be polled with the MRTG software, as shown in Listing 9.2.

Listing 9.2 *Commented interface entry*

```
########
######## This Interface is one of the following
######## - administratively not UP
######## - it is in test mode
######## - it is a softwareLoopback interface
######## - has a unrealistic speed setting
######## It is commented out for this reason.
########
```

(continued)

```
#
# Target[10.0.2.75.3]: 3:public@10.0.2.75
# MaxBytes[10.0.2.75.3]: 193000
# Title[10.0.2.75.3]: remote-gw (No hostname defined for IP
    address): Serial1
# PageTop[10.0.2.75.3]: <H1>Traffic Analysis for Serial1
#    <BR></H1>
#    <TABLE>
#      <TR><TD>System:</TD><TD>remote-gw in </TD></TR>
#      <TR><TD>Maintainer:</TD><TD></TD></TR>
#      <TR><TD>Interface:</TD><TD>Serial1 (3)</TD></TR>
#      <TR><TD>IP:</TD><TD> ()</TD></TR>
#      <TR><TD>Max Speed:</TD>
#          <TD>193.0 kBytes/s (propPointToPointSerial)</TD></TR>
#    </TABLE>
#
#-----------------------------------------------------------------
```

Disabling the interface is a good idea because it is not reasonable to have MRTG poll nonactive interfaces when there is no traffic, thus producing empty graphs. Also, if the interface is enabled and put into service at some future date, it is a simple matter to "uncomment" the interface entry, thus permitting MRTG to monitor the port. The MRTG configuration file uses the HTML formatting language and, in particular, builds a table to format the device information, as denoted by the <TABLE> and </TABLE> tags. The configuration also includes one or more keywords that control which devices are monitored and how data is graphed. Each keyword contains the following syntax:

```
Command [label] args
```

where **Command** is one of the commands shown next, followed by a label enclosed with brackets and one or more arguments or command options.

Each monitored element or interface within the configuration file usually contains the following keywords:

- **Target**
- **MaxBytes**
- **Title**
- **PageTop**

The **target** keyword indicates to MRTG what it should monitor. The basic format is as follows

```
Target[label]: port:community@device
```

The `label` is used as an identifier, so that MRTG can display a group of keywords on one HTML page. The `label` is a combination of the device IP address and interface number. The `port` is the interface number as defined in the `device` that MRTG should poll with the SNMP community string of `community`. The port or interface number must be a valid interface on the device being polled. You can determine the valid interfaces on a given device with the MRTG cfgmaker program. By using this program, you will cause all defined interfaces within a given device to be discovered automatically. Alternatively, using a MIB browser, you can peruse the MIB tree of the device and examine the interface table to discover the interfaces manually. However, if you already know which interfaces you want to monitor, specifying them manually might be the simplest approach. Using the configuration example above, consider the following **Target** command:

```
Target[10.0.2.75.1]: 1:public@10.0.2.75
```

This command will define the label `10.0.2.75.1` and instruct MRTG to monitor traffic from the first interface of the device with the IP address of `10.0.2.75` using the community string of `public`. By default, `MRTG` polls the MIB objects `ifInOctets` and `IfOutOctets` from the specified device and graphs this data over time.

The **Maxbytes** keyword defines the upper limit for any monitored traffic statistics and determines the *y*-axis range for unscaled graphs. For any interface, the **Maxbytes** keyword is normally specified in bytes per second, which can be calculated by dividing the maximum bandwidth of the interface by eight. For example, because 10M Ethernet has a maximum bandwidth of 10Mbps, dividing this by eight (8), we get `1250000` (10,000,000 / 8 = 1,250,000). Setting this value correctly is very important because this will ensure that the graphs display realistic information. For example, in Listing 9.2, the command

```
MaxBytes[10.0.2.75.1]: 1250000
```

defines the maximum of 1,250,000 bytes for the device associated with the label 10.0.2.75.1. Recall that the **cfgmaker** program assigns the MaxBytes value, and the reason this value was chosen is because the interface is of type Ethernet. Having the value for bytes per second handy is important. Therefore, Table 9.1 lists the most common networking interface types. This information has been included here because MRTG doesn't include the maximum bytes per second for the graphs; this is to ensure that they are readable when small traffic loads are graphed.

Table 9.1 *Bytes per second for different interfaces*

Network Type	Bytes per Second
ATM-OC3 (155Mbps)	19,375,000
Gigabit Ethernet (1000Mbps)	125,000,000
Fast Ethernet (100Mbps)	12,500,000
FDDI (100Mbps)	12,500,000
T3/DS-3 (45Mbps)	5,593,250
Ethernet (10Mbps)	1,250,000
Token Ring (16Mbps)	2,000,000
Token Ring (4Mbps)	500,000
T1/DS-1 (1.54Mbps)	193,000
56K	7,000

MRTG also uses the MaxBytes value to detect invalid responses when polling devices for interface traffic statistics.

The **Title** keyword labels the report page and usually includes some information regarding the particular interface that is being monitored. The example

```
Title[10.0.2.75.1]: remote-gw (No hostname defined for IP
    address): Ethernet0
```

defines the title that is associated with the system 10.0.2.75. It contains the hostname, plus the interface (i.e., Ethernet0).

The final keyword, **PageTop**, includes additional information that will be placed at the top of the report. This allows more description of the interface or other information to be placed on the report.

```
PageTop[10.0.2.75.1]: <H1>Traffic Analysis for Ethernet0
   </H1>
```

In this example, the string `Traffic Analysis for Ethernet0` is included when the **cfgmaker** script is executed and further describes what the report represents. The `<H1>` and `</H1>` markers are HTML heading tags. The browser may choose to display the string between these markers in one of many different formats, including centering, bold text, a large font, italics, color, or underlining. Multiple lines may be added to this keyword, and, because HTML normally removes new-line characters, the `\n` sequence must be used if new lines are required.

Using MRTG

After a basic configuration file for the devices has been prepared, it is time to start using MRTG to monitor performance and produce reports on these devices. The command that polls the devices for performance statistics and builds the HTML pages is known as **mrtg**. However, before we can run this command, we must make sure to include the **WorkDir** keyword entry command in the configuration file. This keyword tells MRTG where to create the log files and HTML pages. The syntax of this command is as follows:

```
WorkDir: path
```

where `path` is the absolute pathname of the target directory that will contain all the files needed. After this command has been added to the configuration file, it is time to run **mrtg** with the new configuration to ensure that no syntax errors or other problems have been introduced. This is an important step because it helps to ensure that we catch any problems before we start executing **mrtg** on a more or less permanent basis. Assuming the configuration file being used is called `cisco.conf`, the command

```
# /usr/bin/mrtg cisco.conf
```

runs **mrtg** with this file and immediately attempts to collect SNMP data from the device(s) listed. After the **mrtg** command has finished, it creates a series of files in the directory specified by the **WorkDir** command. Assume, for example, that the `cisco.conf` file contains the following sample entries:

```
WorkDir: /usr/mrtg/www
Target[10.0.2.75.1]: 1:public@10.0.2.75
```

The following files will be created in the `/usr/mrtg/www` directory:

```
10.0.2.75.1-day.gif
10.0.2.75.1-month.gif
10.0.2.75.1-week.gif
10.0.2.75.1-year.gif
10.0.2.75.1.html
10.0.2.75.1.log
10.0.2.75.1.old
```

All of these files have the prefix of the IP address and the interface number and represent the device and port being monitored by MRTG. The `10.0.2.71.1-html` file contains the high-level report, in HTML, previously shown in Figure 9.1. When viewing the MRTG reports, use this file and a standard Web browser to display the interface performance graphs. The files with the `gif` extension are the four graphs that show the daily, monthly, weekly, and yearly usage in bytes per second of the device that the `10.0.2.75.1-html` report file uses. The `10.0.2.75.1.log` and `10.0.2.75.1.old` files contain the SNMP polled data used to build the graphs.

For every interface monitored by MRTG, these seven files will be created automatically. Another good thing about MRTG is that the reports and data files don't consume a large amount of disk space. In fact, MRTG uses a unique method of data storage to minimize the amount of space used in the historical graphs.

To ensure that MRTG captures consistent and complete information from the monitored devices, the MRTG program must be run at regular intervals. One of the best ways to achieve this is to use the `cron` facility. Since the daily graph, which is available on the MRTG report, is averaged over a five-minute period, it is reasonable that **mrtg** should be run every five minutes. A sample **crontab** entry that would do just this is shown here:

```
0,5,10,15,20,25,30,35,40,45,50,55 * * * * /usr/bin/mrtg \
/usr/mrtg/www/mrtg.conf
```

This entry will execute the **mrtg** program every five minutes every day of the week. The * is a wildcard that means *all* for the four time specifications following the `minutes` field. Copy this entry into root's crontab file to have it run on a continued basis.

Customizing MRTG Reports

You can customize the MRTG package to produce differently formatted reports and graphs and to control certain operational aspects of MRTG. To accomplish this, use optional target configuration tags (or keywords) within the MRTG configuration file. The keywords can be divided into two groups: *optional global commands* and *optional target commands*. The global commands affect the operation or behavior of MRTG as a whole, while the optional target commands apply specifically to individual targets or device reports and graphs.

Global Commands

Table 9.2 lists the four global commands supported by MRTG. These optional commands are placed in the configuration file that is used with the **mrtg** program.

Table 9.2 *Optional global commands*

Command	Description
Refresh	Specifies how frequently (in seconds) to update the MRTG report
Interval	Specifies how often **mrtg** is called
Write-Expires	If set to YES, will generate metafiles that control expiration tags for the MRTG reports
IconDir	Tells MRTG to look in an alternative location for GIF images

The **Refresh** command specifies how often, in seconds, the browser should reload the MRTG report page. The default value is 300 seconds, (five minutes). This is a very useful option when it becomes important to precisely control the granularity for the update of the MRTG reports. For example, if it is necessary to have nearly real-time performance information on certain critical devices, lowering **Refresh** to as little as 60 seconds may be appropriate. On the other hand, **Refresh** should be larger for those devices that might be less critical and don't require up-to-the-minute reporting. To reduce the browser refresh rate to one minute, place the following command in the MRTG configuration file:

```
Refresh: 60
```

In order for the refresh value to be effective, it should closely match the interval at which **mrtg** is executed when polling devices. The `crontab` entry previously specified in this section runs **mrtg** every five minutes. If the refresh value is decreased from its default value, the `crontab` entry should also be updated with the same value as well. Consider the situation in which the refresh value is one minute while the execution of the **mrtg** is every five minutes. In this scenario, there would be no point in refreshing the MRTG reports, because the data would only be updated every five minutes by **mrtg**. Clearly, to increase the granularity of the MRTG reports requires that the **mrtg** program run more often to collect additional data points from the devices being monitored.

The **Interval** command specifies how often MRTG is executed. The purpose of this command is to generate in the MRTG report a meta header that controls the time-to-live of the report for caching purposes. Also, the meta header documents the HTML pages with the correct calling interval. If the Web browser being used requires the generation of meta files that control the expiration of the MRTG reports, use the **WriteExpires** command. These metafiles contain tags that specify the expiration of both the HTML and GIF files. Enabling **WriteExpires** will cause MRTG to create additional files in the working directory.

The **IconDir** command can specify an alternative directory (instead of the working directory) to contain icons used by MRTG. It is useful to separate the device report files from the GIF images used with the reports. Thus, to use the `graphics` directory to hold all the images, use the following command:

```
IconDir: /graphics/
```

Note that the directory name must include the trailing "/" character.

Optional Target Commands

Many options control the formatting of the graphs, but only a few affect how the report is displayed. All the keywords described here have the same syntax as the other MRTG commands, such as **Target** and **MaxBytes**. Table 9.3 lists these customization keywords, and a discussion of each follows.

Table 9.3 *MRTG customization options*

Option	Description
AddHead	Like the **PageTop** keyword, this includes the specified entry in the MRTG report. This is a great way to add site-specific information to the MRTG reports
AbsMax	Specifies the maximum value ever to be reached when data is to be graphed
Background	Controls the background color of the MRTG reports
Colours	Overrides the default color scheme
Directory	Places all files related to a given label in the directory specified
Legend	Controls the strings for the color legend
Options	Enables the use of additional Boolean switches, which further control display attributes of graphs
Short-Legend	Overrides the units string, which by default is b/s
Step	Changes the default step or timeout from five minutes (5 * 60)
Suppress	Disables the display of daily, weekly, monthly, or yearly graphs on an MRTG report

Table 9.3 *MRTG customization options (continued)*

Option	Description
Timezone	Controls the time zone that is used. Standard names such as japan are supported
Unscaled	Turns off the vertical scaling of data on graphs on a MRTG report
Weekformat	Controls which UNIX API function is used to format the weekly information displayed in the monthly graphs
WithPeak	Enables display of peak values in graphs on an MRTG report
XSize/YSize	Changes the vertical and horizontal sizes of the MRTG report graphs
XZoom/YZoom	Increases the number of pixels used with a graph
XScale/YScale	Scales both the x and y axes of the graph
Ylegend	Overrides the text displayed for the y-axis for the graph

The **AddHead** keyword adds HTML code between the </TITLE> and </HEAD> HTML tags in the resulting HTML. This is a good way to add any site-specific information to the MRTG reports. For example, to add the ability to Email an individual from the MRTG report, add the following:

```
AddHead[10.0.2.75.1]: <A HREF="mailto:support@monet">Open
    Trouble Ticket</A>
```

Notice that this keyword requires a label and is used to match up the **AddHead** to the existing **Target** command entry.

By default, MRTG scales the vertical axis to ensure that data that is much smaller than the MaxBytes is displayed in such a way that it is visible on the graph. If you want to disable the scaling function, use the **Unscaled** keyword. This command accepts a single string argument that consists of the first letter of the name of the graph that should not be scaled. The string includes d for daily, w for weekly, m for monthly, and y for yearly. Thus, the command

```
Unscaled[10.0.2.71.1]: dw
```

disables scaling for both the daily and weekly graphs.

The **WithPeak** command instructs MRTG to display peak five-minute rates for both incoming and outgoing traffic on device interfaces. Normally, the graphs only contain the average values of the monitored variables. This command takes a single string that contains the first letter of the names of the graphs that should display the peak values. The string includes w for weekly, m for monthly, and y for yearly. In the following example, both the weekly and yearly graphs will contain peak information:

```
WithPeak[10.0.2.71.1]: dw
```

The reason the daily graph is not included in this list is that this graph already shows peak information.

Normally, MRTG displays all four graphs on the interface report. You can use the **Suppress** keyword to remove one or more of these graphs from the report. This keyword takes the same argument as both the **Unscaled** and **WithPeak** commands. To block the display of weekly, monthly, and yearly graphs, use the following command:

```
Suppress[10.0.2.71.1]: wmy
```

To provide a way to better organize MRTG reports and data files, the **Directory** command has been supplied. By default, MRTG saves all the files to the directory specified with the **WorkDir** keyword. The **Directory** command accepts a string argument that represents the name of a directory to which to save all files associated with the label. The commands

```
WorkDir: /usr/mrtg/www/devices
Directory[10.0.2.71.1] gw-1
```

instruct MRTG to save all files associated with the label 10.0.2.71.1 in the directory called gw-1. As you can see, this can be useful in managing a large installation of monitored devices and interfaces because each interface can be saved to its own location. The directory specified with the **Directory** command must exist before MRTG is run because MRTG will not create it. If MRTG is run before this directory exists, it will produce an error message and abort.

The **options** keyword provides further capabilities to customize the way that the MRTG graphs are displayed. This command accepts several Boolean switches, listed in Table 9.4, that toggle attributes to control various graphing options.

Table 9.4 *Options Boolean switches*

Option	Description
growright	Causes graphs to grow from the right side of the graph
bits	Changes the bits per byte
noinfo	Suppresses uptime and device information
no-percent	Suppresses usage percentage information
gauge	Treats polled values as absolute rather than incrementing counters
absolute	Used with gauge values to indicate non-incremental values that are reset when data is obtained

The growright option will cause data to be added from the right side of the graph instead of from the left, which is the default behavior. This also reverses the *x-axis* value for all the graphs.

With MRTG, all the monitored values are displayed in bytes by default. With the bits option, these values may be displayed in bits instead. This has a profound impact on graphs, as the bits value seems to produce a more impressive graph than the graph of bytes. The **noinfo** and **nopercent** keywords suppress information from the MRTG report. In the case of **noinfo**, neither uptime nor additional device information will be displayed. The **nopercent** keyword withholds calculated percent information from the graphs.

The gauge switch treats gathered values as absolute quantities rather than increments to the values displayed in previous polls. This is useful for monitoring information related to disk space, processor utilization, and the number of users on a system. The disk-space monitoring example discussed in the "Monitoring Disk Space" section uses the `gauge` option. The `absolute` switch is used for data sources that reset their values when the data is obtained. This indicates that MRTG doesn't need to calculate the difference between the present value and the previous polled value. The `absolute` value is divided by the elapsed time between the last two polls, which makes it quite different from the `gauge` values previously discussed.

Special Target Names

`MRTG` provides three special target names that can reduce the amount of typing within the MRTG configuration file. These special characters include the caret (^), dollar sign ($), and underscore (_). The text of every keyword that uses the ^ is added to the beginning of every subsequent target that is used. For example, the MRTG sequence

```
PageTop[^]: <H1>The Graphics Lab Network</H1>
```

will be added to every additional **PageTop** keyword command that is found within the configuration file. Thus, given

```
PageTop[10.0.2.75.1]: <H1>Traffic Analysis for Ethernet0</H1>
```

the output on the report will be as follows:

```
The Graphics Lab Network
Traffic Analysis for Ethernet0
```

Whenever `MRTG` encounters a **target** entry, it adds the string `The Graphics Lab Network` to the beginning of each **target** command.

When the **$** character is used instead of the ^, the string that follows is appended to any additional keyword. Thus, given

```
PageTop[$]: <H1> <A HREF="mailto:lisa_ellen@think-
tech.com">Lisa Ellen/A></H1>
```

the above Email link will appear at the end of any **PageTop** entries. Using the example above, the output on the report will be as follows:

```
Traffic Analysis for Ethernet0
Lisa Ellen
```

If you want to replace an existing added value, simply refine it:

```
PageTop[^]: <H1>The Graphics Lab Network</H1>
PageTop[10.0.2.75.1]: <H1>Traffic Analysis for Ethernet0</H1>
```

```
PageTop[^]: <H1>The Engineering Lab</H1>
PageTop[10.0.2.100.1]: <H1>Traffic Analysis for ATM1</H1>
```

In this output, the second instance of **PageTop[^]** overwrites the first and will be used throughout the entire configuration file unless additional **PageTop[^]** keywords are encountered.

Also, previously defined values with ^ and $ can be reset to null, or *unset*, simply by using the characters without any string definitions. Thus,

```
PageTop[^]:
PageTop[$]:
```

resets the keywords to the default state of no value.

The _ character is used with MRTG keywords and specifies a default value for that keyword. In the absence of an explicit keyword value, or the added value, the default will be used, as in the following example:

```
Target[10.0.2.75.1]: 1:public@10.0.2.75
```

The **Target** definition with the label 10.0.2.75.1 can be replicated without the need to use the label string. So,

```
MaxBytes[_]: 1249991
Title[_]: remote-gw (): Ethernet0
Options[_]: growright
PageTop[_]: <H1>Traffic Analysis for Ethernet0</H1>
```

are all valid MRTG entries—because the underscore points back to the 10.0.2.75.1 label.

To reset the underscore, specify an empty value:

```
Options[_]:
```

Master Index

MRTG can be thought of as being *interface-centric*. This means that its main focus is on the interface of the devices being monitored. If MRTG is used to monitor a Cisco router with five interfaces, five separate MRTG reports will be created. Unfortunately, although this structure is sufficient for a small number of interfaces, it becomes difficult to use and manage when faced with a large number of interfaces or the combination of many devices and interfaces. To assist with this task, a script called indexmaker, which produces an index of all the monitored devices and interfaces, has been provided in the MRTG distribution. This script can be found in the `/usr/lib/mrtg` directory. The syntax of `indexmaker` is as follows:

```
indexmaker label config result_file
```

This command supports a number of command-line arguments. Table 9.5 shows many of the more important ones. At a minimum, three arguments are required: the MRTG configuration file, the graph label, and the regular expression that includes all the monitored interfaces that should be added to the index. Because **indexmaker** writes to standard out, the output should be redirected to a file. Thus, the sample command

```
# indexmaker -t 'Summary of Interfaces' *.conf > backbone.html
```

builds a master interface index for all the interfaces contained within the `10.0.2.75` device using the file `backbone.html`.

Table 9.5 indexmaker *command-line arguments*

Option	Description
`-1`	Builds a one-column Web page. Graphs will be stacked on top of one another
`-2`	Builds a two-column Web page. Graphs are placed side-by-side instead of on top of each other. This is the default mode
`-b`	Sets the background color. The default is white (or no color). The value must be specified in hexadecimal format. For example, `#ffffff` is the code for black
`-r`	Uses the specified regular expression to match target interfaces. The default is ".".
`-t`	Sets the `title` of the index page. The default value is `All targets`
`-P`	Sets to parse **PageTop** tags for the graphic name in the index page. This is the default

Table 9.5 **indexmaker** *command-line arguments (continued)*

Option	Description
-p	Doesn't set to parse **PageTop** tags for the graphic name in the index page
-H	Sets the use of <HR> tags between graphics. This is the default
-h	Doesn't set the use of <HR> tags between graphics
-S	Sorts the graphs in alphabetic order. This is the default sort order
-s	Doesn't sort the graphs. They will appear in the same order as found in the configuration file
-N	Adds a sequence number to the beginning of each graph
-n	Does not number graphs. This is the default
-X	Specifies the width for each graph. The default value is 500
-Y	Specifies the height for each graph. The default value is 135
-A	Includes arguments as comments within HTML code
-a	Doesn't include arguments as comments
-G	Adds graphs to the index pages. This is enabled by default
-g	Doesn't add any graphs to the index pages

The indexmaker program can be found in the /usr/lib/mrtg directory. The new file, when displayed, should look similar to the window shown in Figure 9.5. It shows the daily graph for each interface and contains a link to each of the defined pages, which contain the remaining graphs for that interface.

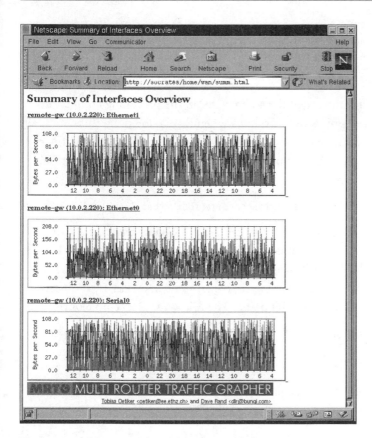

Figure 9.5 *Master index of monitored devices.*

Monitoring Additional Information

MRTG can be used to monitor other information—including additional SNMP objects and non-SNMP information—using the **target** command. The **target** command accepts additional input formats which can be used to monitor and graph information. These formats include direct OID strings, SNMP-abbreviated objects, and custom commands. The direct OID format uses Object Identifier (OID) strings, expressed in fully qualified dotted decimal notation, that specify which object should be monitored by MRTG. *Fully qualified* indicates that the entire path from the root to the object has been supplied. For example, to monitor ifInErrors and ifOutErrors from the device 10.0.2.200, use the following command:

```
Target [10.0.2.200.1]:1.3.6.1.2.1.2.2.1.14.1&1.3.6.1.2.1.2.2.1.20.1\
:public@10.0.2.200
```

This command retrieves both input and output error counts on the interface known as 1.

Notice the use of the **&** character in the preceding command. MRTG requires two variables when displaying data; this character is used as a separator. Alternatively, one could use the SNMP-abbreviated object names instead of the direct OID convention. Thus, the command

```
Target[10.0.2.200.1]:ifInErrors.1&ifOutErrors.1:public@10.0.2.200
```

is functionally equivalent to the previous **Target** command. MRTG knows a limited number of SNMP objects; the list of objects can be expanded by modifying and adding objects to the mibhelp.txt file. This file contains mappings between some SNMP MIB-II objects and fully qualified OID paths. The following is a sample of this file:

```
Descriptor:            ifInErrors
Identifier:            1.3.6.1.2.1.2.2.1.14
ASN.1 Syntax:          Counter32

The number of inbound packets that contained
errors preventing them from being deliverable to a
higher-layer protocol.
```

This file sample shows the ifInErrors object used in the preceding **Target** command and contains a descriptor, identifier, and ASN.1 syntax of the object. The descriptor names the object that MRTG will use and is associated with the identifier string; it can be any string name as long as it is unique within the mibhelp.txt file. The identifier is the fully qualified path name of the object, minus the instance. The ASN.1 syntax refers to the object type and should match the object definition found within the MIB that defines the object. Finally, the entry contains descriptive text that explains the object definition. Although this text isn't required, it is very useful, and its inclusion is recommended when additional objects are added to this file.

Table 9.6 lists SNMP objects that are predefined within the mibhelp.txt file. Consult Chapter 6, "Overview of MIB-II," for additional information about these MIB-II objects.

Table 9.6 *Predefined SNMP* MRTG *objects*

SNMP Object	Object Information
ifOperStatus	Current operational state of the interface
ifAdminStatus	Current administrative state of the interface
ifInOctets	Total number of octets received on the interface, including framing characters
ifInUcastPkts	Number of subnetwork-unicast packets delivered to a higher-layer protocol
ifInNUcastPkts	Number of non-unicast (i.e., subnetwork-broadcast or subnetwork-multicast) packets delivered to a higher-layer protocol
ifInDiscards	Number of inbound packets that were chosen to be discarded
ifInErrors	Number of inbound packets that contained errors preventing them from being delivered to a higher-layer protocol
ifInUnknownProtos	Number of packets received via the interface that were discarded because of an unknown or unsupported protocol
ifOutOctets	Total number of octets transmitted out of the interface, including framing characters
ifOutUcastPkts	Total number of packets that higher-level protocols requested to be transmitted to a subnetwork-unicast address, including those that were discarded or not sent
ifOutNUcast-Pkts	Total number of packets that higher-level protocols requested to be transmitted to a non-unicast (i.e., a subnetwork-broadcast or subnetwork-multicast) address

Table 9.6 *Predefined SNMP* MRTG *objects (continued)*

SNMP Object	Object Information
ifOutDiscards	Number of outbound packets that were chosen to be discarded even though no errors had been detected to prevent their being transmitted
ifOutErrors	Number of outbound packets that could not be transmitted because of errors
ifOutQLen	Length of the output packet queue (in packets)

MRTG supports mathematical operations on the SNMP objects or OID strings. These operators could be used, for example, to group the total number of input errors and output errors for a collection of interfaces instead of just a single interface. Thus,

```
Target[monet]: ifInErrors.0:public@10.0.2.75+ifInErrors.1:public@10.0.2.75
&ifOutErrors.0:public@10.0.2.75+ifOutErrors.1:public@10.0.2.75
```

computes the sum of interface errors for both the first and second interfaces found on the device 10.0.2.75.

Monitoring Disk Space

MRTG also supports the collection of data from custom programs or scripts. For example, MRTG can display disk space usage information. Using the df2mrtg script, available in the contributed software directory, MRTG monitors individual disk partitions and provides disk usage and size information. The following command shows this task:

```
Target[monet]: `/usr/mrtg/bin/df2mrtg -u /dev/hdb2`
```

Placing this line and some additional options in an MRTG configuration file produces, the graph shown in Figure 9.6. Table 9.6 shows that having the ability to collect information from other sources is a very powerful feature of MRTG. As you can see in the figure, the daily graph shows the disk space operating at approximately 120 MB; then at roughly 6:00 P.M. (1800 hours) the disk space plummeted close to zero. This continued for four hours until additional disk space was freed after 10:00 P.M. the same evening to over 180 MB. The monthly graph records the same event, but actual data is compressed into a smaller scale. Therefore, the four-hour window of having no disk space is just a short drop in this graph. These graphs make it very easy to pinpoint disk consummation down to the day and hour and will greatly aid in determining why the event occured in the first place.

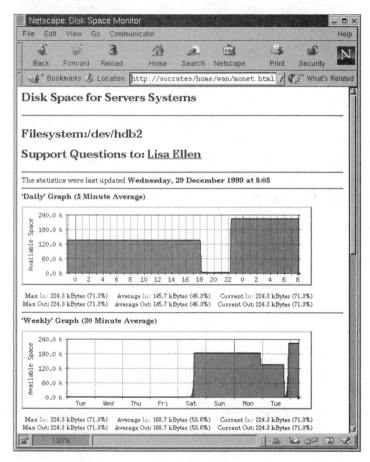

Figure 9.6 *MRTG report on disk space.*

If you are interested in developing custom programs to monitor non-SNMP information, the data returned from the program must be in a format that MRTG understands. Therefore, a program must return four lines of output that include the present state of the first variable, the present state of the second variable, a string indicating the system uptime of the target, and a string indicating the name of the target.

The first two variables are comparable to, for example, incoming bytes per second and outgoing bytes per second. The system update time is indicative of when the system was last rebooted (or when the network management component—the agent—was last restarted). To ensure that the script output is matched with a target, the target name is returned.

In the case of the `df2mrtg` script, the first variable represents the currently used disk space in kilobytes (when the `-u` option is used), and the second variable is a repeat of the first. Because we are only interested in monitoring disk space, the system uptime information and the string representing the target are not needed. Also, depending on the type of data returned with the script, you might need to use the **Options** keyword with either `gauge` or `absolute`, as appropriate. This script also reports other information regarding the disk partitions of the local system. Table 9.7 lists the command-line options.

Table 9.7 df2mrtg *script command-line options*

Option	Description
`-f`	Reports free disk space in the partition
`-s`	Reports the total size of the disk partition
`-p`	Reports free disk space as a percent
`-u`	Reports used disk space

If you want MRTG to graph the free disk space on a partition, use the `-f` option. The `-s` option will report the total size of the partition.

Because MRTG is used to monitor network interfaces, some of the default values and configuration information should be changed when it is used to monitor disk space or other system information. Listed here is the MRTG configuration that closely matches what is appropriate when the `df2mrtg` script is used.

```
Title[monet]: Disk Space Monitor
PageTop[monet]: <H1>Disk Space Usage for System:Monet
```

```
Options[monet]: gauge,growright
MaxBytes[monet]: 314461
AbsMax[monet]: 400000
WithPeak[monet]: ymwd
YLegend[monet]: Available Space
ShortLegend[monet]: Bytes
Legend1[monet]: Current Disk Utilization.
```

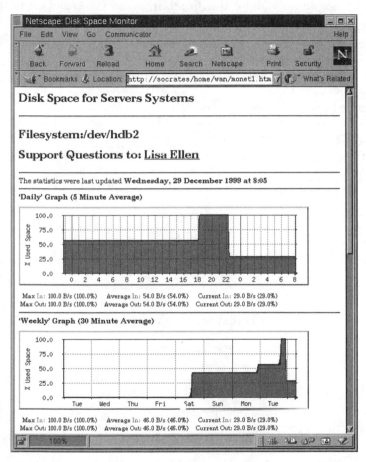

Figure 9.7 *MRTG report on disk usage by percent.*

Because of the flexibility of MRTG and the df2mrtg script, instead of reporting available disk space, we could report percent of disk space available. This is perhaps a better measurement because, by displaying the percent utilization, we can obtain a quick status of the condition of the available disk space without doing any math. Figure 9.7 shows the same partition, but uses the -p option of the script to report on disk percent. As you can see, this graph shows the same information as Figure 9.6, but displaying this information as a percentage is more meaningful and easier to read.

Contributed Components for MRTG

Several modules have been included in the MRTG package to provide support for additional customization of MRTG and monitoring of additional services and devices. Table 9.8 provides a list of these modules found in the /usr/lib/mrtg/contrib directory.

Table 9.8 *Contributed modules for MRTG*

Module Name	Description
ascendget	Provides modem information from Ascend's remote access device
atmmaker	Builds MRTG configuration files for ATM devices
cpumon	Monitors CPU usage from a UNIX system
distrib	Builds network traffic distribution graphs given MRTG log files
get-active	Produces a report of the most active interfaces that are monitored by MRTG
get-multiserial	Monitors dial-in modems on a local UNIX system
GetSNMPLinesUP	Queries SNMP devices for specific objects and returns values to MRTG
ircstats	Collects information on active IRC clients
mrtg-archiver	Archives the MRTG report GIFs given a list of device targets
mrtg-blast	Incorporates tcp-blast output in MRTG
mrtg-dynip	Enables MRTG to monitor dynamic network interfaces

Table 9.8 *Contributed modules for MRTG (continued)*

Module Name	Description
`mrtg-ipget`	Enables MRTG to monitor interfaces expressed with IP addresses instead of instances
`mrtg-mail`	Monitors mail statistics
`mrtgidx`	Generates an MRTG index of monitored devices
`mrtgindex.cgi`	Generates an MRTG index of monitored devices (an improved script)
`ping-probe`	Displays round-trip performance information using **ping**
`portmasters`	Displays modem information from Livingston Portmaster devices
`rdlog2`	Produces traffic displays of devices monitored by MRTG
`rumb-stat`	Obtains low-level statistics from Web servers such as Apache
`TCH`	Monitors modem utilization of USR Total Control modem racks
`xlsummary`	Extracts summary information from the MRTG log files and produces Excel charts

Installation and operation of these tools is found in the directory bearing the same (or similar) name as the script name.

Troubleshooting MRTG Problems

Because the MRTG configuration file consists of plain text, it is relatively simple to introduce syntax errors or other errors into this file during customization. Also, other conditions might exist that produce errors when executing other MRTG programs. Here are some of the most common runtime and configuration problems and proposed solutions.

Error Message/Problem:

```
Rateup WARNING: .//rateup could not read the primary log file for
    10.0.2.50.1
Rateup WARNING: .//rateup The backup log file for 10.0.2.50.1 was
    invalid as well
Rateup WARNING: .//rateup Can't remove 10.0.2.50.1.old updating log
    file.
```

Solution

Don't worry about these errors. They occur once in while but don't pose any serious problem and can be ignored. Unfortuately, there's no way to disable the generation of these messages.

Error Message/Problem:

```
No answer from community@device. You may be using the wrong community
```

Solution

MRTG is having trouble polling a device with the SNMP community string specified in the configuration file. Check to ensure that the correct community string is being used for the device(s) having the problem. Also, make sure the device(s) can be polled from the network using another SNMP tool like snmpget or snmp-walk.

Error Message/Problem:

```
./mrtg rmon
ERROR: I guess another mrtg is running. A lockfile (rmon_l) aged
264 seconds is hanging around. If you are sure that no other mrtg
is running you can remove the lockfile.
```

Solution

MRTG detected a lock file, which indicates that another copy of MRTG is presently running or ran in the past and failed to remove the lock file. Use the **ps** command to ensure that no additional MRTG process is running. If no additional process is running, remove the lock file.

Error Message/Problem:

```
ERROR: I can't find a "target[10.0.2.50.1]" definition
```

Solution

MRTG reports that the **target** keyword command is missing from the configuration file. Add the correct entry in the configuration file.

Error Message/Problem:

```
ERROR: "WorkDir" not specified
ABORT: Please fix the error(s) in your config file
```

Solution

The **WorkDir** command has not been included in the configuration file that was specified with the **mrtg** command. Because this keyword is not optional, MRTG aborts without this definition.

Error Message/Problem:

```
Bareword found where operator expected at (eval 13) line 1, near "1public"
(Missing operator before public?)
Bareword "public" not allowed while "strict subs" in use at (eval 13) line
1. Array found where operator expected at (eval 13) line 1, at end of line
* Problem with '1public@10.0.2.50': syntax error at (eval 13) line 1, near
"1public"
```

Solution

A syntax error was detected in the MRTG configuration file. Check the line indicated within the error message for a missing colon or other syntax errors.

```
Target[10.0.2.50.1]:1public@10.0.2.50
```

Error Message/Problem:

```
SNMP Error:
no response received
SNMPv1_Session (remote host: "10.0.2.200" [10.0.2.200].161
                  community: "public"
                 request ID: 472779887
                 PDU bufsize: 8000 bytes
                    timeout: 2s
                    retries: 5
                    backoff: 1)
SNMPGET: Failed to reach target: "1:public@10.0.2.200". I
tried multiple times!
```

Solution

This error indicates that the device didn't respond to SNMP requests. Check to ensure that the device is alive on the network and the SNMP agent is responding.

Ntop Tool

The ntop program provides a way to determine the systems that are active on a network and the types of traffic sent and received by these systems. Network traffic is sorted by protocol, and some of the most common network protocols are recognized, including TCP/IP and associated protocols. This tool also supports non-IP protocol types such as Decnet, IPX, AppleTalk, and others. Recall the use of ethereal to capture and inspect individual network packets in Chapter 5, "Additional System Utilities and Tools." This tool differs significantly from the tcpdump or ethereal utilities in that it concentrates on providing statistical data about network packets, not their contents. Also, **ntop** doesn't require the use of a Web server; it supports the HTTP protocol internally.

Why use **ntop**? First, it provides a quick and easy way to get an accurate snapshot of network activity without using a network probe or sniffer device. In many cases, a dedicated probe is necessary to track down network problems. In certain situations, however, time is of the essence and **ntop** can be used when it is not possible to obtain a probe quickly because it is deployed and monitoring another network. Second, it might not be possible to attach a probe given certain network configurations, say between a pair of UNIX systems interconnected via a WAN. In this situation, using **ntop** when deploying a probe might be very difficult, if not impossible. Third, where cost is a major consideration, purchasing probes will be far more expensive than installing a public domain software tool.

On the negative side, there is no such thing as a free lunch! Running **ntop** across a number of systems does pose some problems. First, **ntop** places the interface in promiscuous mode, which means that every network packet is being captured, and, as a result, a significant processing load is placed on the system. To address this issue, care should be taken when running **ntop**. Setting up some automated mechanism may remedy any potential problems by ensuring that **ntop** is only run when necessary and, perhaps, not during critical times or peak system usage.

Secondly, using **ntop** may further complicate security policies and procedures because unauthorized access to this tool could result in additional exposure of existing system vulnerabilities and security holes. Don't get the wrong idea about the **ntop** tool; it doesn't introduce any new security problems or vulnerabilities into existing systems. Rather, it provides additional information on any system installed on the network. Luckily, **ntop** has a rudimentary facility to protect the captured network information. It isn't the most rigorous security available, but it provides a reasonable amount of control. This will be discussed further later.

Thirdly, **ntop** doesn't support every networking protocol known to man. In fact, for a public domain tool, its coverage is impressive. It provides a useful set of the protocols prevalent on most networks today. These include IP, IPX, NetBIOS, and Decnet. It also provides higher-level TCP/IP protocols such as FTP, HTTP, DNS, Telnet, and others.

One of the most powerful features of **ntop** is that it provides two viewing modes: Web mode and basic ASCII terminal mode. This is a very unique feature, and **ntop** is one of the first public domain tools that successfully implements multiple robust interface capabilities. However, the most interesting features are found using the Web interface.

In the Web mode, a series of HTML pages are available that provide a number of network traffic statistics reports and additional network-related information. In this mode, a standard Web browser is needed to view these reports and to support multiple simultaneous browser connections. This is a very handy feature when using **ntop** in a distributed network environment where access may originate from more than one location by different users at the same time. When a browser is connected to **ntop**, the main page shown in Figure 9.8 is displayed.

Using Web Mode

To start **ntop** in Web mode, use the -w option followed by a port number. This is the port that the client Web browsers will use to

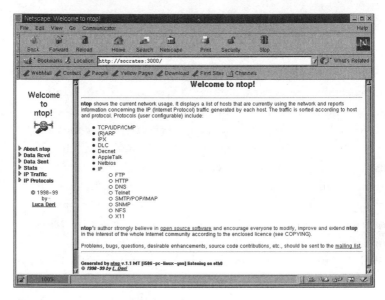

Figure 9.8 *Main ntop Web page.*

connect to the **ntop** program. Thus, to start **ntop** on port 3000, issue the following command:

```
# ntop -w 3000
```

After the tool has started, it displays the following output:

```
ntop v.1.1 MT [i586-pc-linux-gnu] listening on eth0.
Copyright 1998-99 by Luca Deri <deri@unipi.it>
Warning: unable to read file '.ntop'. No security will be used!
Waiting for HTTP connections on port 3000...
```

ntop displays which interface it is using when more than one is installed on the system, and it confirms the specified port used for incoming connections by browser clients. Also, it warns that it was unable to read the security file and, as a result, no security will be used. In this case, any client browser may connect to **ntop** and view the reports. Securing the reports will be covered later.

With Web mode, the main page is divided into two separate frames, as shown in Figure 9.8. The frame on the left-hand side provides a list of report categories that the user may select, while the frame on the right displays a network traffic report. The categories include *About ntop, Data Rcvd, Data Sent, Stats, IP Traffic,* and *IP Protocols.* Each of these contain one or more selectable elements (or reports) that provide detailed information associated with the specified category. The user must click on a category using the left mouse button to expose the elements contained within that category. Each of the important categories (and subsequent reports) are described more fully below.

The screen shots used throughout this section have been taken directly from a Netscape browser while using the **ntop** application. It was felt that actual output integrity (which is a major theme throughout this book) must be maintained at all costs. However, each of the reports was first saved to a new HTML frame. This resulted in new windows being created to display the reports. With Netscape, right-clicking produces a small menu, and one of the menu items provides the ability to save each report using a new frame. The major reason for doing this is so that each report may be contained within a single window. Unfortunately, it's a double-edged sword. When new frames are created, the left panel is removed. As a result, the tree view of each report is not displayed along with each associated report. Also, some of the reports are sigificantly larger than the maximum browser window size and must be displayed in two different frames.

Data-received Category

This grouping of reports shows the actual network traffic statistics for incoming data for all network devices local to the system running the **ntop** tool. The reports include the following:

- All Protocols Report

- IP Report

- Throughput Report

- Network Flows Report

All Protocols Report

This report shows network traffic that was received by the listed network hosts, sorted by network node or network protocol type. This report displays a long table, as shown in Figure 9.9. The figure shows the active hosts, the amount of received data in kilobytes, the percent of network traffic received by each system, and the amount of network traffic broken down by each protocol type. The protocol listed represents the most active on the network. To change the default sort order, simply click on one of the title names. This will force the table to be redrawn based on the new selection.

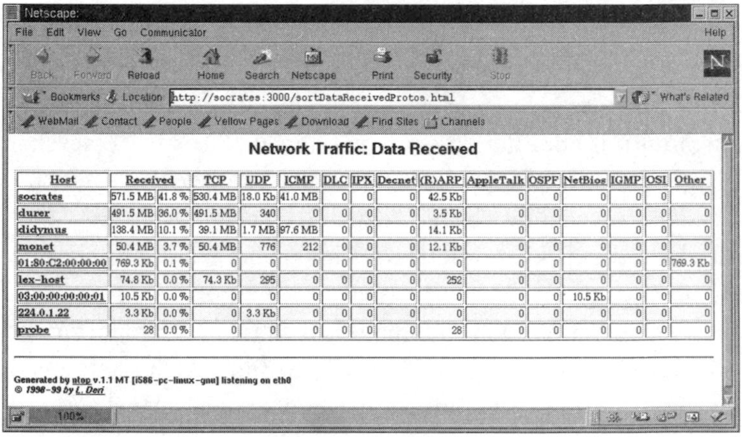

Host	Received		TCP	UDP	ICMP	DLC	IPX	Decnet	(R)ARP	AppleTalk	OSPF	NetBios	IGMP	OSI	Other
socrates	571.5 MB	41.8 %	530.4 MB	18.0 Kb	41.0 MB	0	0	0	42.5 Kb	0	0	0	0	0	0
durer	491.5 MB	36.0 %	491.5 MB	340	0	0	0	0	3.5 Kb	0	0	0	0	0	0
didymus	138.4 MB	10.1 %	39.1 MB	1.7 MB	97.6 MB	0	0	0	14.1 Kb	0	0	0	0	0	0
monet	50.4 MB	3.7 %	50.4 MB	776	212	0	0	0	12.1 Kb	0	0	0	0	0	0
01:80:C2:00:00:00	769.3 Kb	0.1 %	0	0	0	0	0	0	0	0	0	0	0	0	769.3 Kb
lex-host	74.8 Kb	0.0 %	74.3 Kb	295	0	0	0	0	252	0	0	0	0	0	0
03:00:00:00:00:01	10.5 Kb	0.0 %	0	0	0	0	0	0	0	0	0	10.5 Kb	0	0	0
224.0.1.22	3.3 Kb	0.0 %	0	3.3 Kb	0	0	0	0	0	0	0	0	0	0	0
probe	28	0.0 %	0	0	0	0	0	0	28	0	0	0	0	0	0

Figure 9.9 *All protocols report.*

In this example, several hosts have been identified, including `socrates`, `durer`, `rembrandt`, and `224.0.1.22`. These are the active systems presently receiving traffic on the network. However, in the case of `224.0.1.22`, this represents a multicast group, and other systems on the network periodically send traffic to this address. If multicast is enabled on the network, other multicast addresses may be displayed in other **ntop** reports. Also, **ntop** provides a multicast specific report that is discussed later.

This report shows the total amount of received traffic in the second column, expressed in bytes, kilobytes (`KB`), megabytes (`MB`) or gigabytes (`GB`). Also, the received column shows the amount of traffic that each host received, as a percent. In this report, of the listed systems, `socrates` was the recipient of the largest amount of traffic, which represents `41.8%` of the total traffic obtained on the network. The remaining set of columns shows the amount of received traffic based on each of the network protocols supported by **ntop**. The third and fourth columns show the total amount of data that were either `TCP` or `UDP` packets. In this case, `TCP` accounted for the lion's share of traffic.

IP Report

This report uses the same format as the IP Protocols reports, but further defines the TCP/IP protocols that were recorded to include higher-level application functions such as file transfer, remote access, and Web access. Figure 9.10 shows this report.

The columns include total data received by protocols such as FTP, Telnet, HTTP, and others. Although this report contains only a small number of hosts, from a network performance standpoint it provides some very useful information. We can surmise that the FTP protocol is used more than any other protocol listed. This was determined by comparing the total FTP traffic with all other protocols.

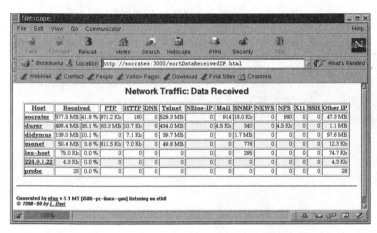

Figure 9.10 *IP report.*

Throughput Report

Figure 9.11 displays this report, which represents a great way to determine actual performance (throughput) of the individual devices on the network. Throughput is defined as the number of network traffic bytes sent over a specified period of time. This report provides three columns: Actual Thpt, Average Thpt, and Peak Thpt. The Actual Thpt column shows the throughput of each system over the last three seconds. Actually, there is a small delay between when the graphic data was collected and displayed and when the browser was last updated. Therefore, the results are a few minutes old and are not completely real-time. The Average Thpt column shows the performance of each system averaged over the period of time that **ntop** was running. Finally, the `Peak Thpt` column represents any spikes in the traffic patterns. By default, the table is sorted by `Actual Thpt` column.

As you can see in the table, the host `socrates` had a large peak of `289.7Kpbs`, but the average was much smaller. When measuring or determining network performance, it is better to take the peak performance numbers with a small grain of salt and consider other factors. That is, the peaks only show how much of the network was used at the highest point during the time the network was being monitored. It is best to also consider the averages because they represent the true nature of the utilization of the network over a longer period of time. The peaks are temporary and fluctuate considerably, while averages reflect more normative behavior.

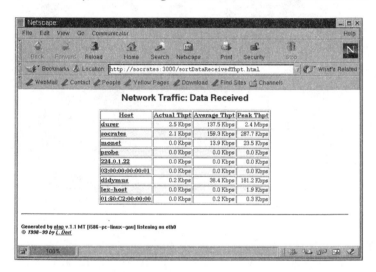

Figure 9.11 *Throughput report.*

Network Flows Report

One very interesting feature of **ntop** is its ability to define custom network flows (i.e., filters) and display the results. Basically, a flow is a filter expression (such as those discussed in Chapter 4, "Core System Utilities and Tools," with `tcpdump`) that is specified on the command line using the `-F` option. For instance, the command:

```
# ntop -F "servermonitor='host durer',session='host socrates\
and monet'" -w 3000
```

defines two different flows. The first filters traffic if either the source or destination address is equal to `durer`. The other captures traffic that goes between `socrates` and `monet`. The names of the flows are simple strings and may contain normal ASCII string characters. Executing this command will display the report shown in Figure 9.12. The figure shows both flows and includes total packet counts and the total number of bytes transmitted or received. Any number of flows may be created, and **ntop** supports many of the filter expression keywords and the syntax supported by `tcpdump` and `ethereal`. These were presented in Chapter 4, "Core System Utilities and Tools," and Chapter 5, "Additional System Utilities and Tools," respectively. Clearly, flows provide a powerful way to provide performance monitoring. The section entitled "Setting Up Flows" discusses creating flows.

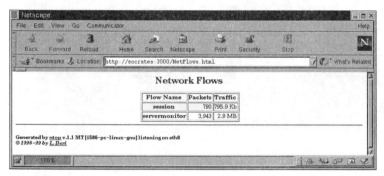

Figure 9.12 *Network flows report.*

Data-sent Category

These reports show the actual network traffic statistics for outgoing data for all network devices local to the system running the **ntop** tool. The reports include the following:

- All Protocols Report

- IP Report

- Throughput Report

All Protocols Report

This report, shown in Figure 9.13, shows the hosts that transmitted traffic on the network. The format of this report is the same as that of the received report, except that this report contains a `Sent` column instead of a `Received` column. This report is useful for tracking down hosts that generate or receive significant numbers of packets. In some cases, this could represent a normal situation reflecting true traffic patterns; on the other hand, it could indicate some type of trouble. It could provide evidence of a misconfigured device or some other undesirable activity. For example, it is interesting to note that the host `durer` transmitted a certain number of `IPX` packets on the network. Regardless of the fact that only a relatively small amount of data was sent using this protocol, this could be a reason to suspect a problem because the network monitored should only contain IP-based traffic. Actually, it is common to have some PC systems transmitting protocols such as `IPX` and `NetBios`, even though the service that uses these protocols is not being used. Further, the number of ICMP packets seems rather high. This could indicate that a large number of ping (or other ICMP messages) requests are flooding the network.

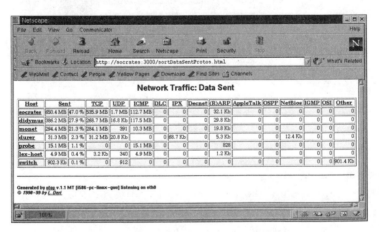

Figure 9.13 *All protocols report.*

IP Report

This resembles the IP Report from the `Data Recd` category discussed in the previous report section. It is interesting to note that in this table, the TCP/IP base activity shows that `Telnet` represents the lion's share of 494.6 megabytes of data transmitted, with `FTP` coming in a distant second with only 40.3 megabytes. Figure 9.14 shows a sample report. These types of reports can come in handy when it becomes necessary to establish which applications are used most. For many companies, HTTP or Web access may be the most significant traffic generator. As you can see, it is very easy to determine which applications are being used the most. If a non-standard protocol is used on the network, but **ntop** doesn't support it directly, it is still possible to add a specific protocol filter and monitor the protocol activity with a flow. Consult the previous report section on how to set up flows.

Network Traffic: Data Sent

Host	Sent		FTP	HTTP	DNS	Telnet	NBios-IP	Mail	SNMP	NEWS	NFS	X11	SSH	Other IP
socrates	650.5 MB	47.0 %	40.3 MB	222	0	494.6 MB	0	4.5 Kb	1.7 MB	0	4.5 Kb	0	0	113.9 MB
didymus	386.5 MB	27.9 %	0	5.4 Kb	0	268.9 MB	0	0	16.8 Kb	0	0	0	0	117.6 MB
monet	294.4 MB	21.3 %	23.0 MB	5.4 Kb	0	261.1 MB	0	0	391	0	0	0	0	10.3 MB
durer	31.3 MB	2.3 %	1.5 MB	13.9 Kb	0	29.4 MB	16.2 Kb	914	295	0	980	0	0	395.9 Kb
probe	15.2 MB	1.1 %	0	0	0	0	0	0	0	0	0	0	0	15.2 MB
lex-host	5.0 MB	0.4 %	0	0	0	0	0	0	340	0	0	0	0	5.0 MB
switch	906.0 Kb	0.1 %	0	0	0	0	0	0	912	0	0	0	0	905.1 Kb

Generated by ntop v.1.1 MT [i586-pc-linux-gnu] listening on eth0
© 1998–99 by L. Deri

Figure 9.14 *IP report.*

Throughput Report

The *data-sent* throughput report has the same format as the *data-received* throughput report. However, this report can speak volumes when it comes to really knowing what is going on in a network. The transmission of traffic can identify the pulse of the network much more so than the received data information. This is true because, when measuring received data, information can come from sources other than the local network. This too is an important performance metric, but having the ability to identify the *heavy hitters* or *power users* on the network is profound.

Consider the table in Figure 9.15, where the host socrates was responsible for a significant amount of the traffic on the network. Note that it had a large spike sometime during the monitoring period. It is also important to note that current Actual Thpt dropped considerably. This is a good thing. If the peak levels had been sustained for a greater period of time, a more in-depth examination of the possible causes would need to be done. Also, it isn't a huge surprise that `socrates` was able to transmit the peak shown. With many powerful workstations and servers, it is a relatively simple matter to exceed network limitations, particularly with high-end systems that contain multiple CPUs. In this example, assume the network was a normal 10 Mbps Ethernet. In this case, `socrates` consumed approximately 25% of the network. However, if we are talking about Fast Ethernet (100 Mbps), only 2.5% of the network was used.

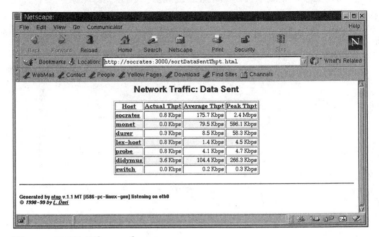

Figure 9.15 *Throughput report.*

Statistics Category

These reports show both overall traffic statistics and other important information regarding the hosts on the network. This category contains the following reports:

- Multicast Statistics Report

- Traffic Statistics Report

- Hosts Report

- Throughput Report

Multicast Statistics Report

This report shows all the multicast packet activity on the network. With multicast, special IP addresses (such as 224.0.0.1) are defined, and systems that provide multicast services, such as Internet TV, will transmit data using these special addresses. Also, information about which devices belong to which multicast groups is also propagated using a standard multicast address. The Multicast Report reveals which hosts are transmitting multicast information. Certain systems, such as Sun workstations and servers, will continue to poll specific multicast addresses to determine if any multicast groups are defined. As a result, these systems will generate traffic despite the fact that no multicast applications are active on those systems.

Generally speaking, to support multicast, the network infrastructure must be configured to support multicast groups propagating and forwarding multicast traffic. If the network isn't configured to specifically support multicast and the reports indicate a significant amount of traffic, then investigation is warranted. If multicast has been set up, it will be important to determine that multicast traffic is directed to only those networks and systems that desire this information. In practice, this is usually automatic because the activation of multicast routing handles many of the details necessary to ensure that multicast packets are forwarded correctly. However, configuration errors or other problems can lead to a network being flooded with unwanted multicast information. In this case, use the Multicast Report to track these down.

Figure 9.16 shows a snapshot of a rather large switched network that contains many systems. The table includes many devices that have transmitted small amounts of multicast traffic. However, a few systems have sent much more. One example is the `cisco-gw2` device. This is the default local router that the system **ntop** was running on, and it has transmitted a significant amount of traffic, as shown in the figure. The only problem is that no workstations on the subnet have been set up to support multicast. As a result, either a workstation on the local network has requested multicast traffic or the router is misconfigured. You may ask, "Why do I see so many devices in the report?" The answer lies in the fact that when a packet is sent using one of the multicast addresses, this information is transmitted across the network to all subnetworks (subnets) that have been configured (or misconfigured) to forward this information. As a result, the report shows all hosts that have transmitted data, regardless of their location within the network. In the case of

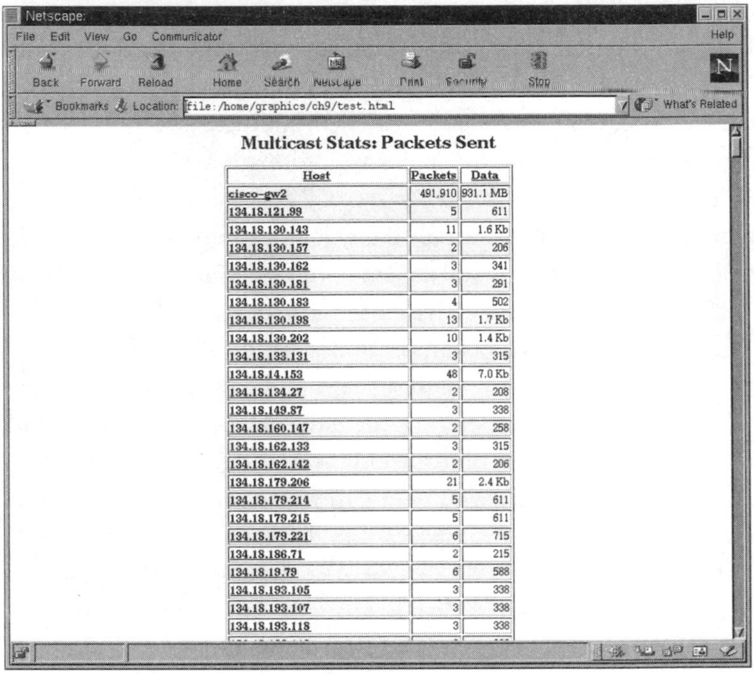

Host	Packets	Data
cisco-gw2	491,910	931.1 MB
134.18.121.99	5	611
134.18.130.143	11	1.6 Kb
134.18.130.157	2	206
134.18.130.162	3	341
134.18.130.181	3	291
134.18.130.183	4	502
134.18.130.198	13	1.7 Kb
134.18.130.202	10	1.4 Kb
134.18.133.131	3	315
134.18.14.153	48	7.0 Kb
134.18.134.27	2	208
134.18.149.87	3	338
134.18.160.147	2	258
134.18.162.133	3	315
134.18.162.142	2	206
134.18.179.206	21	2.4 Kb
134.18.179.214	5	611
134.18.179.215	5	611
134.18.179.221	6	715
134.18.186.71	2	215
134.18.19.79	6	588
134.18.193.105	3	338
134.18.193.107	3	338
134.18.193.118	3	338

Figure 9.16 *Multicast statistics report.*

UNIX hosts transmitting unwanted multicast information, the traffic can be blocked (not forwarded by the local routers) or disabled at the source by shutdown of one or more network services.

Traffic Statistics Report

The global Traffic Statistics Report contains interesting information related to the general performance of the network from a higher-level standpoint. This report contains two tables: the first (shown in Figure 9.17) shows global traffic information, while the other (shown in Figure 9.18) shows protocol distribution utilization.

In the first table, the first three rows contain generic information. With many UNIX systems today, having connections to multiple networks is quite common, and it is easy to monitor the wrong network. The `Nw Interface Type` field reveals which interface the **ntop** program is probing. As indicated previously, it is important to ensure that the correct network is being monitored. The table shows that the first interface, `eth0`, was used. The `Local Domain`

`Name` field shows the name of the domain for the system running **ntop**. Note that this is not a valid domain, but an example.

The `Sampling Time` field is very important as it shows the amount of time the **ntop** program has been active. It is important to remember that in order to gain the most accurate information about network performance, the network must be monitored for as long as possible. This isn't to say that a network should be monitored for a fixed period of time, but rather long enough to establish any common patterns of usage or other interesting or special events. For example, if a particular network task is scheduled once a week, and you want to capture the impact of this task on the network, then the network should be monitored both before and after the event has occurred. It is also important to monitor the network long enough to establish a baseline. The baseline is a measure that represents the normal behavior of the network and is compared to abnormal activity. For many networks, monitoring for a week or two should be adequate enough to determine the baseline. The table shows that **ntop** has been running for approximately 8.5 hours. This time period may be used to glance at the performance of the network, but a longer monitoring period is recommended.

The next section of the table shows some interesting details about the traffic collected. The `Total` statistic represents the total number of frames captured on the interface that **ntop** has been monitoring since it was started. The `Dropped by the kernel` field indicates frames that were dropped due to processing constraints from a UNIX standpoint. Sometimes the system (i.e., the UNIX kernel) will discard packets due to CPU limitations or other temporary limitations. The `Dropped by` **ntop** field shows the number of packets that were discarded by **ntop** due to problems with the packet. Either field may indicate that the system couldn't process the packets fast enough or that one or more filters (or flows) were defined which resulted in **ntop** not using the packet.

The next three rows display the three common packet address types recorded and their associated percentages. They include `Unicast`, `Broadcast`, and `Multicast`. The packet type will reveal to some degree how the network is being used. For example, if the majority of the traffic is multicast-based, then it could be concluded that multimedia applications are the primary source of net-

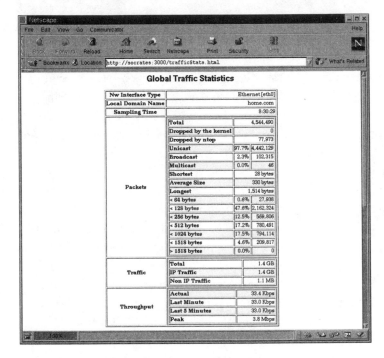

Figure 9.17 *First traffic statistics report.*

work traffic. However, it is important to examine the percentage
very closely. If a large percentage of traffic is either broadcast- or
multicast-based but no network applications have been deployed
to account for this, then a mystery needs to be solved. This is easy
because other **ntop** reports show this information. In general, networks should contain mostly unicast traffic. Unicast traffic is represented by one machine sending information to another. Again,
the network and deployment of applications will ultimately determine the traffic profile.

The remaining rows of the table profile the size of packets
recorded and shouldn't be overlooked. Several years ago, a large
corporation was deploying a new application that involved using a
graphical user interface and back-end database. As the application
was being installed at remote sites around the world, the development and support staff noticed serious performance problems
when using the new application. The problem: The application
was using very small packets between the application interface and
database. The problem was further compounded by the fact that

the network introduced a certain amount of latency for each packet. As a result, the application response time could be measured in minutes not seconds. The heart of the problem was that the application was using only a small fraction of the available network bandwidth. The solution in this case involved changing the application interface to request more information per packet. This ultimately solved the problem, but the behavior was discovered late in the development cycle, which caused application deployment delays and imposed additional development expenses.

The table in Figure 9.17 shows that 47% of the packets were less than 128 bytes each. Also, the running average was only 330 bytes. This is unfortunate because the maximum packet size supported by the network is greater than 1500 bytes. In many situations, the packet size used and the nature of many standard UNIX applications and services can't be altered very easily. Therefore, improvement with standard UNIX services will not be dramatic. On the other hand, custom application development groups should pay close attention to this information so they can detect network-related problems early in the software development life cycle.

One additional note: Within many WAN environments, the maximum packet size is generally smaller than what is available within most local LAN network technologies. This consideration must be examined as well.

The next section, `Traffic`, shows overall totals for network activity. The `Total Traffic` field indicates the total amount of data that was read from the interface. This is the sum of both IP-based and non-IP based network traffic. The `IP Traffic` field shows the total amount of IP traffic, which will include, for example, all upper-level protocols such as ICMP and TCP. The `Total non-IP Traffic` statistic includes protocols such as IPX, AppleTalk, and others. Thus, if we have a mixed network of both IP and AppleTalk protocols, this field would be non-zero and contain the AppleTalk traffic portion. Unfortunately, it appears that the application is inaccurate with respect to these totals because the `IP Traffic` and `non-IP Traffic` fields should equal the value displayed in the `Total` field.

The `Throughput` section measures the observed performance of the interface (packet reception); the previous report sections describe these statistics.

This report contains two additional tables, which are shown in Figure 9.18. The first table, titled `Global Protocol Distribution`, shows the total amount of data (kilobytes) that were sent and received by each major protocol family. For instance, the total amount of data for the `IP` protocol was 1.4Gb, while `IPX` had only 69.8Kb. The report provides an additional protocol breakdown of the `IP` category that includes `TCP`, `UDP`, and `ICMP` with associated protocol values. These values are also displayed to the right of the table in a bar chart format that reflects the percentage of each protocol from the `IP` total. Note that `TCP` represents 81.0% of the IP traffic, whereas `ICMP` represents 18.9%. The reason `UDP` is empty is because the value (from a percent standpoint) is less than one and couldn't be displayed given the scale of the graph. When viewed within the browser, the graph bars are a light blue color. In the associated figures, they appear as a light shade of gray.

The second table shows the total IP traffic sorted by different associated TCP/IP protocols. The first column shows the protocol type, and the second column shows the total amount of data for that protocol. The right side includes the visual representation of the data as a percent. The percentages visual shows the amount of traffic for each protocol. As you can see, the most active protocol was `Telnet`, followed by other non-specific `TCP/IP` protocols. Protocols and/or services that may fall in this category include `remote login`, `finger`, `DNS`, and the like.

Hosts Statistics Report

This report provides additional information pertaining to the hosts found on the network. It includes the following columns: `Host Name`, `IP Address`, `MAC Address`, `Sent Bandwidth`, and `Nw Board Vendor`. Figure 9.19 contains a sample of this report. If the IP address of a host cannot be mapped to a hostname, the `IP address` is used in the `Host Name` column. This is the reason why some of the entries contain both hostname and IP addresses. The IP address field is self-explanatory, and the `MAC Address` column (media access control) contains the hardware address of the host interface that sent/received network traffic. The `Sent Bandwidth` column provides a view of the sent bandwidth for each host on the network. This is

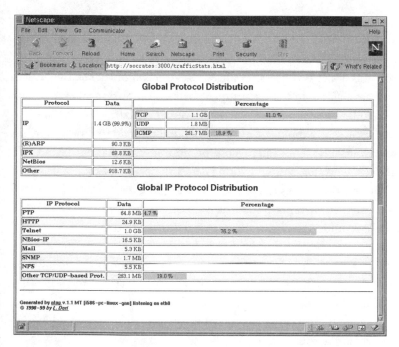

Figure 9.18 *Second traffic statistics report.*

calculated by using the sum of all the traffic sent (not received) to each host and plotting the associated values.

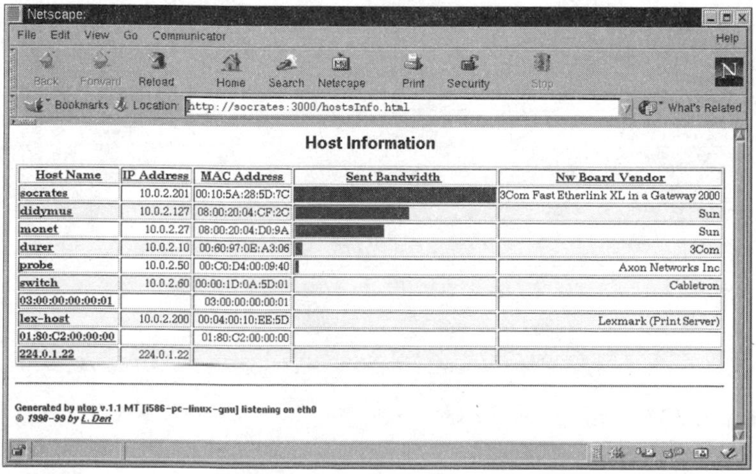

Figure 9.19 *Hosts report.*

The final column contains the vendor of the interface hardware, as derived from the first three bytes from the MAC Address field. Note that not all entries contain an interface vendor, and the 224.0.0.22 contains no MAC address at all. The reason is simple: The two hosts that have MAC addresses but no associated vendors, are server-related low-level addresses used to advertise specific services. The 224.0.0.22 is a multicast address that doesn't map to any specific vendor address, but rather to one or more specific standard MAC address. The **ntop** software didn't detect these addresses, however.

Notice the entries in the Host Name column are underlined. This is because these represent a link to another **ntop** report. The other titles are underlined as well, but for a different purpose. These are used to select the sort order for each column. The hostname (Info about) report provides additional information about the host and includes more detailed traffic information, IP history, and a list of contacted peer systems. Figure 9.20 shows this report for the host socrates. As you can see, some of the information presented in the report can be found in the Host Info report as well.

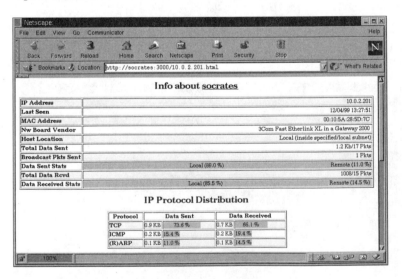

Figure 9.20 *Individual host report.*

The first three items were already discussed. The Host Location indicates that this host is contained within the subnet that **ntop** is monitoring. In other words, the interface that **ntop** is monitoring from is on the same network as the host. Why is this important? It helps to know if this host is local or remote from the perspective of **ntop,** so that the additional information **ntop** reports is interpreted correctly. For example, the Data Sent Stats field gives a graphical representation of the percentages of both local and remote traffic. This information can be used to determine traffic patterns across an internet. In the case of the report shown here, 100% of the traffic is local. If this situation, for example, had been reversed, and 100% of the traffic were remote, it might be necessary to move socrates to another remote network or limit access to this system from the remote location. Total Data Sent represents both the number of bytes and number of packets transmitted from socrates.

The Total Data Sent statistic is a combination of broadcast and multicast traffic expressed in both bytes and number of packets sent. This is a true measure of what this host transmitted on the network, regarding the final destination of the information. The Broadcast Pkts Sent statistic, as its name suggests, indicates the number of packets that used the broadcast address (255) to transmit packets. This includes both IP and datalink broadcast packets. These types of packets are used to send information to all local devices on the network. The Data Received Stats field indicates that all received traffic was local to the system.

The remaining tables include IP Service/Port Usage, IP Session History, and Active TCP Sessions, as shown in Figure 9.21. The IP Session section of the report includes IP activity with which this host was involved. In this case, both TCP and UDP traffic were recorded. The report also provides additional details about the higher-level protocol that was involved in the network activity—that is, higher than either TCP or UDP. As you can see, both ftp and telnet services are listed and additional information regarding these services is provided. In the first table, the ftp activity shown includes the number of sessions for which (times) service was active, the bytes sent/received, and timestamp information.

The Active TCP Session table includes much of the information that can be obtained from the **netstat** command. However, it provides a much easier format in which to review the information than the output of this command. In general, it provides a way to view the state of all TCP-based connections from both a client and a

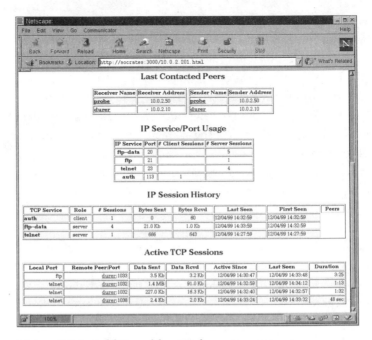

Figure 9.21 *Additional host information report.*

server perspective. The `Client Port` column shows the remote system and TCP port used, which represent the remote end of the connection. The `Server Port`, which is the local end of the connection, also shows the system and TCP port. In Chapter 2, "Simple Network Management Protocol," we discussed how a TCP connection consists of four items: the remote IP address, remote port, local IP address, and remote port. With this report, we can observe the state of each connection. The `State` column provides the current state of all TCP connections. The title for this report is a little misleading because it suggests that only active sessions will be displayed. This report also includes those connections for which termination is pending. Note in this example that there are a number of TCP connections in the `TIME_WAIT` state. This state is entered after either side of a TCP session has been terminated. The large number of sessions in this state is due to the HTTP activity on this system. Because HTTP uses a large number of TCP connections, it is not uncommon to have many outstanding TCP connections pending termination on a Web server.

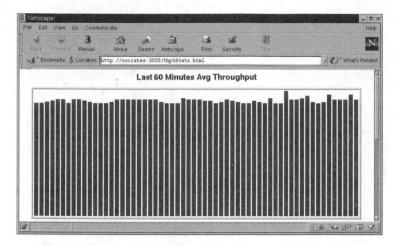

Figure 9.22 *Throughput report.*

The Data Sent and Data Rcvd columns show the amount of data that was sent/received by the connection. The Active Since field shows when (date and time) the connection was first initialized. Also, the Duration field shows how long the connection was active. It is interesting to note that when a connection is no longer active from a TCP standpoint (it's in TIME_WAIT mode, for example), the duration increases until the connection is fully terminated and no longer appears on the report.

Also note that, when possible, **ntop** displays the application name of the service instead of just the TCP port itself. For example, the report shows that several telnet sessions were active between the systems durer and rembrandt. The report displays the port as telnet, not as the normal port number associated with the Telnet application (i.e., 23). The reason **ntop** can do this mapping is because it looks up each of the TCP ports it finds and searches the /etc/services file for an appropriate match.

Throughput Report

This reports contains graphs that show the average throughput for all of the devices on the network being monitored. This is a summary of the traffic for both sent and received packet activity compared to the bandwidth of the network. The graph shown in Figure 9.22 is the first graph displayed in this report. The graph consists of the last hour of monitoring, and each bar represents one minute of time. The scale of the graph is not proportional; the bottom is zero, but the top is not 100%. The report also includes another graphic that represents the last 24-hour running average. The highest bar represents the peak for that time period.

IP Traffic Category

The next five reports display network traffic in more detail, with a particular emphasis on the relationships between each of the devices on the network. The reports include remote-to-local (R->L), local-to-remote (L->R), local-to-local (L<->L), IP Traffic Matrix (Matrix), and local usage by UNIX process (Local Usage) from the perspective of the system running **ntop**. The first three reports share the same general report layout/format, and the remaining two are distinctive.

Remote and Local Reports

Figure 9.23 shows the Remote to Local IP Traffic report. Like many of the other tables, this report lists specific hostnames and IP address information. Also, the report provides links to obtain additional host information, as described previously. They also include two separate tables, one showing the individual traffic for each host, the other showing the totals for all hosts combined. In the first table, the Data Received and Data Sent statistics both contain two columns. The first column shows the amount of data that was either received or sent by each system and expressed in bytes. The second column shows the amount of traffic as a percent for all hosts listed in the table. The second table contains the Total Traffic column, which is a summary of both the Data Received and Data Sent columns from the first table. The next two columns, Data Received and Data Sent, are the summary of the columns with the same name in the first table. The Bandwidth column lists the effective bandwidth utilization as a result of the network traffic monitored.

The two remaining reports provide similar information, but from the point of view of local systems sending/receiving traffic to remote networks and systems and local systems communicating with other local systems. It is left to the reader to export and review these additional reports.

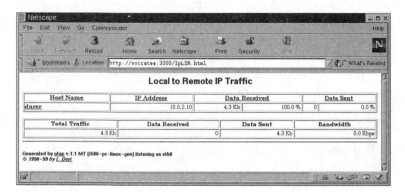

Figure 9.23 *Remote/local IP report.*

Traffic Matrix Report

This report reveals the total amount of traffic going to and coming from each system. Figure 9.24 displays a sample Traffic Matrix Report. The coloring scheme is based on whether and how much the traffic exceeds the performance thresholds listed in Table 9.9. Each of the systems is compared to the largest value that consists of both sent and received values for that system. Depending on the traffic, each system is assigned an appropriate color within their respective cells. In the figure, the cell that intersects hosts socrates and durer is red. Since this book is produced in black and white, the colors appear as dark shades of gray. This cell also contains the total amount of data that was passed between both systems. To maintain symmetry, the cells are repeated because each of the hosts intersect each other twice.

Table 9.9 *Traffic matrix report performance thresholds*

Color	Description
pink	Between 0 and 15% of maximum value
green	Between 15 and 75% of maximum value
red	Over 75% of maximum value

This report is useful for the following reasons. First, it is very easy to determine which systems are communicating with each other. This is important when network traffic exceeds the limitations of the local network and devices must be partitioned to reduce network overhead and increase performance. Knowing the traffic patterns is the first step in effective performance management. Second, it provides totals between systems to determine the heavy hitters. For instance, both `socrates` and `durer` produced the most traffic among all the other systems. From a management perspective, it is important to determine why these two systems generated this amount of traffic. This could be a normal thing or it could be a bad thing; it all depends on which services and/or applications are being offered on these two systems. Using this report and others, it is relative easy to determine what kind of services are being used and to what extent.

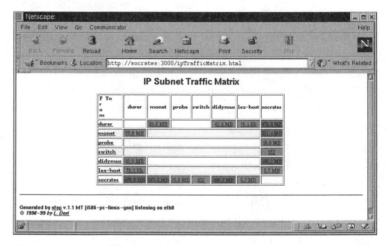

Figure 9.24 *Traffic matrix report.*

One additional note about this report: Each of the intersecting cells between the same systems is blank and contains no values. This is the result of **ntop** monitoring a specific network interface that usually never sees traffic from itself. When a UNIX network process wants to communicate within a system, it may choose to use the loopback interface. As a result, when **ntop** is monitoring real interfaces, it nevers sees this traffic. If you are interested in monitoring activity on the internal network (i.e., loopback), use the -i option to change the default interface when **ntop** is invoked. You may be somewhat surprised by the fact that only a small number of hosts (the loopback address and primary interface address) will be listed in the reports when capturing traffic from the internal network.

Local Usage Report

This report contains two sections: the first shows network usage by each system process, and the other shows network usage by port.

This report is incredibly useful because it provides the ability to probe into which applications and system services are generating and receiving network traffic on a given system. Granted, **ntop** must be running on the local system for this information to be collected, but it is well worth the effort to deploy this tool across the required systems to obtain this information. The report also includes additional useful information, such as the process ID, the user that owns the process, and both sent and received traffic counts. Figure 9.25 shows a sample report of the network utilization by each process only. As you can see, the report table was truncated in the figure; this was due to the length of the table, which would span several screen snapshots if displayed completely. The reason the table is so long is that a typical UNIX server generally contains a fair amount of processes that access the network.

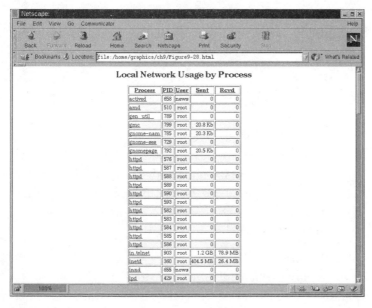

Figure 9.25 *Local usage report (part one).*

The other part of the report shows a mapping between the network port and the UNIX process that uses that port. This is interesting because it provides a way to determine exactly which processes use which network ports. Some of this information may be obtained from the /etc/services file, but not all network applications or services are listed in this file, nor does each entry disclose exactly which process may use a particular port. Figure 9.26 displays a sample mapping report.

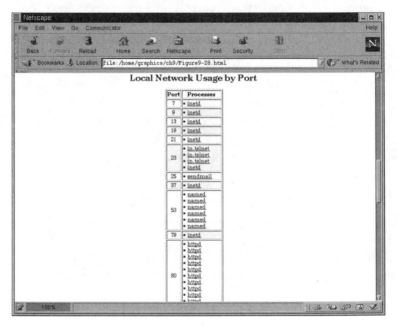

Figure 9.26 *Local usage report (part two).*

IP Protocol Category

Two different reports are included in this category. The first, called Distribution, shows up to three separate tables indicating the flow of traffic. The second report, Usage, shows network protocol usage from a high-level point of view.

Distribution Report

One of the most useful of all the **ntop** reports is the IP protocol Distribution Report, which shows the breakdown of network usage by higher-level protocols. It is similar to the Global Traffic Statistics report shown in Figure 9.17, but contains a detailed breakdown by transport-layer protocol. It reveals the amount of data (sent/received) by protocol type, such as snmp or ftp, as shown in Figure 9.27.

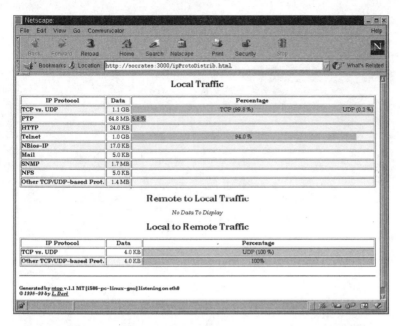

Figure 9.27 *Protocol distribution report.*

This is an important observation because this report clearly shows which applications are used the most versus those used the least. The report contains three tables that include protocol distribution for Local Traffic, Remote to Local Traffic, and Local to Remote Traffic. Each section or table contains three columns: IP Protocol, Data, and Percentage. The IP Protocol column includes the higher-level protocols that **ntop** understands and supports. Those protocols that **ntop** doesn't support are listed under the Other TCP/UDP-based Prot. category. Each protocol has associated Data and Percentage columns that relate the amount of data, expressed in bytes and as a percent of total bytes, in comparison to each of the other protocols.

Using the bar graphs contained within this report, it is relatively straightforward to identify network utilization by protocol or network application. For example, observing the second table shows that, out of all the IP traffic displayed, UDP usage was by far the most significant as compared to TCP traffic.

This report shows high-level protocol or application services, and both the client and server that participated in the traffic exchange. Figure 9.28 displays a sample report that shows ftp,

telnet, snmp, finger, and smtp. Also, it lists both the clients and
server that were using these protocols and services.

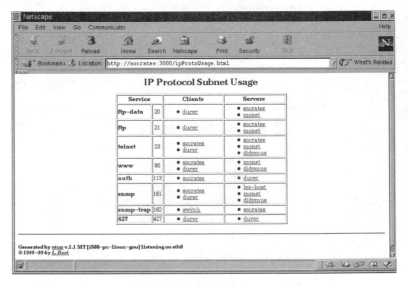

Figure 9.28 *Protocol subnet usage report.*

Using the Command Options

The **ntop** tool supports the command-line options listed in Table
9.10. This software considers a host that hasn't generated or
received traffic since its last poll to be an inactive host. If you are
interested in viewing inactive hosts as well as active ones, use the
-d option. This will show both types when generating reports.
Also, when **ntop** is running in terminal mode, the **-d** key can be used
to accomplish the same purpose. This is useful to display all hosts
regarding their activity status. Another handy option is -i, which
controls the network interface that **ntop** will use to monitor the network. With multi-homed systems, this is an absolute requirement.

If it is necessary to monitor the network by percentage, use the
-p option. This option will display traffic as a percent of total traffic for each system active on the network.

Securing the Web Reports

If you are concerned about security with respect to the reports, no
problem! The **ntop** tool supports a rudimentary but very useful secu-

Table 9.10 *Command-line options*

Option	Description
-d	Shows all hosts, not just active ones
-F	Defines a flow (filter) that is monitored and reported
-l	Shows both local and remote hosts that generate network traffic
-i	Specifies an alternate interface to use
-n	Shows numeric IP addresses instead of names
-r	Controls the delay between screen updates
-p	Shows network traffic as a percent
-w	Enables Web mode

rity feature that can be implemented quickly and easily. When **ntop** is run, it searches for a file called **.ntop** in the home directory of the user starting the process. This file may contain one or more names and associated passwords. When an entry is added to this file, the user is prompted with a login window, as displayed in Figure 9.29.

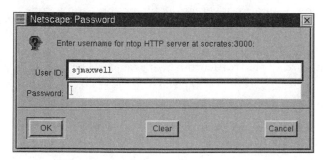

Figure 9.29 *Ntop login window.*

In most instances, it is reasonable that **ntop** be run as the superuser of the system. As a result, an .ntop file can be placed in the directory of the /root file system. To make it as secure as possible, ensure that the file is not readable except by the superuser. The permission of 600 should be sufficient. Assume that we want to pro-

vide access to **ntop** for a handful of users. The following sample
`.ntop` would serve our purpose:

```
netmgr private
tech-1 secret
smaxwell 1ghost99
acartwright 44pleaseread
```

With these entries, any of the four users—netmgr, tech-1,
smaxwell, or acartwright—can obtain access to the **ntop** reports,
provided that they each use the associated password string. Thus,
netmgr would have to use private, and so on. Clearly, this security
feature is very simple, but it does have its weakness. Namely, someone could capture the login sequence with a probe or host-based
software and obtain the name/password pair combination.

Creating Monitoring Flows

The -F option creates new flows within **ntop**. However, the syntax
is a little tricky. The general format using this option is as follows:

```
ntop -F "flow_name='filter expression'[,filter expression]"...
```

When more than one flow will be used, each flow must be followed by the previous one, separated by a single comma with no
spaces in front of the comma. The entire string after the option
must contain double quotes, whereas the filter expression is contained within single quotes. Assume that two new filters are
needed, one to capture all traffic between host chips and dips, and
the other to capture all tcp traffic from host peanuts. The first flow
will be called chipsdips_traffic, and the other is tcp-peanuts.
The following **ntop** command with the associated flows could be
used:

```
# ntop -F "chipsdips_traffic='host chips and dips',tcp-peanuts='host\
peanuts and tcp'" -w 3000
```

In this command, the first flow will capture all traffic either sent
from or received by both chips and dips. The other flow will capture all traffic that contains tcp data and is sent or received by peanuts. Recall that **ntop** supports many of the **ethereal** and **tcpdump**
filter expressions and keyword commands. Therefore, powerful filters can be used to assist with monitoring the network.

Using Terminal Mode

For those who do not want to use the Web interface, the second display mode provides terminal output similar to the UNIX **top** command. Invoke the **ntop** command without the -w option. In this mode, network information is presented in a constantly updated window, as shown in Figure 9.30. This window contains a running status of network utilization sorted by network protocols. Several display options are available that can be used to toggle the information displayed and otherwise control **ntop**. In the window displayed, the network traffic values are represented as a percent. This was enabled by the **p** command. The window only shows a few of the monitored protocols; use the spacebar key to scroll through the entire list of protocols.

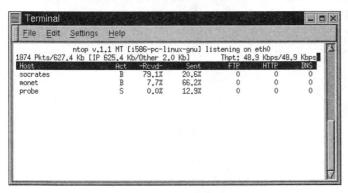

Figure 9.30 *Terminal display mode.*

By default, **ntop** starts in terminal mode. The information presented with the Web interface is available in the terminal mode, but, of course, the data is formatted differently. To review the different reports, **ntop** defines a number of keyboard commands that will alter the displayed report. The keyword command consists of pressing a single letter key without pressing the Enter key.

For example, the **h** command provides help for the **ntop** tool and displays a list of available keyboard commands. Thus, when **ntop** is running, pressing this key (without the Return or Enter) will display the help menu shown in Figure 9.31.

The user is prompted to press a key to return to the main report screen. Even when **ntop** is displaying the help screen, it is still monitoring and collecting network traffic statistics. As you can see in

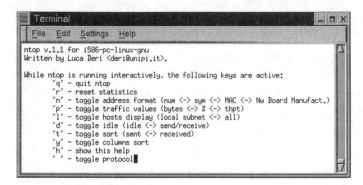

Figure 9.31 *Terminal help mode.*

the help screen, **ntop** shows the supported keyboard commands.
The **q** command is used to halt the operation of **ntop**. The ^c command sequence will accomplish the same thing.

## 10

Linux Control Panel

One of the important features of Linux is that many network administrative chores and tasks have been automated within a graphical user interface (GUI) configuration tool known as the control panel. This chapter provides an overview of the control panel provided with the standard release of Red Hat Linux. Those who are new to UNIX and do not want to edit special network configuration files or use shell commands will find the control panel a welcome aid. Although the control panel doesn't provide the ability to control every aspect of networking, it does provide support for most of the important tasks.

533

The Control Panel

The control panel provides a GUI to a number of network and system configuration tasks. You can use it to do the following:

- control the startup/shutdown of processes or services

- change the date and time

- configure/control printers

- configure network parameters

- configure modem parameters

- load/unload kernel modules

- configure additional system parameters

This tool can be invoked from the GNU Network Object Model Environment (GNOME) interface via the GUI main menu or the command line. To start it from the GUI, single-click on the GNOME *up triangle*, navigate to the System menu, then move to the right and select the Control Panel submenu. Figure 10.1 shows the main GNOME menu and System menu.

Alternatively, the user can acess the control panel from the command line by typing the following:

```
# /usr/bin/control-panel
```

You should be root when running control-panel because it modifies standard UNIX configuration files that require administrator privileges. Despite the fact that control-panel contains several different icons and provides a significant amount of functionality, we are only interested in the areas that relate to networking. However, it is important that a general overview of the other functions be provided as well, with significant emphasis on the network elements as they pertain to network management. A basic overview of the control-panel services is presented first, followed by an in-depth review of the networking related tasks.

The network component of the control-panel, known as the network configurator, configures basic networking services. UNIX contains a large number of configuration files that store

Figure 10.1 *Accessing the control panel.*

important system and networking information in one or more specific formats. Luckily, this tool handles placing the data in the appropriate files and in the correct format. However, as a UNIX administrator, you will need to know where some of the files are located and their associated format because access to the control panel may not be possible or even practical in certain situations.

Starting the control panel displays the main window shown in Figure 10.2. The window contains a single menu, File, plus eight icons. The File menu contains two items: Change Orientation and Exit. The Exit option is self-explanatory, while the Change Orientation option acts as a toggle and will alter the way the icons are displayed. In Figure 10.1, the orientation of the icons is horizontal, and selecting the Change Orientation item will cause the icons to be displayed vertically instead. Selecting the option again will return to the previous orientation.

Run-level Editor

The first icon accesses the run-level manager, which can control systems and/or network services that are activated on startup and services that are deactivated when the system is halted. Linux sup-

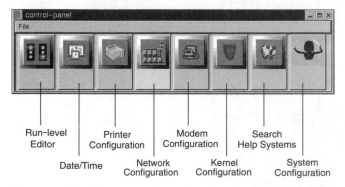

Figure 10.2 *The control panel main window.*

ports the standard *run-level* mechanism, which has its origins in the AT&T UNIX releases, where systems services are invoked and stopped based on different modes or run levels within the system. For instance, Linux usually operates in run level 5, which is known as multiuser mode. This is the primary operating mode when the system is booted and running normally. On other systems such as Solaris, run level 2 is multiuser mode without NFS services, while run level 3 is the normal multiuser mode. A user can determine which run level the system is operating in by using the **runlevel** Linux command. Alternatively, the **uname -a** command can be used.

Changing Date and Time

The next icon changes the date and time of the system. A dialog window is presented that permits the user to select individual components (such as hour, minute, and second) of the current date/time so that they may be changed.

Configure/Control Printers

This icon displays the System Print Manager, which allows you to define, control, and delete system printers. The tool supports the creation of local, remote via Line Printer Daemon (LPD), Windows 95/NT, and NetWare printers. Also, the user can control the printer background process and send test pages to the defined printers as a diagnostic debugging aid.

Network Configuration

This icon represents the network configurator tool that controls basic networking services. This tool defines client domain name server properties, routing information, networking interfaces, and host information. The next section, "Using the Network Configurator," provides more detailed information.

Using Kernel Modules

The Linux system supports dynamic loading of system modules. Modules provide additional functionality or services to the system without having to build a new kernel or restart the system. This icon accesses the `kernel configurator` and permits the loading and unloading of modules on-the-fly. For instance, if the user wants to enable support for a TokenRing network interface, he can do so by loading the `tr` module, which is one of the available modules.

Accessing Help

The `help` icon can be used to configure where the system will search for online documentation. This includes, for instance, the location of man (manual) pages.

System Configuration

The final icon displays the Linux *configurator* tool, which configures and controls a large number of system and network parameters. The configurator software can also be started from the command line using the **linuxconf** command. An overview of the tool appears in the following section.

Using the Network Configurator

As previously mentioned, the `network configurator` provides the ability to configure basic networking parameters. The following tasks can be accomplished using this software:

- configure DNS client configuration parameter

- maintain the hostname database

- configure, alter, or delete network interfaces

- configure network routing

Selecting the `network configurator` icon from the control panel displays the window shown in Figure 10.3.

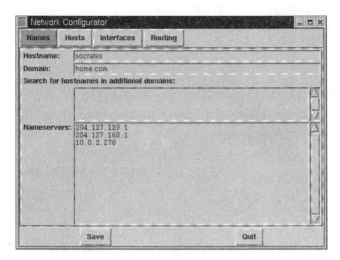

Figure 10.3 `network configurator` *window.*

The top of the window contains a set of buttons that are used to navigate different views or categories. Each button represents a different category. A total of four buttons are provided, and clicking on any one of them will cause the main window to be redrawn with the associated view.

Configuring DNS Parameters

The first button, `Names`, is the default view and is always displayed first whenever the configurator software is invoked. This view is used to define the hostname of the local system and the default domain name. Also, the user can configure the DNS servers to query and search metrics. In Figure 10.3, the name of the system, `socrates`, is contained in the `Hostname` field and DNS domain name, `home.com`, is listed in the `Domain` field. Changing the `Hostname` field will change the name of the system. If you want to list the name of the system while not using the control panel, use the **hostname** command.

The remaining three fields, `Domain`, `Search for hostnames in additional domains`, and `Nameservers`, control the operations of the DNS client software. The three name servers that are defined are 204.127.129.1, 204.127.160.1, and 10.0.2.278. These entries tells the system which name server should be queried and in what order when hostname resolution is used. The search field tells the system which additional domains should be appended to the hostname when querying one of the defined name servers. A name server will be responsible for supporting one or more domains to which specific hosts have been associated. In this case, socrates belongs to the home.com domain, but the system can also query additional hosts that belong to other domains.

The DNS information is stored in the /etc/resolv.conf configuration file, and a change made to the hostname automatically updates these files. Note that any previous information saved in the configuration files will be overwritten with the contents of the fields each time they are saved.

Maintain Host Database

The Hosts button maintains entries with the /etc/hosts file, and selecting this button displays the contents of this file for the current view.

Changes are made only to the local hosts file. If you are running **Note** NIS or DNS, changes made to this file will not affect either of these resolution services.

This system file contains hostname-to-IP address mappings and consists of up to three fields: IP, Name, and Nicknames. The IP address represents the unique address for the designated host. It is not something you just pull out of a hat. This address is specifically assigned to a system or, in the case of using dynamic IP allocation, assigned by a server for the specific host to obtain when the host is booted. Normally, if you are running NIS or DNS, you won't need this file. The bottom line is that all IP addresses assigned to a network must be unique in order for the TCP/IP protocols to function correctly.

Figure 10.4 shows a sample set of hostnames already defined within the local system. These entries only represent mappings between the IP address of the node and some hostname designation. The hostname is strictly for human consumption. The names simply make it easier for people to distinguish one system from another and have no bearing on the operation of the TCP/IP protocols. The networking software uses addresses, not names. Whereas IP addresses are a fixed set of numbers, hostnames are a bit broader. A host can be called anything, and, as shown in Figure 10.4, names can vary in length and include numbers and most valid characters.

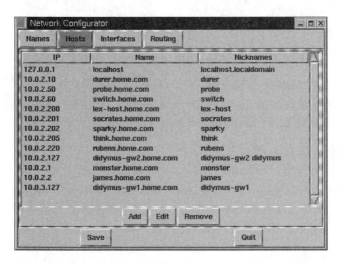

Figure 10.4 network configurator *hosts view.*

As you can see, the Host View window defines three buttons— Add, Edit, and Remove—that assist the user in defining, changing, or removing specific host entries. The view divides each line into three fields that correspond to the /etc/hosts file format. The format includes IP Address, official hostname, and aliases. To add a new host, click the Add button. Once this has been done, a small dialog window will appear that has three blank fields: IP, Name, and Nicknames. Figure 10.5 shows this window.

Assume we want to add a host called monet that has a corresponding IP address of 10.0.2.100; we would add these strings in the appropriate fields within each of the text boxes. Unfortunately, the control panel software doesn't do any error-checking on the format or validity of the information specified within these fields. This means, for example, that the user can input incorrect or even

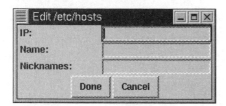

Figure 10.5 *Add Host dialog window.*

badly formatted data and the software will accept it without any warnings.

In practice, most, if not all, UNIX configuration files (including /etc/hosts) don't normally have any built-in mechanisms to ensure that the information entered is indeed correct. Many files, however, do provide some sort of error-checking to pinpoint specific format- or syntax-related errors. This is usually accomplished by running the associated program that is responsible for parsing the specific configuration file and operating on its contents to provide some specific application or system service. Only at this point are any errors detected. The control panel software does provide a rudimentary check; for a valid entry to be accepted, the first and seconds fields must be filled in, while the third is optional and can be left blank.

Once the desired information has been entered, the user must click the Done button. This action will add the entry to the list of existing host mappings. However, the user must save the new configuration by selecting the Save button. If the user doesn't save the new entry and exits the control-panel, the new entry will be lost. Unfortunately, the software doesn't provide a warning if the user decides to exit the software before saving the new host configuration.

To alter an existing host entry, select it from the main window and click the Edit button. The same window shown in Figure 10.5 will be displayed, but it will already include the host information. Change the desired information and click the Done button. If a host is to be deleted from the list, simply select it and click the Remove button.

If you want to really make sure that the entry was added correctly, just use the **grep** command and search for the new hostname from the /etc/hosts file. Thus,

```
# grep monet /etc/hosts
```

will return the following if this host entry was in fact added correctly by the `control-panel` software:

```
10.0.2.100    monet
```

Configuring Network Interfaces

The `Interfaces` button adds, edits, or removes network interfaces from the system. Selecting the `Interfaces` button displays the current defined interfaces in the window shown in Figure 10.6. This window presents the interface configuration information in separate fields and contains some of the same buttons as the `hosts` view just discussed. However, the `interfaces` view has a few extra buttons: `Clone`, `Alias`, `Activate`, and `Deactivate`.

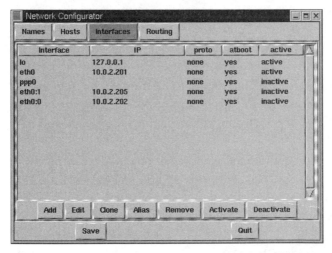

Figure 10.6 `network configurator` *interface view.*

To add an interface to the system, the user must click on the `Add` button and select the type from the interface selection dialog window, shown in Figure 10.7. The user must select the specific interface to configure. The first three interfaces, plus the last one— `PPP`, `SLIP`, `PLIP`, and `Pocket`—are used with either a serial or parallel port that is available on most computer systems. The remaining interfaces—`Ethernet`, `Arcnet`, and `TokenRing`—require a specific hardware interface that must be added to the system before the interface can be used. For instance, should the user desire to configure a second Ethernet interface, the second interface card should already be installed within the system.

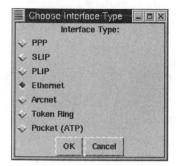

Figure 10.7 *Interface selection window.*

Bear in mind that the user can add a number of interfaces using the control panel, but only the hardware installed will determine whether those interfaces can actually be used.

Depending on which interface type is chosen from the interface selection window, a different set of questions will be presented in a new window. This is because some of the interfaces require different information before they can be set up. For example, selecting the Ethernet type and clicking the OK button displays the window shown in Figure 10.8.

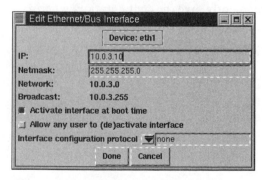

Figure 10.8 *Ethernet interface window.*

When adding a new Ethernet interface, the IP and netmask fields must be completed. If a valid IP address is added to the IP field, then the Netmask, Network, and Broadcast fields are filled in automatically. The Netmask field represents the 32-bit subnet mask that will be used with the IP address to determine the subnet number. The value for the Netmask field is determined by the default mask of the class IP address entered within the IP field. If this value isn't appropriate, change the Netmask to suit the networking requirements.

Check the Activate interface at boot time button if the interface should be started when the system is booted. In most cases, the interface should be enabled on startup so that upper-level protocols or network services will be available. The Allow any user to(de)actvate interface button is supposed to control whether regular non-root users can enable or disable this interface. Unfortunately, this feature doesn't seem to work. The Interface configuration protocol pull-down menu and/or text box specify the method that should be used to obtain additional interface configuration data or IP address information. The two possible methods are Dynamic Host Configuration protocol (DHCP) and Boot protocol (BOOTP) provide a mechanism to retrieve IP address information and other information for a central server. Both require one or more servers to be operating on the network.

Once the interface has been configured, click the Done button. After this, another dialog window will prompt the user to save the interface changes. Figure 10.9 shows this dialog window. Clicking the Save button will permanently save the configuration, whereas the Cancel button will not save the information. Clicking the Cancel button from the interface edit window will delete the change made.

Figure 10.9 *Save dialog window.*

When a new interface has been added, a configuration file is placed in the /etc/sysconfig/network-scripts directory. The file name contains a prefix of ifcfg, followed by the name of the interface. When a new interface called eth1 is created, a configuration file called `ifcfg-eth1` is made. This file contains the interface information shown here:

```
DEVICE=eth1
IPADDR=10.0.2.220
NETMASK=255.255.255.0
NETWORK=10.0.2.0
BROADCAST=10.0.2.255
ONBOOT=yes
BOOTPROTO=none
USERCTL=no
```

As you can see from the output, the file contains a list of names followed by an equal sign, plus an associated value. The major reason for including this information is so that if you have to, you will be able to make a quick change to the script without the aid of the control panel GUI. When an interface has been modified, this file is simply updated with the new information; when an interface is deleted, the file is removed.

If the point-to-point (PPP) interface type (`ppp`) is selected in the window shown in Figure 10.7, then a different configuration dialog window will be displayed. This window, shown in Figure 10.10, contains the required PPP configuration parameters.

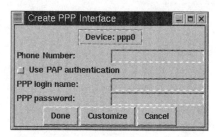

Figure 10.10 *PPP interface dialog window.*

When using PPP, several important pieces of information are necessary in order to ensure that a successful link can be established to the remote end. The first and most obvious is that you must have an account with an Internet Service Provider (ISP) if the connection is going to be used to provide connectivity to the Internet. If this is not the case, you still must have another system that has a modem that can dial. The phone number of the remote system must be placed in the `Phone Number` field. Next, you must have a valid account with a username and password. If you are going to the use the PAP protocol, you must click the Use PAP authentication item. Then, you must enter the user ID (login) and associated password in the PPP login name and PPP password fields, respectively. The final step of the configuration process requires an understanding of connection specifics: system port choices, speed, and other parameters. If you click the Done button, default values that may not be compatible with your environment will be used. It is recommended that you click the Customize button to ensure and/or correct default values not appropriate for your site. Clicking the Done button displays a new window that has four tab panels: Hardware, Communication, Networking, and PAP. Figure 10.11 shows this window.

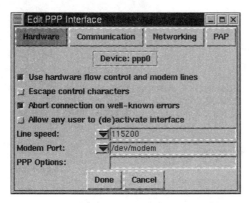

Figure 10.11 *PPP customize window.*

The Hardware panel, which contains the name of the interface being configured, is used to configure some of the low-layer operating parameters needed. In this case, the interface is ppp0. The first checkbox, Use hardware flow control and modem lines, will enable or disable flow control for the modem and the associated port that connects the modem. Flow control ensures that when a connection is established, both modems and ports can control the flow of information without losing any data should errors occur. This checkbox should remained checked in most remote connectivity situations. The Escape control characters option should be disabled because it is used to ensure that any control characters sent will not be interpreted by the local port or modem. The Abort

connection on well-known errors option just means that if one or
more common errors occur, the connection will be terminated.
This option should be enabled because it is a good idea to break
the connection when trouble takes place within the low layer. The
Allow any user to (de)activate interface button is provided to
help non-privileged users enable the interface. This is useful, for
instance, when a temporary problem occurs on the remote end, the
network administrator isn't around to bring the connection back
up when services are restored, and a regular user must assist with
this task.

The next two text boxes contain parameters specific to the
hardware port being used. The Line speed field controls the baud
rate for the physical interface. This should be set to the highest possible rate that the interface can support. Bear in mind that regardless of the setting in this field, the actual rate of the port will be
limited to what the hardware provides. For instance, if the port can
only support 57600 baud, but the line speed is configured for
115200, the 57600 rate will be used despite this configuration setting. Next, the Modem Port field should contain the name of the
physical port to which the modem is connected. By default, a symbolic link is made between the actual port and /dev/modem. It is better to use the symbolic link in this configuration window because
you may want to change the port at a later time, and the
/dev/modem port can be relinked to another port without changing
this configuration. If any special point-to-point configuration
options are needed, they can be added to the PPP Options field.

The Communication panel, shown in Figure 10.12, contains
modem commands and additional parameters such as
expect/response strings. The first field, Modem Init String, resets the
modem before the interface is activated. It is always a good idea to
do this because it ensures that the system can talk to the modem and
that the modem is initialized to a known operating state. The Modem
Dial Command field stores the command sequence for dialing the
phone number located in the Phone Number field. If you are experiencing problems getting a connection to function correctly, check
the Debug connection option. This will cause additional debugging
information to be added to the /var/adm/messages file. The remaining portion of the window defines an expect script sequence that is

used to log in to the remote end. Some systems display a series of login prompts and require responses to these in a particular order. The `expect` script reads these prompts and emits the correct response to the remote system. However, when you use the PAP protocol, these scripts should not be necessary.

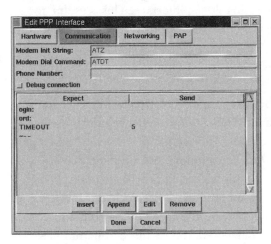

Figure 10.12 *Communication tab window.*

The `Networking` panel, shown in Figure 10.13, provides access to network-layer parameters and options. The `Activate interface at boot time` option should be checked if the interface is to be started when the system boots. This feature would be used, for instance, when the system is used as a route, server, or workstation that requires a remote connection when the system is activated, not just when users log in to the system. When this option is selected, the `ONBOOT` flag is set to `yes` (in the interface configuration file); when the system starts, the `/et/rc.d/rc2.d/S10network` startup script examines this flag and starts any interface that enabled the `ONBOOT` flag.

The `Set default route when making connection` option will configure the local routing table and add a default route to the network associated with this interface. This option is enabled by default. It is very useful in situations when this interface represents connectivity to the Internet and most of the network traffic on this interface. By establishing the default route, it eliminates the need to run a network routing protocol such as RIP or OSPF. In certain sit-

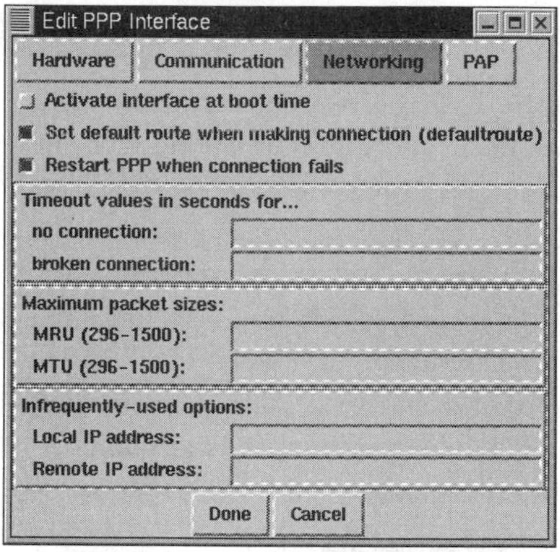

Figure 10.13 *Networking panel.*

uations, it is desirable to run one of these protocols. In many cases, however, the default route approach will be sufficient, particularly in cases when the workstation contains just a single network interface to the outside world.

The `Restart PPP when connection fails` option is also enabled by default, and it makes good sense to restart the PPP service if a connection fails. Since connection failures can be caused by a large number of problems, and some environments want to ensure connectivity whenever a problem happens, connectivity to the remote site will be started automatically. Granted, if a particular problem occurs—say the remote end crashes— restarting the connection over and over won't help. However, when the problem with the remote end is finally resolved, no human intervention is needed to establish the connection at this point. It may become necessary to limit the amount of time spent attempting to establish the remote connection.

The next two text boxes contain timeout values (in seconds) associated with the interface when failures occur on the link. The `no connection` field controls how much time should elapse when a no-connection state is detected on the interface. The `broken connection` field controls the amount of time between connection attempts when the link is terminated either by the remote end or due to some other problem (e.g., trouble in the phone line). The

second section contains packet-size maximums, which, under normal circumstances, don't need to be altered. The final section
defines static IP addresses for both the local and remote network
interfaces. With most ISPs, the IP address information is dynamically assigned and, as a result, no address information should be
included.

The PAP panel stores the username and password for the PAP
login. Figure 10.14 shows this panel, which contains a single sign-
on entry. In this example, the username 2345678@worldnet.att.net
has the associated password of abcdefg-zxcv. The username is formatted according to the ISP naming conventions and usually
implement their own standards for login names.

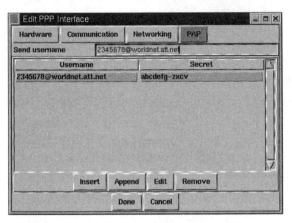

Figure 10.14 *The PAP configuration panel.*

The interfaces panel also contains additional buttons that
maintain and control existing interfaces. The Edit button modifies
parameters of an existing interface. If you want to edit an interface,
first select it with the mouse, then click the Edit button. After that,
a window will be displayed, as shown previously in Figure 10.8.
The next button, Clone, adds a brand new interface by using the
parameters and setting from another interface. Clicking this button
displays the dialog window shown in Figure 10.15. Enter the name
of the new interface that will be a copy (clone) of the interface that
was selected.

Clicking the Done button will create an alias from one of the
existing interfaces. An alias interface is the same as a logical or

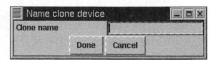

Figure 10.15 *Clone window.*

pseudo-interface. In a nutshell, an alias defines another interface that is a copy of an existing interface but uses a different network address. The primary purpose of an alias interface is to create another network address for the machine. The alias contains all of the parameters and operating characteristics of the original interface.

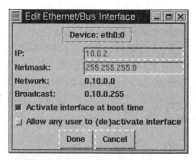

Figure 10.16 *Alias interface window.*

Selecting the `Done` button displays the `Edit Ethernet/Bus Interface` window shown in Figure 10.16. This is the same window that is displayed when editing an existing interface. However, the system adds an alias number after the interface name, separated by a single colon character. In Figure 10.16, a zero has been added to the `eth0` name. This is how the system specifies alias interfaces. In this case, the first alias to the Ethernet interface is named `eth:0`. If another alias is created, it will be labeled `eth0:1`, the third `eth0:2`, and so on. Alias interfaces act and appear to the system as any normal interface, and networking commands such as **ifconfig** can be used as well. For instance, consider the output from the **ifconfig -a** command:

```
eth0        Link encap:Ethernet  HWaddr 00:10:5A:28:5D:7C
            inet addr:10.0.2.201  Bcast:10.0.2.255  Mask:255.255.255.0
            UP BROADCAST RUNNING PROMISC MULTICAST  MTU:1500  Metric:1
            RX packets:1494 errors:0 dropped:0 overruns:0 frame:0
            TX packets:842 errors:0 dropped:0 overruns:0 carrier:40
            collisions:0 txqueuelen:100
            Interrupt:10 Base address:0xfc00

eth0:0      Link encap:Ethernet  HWaddr 00:10:5A:28:5D:7C
            inet addr:10.0.2.254  Bcast:10.0.2.255  Mask:255.255.255.0
            UP BROADCAST RUNNING PROMISC MULTICAST  MTU:1500  Metric:1
            Interrupt:10 Base address:0xfc00

lo          Link encap:Local Loopback
            inet addr:127.0.0.1  Mask:255.0.0.0
            UP LOOPBACK RUNNING  MTU:3924  Metric:1
            RX packets:7890 errors:0 dropped:0 overruns:0 frame:0
            TX packets:7890 errors:0 dropped:0 overruns:0 carrier:0
            collisions:0 txqueuelen:0
```

The output includes three interfaces: eth0, eth0:0, and lo. As you can see, a single pseudo-interface called eth0:0 is defined. Notice that it has all the characteristics of the eth0 interface, but the IP address is different. Additional information regarding alias interfaces can be found in Chapter 4, "Core System Utilities and Tools," under the **ifconfig** section.

The Remove button deletes an existing interface defined on the system. Clicking the Remove button displays a dialog window, shown in Figure 10.17, that will verify the removal of the specified interface. Please note that once the OK button is clicked, the interface is permanently removed.

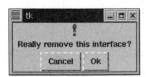

Figure 10.17 *Interface removal verification window.*

As a result, any specific configuration parameters related to the interface shown in the figure will be lost for good. You may want to consider saving a copy of the configuration file related to this interface before it is removed, just in case you need it in the future.

Look in the `/etc/sysconfig/network-scripts` directory for a file with a name that matches the name of the interface that should be saved.

Configuring Routing

The `routing` panel configures the default gateway and adds static routes to the routing table. The `Network Packet Forwarding (IPv4)` option is provided to activate routing between networks that are configured on the system. If the system contains at least two interfaces, and IP traffic needs to be routed between these interfaces, check this option; otherwise it should be left unchecked. Actually, the choice to route is more involved than simply enabling this option. The selection and configuration of a routing protocol is necessary as well, but is beyond the scope of this book. By default, this feature is disabled. Figure 10.18 shows the `routing` panel.

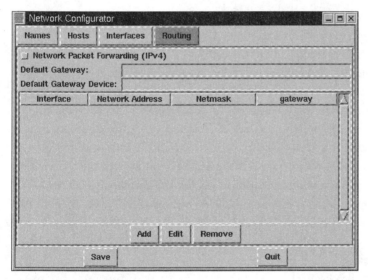

Figure 10.18 *Routing panel.*

The next two fields are used for the default gateway. The *default gateway* (or router) is used when a routing protocol such as `RIP` isn't installed or configured on a system. Using a default router means that if any networks that are not explicitly defined within the routing table must be accessed, the default routing path is used.

Enter either the IP address or valid hostname of the default router
in the Default Gateway field. The Default Gateway Device field
contains the name of the interface that is used to access the default
router. This information is stored in the /etc/sysconfig/network
file.The remaining portion of the panel defines additional static
routing entries. Normally static routes are necessary when the system is not running a routing protocol. To add a route, click the Add
button. This will display a dialog box that has four fields, as shown
in Figure 10.19. A static route requires four items: the network
interface of the route, the network that is routed, the netmask, and
the gateway/router device.

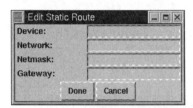

Figure 10.19 *Static route entry.*

The Device field contains the network interface name that will
be used to access the network for the route. The Network field holds
the dotted decimal IP address or valid network name of the network to which the route belongs. The Netmask field determines the
network and node portion, particularly if subnetting is implemented. The Gateway field is the actual IP address of the gateway or
router device that will forward packets to the network defined in
the Network field. Clicking the Done button will save the route entry
to the /etc/sysconfig/static-routes file. Note that if there were
routes previously defined, they would appear in the window displayed in Figure 10.14. As an alternative, the **route** command can
be used to list and add static routing entries. Unfortunately, any
entries added with this command are not saved across system
reboots. Consult the Linux manual page on the **route** command for
additional information. Further, if you want to list the routing
table, you can use the **netstat** command with the -r (for routing)
option. Chapter 4, "Core System Utilities and Tools," fully
describes this command.

Using the System Configurator

The control panel provides access to another system tool, called the gnome-linuxconf. This tool provides a GUI front end to even more network administration configuration tasks. Although this tool is not completed described here, an overview is provided for completeness. Selecting the system configuration icon from the control panel GUI displays the window shown in Figure 10.20.

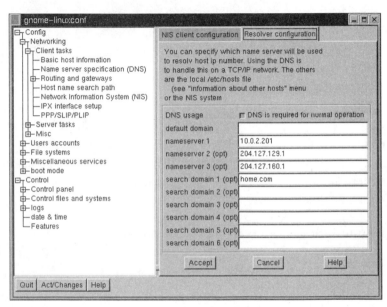

Figure 10.20 *Linux configuration window.*

The gnome-linuxconf window contains a hierarchical tree view on the left, with one or more tabbed panels to the right. The tree view contains two separate root categories, labeled Config and Control, with an associated state box to the left of each category label. Single-clicking the state box either expands or contracts additional items underneath the category. For instance, clicking on the state box for the Networking label will cause additional items to be displayed. Clicking again on the same category will cause the items to disappear. Every time the user selects a category, a new tab panel is displayed to the right. Figure 10.20 shows two panels: NIS client configuration and Resolver configuration. Since the tab panels are cumulative—that is, every category selected displays another panel—the user must explicitly delete a panel by clicking the Quit or Close button associated with that panel.

To aid the reader in learning more about all the functions provided by the gnome-linuxconf configuration tool, Tables 10.1 and 10.2 list and describe each major function.

The root category Config contains several subcategories for configuring networking server applications:

- Networking
- Users Accounts
- File Systems
- Miscellaneous Services
- Boot Mode

The Networking section is divided further into three subcategories: Client Tasks, Server Tasks, and Misc. This section addresses many networking tasks, such as DNS client and server configuration, NFS file system export, Apache Web server setup and configuration, and others. Table 10.1 lists all the tasks available under this Networking category.

Table 10.1 *Available* Networking *category functions*

Main Category	Subcategory	Description
Client tasks		
	Basic host information	Modifies the hostname of the local system and provides access to the interface configuration parameters
	Name server specification	Modifies the DNS resolver configuration file /etc/resolv.conf
	Routing & gateways	

Table 10.1 *Available* Networking *category functions (continued)*

Main Category	Subcategory	Description
	Host name search path	Tells the system the order in which the various name services will be probed; modifies the /etc/host.conf configuration file
	Network information Services (NIS)	Sets up NIS client configuration
	IPX interface setup	Enables IPX network protocols on specific network interfaces
	PPP/SLIP/PLIP	Configures network-layer service on serial or parallel ports; uses standard network control panel
Server tasks		
	Exported file system (NFS)	Sets up file systems that are available for client hosts
	IP aliases for virtual hosts	Creates pseudo-interfaces
	Domain Name Server (DNS)	
	Config	Contains several sub-items for configuring a DNS server
	Add/Edit	Contains sub-items for adding new hosts or modify existing hosts within the DNS database

Table 10.1 *Available* Networking *category functions (continued)*

Main Category	Subcategory	Description
	Security	Contains sub-items for controlling which hosts can obtain DNS zone information
	Apache Web server	
	Defaults	Controls any default configuration options, such as administrator Email address, error log file names, and which TCP port to listen on; includes many other options
	Virtual domains	Provides the means to create virtual Web domains with multiple Web servers
	Sub-directory specs	Permits the configuration of URL paths and directories within the Web server
	Samba file server	
	Defaults	Controls many default configuration options for the Samba server
	Default setup for user's home	Configures the sharing of a disk partition or file system
	Default setup for printers	Non-functional sub-item; clicking on this item does nothing
	Disk shares	Creates multiple independent entry points for the Samba file server

Table 10.1 *Available* Networking *category functions (continued)*

Main Category	Subcategory	Description
	Mail delivery system (sendmail)	
	Basic	Configures the basic operation of the sendmail server
	Anti-spam filters	Controls the creation of mail filters that include relay services
	Ftp server (wu-ftpd)	
	Basic configuration	Configures Email address of administrator, banner file, shutdown message file, and other controlling options
	Virtual hosts	Controls the creation of virtual hosts using the FTP server
Misc	Information about other hosts	Provides access to the /etc/hosts file
	Information about other networks	Provides access to the /etc/networks file
	Linuxconf network access	Creates host filters to restrict access to the Linux configuration server process

The User Accounts category has four subcategories: Normal, Special accounts, Email aliases, and Policies. This category provides many functions for UNIX account administration and associated tasks, including the ability to create new system accounts or modify

existing ones, maintain mail aliases, and control passwords. Table
10.2 provides a complete list of these functions.

Table 10.2 *Available user account category functions*

Main Category	Subcategory	Description
Normal		
	User accounts	Adds, deletes, or removes individual accounts
	Group definitions	Adds, deletes, or removes individual groups
	Change root password	Changes the root password
Special accounts		
	PPP accounts	Creates/modifies special system accounts for PPP access
	SLIP accounts	Creates/modifies special system accounts for SLIP access
	UUCP accounts	Creates/modifies special system accounts for UUCP access
	POP accounts (mail only)	Creates/modifies special system accounts for POP mail access
	Virtual POP accounts (mail only)	Creates/modifies special system accounts for POP virtual mail access
Email aliases		

Table 10.2 *Available user account category functions (continued)*

Main Category	Subcategory	Description
	user aliases	Maintains system mail aliases, which are stored in the /etc/aliases file
	virtual domain user aliases	Maintains virtual system mail aliases
Policies		
	Password & account policies	Controls various parameters regarding system passwords for regular users and accounts
	Available user shells	Controls which command interpreter is the default login shell
	Available PPP shells	Controls which command interpreter is for a PPP user
	Available SLIP shells	Controls which command interpreter is for a SLIP user
	Message of the day	Configures a message-of-the-day string to be presented during normal login

The File systems section contains additional items that help control and maintain file systems. The Miscellaneous services controls the default Linux run levels while the boot mode item is used for lower-level Linux booting configuration and other parameters. All three of these categories are listed in Table 10.3.

The root category Control also contains subcategories that are used to access part of the control panel functions described here

Table 10.3 *Additional functions from* **config** *category*

Main Category	Subcategory	Description
File systems	Access local drive	Makes changes to the /etc/fstab file for local file systems
	Access nfs volume	Makes changes to the /etc/fstab file for NFS volumes
	Configure swap files and partitions	Makes changes to the /etc/fstab file for swap partitions
	Set quota defaults	Controls parameters for disk quotas
	Check some file permissions	Checks file permission of critical files within the /etc directory
Miscellaneous services		
	initial system services	Controls the setting of the default run level
boot mode		
	Lilo	
	LILO defaults (Linux boot loader)	Controls parameters related to the boot of the Linux system
	LILO linux con-figurations	Controls parameters related to the kernel options when booting
	LILO other OS configurations	Defines other operating systems label and boot partition

Table 10.3 *Additional functions from* **config** *category (continued)*

Main Category	Subcategory	Description
	`default boot configuration`	Selects boot parameters to be used when booting the kernel
	`a new kernel`	Configures the booting of an existing Linux kernel
	`a kernel you have complied`	Configures the booting of a new Linux kernel
	`Mode`	
	`default boot mode`	Controls how the system should boot: text mode and network vs. graphic and network. Provides additional control parameters

and a number of administration tasks, like mounting file systems and configuration of system files:

- `control panel`
- `control files and systems`
- `logs`

Table 10.4 lists all the subcategory items under these main categories.

Table 10.4 *Functions available under* `Control` *category*

Main Category	Subcategory	Description
Control		
	`Control Panel`	
	`Activate configuration`	Enables or disables changes made to the system; also, can display the changes before they are committed

Table 10.4 *Functions available under* Control *category (continued)*

Main Category	Subcategory	Description
	Shutdown/ Reboot	Runs the **/usr/bin/shutdown** command
	Control service activity	Enables/disables system services, i.e., those started by the system during normal booting
	Mount/Unmount file systems	Same as the Control service activity item above
	Control config- ured local drives	Same as the Control service activity item above
	Control configured nfs volumes	Same as the Control service activity item above
	Mount other NFS file systems	Same as the Control service activity item above
	Configure supe- ruser scheduled tasks	Maintains a crontab entry for the root account
	Archive configurations	Not implemented
	Switch system pro- file	Controls the use of one or more system profiles that can be activated on com- mand
	Control PPP/SLIP/PLIP links	Enables or disables net- work links
	Control files and systems	

Table 10.4 *Functions available under* Control *category (continued)*

Main Category	Subcategory	Description
	Configure all configuration files	Provides the ability to maintain important system configuration files. Specific files include /etc/HOSTNAME. /etc/aliases. and /etc/exports.
	Configure all commands and daemons	Configures the mapping between system command names and the commands themselves. For instance, **cat** maps to /bin/cat
	Configure file permission and ownership	Controls the permission of files and directories across the system
	Configure Linux-conf modules	Administers Linux modules. Each can be activated or deactivated
	Configure system profiles	Toggles between one or more system configuration profiles
	Override Linux-conf addons	Controls Linux modules
	Create Linuxconf addons	Defines a new Linux module
	logs	
	Boot messages	Displays boot information via boot log file
	Linuxconf logs	Displays the Linuxconf log file

Table 10.4 *Functions available under* Control *category (continued)*

Main Category	Subcategory	Description
	date & time	Controls system date and time settings
	Features	Controls special behavior of the Linuxconf program

tkined Tool—Network Editor

The **tkined** network editor that is available with the Scotty network package provides a graphical user interface (GUI) for a large number of network monitoring and support functions. Also, it provides an interactive editor for creating and manipulating network topology maps. The tool is customizable by the user, and additional networking and system tools can be integrated into the basic package. The software is based on the XWindow system and is available and supported on several different operating system platforms.

tkined Overview

The **tkined** application is a fully featured network manager that provides many of the management capabilities found in some of the more popular commercial products. This tool is considered one of the best public domain network monitoring packages available and boasts many features and functions. The **tkined** application isn't a complicated software package, but it does contain many menu items, submenus, sub-windows, and specific modules. As a result, you must review the basics in order to start using the software right away.

From a functional standpoint, **tkined** does the following:

- discovers networking devices and systems

- creates/maintains network maps and views

- manages SNMP devices

- supports IP monitoring

- creates performance graphs and charts

To start the application, invoke the **tkined** command within a shell prompt:

```
# /usr/bin/tkined
```

Executing the command will display the main window shown in Figure 11.1. By default, the window contains no objects or network devices because a certain amount of customization must be done before **tkined** can monitor your network.

The main window contains a full complement of menu items, a tool selection palette on the left, and a network topology mapping panel. The network mapping panel is used to display a variety of network elements in icon format. The package contains a large number of icons that you can use to represent specific devices and systems, or specific network topologies such as bus and ring that may be found on a network. Finally, you can create different views that contain specific devices, entire subnetworks, charts and graphs, and other items.

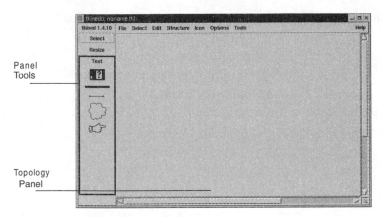

Figure 11.1 *Main* **tkined** *window.*

Topology Views

The package supports the idea of using different views to represent various aspects of the network, such as Cisco routers or a number of critical servers. You can create additional views to house performance graphs or entire subnets. When the application is first started, an empty view is created. The name of the view is displayed in the header of the main application window. The name of the view is also the name of the file in which the view is stored. The default view file is noname.tk, which you can change.

The primary purpose of views is to help divide the network into smaller components. The sheer number of systems on many networks makes it very difficult to monitor the networks, but, by partitioning the network into different elements or compartments, you can make the task much easier. The choice of how to break apart the network is really up to you. The important thing to remember is that you should partition the network into logical or functional areas that best fit your department or company business model.

For instance, let's assume you work for the network group that is primarily responsible for support of the backbone network and Wide Area Network (WAN). Support for specific subnets rests with individual departments, which basically means that devices can be added, moved, or removed for these subnets at any time. As a result, it may not be reasonable to monitor specific end nodes or devices contained within those subnets; instead it would be more interesting to monitor the core backbone devices and WAN components. The topology maps or views created within **tkined** would reflect this monitoring physiology.

In fact, it is in the best interest of all parties for each individual or support group to deploy additional copies of **tkined** to address each specific need and monitoring requirement. Using multiple copies of **tkined** on the same system is one possible approach to this situation.

Network Discovery

One powerful use of **tkined** is to dynamically discover the network devices within a single subnet, multiple subnets, or individual devices. One of the primary objectives for a network manager is to quickly and easily integrate the topology of the network into the tool. To begin the discovery process, select the IP Discovery submenu from the Tools main menu. A new menu called IP-Discovery will be displayed to the right of the tool menu. Figure 11.2 shows this new menu. It contains an option, Discover IP Network, that queries devices using ICMP and SNMP protocols in an attempt to learn the network topology. Selecting this option displays the subwindow shown in Figure 11.2.

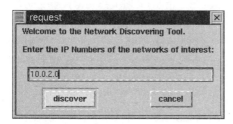

Figure 11.2 *Network discovery request window.*

The dialog window requires the user to enter a valid IP network address or group of addresses followed by spaces. As shown in Figure 11.2, the 10.0.2.0 network will be discovered when you click the discover button. Clicking this button also displays the window shown in Figure 11.3.

The window shows the progress of the discovery and the specific steps that were involved. The discover process shown in Figure 11.3 took only 66 seconds to complete and found seven nodes on the network. Given the number of nodes, the time required

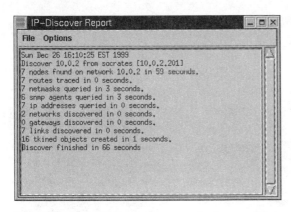

Figure 11.3 *Discovery status window.*

doesn't represent a problem. However, on a large network, the discovery process could take a lot longer. Note that **tkined** has detected those devices that support SNMP and those that do not. In the example, the application found six SNMP agents, which is correct for this network. We will see later on that **tkined** supports a significant number of functions based on SNMP and that accurate detection of SNMP devices is paramount. The other important information regarding the status window is the count of the number of objects that were created. Figure 11.3 indicates that a total of 16 objects were created. Since there were seven devices, each one has an individual icon, a network connection object, and two networks.

Once the discovery is complete, **tkined** attempts to render the topology and devices with the networking topology panel. Figure 11.4 shows the results of probing the `10.0.2.0` network. Notice that the icons are a little unorganized and that the default icon is used for all the devices. You can customize the topology map and move the objects around to make the map a bit more visually appealing. Unfortunately, if you want to use more representative icons, you must assign them manually.

To move an icon around, simply select the object and then, pressing both mouse buttons, move the icon to the desired position and release the mouse. To help track your actions, the software displays a square box as a guide that moves as the mouse is moved. You can move all objects within the topology view around in this manner.

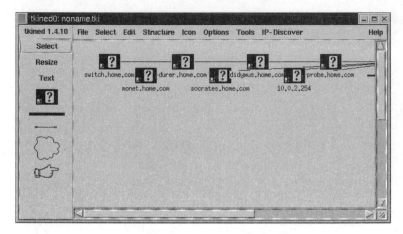

Figure 11.4 *Discovered network topology.*

To replace the default icon for an object, select the object and go
to the `Icon` menu, then click on the `Node` option. When a list of system types appear, select the one that matches the device you are
changing, as shown in Figure 11.5. After this, the device's icon will
change to the type you have specified. As you see from the list, a
large number of different icons are available for systems. The menu
also contains additional options that have icons for networking
devices like switches and routers. The `Network Device` option contains icons for a bridge, concentrator, switch, router, terminal
server, and Cisco router. The `Peripherals` option has icons for the
following devices: modem, phone, printer, laser printer, HP plotter,
HP Deskjet, and HP Scanjet. The `Misc` option contains generic icons
such as a small box, normal box, big box, and connector.

The tool is also flexible enough to permit you to use custom
icons and apply them to objects. Consult the "Customization" section for additional information. Once all the default icons have
been replaced with more representative ones and the objects have
been moved around to make the map more readable, the map
should represent the network more accurately. The network discovery from the previous example produced the topology view
shown in Figure 11.6.

In the `home.com` topology view of this test network, each of the
device icons has been changed to correspond to the actual device it
represents. Note that Linux systems use a custom icon that was

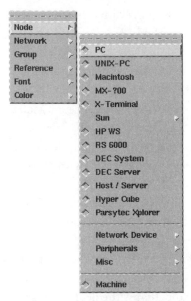

Figure 11.5 *List of device icons.*

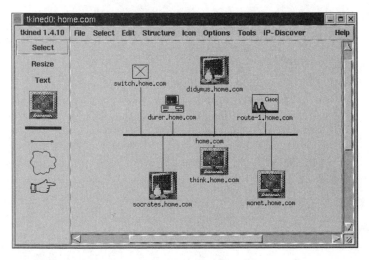

Figure 11.6 *Completed topology view.*

added to **tkined** after installation. You won't find this icon in the
standard list of available icons. Bear in mind that you can assign
any system icon to a device object, regardless of the object; no
internal mechanism or rule will prohibit this action. The only

exception to this is when it comes to assigning different icons to incompatible types. For instance, the tool will not permit a network type (such as `10MB Ethernet`) to be assigned a device icon, and vice versa. The `10MB Ethernet` network type represents a horizontal line that connects one or more nodes.

In certain situations, this may pose a problem because if an icon for a device doesn't represent the actual device, it can be mistaken for another. In practice, this problem can be diminished because actions to a device should be based on not only the icon image, but the device's label as well.

You may be wondering, "Why should I use autodiscovery if I have to assign the icons myself and clean up the view too?" Well, this is a good question. However, there is more to the discovery process than meets the eye; the tool does a good job of building a list of all the devices on the network and creating individual objects for them. It also assigns each one a label that is the device's hostname. Further, it detects which devices support SNMP as well and assigns default parameters for the collection of SNMP information.

Despite this, you may prefer to manually set up the network topology views yourself. The next section will show you how.

Using the Tool Panel

The **tkined** editor provides several tools on the left side of the main window that you can use to build your own or make changes to existing topology maps. Figure 11.7 shows a cut-away view of the tool palette from the main window.

The tool palate contains the following tools:

- Selection
- Resize
- Text
- Device
- Network
- Connection
- Group
- Reference

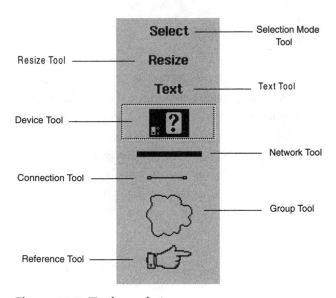

Figure 11.7 *Tool panel view.*

Selection Tool

This item is really more of a mode than a tool; it enables a selection mode that indicates whether the mouse will be used for selecting existing objects on the topology view. You will need to use this mode when changing object attributes and parameters or deleting objects. Enabling this mode changes the mouse pointer to a black-filled left-handed arrow (▶). You may select an individual object by left-clicking it. To select a group of objects, left-click the mouse and drag the mouse over the objects that you wish to select. At this point, the mouse pointer will change to a (↘), and a rectangle or rubberband will be shown, which encompasses all the objects selected.

To delete an object, select it, and then select the Delete option from the Edit menu or use the equivalent keyboard command, **^d** (**control+d**).

Resize Tool

This tool provides the ability to resize network topology and graph/stripchart objects. To enlarge or reduce one of these objects, first left-click the object. Next, select the Resize tool, left-click on one of the four object handles, and drag the object to the desired position and release the mouse button.

Text Tool

This tool adds text objects to the topology view. Adding static text information can improve the appearance of the view and provide vital information. For example, if the view includes different sub-views that contain multiple subnets, you can add specific labels for each of the subnets. When this tool is selected, the mouse pointer changes to a crosshair (I). You can control these objects just like you would any other element associated within a particular view.

To add a textual object, highlight the text box by selecting it. Next, single-click the left button on the mouse within the topology view area and begin typing the label. If you want to edit an existing view, right-click the mouse at the point in the text where you want to make the modification.

Device Tool

When selected, this tool permits the user to create device objects. This is the primary way to add additional devices to a topology map. Selecting this tool changes the mouse pointer to a plus sign (+). The icon is the default device graphic, which you can change by selecting another icon from the `Icon` menu.

To create an object, simply left-click on the topology view once the mouse pointer has changed to a plus sign (+).

Network Tool

This tool creates network icons that interconnect device objects. The standard network topology icon is the bus, which can't be changed. However, the thickness that represents a bus network topology can be changed depending on the type of network specified. Use the `Network` option in the `Icon` menu to change the network topology icons located on the topology view.

To create a network object type, select the network object with the left button of the mouse. Next, move the mouse over to the topology view area. Then, left-click to mark the beginning of the network, then drag to the right until the desired length of the network (or line) has been established.

Connection Tool

The Connection tool makes connections between individual device objects and one or more network topology objects. Device objects may interconnect to one or more network objects, but using the Connection tool to link two network objects is not supported. The only way to interconnect network elements is by using one or more device objects.

To connect a device object and network element, select the Connection tool. Move to the topology area. Notice that the mouse pointer will change to a (+). Next, left-click on the device object and begin dragging the pointer toward the network object that you want to connect to. The software will display a connecting line that is tracked to the mouse. Then left-click to complete the operation.

Group Tool

This tool is primarily used to combine a group of individual objects into a single object. For instance, a collection of workstations might be organized into subnet views. Therefore, the top-level topology view might include group objects that contain additional device objects or other elements.

To create a new group, simply select the elements that should be included in the group, plus the new group object, and select Join Group in the Structure menu. Access to the members of the group object is achieved by expanding the group. Figure 11.8 shows two groups called Subnet 134.110.1.0 and Subnet 134.110.2.0. In this example, the default icon for each group has been changed to represent a bus network topology.

To expand a specific group, select the group element and execute the expand option in the Structure menu. The icons that were once hidden will now be visible to the view, which is displayed in Figure 11.9. The group facility can organize a large network. Also, the icon associated with a group can be changed in the same manner as individual device objects. The group icons available are listed via the Group option in the Icon main menu.

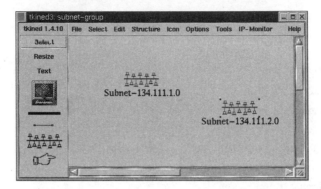

Figure 11.8 *Sample view that contains group objects.*

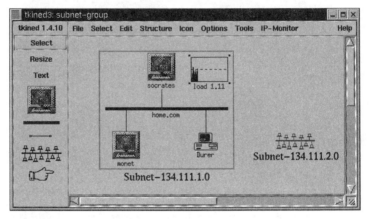

Figure 11.9 *Expanded group.*

Reference Tool

This tool creates links to existing topology views that can be accessed using an individual icon element. Reference objects provide a shortcut to another instance of a **tkined** view. The topology view displayed in Figure 11.10 shows three different reference links: Accounting Subnet, Performance, and Backbone.

To access the view behind the reference link, right-click the icon and select the Open (this view) option. This will display the view that is linked to this reference object over the existing panel. Figure 11.11 shows a sample of the view associated with the Accounting Subnet reference object.

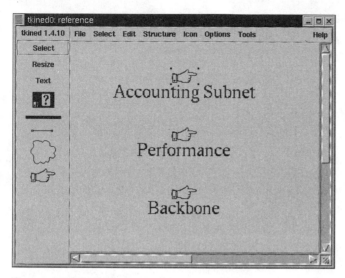

Figure 11.10 *Reference objects.*

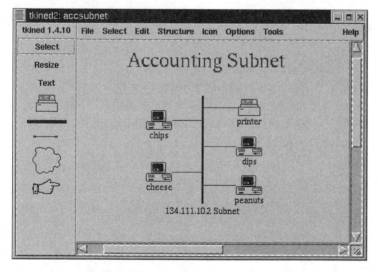

Figure 11.11 *Referenced view.*

Building Views

When building topology views, you must use the tool palette discussed in the previous section. This section provides step-by-step instructions for creating custom network views that match the physical or logical topology of your network. Two major approaches to designing a topology view are available: *physical* and *logical*. A physical topology view mimics the way the physical network is installed or connected.

For example, consider an Ethernet network that contains a single LAN switch with several workstations interconnected to the switch. We can map all of the physical elements of this network, including the cabling that connects each of the nodes to the switch, as shown in Figure 11.12. From the network diagram, we can determine the office drops used by each workstation, the punch-down location that each office drop uses, and the mapping between a switch port and an individual workstation. The numbers enclosed within the rectangle closest to the devices represent the office drops, while the other boxes are patch panel locations. Usually many details are presented in a physical network layout, such as the location of equipment (the switch, for instance) and other associated information. Usually physical network diagrams are the hardest to maintain because any little change, such as a workstation being added or deleted, can render it inaccurate.

The network manager must be diligent in keeping this information up-to-date, which can be a full-time occupation by itself.

A logical network view usually presents the network at a much broader and higher level. Logical views show the relationship of nodes and network devices from a purely conceptual level and don't necessarily include details regarding physical connections, switched port mapping, and other information. Figure 11.13 shows an example of this type of topology.

It is common for many network managers to use both approaches when building views. Therefore, the network topology views start out at a high level and, through a series of views, become increasingly more detailed.

Before building a topology, it is also recommended that you determine which topology type— logical, physical, or both—will be used. Also, in an effort to ensure that the topology view will be effective and useful, it is important to consider the ways in which the networks are viewed and supported within the local environment. For example, a large corporation might delegate administrative authority for each of the subnets to each of the departments. As a result, the central network group focuses mainly on the corpo-

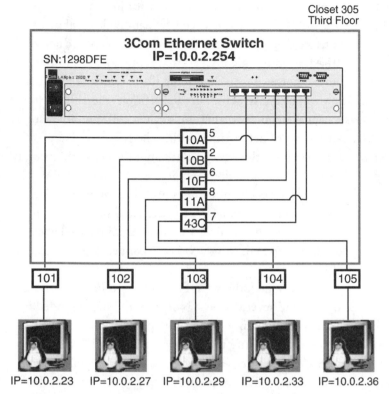

Figure 11.12 *Physical topology example.*

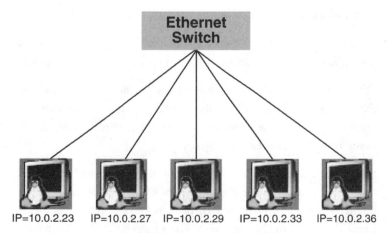

Figure 11.13 *Logical topology example.*

rate backbone. Therefore, a topology view for just this portion of
the network will be built, while each of the individual subnet owners maintains a topology view for just their portion of the network.

Using **tkined,** a set of logical views that represents one of the
most common approaches to describing the network of a mid-size
corporation will be constructed. In this example, the corporation
employs a Management Information Services (MIS) group responsible for all aspects of networking within the company. Each
department is assigned their own subnet, but the network group is
responsible for maintaining connectivity between nodes within the
subnets, and between each subnet and backbone network. The
company is based in Boston, Massachusetts, and is situated within
a campus of three buildings all very close in proximity to each
other. Also, the group maintains a WAN to connect many sales and
support offices.

Since the network includes both LAN and WAN components, it
is necessary to build several views. Note that the step included in
this section involves creating objects for actual devices on the network. You should substitute the specific devices for the actual
devices available on the network. To build each view will require
many individual steps. The sections that follow provide step-by-
step instructions for building a LAN view and a WAN view.

LAN View

To build a LAN view, follow these steps:

- Create a new directory to contain all the views. In this example,
  the directory /home/network-views is created for this purpose.

- Obtain a clean (new) view by selecting the New View option in
  the File menu. This will display an empty view. If you don't
  want to create a new view, just delete the unwanted objects to
  make room for additional objects.

- Since the default view of noname.tki is used, rename the view to
  top-level-view by selecting the Save As... option in the File
  menu. A dialog window will appear as shown in Figure 11.14.
  Enter the name of the new view and click the Select button.

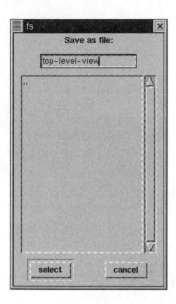

Figure 11.14 *Save As dialog window.*

- Using the left mouse button, select the Group tool. A transparent border should appear around this tool, indicating that it is active. When the mouse is moved in the topology view region, the mouse pointer changes to a symbol.

- Single-click the left mouse button to select the first group object. Next, right-click on the same object and select the Edit all Attributes... pop-up menu option. A new dialog window will appear, as shown in Figure 11.15. You can change the label (or name of the object) in this window. By default, it contains the label of group1. Next, enter the new label of LAN and click the Set Values button.

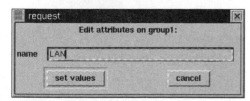

Figure 11.15 *Object attribute dialog window.*

- At this point, you should have a window that resembles Figure 11.16. If you do not, please review the previous steps to ensure that they were done correctly.

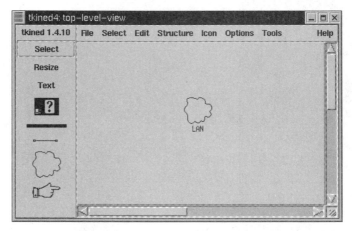

Figure 11.16 *Logical view.*

- Is is important to periodically save any modifications made to the view. Therefore, select the Save option in the File menu. A dialog box requiring confirmation to update the view will appear, as shown in Figure 11.17. Click the Replace button to save the most recent changes. In this example, the top-level-view file will be updated.

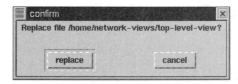

Figure 11.17 *Confirm dialog box.*

- Select the Network tool. Then, create a network that will represent the backbone network for the corporation. Left-click the mouse, release the button, drag the cursor to the right, and then left-click again. In this example, the backbone includes a series of Cisco routers interconnected via Gigabit Ethernet interfaces. Note that the tool hasn't been updated to include icons for Gigabit networking devices. Instead, it will just use the icon associated with FDDI.

- Change the network object type. Select the Select tool. Next, select the network icon just created by clicking the left mouse button. Then, select the FDDI option in the Icon->Network menu.

- Change the name of the network object to Backbone by modifying the Edit All Attributes... pop-up menu item. Note that this dialog window displays objects that can be changed. Modify the name field only.

- Add the Cisco router devices by selecting the device object tool and using the left button to create four device objects. If the actual network doesn't contain Cisco equipment, use the generic device types. Also, alter the number of devices to match your network environment.

- Click the Selection tool and select all the objects just created. Change the default icons for these devices to use the Cisco icon by selecting the Cisco option in the Icon->Node-> Network Device menu.

- Connect each of the Cisco devices in the backbone network. Select the Connectivity tool, left-click on one of the Cisco devices, and then left-click on the network object. Repeat this for each of the Cisco objects.

- Change the IP address information and the name of the devices created just by editing the attributes of the object. With device objects, two object elements are listed in the dialog box, as shown in Figure 11.18. In this example, one of the Cisco routers is called cisco-gw1.home.com. with the IP address of 10.0.1.1.

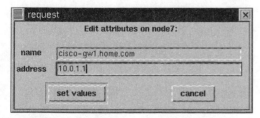

Figure 11.18 *Object attribute dialog box.*

- Move the entire backbone network into the LAN group. Select all the Cisco devices, network and associated network objects, plus the LAN group object. Select the Join Group option in the Structure menu. Once you do this, the backbone network will be contained within the LAN group object.

- To access the individual objects within a group, use the expand option in the Structure menu. You can also expand the group by selecting the group object and using the right mouse button to select the Expand group from the pop-up menu.

- Once expanded, the elements within the group are displayed within a gray rectangle, as shown in Figure 11.19.

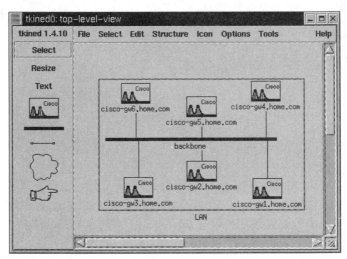

Figure 11.19 *Group view.*

- You can add a background image to this topology map to make the view more representative. Currently only X11 bitmap files are supported. To add an image, select the Import... option from the File menu and input the filename that contains the background image.

- In this example, a background image of the state of Massachusetts has been added to the topology view called ma-image.xbm because the company is based in the state. Since the image is rather large, it was necessary to move the entire image from the top left corner of the window to the lower right corner. Also, the LAN group object was moved over to the city (Boston, in this case) in which the corporate office is located. To move the object, simply left- and right-click on the object and drag it with the mouse. Release the button at the desired location.

- Add a descriptive title to the view. Select the Text tool and left-click within the area where you want to place the new title. Possible titles include: Corporate LAN, Backbone Network, and Corporate Network, and the like. If the title isn't at the desired location, move it with the mouse using the same procedure discussed in the previous step. Figure 11.20 shows the completed view.

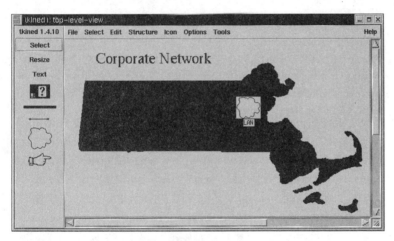

Figure 11.20 *Completed LAN view.*

WAN View

To build a WAN view, follow these steps:

1. Create another tkined view by selecting the New View option in the File menu.

2. Save the new view to a file called WAN-view within the /home/networkviews directory.

3. Since the company maintains different offices throughout the country, it is reasonable to use a map of the United States to show the location of individual devices that are within the

WAN. Therefore, import the background image called `usa-image.xbm`.

4. Create devices that are used to support the WAN. This includes routers, modems, and any other associated devices. For our example, a total of four routers have been added to the view: `wan-remote.home.com`, `fl-gw.home.com`, `tx-gw.home.com`, and `ca-gw.home.com`.

5. Create connectivity objects between each of the routers showing the correct topology of the network.

6. Add a descriptive label using the Text tool.

7. Now that you have completed this view, you should make a link from the first view (`top-level-view`) to the `WAN-view`. You can do this by creating a reference object on the `top-level-view`. To add this object to the view, select the reference icon with the left mouse button. Next, left-click on the topology map where the object should be placed.

8. Once you create the reference object, you must add it to the `WAN-view`. To do this, right-click on the reference object to display the dialog box shown in Figure 11.21. Enter the name `WAN-view` in the `name` field to serve as the name of the object. Next, specify the full pathname and filename of the file that contains the `WAN-view` topology map. In this example, the path and file is `/home/network-views/WAN-view`. Click the `Set Value` button to save this information.

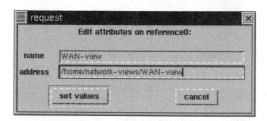

Figure 11.21 *Reference object attributes dialog window.*

9. To ensure that the reference object link is operational, right-click on the object link and, when the pop-up window appears, select the `Open (this view)` item. If the link is working, a `WAN-view topology map` should replace the existing view, as shown in Figure 11.22.

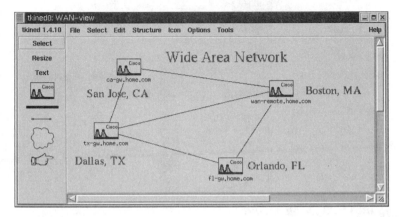

Figure 11.22 *WAN topology view.*

Using Background Images

Images that represent many US states are located in the `images` directory on the top level of the CD-ROM. These images can be used as backgrounds within **tkined** topology views. Under this directory, a `README.txt` file contains additional information on retrieving and using these images.

Managing the Network

At this point, network topology views should have been created either through the automated discovery process or manually. In any event, it is assumed that network elements such as routers and network switches have been created and we can now begin to use some of the power features of **tkined** to manage these individual devices.

Many of the device management capabilities are accessed with the `Tools` menu, displayed in Figure 11.23. This menu provides access to a large set of management functions.

Each of the tasks found on the `Tools` menu can be divided into the following categories:

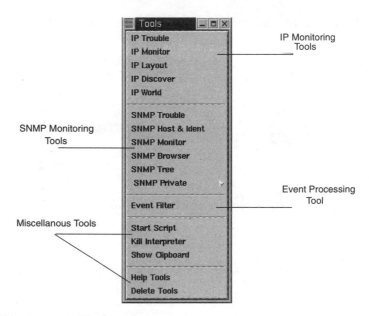

Figure 11.23 *Tools menu.*

- Internet Protocol (IP) monitoring

- SNMP monitoring

- event monitoring and processing

- miscellaneous tasks

Most of the options, when selected, create a new dynamic menu to the right of the `Tools` menu. For example, selecting the `IP-Trouble` option adds a new menu, `IP-Trouble`, to the main menu bar, as shown in Figure 11.24. The removal of the menu is not automatic, however; the user must delete the menu manually by selecting the last `Tools` menu option, `Delete IP-Monitor`.

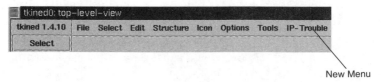

Figure 11.24 *Addition of new menu on main menu.*

The IP monitoring menu includes the five submenus listed in Table 11.1. Some of the monitoring functions use the remote procedure call (RPC) facilities of the target devices to gain management information. Therefore, this facility must be active in order for these monitoring functions to work correctly.

Also, many of these functions require a selection of one or more target systems in order to perform a specific task. Therefore, functions selected from the menus will not execute without a target selection.

Table 11.1 *IP monitoring menu submenus*

Submenu	Description
IP Trouble	Tools used to diagnose specific connectivity or system-related problems
IP Monitoring	Tools used to monitor specific services
IP Layout	Options to control the layout of one or more topology views
IP Discover	A tool used to discover all the devices and systems on a given network
IP World	A visual traceroute facility

IP Trouble Submenu

The IP-Trouble submenu contains a large number of functions that help diagnose specific system and connectivity problems. It is the front end for many of the common UNIX network and system commands such as **ping, traceroute, telnet, finger,** and **whois**. Figure 11.25 shows the submenu as a self-contained window. All of the menus available under **tkined** can be "torn off" and accessed via a regular window. See the "Menu Reference" section for instructions on how to activate a tear-off menu.

The options listed in this submenu are described next.

Figure 11.25 *IP trouble submenu.*

Ping

This option implements the standard ping services to determine general network connectivity. Chapter 4, "Core System Utilities and Tools," discusses this command. It displays a result window that shows the round-trip time for the ICMP (ping) response when the command is successful. If the task fails, a `not reachable` message is displayed instead.

Multi Ping

This option provides the ability to alter some of the ping options when checked for general network connectivity. Invoking this function causes the application to display the dialog window shown in Figure 11.26. This window contains two scroll elements that can be used to vary the number of bytes and the maximum amount of bytes that is sent with each ICMP request. The number of bytes sent determines the number of ICMP requests that are transmitted.

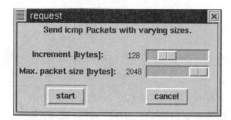

Figure 11.26 *Multi ping dialog window.*

Click the `Start` button to begin issuing the ICMP requests. Using the default values, a total of 17 requests are sent, as shown in the result window displayed in Figure 11.27. This tool is most useful for obtaining generic performance information from one or more network devices in a more automated fashion.

Figure 11.27 *Ping result window.*

Netmask

This option displays the defined subnetwork mask used by the target host. Upon success, it displays a message similar to: `Netmask for monet.home.com [10.0.2.27] 255.255.255.0` for the host `monet`, indicating the use of `255.255.255.0` (24 bits) for the subnet mask. If the tool is unable to obtain this information, it displays an empty mask list of 0.0.0.0.

Traceroute

This option implements the standard traceroute services to determine the routing path between the local system that is running **tkined** and the remote target system. It displays the same output in the same format as the standard **traceroute** command. Chapter 4, "Core System Utilities and Tools," discusses the **traceroute** command.

Telnet and Rlogin

This option provides generic remote access to the target system invoking either the **telnet** or **rlogin** services. When either are selected, they display a new window with a login prompt. Note that if two or more target hosts have been selected, an appropriate number of terminal windows will be created.

Daytime, Finger, DNS Info, Whois, and NTP Info

Each of these options obtains miscellaneous information about the target host and displays a result window that contains either the information or any error messages.

TCP/RPC Services

Both of these options attempt to discover which TCP port and/or remote procedure call (RPC) services are running on the remote target. In the case of TCP services, the output is similar to the **nmap** command explained in Chapter 5. This option will retrieve all the RPC services currently running. Probing a Sun server system called bubbles obtained the output shown in Figure 11.28.

NFS Exports/NFS Mounts

These options list any exported file systems or mounted file systems on the remote target.

Host Status

This option provides the ability to execute a **vmstat** command on a remote target host via the **rstatd** process. This command provides

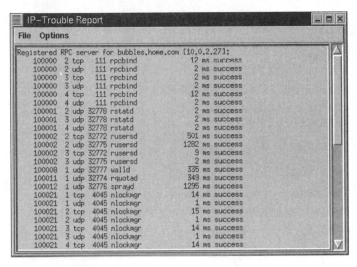

Figure 11.28 *RPC services listing.*

uptime information as well. When executed, it displays a dialog window that permits the user to alter the polling interval. This interval controls the amount of time between each query cycle. Figure 11.29 shows this window.

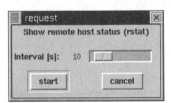

Figure 11.29 *Interval dialog window.*

Figure 11.30 shows a sample of the output that is generated by executing this task.

Ether Status

This option provides the ability to obtain Ethernet-like statistics from the remote target system via the `etherd` process. Like the `Host Status` function, it displays a dialog window that allows the user to alter the polling interval.

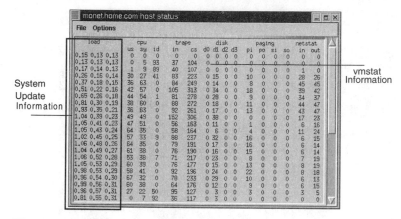

System
Update
Information

vmstat
Information

Figure 11.30 *Remote result window.*

Set Parameter

This option displays a dialog window that permits the user to change some basic parameters associated with options contained within the IP-Trouble menu.

The window contains four items; the first three control the general operating characteristics of the **ping** command, while the other controls the limit of the number of hops used with the **traceroute** command.

Figure 11.31 *IP-Trouble parameter window.*

Help IP-Trouble

This option displays a new window that contains generic help on all the IP-Trouble menu options. This is useful for searching the menus for specific options, but it doesn't provide specific details regarding each option.

Delete IP-Trouble

This option removes the IP-Trouble menu from the main window.

IP Monitoring Menu

The IP-Monitoring menu, shown in Figure 11.32, provides fault-monitoring tasks relating to the performance behavior and network connectivity of a UNIX system. Some of the menu options create performance graphs on the topology panel. As you will see, these graphs are one excellent way to monitor specific information on a continued basis.

Figure 11.32 *IP monitoring menu.*

The options listed in the IP Monitoring menu are described next.

Check Reachability

This option monitors network device reachability and provides a different way to indicate when problems occur. To enable this feature, simply select the target devices that should be monitored and select the Check Reachability option. When network connectivity is interrupted, either due to a network or device problem, the

associated topology device icon that represents the monitored system will blink and turn red. Figure 11.33 shows a topology view
with a device (called `route-1.home.com`) that failed the reachability
test. Its icons have changed to indicate that this problem has
occurred.

In the figure, the icon appears white. This is because the icon is
blinking between white and red colors on a continuous basis; when
the screen snapshot of the window was taken, the icon was white
at that time. When connectivity is restored to the system, the icon
returns to normal. This provides a visual mechanism to alert when
a particular device or system is down.

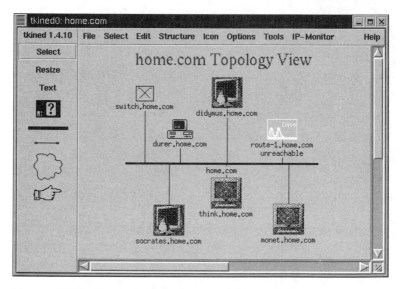

Figure 11.33 *Device's icon change to denote failure.*

Bear in mind that factors not related to a system can cause it to
appear to be down. For example, in many networks, a switch or
other networking device provides connectivity between the target
monitored systems and the host that is running the monitoring
software. For instance, consider the network shown in Figure
11.34.

This network consists of three primary devices and two 3Com
LAN switches interconnected via a Cisco router. If either `Router B`
or `Switch C` fails for any reason, connectivity between the moni-

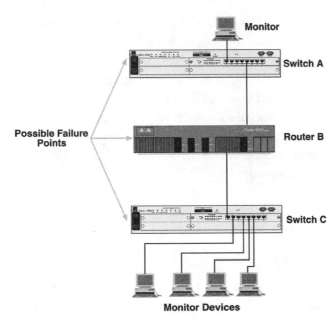

Figure 11.34 *Possible monitoring failures.*

tored systems and the monitoring device will appear to be down. In reality, an intermediate device has caused this problem. The solution? Plan on monitoring more than just the systems and other important workstations. Take into consideration the entire path between each of the critical systems to the network that will provide the primary monitoring services.

To go a step further, let's consider the example where all the devices are being monitored and the power supply in Switch C decides to take a vacation and become inoperative. At this point, assuming the switch doesn't contain redundant power supplies, the switch is dead in the water. From a **tkined** perspective, the devices attached to this switch and the switch itself have become disconnected from the rest of the network. The topology view now contains a bunch of blinking icons. The problem now becomes, which device(s) are really down?

The answer to this question, unfortunately, requires some amount of knowledge about the network topology. An experienced network troubleshooter might examine the topology and determine the best place to start looking for the most likely cause. The first step in a situation like this is to begin to isolate the problem. To some degree, the **tkined** tool has done this for you; it shows which part of the network is experiencing trouble. It will be important to examine the problem in stages, ensuring connectivity along the way. For example, if you see that a particular switch is down, attempt to establish reachability to the device closest to the switch. Keep probing each neighbor of the affected system until you have determined the root cause, which in this case, requires the replacement of a failed power supply.

Round-Trip Time

This option produces a stripchart graph that shows the round-trip delay using the Internet control message protocol (ICMP). What is interesting about this feature is that the graph is added to the topology panel alongside the device icon. In essence, this tool provides the ability to visually see the behavior of the system and associated path network to the system. This means that specific views can be created to display performance-related information. Consider the view displayed in Figure 11.35, which shows two servers, each with an associated round-trip time (RTT) graph. All is well with both systems because the RTT is one millisecond. This indicates that the network paths between the system running **tkined** and the target hosts are free from congestion or other problems that could affect network performance.

System Load, CPU, Disk, and Interface Activity

Each of these options provides monitoring capabilities just like the round-trip time graph above. When selected, each will create a stripchart graph as shown in Figure 11.36. In this figure, a new view specific to a single system called monet was created. The view contains five different graphs that indicate round-trip delay, system load averages, CPU activity, network interface performance, and disk activity.

Understanding the performance information presented in the graphs requires knowing the output of certain UNIX monitoring commands. It is beyond the scope of this book to examine each of the system administration monitoring tools. Therefore, the reader

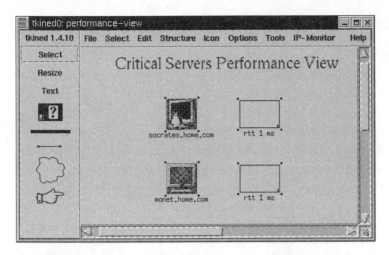

Figure 11.35 *Performance-specific view.*

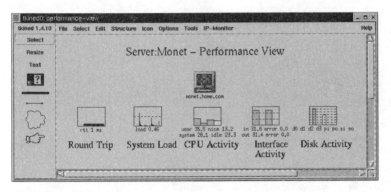

Figure 11.36 monet *performance view.*

should research **vmstat, rstatd, uptime,** and related commands for additional information.

The layout of the view isn't critical, and, with a little imagination, custom views can be pieced together that are functional yet easy to use. If many systems require the amount of monitoring shown in Figure 11.36, it is recommended that each of the system views be created separately and even linked with its own reference icon. Alternatively, group elements can be used instead of reference icons; the choice is really up to you.

Ethernet Load/Active Users

The `Ethernet Load` option shows the network load of the default interface, as reported by the etherd process. The `Active Users` option provides a list of all the users logged in to a particular system.

Monitor Job Info/Modify Monitor Job

These options provide the ability to monitor and alter the **tkined** monitoring processes. You can list every presently running monitoring task executed by **tkined** using either of these options. The `Monitor Job Info` option simply lists all the active processes, whereas the `Modify Monitor Job` option permits the user to alter certain operating parameters or even kill a particular process. Figure 11.37 shows the window displayed when the `Modify Monitor Job` option is selected.

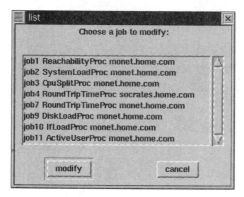

Figure 11.37 `Modify Job` *selection window.*

This window contains a list of monitoring jobs from which the user can select a single job to review or modify. To modify a particular job, select it and hit the `Modify` button. As a result, a new window will be displayed, as shown in Figure 11.38. This window controls the monitoring interval, job status, falling and rising threshold values, and threshold actions, and provides the ability to stop a monitored task. If you want to stop the job, use the `Kill Job` button.

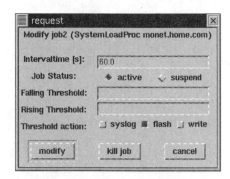

Figure 11.38 Modify *monitoring task window.*

Set Parameter

This option provides the same functions as the IP-Trouble menu option but contains an additional toggle switch that controls the creation of graph diagrams. By default, the value is false.

Delete IP-Monitor

This option deletes the IP-Monitor menu. However, if monitoring jobs are active, selecting this menu option will display a dialog box informing the user that pending tasks are still operating. Deleting the menu means that any monitored jobs will be stopped. The user is given the choice of killing those tasks and exiting the menu or canceling the delete-menu task all together. Deleting the IP-Monitor menu automatically removes certain graphs, such as interface activity and disk activity, from the topology view.

IP Layout Menu

The IP-Layout menu contains functions that control how a topology view will be organized. The options on this menu are good for handling situations where an IP discovery process was executed and a large number of network device elements have been created. This menu provides a way to automate how the devices are laid out and positioned on the view. Figure 11.39 shows the IP-Layout menu.

The options listed in the IP Layout menu are described below.

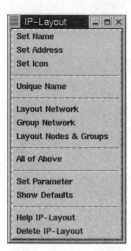

Figure 11.39 *IP layout menu.*

Set Name, Address, and Icon

These menu options cause what is displayed in an object's label area to include either the object name, address, or icon name. For instance, to make each device contain the address within the label, select the Set Address menu option.

Unique Name

This option will strip off domain name extensions for each selected icon element. The purpose of the option is to shorten the name of each object so that it includes just the host portion of the name, not the domain name.

Layout Network, Group Network, and Layout Nodes & Groups

These menu options provide automated tasks to assist with the organization of a topology view that contains many objects. You can also use them with a small number of devices, but it may be easier to lay these out using a manual approach, particularly if the view will contain a custom look. The Layout Network option will position all nodes that are attached to a given network around that network in an orderly fashion. The Group Network option will make all members of a given network into members of a group, which will be named after the address of the network. The Layout Network option attempts to control the layout of groups and individual device objects together on a view. Unfortunately, the layout of these objects isn't what one would expect. This function lays groups out in a reasonable manner, but it places device objects on top of each other, which is not all that useful. It is recommended that objects be laid individually or by using one of the other automated layout menu options.

All of the Above

This option seems to suggest that it will execute each of the menu items above it. When we selected this option, it started to change the name of the object elements to the complete name. The **tkined** application crashed after this. Even after repeated attempts, the option either didn't complete the task or caused the application to stop. Therefore, it is recommended that you do not use this menu option.

Show Parameter

This option displays a new window that contains menu layout parameters that the user can alter. In practice, you won't need to change the default values and you can ignore this option.

Delete IP-Layout

This option closes the IP-Layout menu. Executing this task doesn't affect any previously executed layout tasks, existing object elements, or associated topology views.

IP Discover Menu

The IP-Discover menu automates the process of collecting and inventorying network devices for the purpose of building one or more topology views. The process of conducting a discovery is covered in the "Network Discovery" section at the beginning of this chapter. A note of caution is warranted here because a network discovery process can adversely affect network performance if used incorrectly or too often. Following these rules when using the automated discovery process will help keep problems to a minimum:

- Discover only those networks that you actually work with or have the network owner's permission to inventory.

- Never leave the discovery process active without someone monitoring the process. Because the process of inventorying large networks is a time-consuming task, it may take several days to fully discover the network. It may not be a good idea to start the process and walk away. If a problem that adversely affects the rest of the network occurs, it is better to know of the problem before the user community (or your boss).

- When inventorying a large network, it is better to discover the network in smaller portions than attempt to do the whole thing and let the process span several days. The major argument against large discoveries is that they tend to cause network-related problems should the software crash or otherwise probe the network continuously as a result of a software bug or other problem.

- Be informed about the exact nature of the discovery process. Knowing which SNMP MIB objects and other elements are queried to inventory the network is important.

Figure 11.40 IP-discover *menu.*

The options listed in the IP-Discover menu are described here.

Discover IP Network

As shown in the section, "Network Discovery," this option invokes the discovery process for an IP-based network. Unfortunately, as of this writing, **tkined** does not support other network-layer protocols, such as IPX. Selecting IP Discover option will display a new dialog window. This new window contains a text box that permits the user to add one or more destination network addresses to discover.

The discovery process uses both ICMP and SNMP to inventory and query devices on the network.

Discover Route

This menu option will conduct a discovery of the route to a destination host or other device. When the route to the remote destination has been established, a series of routers (gateways) and network icons that represent the network path from the local system to the remote system are created. This type of discovery is most useful when attempting to learn more about the individual nodes that are used when reaching a remote system.

Show RPC/TCP Server

Both of these options attempt to probe a remote RPC or TCP destination service to see if it is currently operating and accepting service connections. When selected, each displays a dialog box that contains a list of remote server processes to query. Selecting the RPC option displays a server list, as shown in Figure 11.41.

In the figure, the mountd process was selected. This process is used when remote mounting of a file system is configured on a system. The major purpose of these menu options is to attempt the discovery of a small class of the devices and systems. For example, it is possible to search for all systems that provide remote filesystem mounting capabilities. The list of remote services shown in the dialog window represents many of the standard services for most UNIX systems. Therefore, it should not be difficult to inventory the network with just about any service that is needed.

Resolve Email

This menu option provides a mechanism to determine the location of electronic mail systems that provide a mailbox for a given Email user. When selected, this option displays a dialog box that permits the user to add an Email address within a text field. This function is used mostly to identify which systems are used to support Email and to monitor those specific systems.

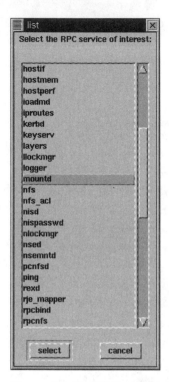

Figure 11.41 *RPC server query list.*

Set Parameter

This option controls generic operational parameters for the discovery menu options. In practice, you won't need to change the default values and can largely ignore this option.

IP World Menu

The IP-World menu provides a visual traceroute feature that when given a destination, will record the routing hops on a world map. Since this menu provides the same basic services as the **xtraceroute** command that was discussed in Chapter 5, "Additional System Utilities and Tools," this option isn't described here.

SNMP Menu

The SNMP-related tools provide a way to query for specific SNMP information and to monitor MIB objects. Generally speaking, these services amount to having a way to interrogate SNMP agents in an automated fashion.

SNMP-Trouble Menu

The SNMP-Trouble menu, shown in Figure 11.42, provides options to query devices for specific information. When specific problems occur, use this menu to learn more about the problem and implement a solution.

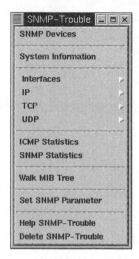

Figure 11.42 SNMP-Trouble *menu.*

The options in the SNMP-Trouble menu are described below.

SNMP Devices

This option provides a generic test to determine which of the selected devices on the topology panel respond to SNMP requests. The system.SysDescr.0 MIB-II object is queried as a result of selecting this option. The option is provided as a quick way to establish basic SNMP connectivity to network devices.

System Information

This option shows generic SNMP information about the target system. It provides the equivalent of a walk on the MIB-II system group, as shown in Figure 11.43.

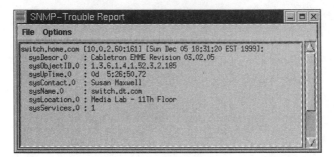

Figure 11.43 *System information display window.*

Interfaces, IP, TCP, and UDP

These menu options provide access to objects associated with the MIB-II group. Each option contains one or more sub-options for displaying specific MIB tables or group information.

ICMP and SNMP Statistics

Like the options above, these menu options provide access to additional MIB-II objects.

Walk MIB Tree

Like the UCD **snmpwalk** command, this menu option provides an automated way to walk a MIB tree. Given an MIB group, it walks the entire MIB tree until the end of the MIB is detected.

Set SNMP Parameter

This menu option permits the user to alter some of the default SNMP parameters that are shared by all the menu functions. Selecting this option displays the window shown in Figure 11.44.

The window contains some of the basic SNMP parameters, such as community name, SNMP (UDP) port, timeout values, and so forth. If the network uses nonstandard community strings (which is strongly encouraged), this would be the place to enter the appropriate value.

SNMP-Host Menu

The SNMP-Host menu is used to retrieve specific objects from the HOST-RESOURCE MIB. This MIB provides system-specific objects related to storage, file systems, and process information.

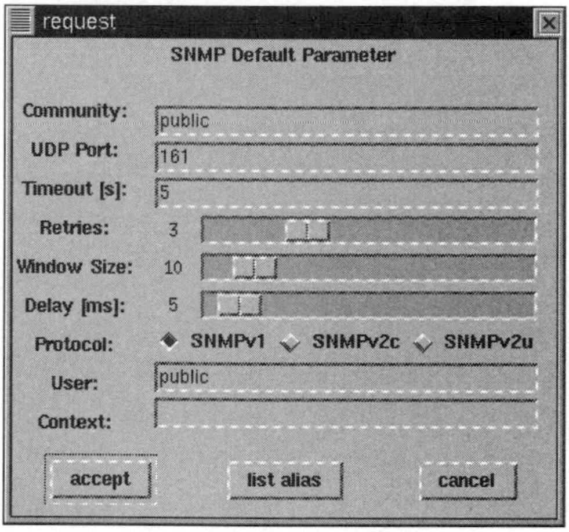

Figure 11.44 *SNMP parameter options window.*

Since a description of this MIB is beyond the scope of this book, this menu will not be described.

SNMP-Monitor Menu

This menu provides access to options for the monitoring of specific MIB objects. Figure 11.45 shows the SNMP-Monitor menu. The basic purpose of this menu is to provide continuous monitoring of device elements to determine abnormal conditions or other problems.

Figure 11.45 SNMP-Monitor *menu.*

The SNMP-Monitor menu options are described next.

Monitor Variable

One of the most important tasks that **tkined** has to offer is the ability to monitor one or more specific MIB objects. Selecting the `Monitor Variable` option displays a dialog window that permits the user to enter an MIB object name, as shown in Figure 11.46.

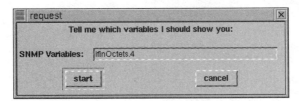

Figure 11.46 *Monitor dialog window.*

You can add any valid MIB object name to this text box. Selecting the `start` button creates a graph on the topology view with the values of this object. In Figure 11.46, the MIB-II object `ifInOctets.4` was entered. Recall from Chapter 6, "Overview of MIB-II," that this object contains the total number of incoming bytes for for the fifth interface on the system. Once **tkined** starts to monitor this object, a historical graph can be maintained to show the amount of network traffic going into this interface. Figure 11.47 shows a sample stripchart that tracks the `ifInOctets.4` object.

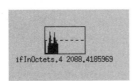

Figure 11.47 *Stripchart of the* `ifInOctets` *object.*

Interface Load

This option provides a stripchart for each interface within the target system. It is useful for viewing all the interfaces of a particular set of devices at the same time.

TCP Service User

This option provides a count of the users accessing or using a particular TCP service. It is a good way to capture heavy use of certain protocols and services such as Web access, file transfer, and mail.

Menu Reference

This section provides an overview of the generic application menus. To accomplish specific actions or tasks, review the following sections for a detailed explanation of application functionality.

The menus provided by **tkined** are used to access much of the application's functionality. With the exception of the Tools menu, all other menus are described in the section. The Tools menu is explained in the last section, "Managing the Network."

The main window contains the following submenus: File, Select, Edit, Structure, Icon, Options, Tools, and Help. These submenus can be accessed from the main window or made into separate windows. The latter feature, known as a tear-off menu, provides an additional convenience for the user by transforming the menu into an independent window. To tear off a menu, select the first dashed line separator located on the top of the menu frame. Once you do this, a new window that contains the associated menu will appear. Figure 11.48 shows the top tear-off bar for the Help menu.

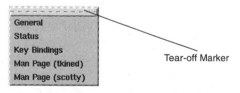

Figure 11.48 *Help menu tear-off menu.*

The Help menu provides generic on-line information regarding the **tkined** application and features. One of the more important items is the **tkined** man page, which will be displayed when the user selects the Man Page (**tkined**) menu option. Also included is the Scotty man page, which provides a detailed overview of the Application Programming Interfaces (APIs) for the Tool Command Language (TCL).

Generally speaking, you can execute most of the menu functions via a corresponding keyboard equivalent that can be used instead of selecting menu options with the mouse.

The `File` menu contains options used to create and maintain network views. Figure 11.49 shows the `File` menu. The `Clear` option deletes the currently displayed view. The application will prompt for confirmation before the operation is completed. Deleting the existing view automatically creates another empty view. If the user deletes a view that isn't already saved to a file, then the view will be lost forever. The `Open...` menu option restores and displays a pre-existing view from a UNIX file. Displaying an existing view will create a new **tkined** window, and the filename of the view will be placed within the window title.

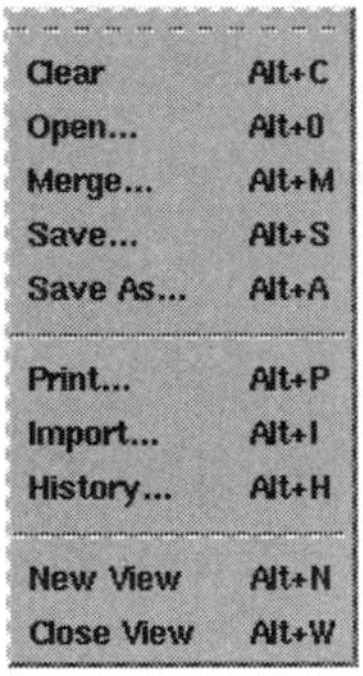

Clear	Alt+C
Open...	Alt+O
Merge...	Alt+M
Save...	Alt+S
Save As...	Alt+A
Print...	Alt+P
Import...	Alt+I
History...	Alt+H
New View	Alt+N
Close View	Alt+W

Figure 11.49 `File` *menu.*

The `Merge...` item can be used to combine different views into a single one. The `Save...` option saves the currently displayed view to a file. The user is prompted for the filename. The `Save...` option makes a copy of the view and places it in a different file. The `print...` option prints the current active view.

The `Select` menu offers a variety of options that select and highlight a number of objects. Figure 11.50 shows this menu. The first option, `Select All`, selects all the objects contained within the topology view. The `Select Neighbors` option selects an adjacent object that interconnects an existing selected object. The `Select member` option selects all members of a view. The remaining menu options provide the ability to select objects based on the type,

Figure 11.50 Select *menu.*

name, address, label, and attribute. Each of the options displays a dialog window so that appropriate input can be collected by the user. For example, selecting the Type... option displays the dialog window shown in Figure 11.51, which permits the user to choose the type of object from a list of predefined menu items.

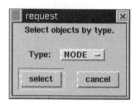

Figure 11.51 Selection by type *dialog.*

Figure 11.52 shows the available types that can be chosen from the selection list. The list contains all the objects types that are supported by the software. Selecting an object type and clicking the Select button will select all objects on the main topology panel that meet the criteria. In this case, only the node types will be highlighted. The Name..., Address..., and Label... options permit the user to input an expression string that is compared to all the objects within the topology view for that particular attribute. The remaining option, Attribute..., provides the user the ability to further define a selection criteria by using additional object definitions. One possible attribute, for instance, is the topology map to which an object belongs.

The Edit menu contains a number of items used to modify object attributes and control the placement of objects on the view,

Figure 11.52 *Type selection.*

and generic editing options such as Cut, Copy, and Paste. Figure 11.53 shows the Edit menu.

The first item, Attribute, is a submenu that can add, modify, or delete an object attribute. This submenu contains three options: Create..., Delete..., and Edit....

Each object defined in the topology view contains both standard and custom properties (attributes) that provide additional information or configuration parameters.

Figure 11.53 *The* Edit *menu.*

The standard attributes associated with all node objects include Name, Address, and SNMP:Config. The Name represents the official hostname of the object, and the Address is the IP address of the object. The SNMP:Config property contains the command-line options that are used when specific SNMP operations are performed on the object. Additional user attributes may be defined.

Using this menu, only custom properties and `SNMP:Config` objects may be deleted or edited.

To create a new property, first select the object or group of objects with which you want this new property to be associated. Then select the `Create` option in the `Attribute` menu. This will cause a dialog window, as shown in Figure 11.54, to appear. Enter the name of the new attribute in the `Name` field. The name can be anything you want, but it should be representative of the value being entered. For example, a new attribute called `snmp_version` can contain the version of the SNMP protocols that is supported by the device. In the case where devices support more than one version, the value indicates the highest level of support. Next, enter the value associated with this property, and, for this example, assume that the devices support all versions. As a result, enter the value of 3, as shown in Figure 11.54. Finally, click the `Create` button to save the new attribute and apply it to the objects that were previously selected.

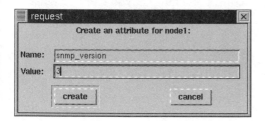

Figure 11.54 *Create New Attribute window.*

The next menu option, `Set Label...`, alters the object label. The label is listed directly below the object icon.

The `Structure` menu, shown in Figure 11.55, contains options used to control the organization of the group and group members. Also, the menu provides functions to control the placement of objects in relation to other objects.

The first two options control how the objects are displayed when one object is placed on top of another object. The first option, `Bring to Front`, brings a hidden object to the foreground, while the `Send to Back` option does the opposite. These options are most useful when a smaller object that was created after a larger

Figure 11.55 `Structure` *menu.*

one was created, needs to be placed in front of the larger one. The remaining options maintain groups.

The `Icon` menu options assign icons to object elements. A large collection of icons are available with **tkined** that include icons for UNIX systems, network devices like routers and switches, and network topology icons for Ethernet and other network topologies. There are some basic rules about the appropriate device types that can be assigned to certain icons. For example, you can't assign a network element (such as FDDI) to a device icon that represents a Linux system.

Figure 11.56 `Icon` *menu.*

The use of this menu, shown in Figure 11.56, should be fairly intuitive. As you can see, a series of submenus are used to access individual icons that have been sorted by type. The `Options` menu controls basic elements of the topology views, such as page size and orientation. Also, the tool palette can be placed on the top of the window versus the left side. The defaults of the options should be accessible to most users. Figure 11.57 shows the `Options` menu.

Figure 11.57 Options *menu.*

Tools at a Glance

Table A.1 provides a quick summary of the tools described in this book. Each tool is categorized into one or more network management classifications related to the functions it performs.

Table A.1 *List of tools described in this book*

Tool	Description	Performance Management	Configuration Management	Diagnostics Management	Page
arp	Monitors and controls ARP cache		✓	✓	106
arpwatch	Monitors ARP activity			✓	184
control-panel	GUI-based configuration tool		✓		534
ethereal	GUI-based packet capture			✓	188
fping	Fancy ping	✓		✓	210
ifconfig	Interface configuration		✓		115
ping	Determines number of active device(s) on network	✓		✓	143
mibiisa	Sun MIB-II SNMP agent	✓	✓	✓	391
mrtg	Network performance graphing tool	✓		✓	466
netstat	Network statistics	✓		✓	125
ntop	Network traffic monitor	✓		✓	500
nmap	Network port scanner			✓	218

Table A.1 *List of tools described in this book (continued)* •

Tool	Description	Performance Management	Configuration Management	Diagnostics Management	Page
snmpbulkwalk	Enhanced SNMP retrieval			✓	451
snmpconf	Automated SNMP configurations		✓		454
snmpd	UCD SNMP agent			✓	448
snmpdelta	Formats SNMP data			✓	422
snmpget	Regular SNMP retrieval			✓	425
snmpgetnext	Retrieves multiple SNMP objects			✓	427
snmpnetstat	Retrieves network statistics from SNMP entity			✓	429
snmpset	Alters SNMP configuration information		✓		434
snmpstatus	Retrieves important SNMP data			✓	437
snmptable	Retrieves SNMP table data			✓	440
snmptest	Tests SNMP connectivity			✓	443

Table A.1　*List of tools described in this book (continued)*

Tool	Description	Performance Management	Configuration Management	Diagnostics Management	Page
snmptrap	Sends SNMP traps			✓	445
snmptrapd	Receipt of SNMP traps from network			✓	446
snmpwalk	Retrieves either a group or entire MIB tree			✓	450
tcpdump	Packet capture program			✓	153
tkined	Network editor used to create topology maps and manage network devices	✓		✓	568
tkmib	SNMP MIB browser		✓	✓	458
traceroute	Displays routing paths	✓		✓	171
xtraceroute	Displays routing path information	✓		✓	239

Installation Procedures and Software Notes

Use the following installation procedures to install the tools described in this book. Many of the packages have been made available on a CD-ROM that is located on the inside back cover. The software can also be obtained via the Internet. Because some of the tools may have been updated since the publication of this book, pointers to alternative sources (where applicable) have been provided. Additionally, some of the tools are also available in source code form; as a result, procedures for building these packages are included as well.

Table B.1 contains a list of all the tools discussed within this book. The table also includes a column that indicates whether the tool is included on the CD-ROM, the directory where it can be found, and any alternate Internet sources for where the tool can be located. This information is provided because some tool owners provide updates on a periodic basis, and newer versions can be downloaded directly from the Internet.

Table B.1 *Directory of tool information*

Tool	On CD-ROM	Directory On CD-ROM	Alternate Source
Chesapeake's Subnet Calculator	Y	ccci	`http://www.ccci.com/tools/subcalc/index.html`
arp	N	NA	NA
control-panel	N	NA	NA
ethereal	Y	ethereal	`http://ethereal.zing.org`

fping	Y	fping	`ftp://ftp.staford.edu/pub/packages/fping/fping2.2b1.tar.gz`
			`ftp://sesame.hensa.ac.uk/ftp/mirrors/ftp.kernel.org/pub/software/admin/mon/fping2.2b1.tar.gz`
			`ftp://www.wooten.net/ftp/pub/unix/att/tcputils/fping.tar.z`

ifconfig	N	NA	NA
ping	N	NA	NA
netstat	N	NA	NA
nmap	Y	nmap	`http://www.insecure.org/nmap`
ntop	Y	ntop	`ftp://ftp.unipi.it/pub/local/ntop`
mibiisa	Y	sunagent	`http://www.sun.com/solstice/products/ent.agents`
mrtg	Y	mrtg	`http://eestaff.ethz.ch/~oetiker/webtools/mrtg/pub/`

Table B.1 *Directory of tool information (continued)*

Tool	On CD-ROM	Directory On CD-ROM	Alternate Source
snmpd	Y	ucd	Part of the UCD package
snmpdelta	Y	ucd	Part of the UCD package
snmpget	Y	ucd	Part of the UCD package
snmpgetnext	Y	ucd	Part of the UCD package
snmpnetstat	Y	ucd	Part of the UCD package
snmpset	Y	ucd	Part of the UCD package
snmpstatus	Y	ucd	Part of the UCD package
snmptable	Y	ucd	Part of the UCD package
snmptest	Y	ucd	Part of the UCD package
snmptranslate	Y	ucd	Part of the UCD package
snmptrap	Y	ucd	Part of the UCD package
snmptrapd	Y	ucd	Part of the UCD package
snmpwalk	Y	ucd	Part of the UCD package
snmpbulkwalk	Y	ucd	`ftp://ftp.ece.ucdavis.edu/pub/snmp/ucd-snmp.tar.gz` `ftp://sunsite.cnlab-switch.ch/mirror/ucd-snmp/ucd-snmp.tar.gz` `ftp://ftp.win.or.jp/pub/network/snmp/ucd-snmp/ucd-snmp.tar.gz`
snmpconf	Y	snmpconf	`http://www.net.cmu.edu/projects/snmp` `ftp://ftp.net.cmu.edu/pub/snmp/snmpconf/snmpconf-V1.1.tar.gz` `ftp://ftp.net.cmu.edu/pub/snmp/cmu-snmp-V1.13.tar.gz`
tkined	Y	scotty	`http://wwwhome.cs.utwente.nl/~schoenw/scotty/` `ftp://ftp.ibr.cs.tu-bs.de/pub/local/tkined`
tkmib	Y	ucd	Part of the UCD package

Table B.1 *Directory of tool information (continued)*

Tool	On CD-ROM	Directory On CD-ROM	Alternate Source
traceroute	N	NA	NA
xtraceroute	Y	xtracroute	http://www.dtek.chalmers.se/~d3august/xt/index.html

Using RPM to Install Software Packages

You can install the following packages using the GNOME Red Hat Package Manager (RPM) installer:

* Ethereal
* MRTG
* nmap
* ntop
* xtraceroute

Many of the packages found on the CD-ROM are in the RPM package format. As a result, you can install these tools using the RPM installation tools found with Linux. Two different versions of the RPM are available on Linux, and either one can be used to install the software tool. The first, called rpm, is a command-line interface. The other, which provides a GUI interface, is called **gnorpm**.

The CD-ROM contains several RPM packages, and the procedure for installing each one is the same. Therefore, only a single package will be shown in the procedure that follows.

Mount the CD-ROM

1. Mount the CD-ROM that was supplied with this book. Once the CD-ROM is placed in the CD drive, issue the following command:

```
mount -o ro /dev/cdrom /mnt/cdrom
```

This command will mount the CD-ROM under the /mnt directory. The rest of the procedure will use this directory as an example.

Using the Command-line RPM Tool

1. Change to the directory that contains the RPM packages that are located on the mounted CD-ROM:

```
cd /mnt/cdrom/linux
```

2. Invoke the rpm tool to install the desired package. In this example, the xtraceroute package will be installed:

```
rpm --install xtraceroute-0.8.13-1.i386.rpm
```

If you do not encounter errors, then the package is installed sucessfully. If the package is already installed, then the following error message will display:

```
error: package xtraceroute-0.8.13-1.i386.rpm is already
    installed
```

Using the RPM GUI

1. Start the RPM installation tool as the root user, by issuing the following command:

```
/usr/bin/gnorpm
```

Executing this command displays the window shown in Figure B.1.

This is the main **gnorpm** installation window from which you can install, query, verify, and remove packages. You can perform other tasks here as well, such as searching for a particular package and upgrading one or more of them. Together, these functions make the **gnorpm** tool a very important tool for the network and system administrator.

2. Use the panel on the left to inspect packages that have already been installed on the system. Using this tree view, you can navigate through each of the folders, thus revealing additional folders and ultimately, individual packages. If you want to remove

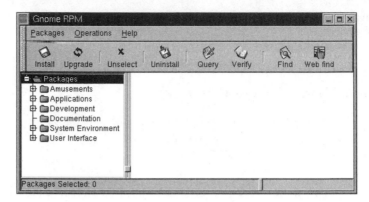

Figure B.1 *GNOME RPM main window.*

one or more packages, simply select the package(s) and click
the Uninstall button.

Figure B.2 *Installation window.*

3. Next, click the Install button located to the far left side of the
   window. A new sub-window will be displayed, as shown in Figure B.2. Selecting the Install... submenu from the Operations
   menu will also cause this window to appear. The window displayed contains an empty panel because no packages have been
   selected to be loaded on the system. We must now select the
   packages we would like to install. To do so, we must click the
   Add button. When we do so, the Add Package dialog window
   will appear, as shown in Figure B.3. It is here that we select the
   package that we would like to install.

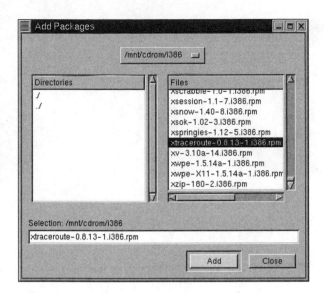

Figure B.3 *Add Packages window.*

Note that the default file location is displayed in the /root directory. You must now navigate to the location where the RPM packages reside. In our case, we need to select the directory in which the CD-ROM has been mounted. The CD-ROM will be mounted under the /mnt directory. The full path of the package includes the following:

/mnt/cdrom/linux

Once you have selected the xtraceroute-0.8.13-1.i386.rpm package, click the Add button. This places the xtraceroute package in the Install window, as shown in Figure B.4. Dismiss the Add Packages window by clicking the Close button.

4. Before you install the software, it may be a good idea to query the package to see what it contains and where the package files will be placed. Also, you might be able to learn more about the package. Clicking the query button will display the window shown in Figure B.5.

As you can see, this window provides summary information about the xtraceroute package, a scrollable list of the files related to the package, and a couple of buttons. The Install

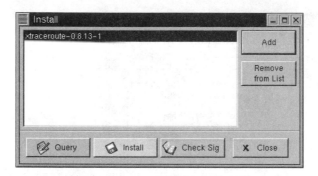

Figure B.4 *Install window with selected package.*

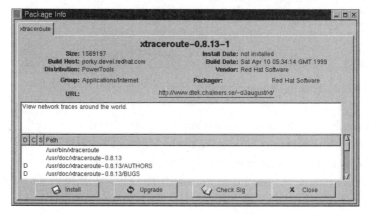

Figure B.5 *Query package window.*

button will continue the install, the `Upgrade` button will upgrade
the package if an older version already exists, and the `Check Sig`
button will ensure that the package contains the correct digital
signatures. These signatures are used to verify that the package
is complete. Finally, the `Close` button will dismiss this window
without doing anything else.

5. At this point, you are ready to install the package. Therefore,
click the `Install` button. The window shown in Figure B.6
shows the installation progress using a progress bar.

Once the progress window disappears, and if no errors have
occurred, the package is installed.

The **gnorpm** installer detects when an application has already
been installed. As a result, if the user attempts to install a package

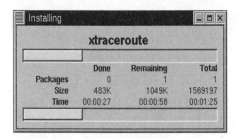

Figure B.6 *Progress window.*

that is already on the system, the software displays a warning message, as shown in Figure B.7.

Figure B.7 *Warning message dialog window.*

Non-RPM Package Installation Procedures

The following packages are either not available in RPM format or require special installation instructions:

- subnet calculator

- fping

- snmpconf

- Sun agent

See the beginning of this appendix for specific instructions on accessing and mounting the CD-ROM.

Installing the Chesapeake Software

The installation procedure for the subnet calculator includes the following steps:

1. Obtain the *tar* archive from the CD-ROM or at the Internet address listed in Table B.1. If you are getting the archive from the Internet site, you must do the following:

   - Fill out the Registration form

   - Agree with the License Agreement

   - Download the `subcalc.tar.Z` file

   If you are getting a package from the CD-ROM, copy the *tar* archive to a new directory:

   ```
   cp /mnt/cdrom/ccci/subcalc.tar.Z <directory>
   ```

2. From the directory to which the `tar` archive was saved, run the following commands:

   ```
   uncompress subcalc.tar.Z

   tar xvf subcalc.tar

   [lots of output]
   ```

3. Load the `subcalc.html` file in your favorite Web browser. This HTML file is located in the same directory as where the archive file was untarred.

Installing the FPING Software

The installation procedures for the fping package include the following:

1. Obtain the fping package from one of the sites listed in Table B.1 or from the CD-ROM available with this book. If you are interested in installing just the binary of this program, follow steps 1 and 2; disregard the remaining steps.

2. Uncompress the GNU archive:

   ```
   gunzip fping-2.2b1.tar.gz
   ```

3. Untar the archive into the directory you will be using to contain the source code or binary:

```
tar xvf fping-2.2b1.tar
```

4. Normally, the untarring will create a new directory whose name begins with **fping-2.2b1** and ends with the software version number. Change to this directory:

```
cd fping-2.2b1
```

5. Next, run the **configure** command from this directory:

```
./configure
```

```
[lots of output]
```

After several pages of output, the configure program will ask a small number of questions.

```
[questions here]
```

6. If no errors were encountered, run the **make** command:

```
make
```

```
[lots of output]
```

7. After the make has finished, and if no serious errors were displayed, install the package by running the following command:

```
make install
```

```
[lots of output]
```

If you encounter a problem during the installation, consult the READ.ME file, which can be found on the top-level directory of the **fping** distribution.

Installing the Sun Agent

To install the Sun agent on an older release of Solaris using the Solaris 2.6 CD-ROM, follow the procedure outlined here and execute the commands as the superuser.

1. Obtain the software package from one of the sites listed in Table B.1 or from the CD-ROM available with this book.

2. Mount the CD-ROM into the system (or use the volume manager).

3. Change the directory to the CD-ROM:

```
cd /cdrom/sol_2_6_sparc_smcc_svr/s0/Solaris_2.6/Product
```

4. Install the SUNWascom package:

```
pkgadd -d . SUNWascom
[lots of output]
```

5. Install the SUNWsasnm package:

```
pkgadd -d . SUNWsasnm
[lots of output]
```

6. Install the SUNWadmi package:

```
pkgadd -d . SUNWadmi
[lots of output]
```

7. Install the SUNWmibii package:

```
pkgadd -d . SUNWmibii
[lots of output]
```

8. To activate the agent, reboot the system or use the system startup script:

```
/etc/reboot
```

or

```
/etc/inid.d/init.snmpdx start
```

Sun Agent Package Information

The Sun agents started shipping standard with Solaris 2.6. The binary package is available for both SPARC and Intel; therefore, it can only be installed on Solaris systems on either of these platforms. The standard Solaris 2.6 and 2.7 CD-ROMs contain the packages for the Sun Enterprise agents. The agents are also available and can be downloaded via the Sun Web site if you don't have access to the Sun Solaris CD-ROM. The agents can be installed on Solaris 2.4 and 2.5 versions. Because previous releases didn't include the agent, installation of these versions of Solaris will require the pkgadd system utility. The packages that are required as well as a list of the components within the package for the Sun agents are listed here:

- SUNWascom

- SUNWsasnm

- SUNWsadmi

- SUNWmibii

SUNWascom

This package contains configuration and common files for the other packages, which can be found in the `/etc` and `/var` directories. These other packages include `/etc/snmp/conf/snmpd.conf` and `/var/snmp/mib/sun.mib`.

SUNWsasnm

This package contains the `snmpdx` master agent, the master agent MIB file, `snmpdx.mib`, the system startup file, `init.snmpdx`, and additional system libraries.

SUNWsadmi

This package contains the DMI portion of the agents. Despite the fact that the DMI functionality won't be used, it should be installed as well.

SUNWmibii

This package contains the `mibiisa` system agent.

Sun Agent Startup Information

The Sun SNMP agent and master agent are available only on the Solaris platform. They are shipped standard on the present version of Solaris but can be installed on previous releases as well. For the SNMP agents to be available at all times, they should be started when the system is initialized or rebooted. The Sun agent ships with a startup script and is set up when the software is installed. The startup script, `init.snmpdx`, which is found in the `/etc/init.d` directory, starts the master agent automatically. Once the master agent is running, it starts any configured subagents and, by default, starts the `mibiisa` system agent. Listing B.1 shows the startup script:

Listing B.1 *Agent startup script*

```
1   #!/sbin/sh
2   # Copyright 01/17/97 Sun Microsystems, Inc. All Rights Reserved.
3   #pragma ident   "@(#)init.snmpdx 1.11 97/01/17 Sun Microsystems"
4
5   #
6   # Return pid of named process in variable "pid"
7   #
8   pidproc() {
9           pid=`/usr/bin/ps -e |
10                  /usr/bin/grep $1 |
11                  /usr/bin/sed -e 's/^  *//' -e 's/ .*//'`
12  }
13
14  #
15  # Kill named process(es)
16  #
17  killproc() {
18          pidproc $1
19          [ "$pid" != "" ] && kill -9 $pid
20  }
21
22  case "$1" in
23
24  'start')
25          if [ -f /etc/snmp/conf/snmpdx.rsrc -a -x /usr/lib/snmp/snmpdx ]; then
26                  /usr/lib/snmp/snmpdx -y -c /etc/snmp/conf
27          fi
28
29          ;;
30  'stop')
31
32          killproc snmpdx
33          killproc snmpv2d
34          killproc mibiisa
35          ;;
36
37  *)
38          echo "Usage: /etc/init.d/init.snmpdx { start | stop }"
39          ;;
40  esac
41  exit 0
```

Like most startup scripts on Solaris, this script provides the ability to either start or stop the master agent and subagents. A case statement provides the logic to determine which argument is given

on the command line and takes appropriate action. If the string
`start` is specified, then everything between lines 25-29 is executed.
If the `stop` string is used, then everything between lines 31-35 is
executed. When the system starts, it executes this script with the
`start` argument. When the system is being brought down, the
script is started with the `stop` argument. The `*)` label (on line 37) is
provided when the script is being executed on the command line. If
either the `start` or `stop` argument isn't provided, the script uses
this to match anything that results in a usage string being displayed.

When the script starts the agent processes, it first checks to
ensure that the `/etc/snmp/conf/snmpdx.rsrc` file exists and is a regular file, and then checks to see if the `/usr/lib/snmp/snmpdx` is executable. If either of these tests fails, the script just silently stops
without starting the agents.

When the script is invoked to stop the agent processes, it uses
the **killproc** (lines 8-12) function with the name of each agent name
to stop the agents. Before the **killproc** function actually kills each
agent process, it checks to see if each of these processes is in fact
running by invoking the **pidproc** function. This function executes the
ps command followed by a **grep** for the match of the agent name. If
the agent is running, it will return a process id. If not, the null
string `""` is returned. The last step is to issue the **kill-9** command
with the process ID of each running agent.

The script is designed to be used both during and after the system has been booted. For example, to stop the agent processes, use
the following command:

```
# init.snmpdx stop
```

To start the agents, use the following:

```
# init.snmpdx start
```

Installing the UCD Package

The installation procedure for the UCD package includes the
following steps:

1. Obtain the `fping` package at one of the Internet addresses listed
   in Table B.1 or from the CD-ROM available with this book.

2. Uncompress the GNU archive:

```
gunzip ucd-snmp-4.0.1tar.gz
```

3. Untar the archive into the directory you will be using:

```
tar xvf ucd-snmp-4.0.1tar
```

4. Normally, the untarring will create a new directory whose name begins with ucd-snmp and ends with the software version number. Change to this directory:

```
cd ucd-snmp-4.0.1
```

5. Next, run the **configure** command from this directory:

```
./configure
[lots of output]
```

After several pages of output, the configure program will ask a few questions.
```
[questions]
```

6. If no errors were encountered, run the **make** command:

```
make
[lots of output]
```

7. After the **make** has finished, and if no serious errors were displayed, install the package by running the following:

```
make install
[lots of output]
```

If you encounter a problem during the installation, consult the Frequently Asked Questions (FAQ) file and additional documentation that comes with the package. The FAQ.txt file is located at the top level of the installation directory.

The UCD packet is available in the public domain; as such it must be retrieved and subsequently installed. It is provided either in source or binary form. The binary form is easiest to install because the package doesn't need to be compiled. However, if you want to build the UCD from scratch, you will need a compiler and a little bit of patience. The procedures for installing the binary and source releases have been provided on the following pages.

Directory Layout

The UCD package (version 3.5) consists of the following directories:

- `agent`
- `apps`
- `etc`
- `local`
- `m`
- `man`
- `mibs`
- `ov`
- `s`
- `snmplib`

The `agent`, `apps`, `local`, `m`, and `s` directories contain source code, shell scripts, and header files, which constitute the bulk of the package. In particular, the `apps` location contains the source for all the SNMP tools (such as `snmpget` and `snmpset`), and the `agent` location is where the SNMP agent and trap handler source files (`snmpd` and `trapd`) reside. The `snmplib` directory contains the source to the SNMP APIs. The `mibs` directory contains a list of MIB files that the agent supports, and the `ov` directory contains files that are used for integration into the HP OpenView software package. The `etc` directory contains the agent configuration files needed to implement SNMP security.

The UCD agent must also be configured to start when the system is brought up. The version of the UCD package described in this book doesn't contain a startup script, and, as a result, the Sun agent startup script has been altered to include the UCD agent. Listing B.2 shows the code fragment used to start the UCD agent; it can be included in its own startup script.

Listing B.2 *UCD agent startup*

```
#
# Start the UCD Agent
#
if [ -f /usr/local/share/snmp/snmpd.conf -a -x /usr/local/
sbin/snmpd ]; then
        /usr/local/sbin/snmpd
fi
```

By default, the UCD agent listens on well-known port 161. If the agent must use another port, change the preceding command by including the -p option followed by the new port number.

Installing the snmpconf and CMU Software Packages

The installation procedure is as follows:

1. Obtain the snmpconf and CMU Library packages at one of the Internet addresses listed in Table B.1 or from the CD-ROM available with this book.

2. Determine a location for the software. Possible directories include the following:

   `/usr/local/snmp` and `/usr/local/snmpconf`

   Create the appropriate directories:

   `mkdir /usr/local/snmp` and `mkdir /usr/local/snmpconf`

3. Uncompress the CMU archive:

   `gunzip cmu-snmp-V1.12.tar.gz`

4. Uncompress the snmpconf archive:

   `gunzip snmpconf-V1_1_tar.gz`

5. Untar the CMU archive into the directory you will be using:

   `cd /usr/local/snmp`

   `tar xvf cmu-snmp-V1.12.tar`

   a. On Solaris, it is necessary to modify the source.

   b. Add the include file `<sys/sockio.h>` in the `snmp_extra.c` file after the other entries.

   Remove extra spaces next to the line `version.o` in **makefile.**

6. Next, run the **configure** command from this directory:

   `./configure`

   `[lots of output]`

   After several pages of output, the configure program will ask a small number of questions.

```
[questions]
```

7. If no errors were encountered, run the **make** command:

```
make
```

```
[lots of output]
```

8. If no errors were encountered, run the **make install** command:

```
Make install
```

```
[lots of output]
```

9. Untar the `snmpconf` archive into the directory you will use:

```
cd /usr/local/snmpconf
```

```
tar xvf snmpconf-V1_1_tar
```

10. Next, run the **configure** command from this directory:

```
./configure
```

```
[lots of output]
```

11. If no errors were encountered, run the **make** command:

```
make
```

```
[lots of output]
```

12. After the **make** has finished with no serious errors, install the package by running the following:

```
make install
```

```
[lots of output]
```

13. Invoke a `csh` and add the `/usr/local/lib` library path to the `LD_LIBRARY_PATH` variable:

```
csh
```

```
set LD_LIBRARY_PATH /usr/local/lib
```

If you encounter a problem during the installation, consult the `README` and `INSTALL` files that come with the package. These are located at the top level of the directory in which the software was installed.

Glossary of Networking/ Network Management Terms

Like many different technologies and industries, networking and network management have their own subculture and language. This glossary has been provided to bridge the gap and explain some of the more common terms used in this book and in the industry.

Table C.1 *Terms and definitions*

Term	Meaning
100Base-TX	Known as Fast Ethernet; a 100 Mbps LAN technology based on the CSMA/CD network access method using two-pair Category 5 UTP cabling. Additional media types include 100Base-FX (fiber optic cable) and 100Base-T4 (four-pair Category 3 cabling UTP)
10Base-T	A 10 Mbps LAN technology that uses the CSMA/CD network-access-method-based IEEE 802.3 specifications. Additional media types include 10base2 (Thinnet, using thin coaxial cable), 10Base5 (ThickNet, using a large coaxial cable), and 10BaseFL (using fiber optic cable)
ACK	Acknowledgment; a response to a specific request. For instance, TCP provides acknowledgment for each packet transmitted
Agent	A software component found within networking devices or operating system processes that responds to queries from one or more network managers
arp	The UNIX command that displays or manipulates the ARP cache
ARP	Address Resolution Protocol; a network protocol that is responsible for mapping lower-layer network addresses (such as Ethernet) to higher-layer addresses (such as the Internet Protocol)

Table C.1 *Terms and definitions (continued)*

ARP cache	A list of ARP entries that consists of an IP address and datalink address used by a node on a TCP/IP network
ATM	Asynchronous Transfer Mode, a standard for cell relay that can be used to carry voice, data, and video in small 53-byte-size cells
Attachment Unit Interface	Known as AUI; defines the specification between an Ethernet media access unit (MAU) and DTE device; specifies how an Ethernet device connects to a transceiver used on a 10Base5 network
Backbone	A core LAN or WAN that uses one or more high-speed networking technologies with smaller networks branching off of them. LAN backbones connect different departments or groups of users. WAN backbone networks often provide connections to regional or remote locations
BER	Basic Encoding Rules. Standard method for encoding values of each ASN.1 type as a series of string octets or bytes
Bandwidth	Commonly used to describe the carrying capacity of a digital network facility that is typically measured in bits-per-second (bps). For example, 100 Base-T Ethernet is said to have the capacity of 100 Mbps
BootP	Bootstrap Protocol based on the UDP network-layer protocol; provides a means to assign a host a dynamic IP address

Table C.1 *Terms and definitions (continued)*

Broadcast address	A special address used to simultaneously broadcast information to all stations on a network. Examples include IP broadcast (134.111.10.255) and Ethernet Broadcast (FF:FF:FF:FF:FF:FF)
Broadcast domain	A collection of network devices that share the same physical or logical network. Broadcast domains can be confined to a series of switched ports. When a broadcast occurs on this network, only those devices within the domain will receive it
Community string/ community name	A string that provides password protection with SNMPv1 agents. If the SNMP manager has the community string, it is permitted to modify any object writable within the agent's MIB
CMIP	Common Management Information Protocol; an ISO standard for network management that provides some of the same functions as SNMP
Datalink Protocol	A low-level network protocol that functions on OSI model layer 2. It refers to the frame format and communications protocol. Popular datalink protocols include Ethernet, FDDI, and ATM
Enterprise MIB	A vendor-specific MIB that is defined under the enterprise branch and located under the iso.dod.internet.private branch. Many vendor MIBs such as Cisco and 3Com use this branch

Table C.1 *Terms and definitions (continued)*

Extensible agent	An SNMP agent that can be extended to include additional functionality by altering one or more configuration files or adding some custom functions
Get	An operation used to obtain the value of an MIB object from an SNMP agent. It serves as the primary way an SNMP manager retrieves MIB values
GetNext	Similar to the SNMP Get, this SNMP operation retrieves the "next" object in the MIB tree
Host resource MIB	The MIB that provides access to system-level objects such as memory usage, disk usage, running processes, etc. The UCD Agent provides access to these MIB objects
HPOV	Hewlett-Packard OpenView; one of the most popular network management packages
Internet Protocol	The Internet Protocol (IP) provides best-effort packet delivery and routing layer services. This protocol operates on layer 3 of the OSI model
Master agent	A central controlling agent that intercepts SNMP requests on the standard port and forwards these requests to one or more subagents. Usually, the subagents must be configured to function with the master agent
MIB	Management Information Base; defines objects contained within SNMP device agents that are used to manage the device

Table C.1 *Terms and definitions (continued)*

MIB-II	A standard MIB that provides access to a core set of objects defined in several groups. These include system interfaces, at, ip, icmp, tcp, udp, egp, and transmission
MIB browser	A user program that provides a hierarchical view of MIB objects for display or modification of individual object values
Multicast	An address that uses the class D range (224.0.0.0-240.0.0.0) for the destination IP address. Multicast represents a more effective mechanism than traditional unicast delivery for sending information to a large collection of devices
OSI	Open Standard Interconnection model. The model defines seven layers that are responsible for establishing connectivity between network devices
OUI	Organization Unique Identifier; part of the datalink address that represents the vendor of the equipment; used to identify datalink frames
Out-of-band management	Refers to the ability of a device to support remote management capabilities using a special interface that is not used for general connectivity
Packet	A generic term that describes the messages transmitted across a network. Packets contain a source, destination, and other associated information
PDU	Protocol Data Unit; the packet for SNMP message types. SNMP defines several PDU types: get-request, set-request, get-response, and trap

Table C.1 *Terms and definitions (continued)*

Probe	A device that attaches to a network that collects performance and packet information for later analysis and reporting. Probes usually implement RMON or some other network performance monitoring protocol
Polling	The act of retrieving specific information (MIB objects) from one or more agents. A manager is said to poll the agents for required information
RMON	Remote Monitoring Protocol. RMON is responsible for collecting network traffic and protocol information within a network probe. Many vendors have implemented RMON within their networking products
SAN	Storage Area Network. A network topology that integrates mass storage management hardware (i.e., disk farms) to computer systems using a standard-based networking infrastructure
Set	The operation used to change one or more MIB objects within an agent. An SNMP set operation requires security authentication to complete this task
SNMP	Simple Network Management Protocol. SNMP is the management protocol that provides management capabilities to individual systems and devices. SNMP defines a manager, agent, and MIBs
SNMPv1	The first version of SNMP. This version included the core framework, SMIv1, and MIB-II definition

Table C.1 *Terms and definitions (continued)*

SNMPv2	Enhancements to the SNMPv1 framework; includes new SMI, additional SNMP PDUs, and changes to MIB-II groups and objects
SNMPv3	New SNMP version that provides a robust framework for security
SMI	Structure of Management Information; a general framework for the definition and construction of an MIB
State machine	A model that contains a fixed number of states and actions to transition from one state to another. TCP uses a state machine model for protocol operations
Subagent	An SNMP agent that has been configured to function with a master agent. All SNMP requests come from the master agent, and the subagent listens for SNMP requests on a different port
TCP	Transmission Control Protocol; OSI transport layer 4 protocol that is responsible for reliable data transport from one machine to another. TCP is used extensively throughout the Internet
Topology	A physical or logical layout of a network that consists of networking devices such as switches, routers, and individual workstations and servers
Tivoli	A network management package that provides a large number of management services. Services include software distribution, UNIX account administration, and remote system management

Table C.1 *Terms and definitions (continued)*

Trap	A message sent from an SNMP agent to a manager. Trap messages may include ColdStart, WarmStart, LinkDown, and LinkUp. Enterprise traps (EnterpriseSpecific) contain vendor-specific information
trapd	A UNIX program that listens for incoming traps from the network using port 162. Trap messages can be logged or deleted, or they can invoke additional actions if they fit a certain pattern or profile
UDP	User Datagram Protocol; a lightweight transport layer protocol that provides no guarantee of information delivery
Unicast	A datalink frame sent from one system to another. A unicast frame is directed to a specific device on a network
URL	Universal Resource Locator; a pathname that contains a host name plus a directory path to retrieve a particular Web page
Variable binding list	A field with an SNMP PDU containing specific MIB objects and associated values
Virtual LANs	Virtual Local Area Network (VLAN); a logical collection of networking devices (servers, workstations, etc.) that are contained within a single broadcast domain
WAN	Wide Area Network; a network that is spread out over a large geographic area or based on WAN technologies such as ATM, Frame Relay, PPP, and others.
WWW	World Wide Web; a collection of Web sites that span the globe

Index

Symbols

. (dot) 25
   accessing 25

A

abstract syntax notation (ASN.1)
   see ASN.1
access control list (ACL) 19
access mode 31, 297
Accessing Objects 37
ACK segment 75, 77, 80
address primitives 163
Address Resolution Protocol (ARP)
   see ARP 66
agent 4, 23
   architecture 55
   determining functionality of 6
   extensible 7, 8
   external behavior 5
   internal behavior 6
   master agent 55
   master and 54
   master/subagent architecture 55
   multiple 7
   overview of 326
   port contention problem 55
   public domain 6
   SNMP 5
   subagent 54
agent functional diagram 8
AgentX 56
alarms 15
application data types

counter 29
displaystring 29
gauge 30
networkAddress 30
opaque 30
TimeTicks 30
Application Layer 60
Application Programming Interface
   (APIs) 13, 613
ARCHIE 69
architecture 13
arithmetic operators 168
arithmetic primitives 164
ARP 66, 95, 96
   --display option 110
   -a option 110
   -d option 112
   -f option 114, 115
   -n option 110
   -s option 112
   -v command example 107
   Address field 108
   advantages 97
   C flag 109
   cache 98, 99, 106
   command character format 107
   command-line options 107
   datalink address format 100
   deleting an ARP cache 112
   description 106
   Flag Mask field 108
   Flag Mask field options 108
   hardware type 98
   hardware type field 98
   hlen field 98

Software and Information License

The software and information on this diskette (collectively referred to as the "Product") are the property of The McGraw-Hill Companies, Inc. ("McGraw-Hill") and are protected by both United States copyright law and international copyright treaty provision. You must treat this Product just like a book, expect that you may copy it into a computer to be used and you may make archival copies of the Products for the sole purpose of backing up your software and protecting your investment from loss.

By saying "just like a book," McGraw-Hill means, for example, that the Product may be used by any number of people and may be freely moved from one computer location to another, so long as there is no possibility of the Product (or any part of the Product) being used at one location or on one computer while it is being used at another. Just as a book cannot be read by two different people in two different places at the same time, neither can the Product be used in two different places at the same time (unless, of course, McGraw-Hill's rights are being violated).

McGraw-Hill reserves the right to alter or modify the contents of the Product at any time.

This agreement is effective until terminated. The Agreement will terminate automatically without notice if you fail to comply with any provisions of this Agreement. In the event of termination by reason of your breach, you will destroy or erase all copies of the Product installed on any computer system or made for backup purposes and shall expunge the Product from your data storage facilities.

Limited Warranty

McGraw-Hill warrants the physical diskette(s) enclosed herein to be free of defects in materials and workmanship for a period of sixty days from the purchase date. If McGraw-Hill receives written notification within the warranty period of defects in materials or workmanship, and such notification is determined by McGraw-Hill to be correct, McGraw-Hill will replace the defective diskette(s). Send request to:

Customer Service
McGraw-Hill
Gahanna Industrial Park
860 Taylor Station Road
Blacklick, Ohio 43004-9615

The entire and exclusive liability and remedy for breach of this Limited Warranty shall be limited to replacement of defective diskette(s) and shall not include or extend any claim for or right to cover any other damages, including but not limited to loss of profit, data, or use of the software, or special, incidental, or consequential damages or other similar claims, even if McGraw-Hill has been specifically advised as to the possibility of such damages. In no event will McGraw-Hill's liability for any damages to you or any other person ever exceed the lower of suggested list price or actual price paid for the license to use the Product, regardless of any form of the claim.

The McGraw-Hill Companies, Inc. specifically disclaims all other warranties, express or implied, including but not limited to, any implied warranty of merchantability or fitness for a particular purpose. Specifically, McGraw-Hill makes no representation or warranty that the Product is fit for any particular purpose and any implied warranty of merchantability is limited to the sixty day duration of the Limited Warranty covering the physical diskette(s) only (and not the software or information) and is otherwise expressly and specifically disclaimed.

This Limited Warranty gives you specific legal rights; you may have others which may vary from state to state. Some states do not allow the exclusion of incidental or consequential damages, or the limitation on how long an implied warranty lasts, so some of the above may not apply to you.

This agreement constitutes the entire agreement between the parties relating to use of the Product. The terms of any purchase order shall have no effect on the terms of this Agreement. Failure of McGraw-Hill to insist at any time on strict compliance with this Agreement shall not constitute a waiver of any rights under this Agreement. This Agreement shall be construed and governed in accordance with the laws of New York. If any provision of this Agreement is held to be contrary to law, that provision will be enforced to the maximum extent permissible and the remaining provisions will remain in force and effect.